ORGANIZATION

AND

REVOLUTION

D0169067

ORGANIZATION

AND

REVOLUTION

WORKING-CLASS ASSOCIATIONS IN THE

GERMAN REVOLUTIONS OF

1848-1849

BY P. H. NOYES

PRINCETON, NEW JERSEY

PRINCETON UNIVERSITY PRESS

1966

PREFACE

I ATTEMPT HERE to analyze the role played by the workers and their associations in the course of the two years of the German revolutions of the mid-nineteenth century. The revolutions of 1848-1849 influenced, if only in a negative fashion, much of subsequent German history and, with it, the history of Europe. It is important for those outside Germany, as well as those within, to know what happened in those years and what was the nature of the failure of the revolution and of liberal Germany. Part of this failure, a large but often unmentioned part, was due to the failure of the workers' associations.

In the course of the preparation of this book, I have been helped by a number of German scholars and librarians who introduced me to the sources on which a study of the workers' movement of 1848 must be based. In particular, I should like to thank the late Werner Blumenberg, head of the German section of the International Institute for Social History in Amsterdam, and Dr. Kurt Koszyk, director of the *Westfälisch-Niederrheinische Institut für Zeitungsforschung* in Dortmund, for their help and advice. In addition, I received welcome assistance from the staffs of the *Bundesarchiv* and the *Stadtarchiv* in Frankfurt am Main, the *Stadtbibliothek* in Cologne and the *Ratsbibliothek* in East Berlin.

The book represents a revised version, reduced in size and expanded in scope, of a doctoral thesis submitted to the University of Oxford. It has profited, in its various forms and stages, from the suggestions of a number of

v

readers. My thesis supervisor, Mr. A. J. P. Taylor, contributed more than perhaps he knows, or would wish to admit, through advice, encouragement, incisive comments and above all the example of the industry and intelligence which are necessary for the writing of history. I am also indebted to Professors Peter Gay, Donald G. Rohr and Fritz Stern, and to Messrs. F. H. Hinsley, James Joll, Gerald Stearn and A. H. Walker, all of whom have read one or more versions. I have tried to follow their advice as much as the evidence and my own judgment permitted; I remain extremely grateful for it even in those cases in which I have been stubborn or obtuse about accepting it. I am of course responsible for all errors of fact or opinion that remain. I should note in particular that translations from the German, with a very few exceptions indicated in the text, are my own; I have tried, I hope with some success, to reproduce the effect, both awkward and eloquent, of the language in which the petitions and pamphlets of the 1848 workers' movement were cast.

I have also received generous financial support which has helped at various stages in the preparation of the book. The initial research was undertaken while I was studying at the University of Oxford as a Marshall Scholar; I am, and shall always remain, most grateful to the Marshall Aid Commemoration Commission of Great Britain for its support during those years. In the final stages I was aided by typing grants from the office of the Dean of the Graduate Faculties of Columbia University and from the William A. Dunning Fund administered by the History Department of that university.

I have been assisted in what are often considered the mechanical aspects of producing a book in ways which were far from mechanical. Miss Marie T. Eckhard typed the final version with precision and care. Mr. Robert

Palmer kindly undertook to prepare the index. Proof reading was aided by a task force of friends and colleagues who gathered at a rather trying time to give assistance far beyond the call or claims of friendship; I can record, but only inadequately express, my gratitude.

Finally, in ways too multitudinous to mention, I was helped by my parents and by my wife Helen, herself a student and teacher of history; it is their book too.

PHN

New York City
December 1965

CONTENTS

PREFACE   v

INTRODUCTION   1

SECTION I: Pre-March

  CHAPTER 1 · The Condition of the Working Class
           in Germany in the 1840s   15
  CHAPTER 2 · Socialist Theories and Workers'
           Clubs   34

SECTION II: Barricades, Meetings and Clubs—
Spring of 1848

  CHAPTER 3 · The March Days   57
  CHAPTER 4 · Alternatives to Organization—
           Government Action   81
  CHAPTER 5 · Alternatives to Organization—
           Radical Leaders   99
  CHAPTER 6 · The Beginnings of Organization   124

SECTION III: The Rival Congresses—Summer of 1848

  CHAPTER 7 · The Artisan Congresses and the
           Guild Movement   163
  CHAPTER 8 · The Workers' Congresses and the
           Attack on the Guilds   192
  CHAPTER 9 · The Frankfurt Assembly and the
           Workers' Demands   221

SECTION IV: The Closing of the Ranks—Autumn,
Winter and Spring, 1848-1849

  CHAPTER 10 · The Democratic Deadlock   265
  CHAPTER 11 · The Growth of Organization   290
  CHAPTER 12 · The Failure of the Governments   315

CONTENTS

SECTION V: Defeat and Dissolution—1849 and After

CHAPTER 13 · The May Uprisings and the
Workers' Associations   341

CHAPTER 14 · The Final Congress and the End
of the Associations   360

CONCLUSION   376

SELECTED BIBLIOGRAPHY   381

INDEX   395

"Nur der verdient die Freiheit, wie das Leben,
Der täglich sie erwerben muss."

—GOETHE, *Faust*

"Erst kommt das Fressen, dann kommt die Moral."
—BRECHT, *Die Dreigroschenoper*

INTRODUCTION

"THE NEXT revolution will not be political; it will be a social one. No longer will it have some hollow political theory for its battle cry, but hunger against gluttony, nakedness against luxury." So wrote the perceptive Prussian noble Joseph Maria von Radowitz in 1846.[1] His prediction was soon echoed by others. Tocqueville noted "the gale of revolution in the air" and prophesied in the following year that:

> Before long, the political struggle will be restricted to those who have and those who have not; property will form the great field of battle; and the principal political questions will turn upon more or less important modifications to be introduced into the rights of property. We shall then have once more among us great public agitations and great political parties.[2]

And Marx and Engels, in the *Communist Manifesto* published in February of 1848, spoke of the "specter of Communism" which was haunting all Europe and which foreshadowed the coming proletarian revolution.

[1] From *Gespräche aus der Gegenwart über Staat und Kirche,* quoted by Ernst Benz, "Franz von Baaders Gedanken über den Proletair. Zur Geschichte des vor-marxistischen Sozialismus," *Zeitschrift für Religions- und Geistesgeschichte,* vol. 1 (1948), p. 124.

[2] *The Recollections of Alexis de Tocqueville,* trans. Alexander Teixera de Mattos, ed. J. P. Mayer, New York, 1959, p. 11. That Tocqueville thought this prediction to be fulfilled by the actual course of the revolution in France may be seen from pp. 74-81 or from his account of the June days, pp. 150ff.

1

Prediction of social revolution was a commonplace of the mid-1840s. The "social question," the problem of poverty and the proletariat, the emergence of the working class as a political force, these features—it was widely believed—would distinguish the revolutions of the mid-nineteenth century from all that had gone before.

Though predicted, the social side of the revolutions of 1848 has often been ignored by subsequent historians, or, if not ignored, its importance has been minimized. The year 1848 has been seen in purely political terms; liberalism and nationalism are regarded as the issues of the revolution, the middle classes and the "intellectuals" as the revolutionaries. Though broader or more elemental issues may at first have moved the mobs to riot and revolt, though the revolution may have had some basis in the reality of social and economic demands, the reality—so runs one influential interpretation of 1848—soon disappeared. "The proletariat was defeated in Paris, the peasants were bought off in the Habsburg Monarchy. The social forces behind the revolution, disjointed and insufficient from the very outset, were thus practically eliminated." [3]

But at least in Germany the revolution continued on into the following year, 1849, and there were renewed outbreaks of violence. The working classes who had manned the barricades in March continued to agitate and to organize to improve their lot. The background of working-class activity, the outbreak of strikes and the rise of the workers' associations remain an essential feature of the revolutions of 1848-1849 in Germany. The problem is rather that the group which contemporaries

[3] L. B. Namier, *1848: The Revolution of the Intellectuals*, London, 1946, p. 23. Namier's views on 1848 have found widespread acceptance; see, for example, A. W. Palmer, *A Dictionary of Modern History, 1789-1945*, Baltimore, 1964, p. 273: "With few exceptions, the revolutions were the work of middle-class intellectuals."

2

regarded as the working class refuses stubbornly to be brought under the conventional categories of class analysis.

*

Artisans, and not industrial workers, were the major source of mass revolutionary unrest in mid-nineteenth century Europe. In England it was the depressed and declining handloom weavers who formed the core of the Chartist movement; in France it was a Paris where small craftsmen still predominated that fought the classical social-revolutionary battles of the June Days; in Germany the artisans provided the force, or potential force, which lay behind the revolutions of 1848. Threatened with extinction or submersion in the mass of the proletariat, the artisans revolted, sometimes in the name of their traditional guilds, sometimes paradoxically in the name of that "working class" whose very formation they sought to avoid. Indeed the decline of the artisans, or rather their changed position, may well account for the decreasing danger of revolution in the latter part of the century.

But the forces of revolt must be channeled before a revolution can successfully occur.[4] Organization is essential for revolution; social discontent must find some organized outlet before it can be felt politically or have revolutionary effects. This channeling may initially come from a variety of circumstances, from the concatenation of events which, for example, produced the crisis in France of 1789 and the simultaneity of revolutions

[4] One of the greatest historians of revolution, himself—unlike most others—an active revolutionary as well, put the problem of organization and revolution succinctly: "Only on the basis of a study of political processes in the masses themselves, can we understand the role of parties and leaders. . . . Without a guiding organization the energy of the masses would dissipate like steam not enclosed in a piston-box. But nevertheless what moves things is not the piston or the box, but the steam." Leon Trotsky, *The Russian Revolution*, ed. F. W. Dupee, New York, 1959, p. xi.

throughout Europe in 1848. But for such outbursts to become successful revolutions, for the revolutionary pressure to be maintained, organization is necessary, the sort of organization which, to cite again the example of the first French revolution, the Jacobin clubs and the Paris sections were able to provide in the years following 1789.[5]

The nineteenth century was *par excellence* a century of organization: hosts of associations sprang up, from secret revolutionary conspiracies and public political parties to trade unions, singing and gymnastic clubs, temperance and ladies' political societies. As the old bonds of a stratified, hierarchical society broke down, people sought to attach themselves to organizations that would give them some position in society beyond anonymous membership in an economic class. The artisans were particularly susceptible to this drive for organization; the guild traditions provided a link between the old concept of society and the newer forms of organization. They also provide the connection between the "primitive rebels" who have been found throughout the history of western Europe and the "modern" social movements of the nineteenth and twentieth centuries.[6]

Yet organization, though necessary for revolution, can undermine a revolution as well. Organization can become an end in itself; rival associations can cut across each other's support, separating the organized expression of a revolution from its base in mass movements. The

[5] The way in which the popular movement in the French Revolution was channeled has only recently been explored; see, for example, George Rudé, *The Crowd in the French Revolution*, Oxford, 1959, and Albert Soboul, *Les sans-culottes parisiens en l'an II*, Paris, 1958. No similar work has yet been done on the popular movement in 1848 though it was probably equally important, if only negatively so, for the revolutions in that year.

[6] On the survivals of the earlier sort of rebellion see E. J. Hobsbawm, *Primitive Rebels, Studies in Archaic Forms of Social Movement in the 19th and 20th Centuries*, Manchester, 1959.

4

attempt to formulate precise goals for revolutionary associations may reveal the conflicts in these goals, destroying the unity of the initial revolutionary outburst.

This is what happened in Germany in 1848. The discontent necessary to support a revolution was there among the workers and artisans; the necessity for organization was realized in the months following the March Days. It was indeed a phenomenally fertile period in organizational ideas; within a few years or even months most of the schemes for labor organizations, trade unions and cooperative societies which appeared in the nineteenth century were outlined and, what is more remarkable, put into practice, however short lived. But the organizations ultimately failed to provide adequate support for the revolution, revealing instead the rifts within the working class and cutting off that class from the official middle-class leaders of the revolution in the Frankfurt Assembly or the governments of the separate German states. The German revolutions and the working-class associations of 1848 were failures with crucial results for the liberalism and nationalism of the official side of the revolution and for the German labor movement as well.

This book seeks to analyze this failure in detail, describing stage by stage the development and disintegration of the working-class forces behind the revolution. At the same time it seeks to present a picture of the heterogeneous elements within that class. An upheaval such as a revolution lifts the lid off society, allowing a glimpse, not normally available, of lower social strata. The year 1848 revealed the anxieties and aspirations, the way of life, of the mid-nineteenth century German artisans and laborers; it allows the historian to paint the portrait of a class in crisis.

✿

Historians of the German revolution of 1848 have suffered more than most from what one writer has called "the curse of contemporaneity, from the tendency to interpret it in the light of developments subsequent to it and very frequently irrelevant to it." [7] There is a vast literature in German on the events of 1848, the liberal and nationalist revolution, and a much smaller body of work on the social and economic side of these events. Both types are marred by the attempt to use 1848 as a peg on which to hang an argument about the later history of Germany.

Immediately following the revolution, conservative historians saw in its defeat all the dangers inherent in liberalism and the demands for constitutional government, while nationalists argued that the failure of revolution proved the necessity of the solution to German unification which Bismarck evolved. Later, after the collapse of the Reich and the establishment of the Weimar Republic, many writers came to regard the revolutions as the first growth of a "democratic" Germany, the ancestor of the new German republic. Even so scholarly a piece of work as Veit Valentin's two volume history, though it remains the most comprehensive account of the revolutions, suffers from a tendency to lament the "lost opportunities" of the German past and to praise the German "spirit" which the liberals represented. [8]

[7] Theodore S. Hamerow, "History and the German Revolution of 1848," *The American Historical Review*, vol. 60 (1954), p. 28. Professor Hamerow provides a most useful survey of the writings on the revolution.

[8] *Geschichte der deutschen Revolution von 1848/49*, Berlin, 1930-1931. It is interesting to note that the faulty emphasis of this work is exaggerated in the abridged and inaccurate English translation, which omits a large portion of the social and economic sections, especially those dealing with the artisans' movement. (Veit Valentin, *1848, Chapters of German History*, trans. Ethel Talbot Scheffauer, London, 1940.)

Since the second World War writings on 1848 have often shown similar biases, hunting out the origins of either a liberal democratic or socialist revolutionary past or showing that the weaknesses of this past led inevitably to the "German catastrophe" of the twentieth century. It has become increasingly evident, however, that the revolutions cannot be understood apart from their social background, and a number of recent studies have emphasized the social and economic factors behind the revolution, pointing to the need for a detailed analysis of the role which the workers played.[9] Yet apart from these general surveys no work has appeared on the subject outside the communist camp, and the rise of the workers' associations in 1848 remains a neglected field of study.

*

There is a second stream of writing on 1848 which has dealt in some detail with aspects of the workers' movement, but it is one which remains confined within the narrow banks of a particular bias. Initially left-wing criticisms of the revolution were given utterance by Karl Marx and his followers, both during 1848-1849 in the columns of the *Neue Rheinische Zeitung* which Marx edited in Cologne and afterward in the articles which were written by Engels and published under Marx's name in Horace Greeley's *New York Tribune* in 1851-1852.[10] The role and position of Karl Marx in

[9] Rudolph Stadelmann, *Soziale und politische Geschichte der Revolution von 1848*, Munich, 1948; Jacques Droz, *Les Revolutions Allemandes de 1848*, Paris, 1957; and Theodore S. Hamerow, *Restoration, Revolution, Reaction: Economics and Politics in Germany, 1815-1871*, Princeton, 1958. Hamerow in particular emphasizes the role of the artisans; see also his article, "The German Artisan Movement 1848-49," *Journal of Central European Affairs*, vol. 21 (1961), pp. 135-152.

[10] The articles were later brought out as a book, *Revolution and Counter-Revolution or Germany in 1848*, ed. Eleanor Marx Aveling, London, 1896.

1848 has been, since the time of the revolutions, the starting point for most writing in Germany on the workers' movement. Yet Marx's position in 1848 was a peculiar one; and for a variety of reasons—because of his background, because of the theories he held about the way in which a revolution must develop, because of the situation in Cologne where he chose to work—Marx remained largely aloof from the workers' movement and was in turn ignored by the mass of workers.

All studies which have appeared in Germany on the workers' movement have, however, been written from a socialist and usually a Marxist point of view. The standard work on the subject is subtitled "A Contribution to the Theory and Practice of Marxism." [11] The more recent work by Karl Obermann and others which has appeared in the (East) German Democratic Republic since the second World War is replete with communist cant and is largely vitiated by the desire to justify the actions and glorify the role of Marx in the revolutions.[12] In spite of this obvious bias, the interpretation by Marxists of Marx's role in the 1848 workers' movement has been accepted by many non-Marxist historians as well.[13]

[11] Max Quarck, *Die erste deutsche Arbeiterbewegung, Geschichte der Arbeiterverbrüderung 1848/49,* Leipzig, 1924. An earlier study, George Adler, *Die Geschichte der ersten sozial-politischen Arbeiterbewegung in Deutschland,* Breslau, 1885, is less obviously Marxist but emphasizes the alliance between the socialists and the workers and the socialist influence on the working class, pp. iii-iv, 291, 309, and regards Marx as one of the most prominent leaders of the workers in 1848, pp. 316-317.

[12] Karl Obermann, *Die deutschen Arbeiter in der ersten bürgerlichen Revolution,* Berlin, 1950, also issued in a somewhat expanded version as *Die deutschen Arbeiter in der Revolution von 1848,* Berlin, 1953. Another typical East German product on this subject is Elizabeth Todt and Hans Radandt, *Zur Frühgeschichte der deutschen Gewerkschaftsbewegung, 1800-1849,* Berlin, 1950.

[13] Koppel Pinson, for example, begins his comments on the 1848 workers' movement with the statement that "here the di-

Apart from overemphasizing the role of Marx, the socialist and Marxist histories of the German revolution make two further mistakes, both of which, it is hoped, are corrected here: they underestimate the essential role of the artisans and they neglect to a large extent the drive for organization on the part of the workers.

The working class in Germany in 1848, it must be repeated, was not a modern "industrial proletariat"; it was composed primarily of artisans, trained in the guild system to carry out the old skilled trades which were being threatened by the use of machines, the factory system and the growing competition from abroad. In the course of 1848-1849 these workers formed into associations in order to protect their interests, associations which were based more on the medieval guilds than on any idea of action by a conscious and unified working class. Paradoxically these associations often adopted the slogans of socialism, both those used by Marx and those of "Utopian" socialists who had preceded him. Indeed the gap between the aims of the workers' movement of 1848 and the vocabulary used to describe those aims was one of its fundamental weaknesses.

The associations remained largely the product of the decline of the handicraft trades. They organized strikes, held congresses, explored a number of means of working-class self-help and petitioned the legislative bodies of the German states, above all the National Assembly in Frankfurt, to come to their aid, to prevent through the prohibition of trade freedom and the support of the guilds the decline of handicraft production. They were on the whole unsuccessful in obtaining their ends. The causes of the failure of the revolution must be sought

rect influence of Marx and Engels was of paramount importance" and refers later on to "Marx, Engels and other proletarian leaders" of the revolution. *Modern Germany: Its History and Civilization,* New York, 1954, pp. 85, 89.

as much in the weaknesses of these associations as in
the attempt to draft a German constitution at Frankfurt
or in the conflict of national rivalries in eastern Europe.
Indeed Bismarck, in the version, probably incorrect, of
the famous speech to the Budget Commission of 1862
given in his memoirs, lists "associations" (*Vereine*) along
with speeches and majority decisions as the great mistakes of 1848.[14] The collapse of the workers' associations
into internecine quarrels and hostility to the institutions
of the middle-class liberals removed the force which
stood behind the initial success of the revolution.

What brought the workers and artisans into the streets
in March of 1848? What did they want out of the
revolution? What did they seek to do with it? What
were the purposes and functions of the organizations
which they set up? What influence did the workers
and their organizations have on the course of events
during 1848 and 1849? These are the questions to which
this study seeks an answer.

*

Three main groups of sources have been used in order
to answer these questions. First, the publications of
the workers' associations themselves are essential to the
understanding of the workers' movement. These include
the proceedings of a large number of the working-class
congresses which were held throughout Germany during
1848-1849 and sought to unite the workers, sometimes
in a particular trade, sometimes for the whole country,
in order to form some sort of workers' organization and
exert pressure on the rest of the country. There are
also in existence a large number of the statutes of the

[14] *Gedanken und Erinnerungen,* Munich, 1952, p. 232. This is,
of course, the famous "blood and iron" speech, though the original phrase, and the phrase as Bismarck remembered it, appears
to have been "iron and blood."

workers' associations, both local and national, and these too have been consulted. In addition the associations often published newspapers which reported the activities of the workers' organizations and discussed their problems.[15]

Secondly a number of newspapers, particularly the *Berliner Zeitungs Halle* and the *Neue Rheinische Zeitung* but many others as well, interested themselves in the "social question," though they often ignored the growth of the workers' associations; these newspapers give a picture of the general background of poverty and misery, of workers' riots and unrest against which the story of the workers' associations and the revolution must be told. Also for this purpose, the collection of street placards and pamphlets in the library of the municipal council in East Berlin provided a valuable source for the day-to-day happenings in that city and the social background of these events.[16]

Finally, the petitions which the workers and artisans drew up and sent to the National Assembly in Frankfurt am Main form one of the main sources for the investigation of the workers' movement in 1848 and provide the clearest statement of just what it was the workers hoped to gain from the revolution. Taken along with those from other groups, the petitions represent a cross section of the demands which lay behind the revolution, similar perhaps to that provided by the *cahiers des doléances*

[15] As far as I know, the only newspaper of a workers' association exerting influence on a national level in 1848 that I have been unable to find is *Der Gutenberg*, which was published by the national printers' union. A copy of this paper existed in the library of the Printers' League in Berlin before 1939; by the end of the war both the library and the paper had disappeared.

[16] *Plakate und Flugschriften zur Revolution 1848/49*, Ratsbibliothek, Berlin (East). The collection contains 11 portfolios with over 1,200 street placards and broadsides in addition to more than 300 pamphlets dating from the period of the revolution.

drawn up before the meeting of the French Estates General in 1789. Yet these petitions have been almost completely neglected even by historians who have concerned themselves with the social side of the revolution. The workers' petitions—several thousand of them—may be found in the archives of the Economic Committee of the Frankfurt Assembly, which sifted and analyzed them and debated the extent to which the workers' demands could be enacted into law.[17] The archives of the Economic Committee, together with the debates of the Assembly itself, furnish ample evidence of the ultimate inability of the middle-class delegates at Frankfurt to deal with the demands of the workers.

These demands may also be seen in a second collection of petitions, those sent to the Artisans' Congress which met in Frankfurt during the summer of 1848.[18] Together the two groups of petitions provide eloquent testimony to the desperation with which the workers of Germany faced the changing economic conditions of the mid-nineteenth century.

The nature of these conditions and the response of the German workers during the period before the March revolutions must be considered before going on to the events of the revolution itself.

[17] *Akten der Nationalversammlung, Volkswirtschaftlicher Ausschuss,* 55 vols., Bundesarchiv, Frankfurt am Main.
[18] *Akten des Handwerker-Kongresses zu Frankfurt am Main,* 3 vols., Stadtarchiv, Frankfurt am Main.

SECTION I
PRE-MARCH

CHAPTER 1

THE CONDITION OF
THE WORKING CLASS IN GERMANY
IN THE 1840s

THE THIRTY-EIGHT states of the German Federation stood on the threshold of the Industrial Revolution in the years before 1848. Predominantly agricultural, with economies based on the peasant and the farm, the guild and the artisan, Germany was "in many ways medieval and in many places less vigorous than it had been in the days of Dürer and Holbein." [1] But a variety of factors—the freeing of the serfs, the break-up of the guild system, the campaign for internal free trade and the foundation of the Zollverein—was transforming the old system. Industries slowly began to appear, in the Rhineland, in Saxony and Silesia, around Berlin. By 1848 there did exist in Germany a "working class."

The working class of 1848 was not, however, a unified, self-conscious body; the radicals and democrats of 1848 were to note to their sorrow that there was no "ideal proletariat" to carry out the revolution.[2] Rather the working class was of mixed origins: failed or failing master craftsmen, journeymen frustrated in advancement by the guild system, skilled tradesmen put out of work by the new techniques of production, casual and day laborers and that mass of economic misfits Marx called

---

[1] J. H. Clapham, *The Economic Development of France and Germany, 1815-1914*, Cambridge, 1936, p. 82.

[2] See the report of the Central Committee to the second Democratic Congress, held in Berlin in October 1848, quoted by Gustav Lüders, *Die demokratische Bewegung in Berlin im Oktober, 1848*, Berlin, 1909, pp. 152-156.

the *Lumpenproletariat*. Factory workers, where they existed, often considered themselves to be superior to the common run of workers; the machine builders were held to be the "aristocrats" of the Berlin labor force.[3]

Nor was the line between the working class and the lower middle class, the *Kleinbürgertum*, one which could be drawn with any precision. Indeed it has been argued that "there was strictly speaking, in Germany, neither a powerful bourgeoisie nor a powerful working class [4] but only an industrial lower middle class which began to release certain groups upward and downward." [5] The poor journeyman who failed to obtain advancement in his trade guild and joined the ranks of the factory workers and the rising manufacturer were both initially members of the same social group and both products of the same crisis—the collapse of many of the old artisan trades.

The difficulty in defining the working class of 1848 lies partly in the drastic and complex changes which were occurring in the very concept of "class" and the vocabulary of social description. The emergence of the working class coincided with the emergence of the idea of class itself as distinct from status or estate: *Klasse* began to replace *Schicht* or *Stand* in contemporary nomenclature. The old German states had been regarded as static societies composed of estates. The economic forces which produced a working class saw the destruction of the medieval ideal of hierarchic or corporative estates which were equated with society, though many, from Frederick William IV of Prussia to the members of the entrenched guilds, still clung to it. The

[3] Stephan Born, *Erinnerungen eines Achtundvierzigers*, Leipzig, 1898, p. 122.

[4] *Vierten Stand*—literally "fourth estate." There is no adequate translation in English for this phrase and therein lies the problem of discussing the German working classes in 1848.

[5] Stadelmann, *Soziale und politische Geschichte*, p. 156.

16

concepts of "state" and "society" separated; the individual's rights in one were not to be determined, fixed or limited by his function or position in the other. Liberals demanded political rights for all; socialists preached class war. Both were ready for revolution; neither realized the true nature of the conditions under which the revolution would take place.[6]

The growth of population was in Germany, as in Britain, "the dominant event of the nineteenth century." [7] Between 1800 and 1850 the population of the German states swelled from 23 million to 35 million, an increase of over 50 per cent; two thirds of this increase occurred in the period after 1820. The rate of increase varied considerably between the different states. The Prussian population grew by 60 per cent from 1816 to 1846;

[6] For the distinction between "state" and "society," "status" and "class," see the two highly illuminating articles by Werner Conze, "Staat und Gesellschaft in der frührevolutionären Epoche Deutschlands," *Historische Zeitschrift*, vol. 186 (1958), pp. 1-34, and, more importantly for the study of the working class, "Vom 'Pöbel' zum 'Proletariat,' Sozialgeschichtliche Voraussetzungen für den Sozialismus in Deutschland," *Vierteljahrschrift für Sozial- und Wirtschaftsgeschichte*, vol. 41 (1954), pp. 333-364. The first of these articles has now been published in an expanded version along with essays illustrating the topic by a number of Conze's students in Werner Conze, ed., *Staat und Gesellschaft im deutschen Vormärz 1815-1848*, Stuttgart, 1962. On the older conception of German society, see Leonard Krieger, *The German Idea of Freedom, History of a Political Tradition*, Boston, 1957, pp. 8ff.; Franz Schnabel, *Deutsche Geschichte im neunzehnten Jahrhundert*, Freiburg im Breisgau, 1933, vol. 1, p. 13. The distinction between *class* and *status* is a fairly common one among sociologists; see Max Weber, *Essays in Sociology*, trans. H. H. Gerth and C. Wright Mills, New York, 1946, pp. 180-185. A discussion of similar developments in England may be found in Asa Briggs' article, "The Language of 'Class' in Early Nineteenth-Century England," *Essays in Labour History*, ed. Asa Briggs and John Saville, London, 1960, pp. 43-73; see also Raymond Williams, *Culture and Society, 1780-1950*, New York, 1959, introduction.

[7] So it was called by J. H. Clapham, *An Economic History of Modern Britain*, vol. 1, *The Early Railway Age*, Cambridge, 1926, p. vii.

that of Austria-Hungary rose by only 25 per cent between 1818 and 1846.[8]

The mass of population was still overwhelmingly rural. In 1850 approximately 70 per cent lived in the country or in villages of less than one thousand inhabitants; the figure had been 90 per cent at the beginning of the century.[9] The rural situation was thus far from static. Improvements in agricultural techniques such as deep plowing, the planting of a greater variety of crops and the use of artificial fertilizers had rapidly increased the productivity of German agriculture. More importantly, the movement to free the serfs, beginning with the Prussian decree of October 9, 1807, sweeping through the smaller states in the 1820s and 1830s and culminating with the abolition of the last labor dues, especially the Austrian *robot*, in 1848, both stimulated production and created a considerable problem of overpopulation in the rural areas. The dangers and difficulties of the "agrarian proletariat," the *unterbäuerliche Schicht* of the German villages, were much discussed in contemporary pamphlet literature. The villages themselves, the leading feature of German agricultural life which once could be said to "hold the people together, fostering a spirit of association," [10] were plagued with excess labor, with

[8] Jürgen Kuczynski, *Die Geschichte der Lage der Arbeiter in Deutschland von 1789 bis in die Gegenwart*, vol. 1, pt. 1, *1789 bis 1870*, Berlin, 1954, p. 34. Britain in the same period (1800-1850) showed a population increase of nearly 70 per cent, France of but slightly more than 30 per cent. Georg von Viebahn, ed., *Statistik des Zollvereinten und nördlichen Deutschlands*, Berlin, 1862-1868, vol. 2, p. 251; Jerome Blum, *Noble Landowners and Agriculture in Austria, 1815-1848*, Baltimore, 1948, p. 43.

[9] Viebahn, *Statistik*, vol. 2, p. 147; Gustav Schmoller, *Zur Geschichte der deutschen Kleingewerbe im 19. Jahrhundert, Statistische und nationalökonomische Untersuchungen*, Halle, 1870, pp. 189-190; Friedrich Lütge, *Deutsche Sozial- und Wirtschaftsgeschichte, Ein Ueberblick*, Berlin, 1952, p. 307.

[10] Thomas Banfield, an Englishman who visited Germany in 1845, spoke in praise of the German villages as a force for order

18

large numbers of landless peasants or those with holdings too small to support themselves. Faced with unemployment in the villages, with the decline of the smaller agricultural holdings and the breakdown of home industries, especially of weaving and spinning, the workless peasant moved whenever possible to the towns and cities, seeking employment in the new industries or swelling the ranks of the handicraft workers.[11]

The growth of the towns was perhaps the most marked feature of the period. Berlin grew by 110 per cent between 1819 and 1846, Vienna by 81 per cent in the same period, so that by 1848 they each had a population of over 400,000. Apart from these two there were few cities of any great size; only Hamburg and Breslau exceeded 100,000 in 1848, while four other cities (Munich, Dresden, Königsberg and Cologne) were approaching that mark.[12] It was not the larger cities so much as those of middle size that grew most. Partly because of the difficulties of traveling from one state to another and partly because of the lack of industry, the peasant or day laborer turned often as not to the nearest town of any size in his search for employment.[13]

＊

and improvement. In them, he declared, "the first attempts at association have been made." (*Industry of the Rhine,* London, 1846-1848, vol. 1, p. 83.)

[11] On the peasant proletariat in the 1830s and 1840s, see Conze, "Vom 'Pöbel' zum 'Proletariat,'" pp. 348-349.

[12] For the population of Berlin, see E. H. Müller and C. F. Schneider, *Jahresbericht des statistischen Amtes im königlichen Polizei-Präsidio zu Berlin für das Jahr 1852,* Leipzig, 1853, p. 7; the other figures are cited by Namier, *Revolution of the Intellectuals,* pp. 5-6, n. 2.

[13] For example, Stettin, the chief Baltic port for Prussia, increased its population by some 77 per cent between 1819 and 1847, although in the later year it still contained only some 45,000 inhabitants. *Mittheilungen des Centralvereins für das Wohl der arbeitenden Klassen,* Aug. 15, 1849. Also Banfield, *Industry of the Rhine,* vol. 2, p. 235.

In Germany the existence of cheap labor came first and was followed, all too slowly in many areas, by the development of industry. By the time of the 1848 uprisings the beginnings of industry were present, but only the beginnings. There were few industrial centers in the modern sense. Mining, for example, was carried out in rural areas; the miners were peasants who farmed small holdings at the same time that they worked the mines. In the Ruhr the Krupp factory employed only 122 workmen in 1846. Though the Borsig works on the outskirts of Berlin beyond the Oranienburger Tor had 1,200 employees, the average number of workers in the machine building factories in all of Prussia was only 58. There were only 1,261 steam engines for industrial purposes in Prussia and only 1,631 in the whole of the Zollverein.[14]

Manufacturing was most often carried on by master craftsmen, together with their journeymen and apprentices, working at home or in small workshops, either individually or as the employees of some entrepreneur who hired out the work and the materials. This held for a variety of trades and areas, ranging from the cutlery industry of Solingen to the textile trade of Saxony and Silesia. A few factories did exist in these areas, but they were regarded as exceptions and often treated as unwanted interlopers by the craftsmen. "Germany in general could in no sense be called capitalistic." [15] The

[14] Banfield, *Industry of the Rhine*, vol. 2, p. 75; Clapham, *Economic Development of France and Germany*, p. 92; Pierre Benaerts, *Les origines de la grande industrie allemande*, Paris, 1933, *passim; Die Verbrüderung, Correspondenzblatt aller deutschen Arbeiter*, Apr. 2, 1849; Hermann Müller, *Die Organisationen der Lithographen, Steindrucker und verwandten Berufe*, Berlin, 1917, p. xx.

[15] Clapham, *Economic Development of France and Germany*, p. 85.

artisan or handicraftsman provided the basis of German industry.

The predominance of artisans may be seen from an examination of the figures compiled by the Prussian Statistical Bureau under the direction of Friedrich Dieterici.[16] In 1846 the Prussian industrial class may be divided into the following groups:

master craftsmen	10.0
journeymen and apprentices	9.0
independent handicraft workers	33.0
servants and day workers	28.5
factory workers	12.5
trade and commerce	7.0
total	100.0

The first three groups constitute the class of handicraftsmen; taken together they represent some 52 per cent of the industrial class. On the other hand, the figure of 12.5 per cent given for factory workers must be modified; Dieterici included in this group all workers employed in the weaving trade and many of these worked not in factories but in their own homes under a putting-out system. Excluding the master craftsmen, the industrial working class comes to 27.2 per cent of the total male population of Prussia over fourteen years of age; the factory workers (in Dieterici's sense) constitute only 4.2 per cent. Such was the Prussian working class on the eve of 1848.

Contemporaries did indeed refer to this group as a "working class" and even as the "proletariat," though they were often somewhat hazy as to just what they meant by these terms. The anonymous author of a pamphlet entitled *Reflections of a German Proletarian*

[16] F. W. C. Dieterici, *Mittheilungen des statistischen Bureaus in Berlin*, Berlin, 1849, pp. 68-80.

which appeared in Munich at the outbreak of the revolution offered the following definition:[17]

The proletariat is that class which does not have sufficient property to feed itself on the proceeds of the same but must support itself through manual labor, which however only exists during the periods of well-ordered government and political stability. Also to be counted as proletarians are those small property owners or artisans whose income is no sooner affected by some small event in the life of society than it does not suffice to support them.

Another anonymous pamphleteer spoke of the working class which "consists of the just—since propertyless—classes, the proletarians, the mass of the workers who are despised as a 'mob' and mistreated by the bourgeoisie, debased by money, or [by] the aristocracy, proud of its family tree." In this class the author included small master craftsmen, their journeymen, apprentices and assistants, factory workers and manual laborers, daily wage earners as well as students, artists and writers! [18] And the city chronicler of Nuremberg referred to the "proletariat" simply as "a new word for people who have no money." [19] The idea of a "working class"

[17] *Betrachtungen eines deutschen Proletariers,* Munich, 1848, p. 19.

[18] *Contre-Revolution in Berlin oder Bürger und Arbeiter,* Berlin, 1848. The pamphlet ends with the stirring declaration, typical of the time: "The intelligentsia and the workers: they are one!" This attitude is not so farfetched however; actors and artists, for example, both thought of themselves as members of the working class—superior ones to be sure—and petitioned the Frankfurt Assembly to be included in the regulations for workers' guilds. *Akten des volkswirtschaftlichen Ausschusses,* vol. 10, minutes for committee meeting, Apr. 28, 1849; vol. 17, petition of artists in Paderborn in Westphalia.

[19] Quoted by Ludwig Brunner, *Politische Bewegungen in Nürnberg im Jahre 1848 bis zu den Herbstereignisse,* Heidelberg, 1907, p. 37.

had thus gained considerable currency, though the workers to whom the term was applied were a very mixed group indeed.

The existence of a working class at this time is a denial of the proposition that such a class is the product of the Industrial Revolution, a refutation of the dictum that "the proletariat follows the capitalistic form of production as its shadow." [20] Rather in Germany the process seems to have been reversed: the growth of the proletariat, or what contemporaries regarded as a proletariat, preceded the full development of capitalism. Indeed the extension of the factory system was regarded as a partial solution to the problem of an underemployed working class otherwise dependent on the old trades and hampered by guild regulations. "The sickness for Germany," wrote Peter Reichensperger in 1847, "lies not in the excess of population, not in the machine system nor in the superfluity of industrial factories in general; rather it lies precisely in the lack of those machines and factories which ought to create work and employment for *our* workers instead of the English." [21] A contemporary Englishman explained the quiescence of German factory workers in the face of low wages and long hours by this "excess of supply over demand for labour." [22] The factory workers were relatively secure, relatively well off, and they knew it: this accounts to a large extent for the conservative role the factory workers were to play in the coming revolution.

＊

The members of the old established handicraft trades and the medieval guilds constituted the largest section

[20] Werner Sombart, *Socialism and the Social Movement in the Nineteenth Century,* New York, 1898, p. 9.
[21] Quoted by Conze, "Vom 'Pöbel' zum 'Proletariat,'" p. 361.
[22] Banfield, *Industry of the Rhine,* vol. 2, p. 41.

of the working class. In Prussia in 1846 this group came to some 14 per cent of the entire population; moreover, it was an expanding group, having increased in size by some 87 per cent since 1816, that is, at a rate substantially greater than that at which the total population was growing. Elsewhere, in Bavaria, for example, and Baden, and most of all in Saxony, the guild handicraftsmen formed an even more dominant element in the working class.[23] This growth in size runs counter to the general picture of decline; indeed the declining position of the artisans was partly a result of their increased numbers.

Moreover the artisans as a group were changing in composition. Master craftsmen still exceeded their assistants in number but, whereas at the end of the Napoleonic Wars there were in Germany nearly twice as many masters as there were journeymen and apprentices, the proportion in 1846 was something like ten to nine. The increase in the number of journeymen and apprentices was an accelerating phenomenon, largely confined to the years after 1830.[24] The change led to a severe conflict of interest between the journeymen and the masters. The latter, fearing competition and overcrowding of the market, attempted to increase the difficulties of entering a trade, raising the standards of the entrance examinations or even establishing arbitrary limits on the numbers to be admitted. The journeymen found their way blocked, their hope of achieving the rank of master foiled and themselves condemned to a lower

[23] Schmoller, *Geschichte der deutschen Kleingewerbe,* pp. 65, 71, 139-140.

[24] Schmoller, *Geschichte der deutschen Kleingewerbe,* pp. 168-169. Stephan Born noted that the most important division in the German working class was between the masters and the journeymen. "There were," he remarked, "two age levels, not two classes." *Erinnerungen,* p. 136.

standard of living.[25] Opposition between masters and journeymen was not a new feature; many examples can be found in the eighteenth century and before. But then the journeymen remained among the strongest supporters of the guilds. Now they were ready to ignore, perhaps because they were forced to, the fixed course prescribed by guild regulations; they began to look for revolutionary remedies and lent an eager ear to the socialist agitators they met abroad, in Paris or Switzerland, during their *Wanderjahre*.[26]

The masters were themselves divided. A few were prosperous, employing large numbers of journeymen or at least as many as the guild regulations would allow them, achieving a substantial income and enjoying a position of considerable importance in their communities, retaining only nominally the position of artisan.[27] Most, however, worked without assistants and had a standard of living little if any better than the mass of journeymen. There was great fear among the master craftsmen of sinking into the working class, of being, in the words of the petition the guilds of Eschwege in Electoral Hesse were to send to the Frankfurt Assembly, "forced into the abyss of the proletariat." [28]

[25] One symptom of the increasing gap between masters and journeymen was that the latter now found it more difficult to find wives among the daughters of the former, who came to regard a mere journeyman as beneath their social position. E. F. Goldschmidt, *Die deutsche Handwerkerbewegung bis zum Siege der Gewerbefreiheit,* Munich, 1916, p. 12; Veit Valentin, *Frankfurt am Main und die Revolution von 1848-49,* Berlin, 1908, p. 104.

[26] Rudolf Stadelmann, Wolfram Fischer, *Die Bildungswelt des deutschen Handwerkers um 1800, Studien zur Soziologie des Kleinbürgers im Zeitalter Goethes,* Berlin, 1955, pp. 70ff.

[27] Stadelmann and Fischer give biographical sketches of several such figures, *Bildungswelt,* pp. 117ff., 158ff., 168ff.

[28] *Akten des volkswirtschaftlichen Ausschusses,* vol. 12. The petition noted that those already belonging to the "proletariat" came "in large part . . . from the sick stem of the artisan class."

In fact it seemed to some that the *Handwerkerstand* could itself be divided into two "classes." Gottfried Kinkel, the radical professor of history at the University of Bonn, summed up the position of the artisans in 1848 in the following words:[29]

> In the handicraft trades the struggle of capital and labor, the angry opposition of the aristocracy and the proletariat, rages more deeply than in the other estates. Half the artisans belongs to the bourgeoisie and visits the casinos . . . ; the other half sends its children to the poor house and lives a mean and miserable life on its daily earnings. Among the artisans themselves an aristocracy has arisen—namely, *the aristocracy of the better coat.*

❖

The crisis of the handicraft trades was a complex one, going beyond the impoverishment of the artisans. A simple picture of decline is inadequate. Indeed the crisis did not hurt all artisans nor was it evident at all times. The years following the end of the Napoleonic Wars were ones of relative stability and even prosperity for the small trades; the decline set in only in the late 1830s, perhaps not until the financial crisis of 1839, and then more markedly in the 1840s, producing the unrest that broke out with the Silesian weavers' revolt of 1844 and fed into the revolutions of 1848. Even then not all trades were affected. The blacksmith in the village, the mason and carpenter in the city, were still needed for local work. But tailors, shoemakers, printers,

[29] *Handwerk, errette Dich! oder Was soll der deutsche Handwerker fordern und tun, um seinen Stand zu bessern?* Bonn, 1848, pp. 5-6. Kinkel dedicated his pamphlet to the Economic Committee of the Frankfurt Assembly and called for legal protection from the state for the handicraft trades together with direct material aid and the granting of the right of free association. These were in essence the demands of the German workers of 1848.

weavers and even cigar makers (the groups that were to be most active in 1848)—all of these could be and were hurt by competition from other cities and other countries and by the improvement in methods of production.[30] At the same time, the use of machines created new opportunities for mechanical artisans.

Two factors in particular undermined the position of the traditional handicraft trades: the foundation of the *Zollverein* in 1834 and the growth of the railways, which expanded rapidly from the first line in 1835 (five miles of track from Nuremberg to Fürth), so that by 1848 there were 3,000 kilometers and the railway age for Germany could be said to have begun.[31] Schmoller indeed saw the railways as the chief cause of the collapse of the small handicraft trades. For the competition of trade from the farthest reaches of the German states as well as increasingly cheap goods from Britain and Belgium attacked the position of many of the handicraft trades before industrial production was of great importance in Germany itself.[32]

The importance of trade accounts for the intensity and the particular focus of debates on laissez-faire in Germany. The interests which fought against free trade in Germany were different from those in England. There the controversy centered on the protection of agriculture. In Germany a greater range of positions could be found. Many accepted Friedrich List's arguments for internal free trade and protection abroad. But the problem was

[30] Among the collapsing trades was also that of the wig makers, a direct casualty of the decline of the fashions of the old regime.

[31] Jürgen Kuczynski, *Die wirtschaftlichen und sozialen Voraussetzungen der Revolution von 1848/49*, Berlin, 1948, p. 15.

[32] Schmoller, *Geschichte der deutschen Kleingewerbe*, p. 166; the railways changed in particular the pattern of the *Wanderjahre* of the journeymen, cf. Stadelmann and Fischer, *Bildungswelt*, p. 74.

complicated by the question of the protection of the handicraft trades and the preservation of the guild system. Indeed two concepts were involved though they were not always clearly separated by contemporaries. The German word *Gewerbefreiheit* means literally "trade freedom" and is perhaps best translated as "free entry into trades." This, for the workers and artisans, was a far more important issue than simply *Freihandel* or free trade in the English sense.[33] For many observers the troubles of the artisans started with the introduction of trade freedom, or free entry into trade, in the Rhineland by the French during the Napoleonic Wars and the subsequent reforms of Stein and Hardenberg, particularly the laws of 1810-1811 which sought to establish this free entry throughout Prussia. "From this time," declared one pamphleteer of 1848, "dates the impoverishment of the industrial class." [34]

The French and Prussian efforts to reform the guild system were in some respects not new; indeed they may be seen as the culmination of eighteenth century attempts at codifying guild laws, attempts which date back to the instructions of the Imperial Diet of 1731, calling on all the German states to reform the regulations of the guilds. And in spite of the French and Prussian reforms the guild system remained intact throughout most of Germany. Even in Prussia the laws of 1810-1811

[33] The German economic historian Lütge treats *Handelsfreiheit* as simply a subdivision of the general problem of *Gewerbefreiheit*. *Sozial- und Wirtschaftsgeschichte*, p. 329.

[34] C. F. Wesenfeld, *Beschränkte oder unbeschränkte Gewerbefreiheit, Eine Zeitfrage,* Berlin, 1848, p. 3. The laws of 1810-1811 are analyzed in detail in Kurt von Rohrscheidt, *Vom Zunftzwange zur Gewerbefreiheit, Eine Studie nach der Quellen,* Berlin, 1898, bks. 2 and 3; Hugo Roehl, *Beiträge zur Preussischen Handwerkerpolitik vom Allgemeinen Landrecht zur Allgemeinen Gewerbeordnung von 1845,* Leipzig, 1900, pp. 107-155.

were never thoroughly applied nor were they extended to the portions of Saxony acquired in 1815.

A fixed period of apprenticeship under a qualified master, several years of travel and work as a journeyman—the *Wanderjahre* much extolled by German poets of the period—and the passing of a set of stiff examinations were required for entry into most trades. There were a number of anomalies: often simple articles, a lock, a table, a loaf of bread, were made by guild members, supposedly the more skilled among the workers, while complex ones, a piano, for example, or scientific instruments, were not. Guild and nonguild workers were joined in similar or related jobs. Masons and carpenters belonged to guilds, but architects, construction workers and shipbuilders did not; the ironsmiths belonged but the machine builders did not. The Prussian regulations were codified in the industrial ordinance (*Gewerbeordnung*) of January 17, 1845, which marked a further advance toward industrial freedom and was put through over the protests of many of the handicraft workers. The rights of guilds to limit the number of apprentices were abolished; their power of examination and control over the entry into trades was limited; the requirement of *Wanderjahre* for journeymen (and with it their guaranteed support) was dropped. Still the guilds remained in forty-two different trades, some new guilds were founded where none before had existed, and police permission was often substituted for guild membership as a requirement for the practicing of a trade.[35]

[35] Goldschmidt, *Die deutschen Handwerkerbewegung*, pp. 10-11, 14-15; Schmoller, *Geschichte der deutschen Kleingewerbe*, pp. 83ff.; Roehl, *Beiträge*, pp. 251ff.; Hugo C. M. Wendel, *The Evolution of Industrial Freedom in Prussia 1845-1849*, Allentown, Pa., 1918, pp. 8, 23-47.

Elsewhere the guilds were in an even stronger position than they were in Prussia. The whole effect of the French reforms in Electoral Hesse was counteracted with the restoration of the guilds there in 1816. A Württemberg ordinance of 1838, while freeing thirteen trades from the requirement of guild membership, retained this requirement for some fifty others, including many of the most common. In Bavaria, with the exception of the Rhenish Palatinate which had been occupied by the French, the guild system remained and a law of 1834 limited the previously existing privileges of officials in granting exceptions to the entry regulations. In Saxony, in spite of its growing textile industry, guild regulations and compulsory guild membership were strictly enforced under a law of 1840, and the country retained the highest proportion of artisans to total population among the members of the *Zollverein*.[36]

Yet legal protection was probably inadequate to preserve the position of the guilds. The problem was not simply the impoverishment of the artisans. Beyond economic grievances lay the devotion of many of the members of the guilds to an entire way of life, a culture with deep roots in the past, an ethos which had established the guild members as men of status and stature in the community. Contemporary literature paid considerable attention to the moral effects of the collapse of the artisan guilds as well—the undermining of the restraint and educational benefits which a respected master provided for apprentices and journeymen. The 1840s saw the breakdown and threatened destruction of a system which had grown up in the later Middle Ages

[36] Hamerow, *Restoration, Revolution, Reaction,* pp. 26-29; Rudolf Bovensiepen, *Die kurhessische Gewerbepolitik und die wirtschaftliche Lage des zünftigen Handwerks in Kurhessen von 1816-1867,* Halle, 1907, p. 13; Richard Lipinski, *Die Geschichte der sozialistischen Arbeiterbewegung in Leipzig,* Leipzig, 1931, vol. 1, p. 46.

and survived largely untouched at least until the beginning of the nineteenth century.[37]

＊

There was also throughout Germany more than ample cause for the workers to demand simple, physical improvement in their standard of living. Many were hungry; many lived in abject poverty.[38] Long hours (12 per day was a minimum and 14 or even 16 quite usual) and low wages were a common and constant complaint. In Berlin, for example, wages ranged from less than 1 thaler per week (approximately 84 cents at the contemporary exchange rates) to 5 or 6 thaler in the most skilled and exclusive trades. Printers, who were considered to be well off among the handicraft workers, received 3 thaler, 15 silbergroschen per week, and this at a time when the barest minimum upon which it was possible to live for a single worker with neither wife nor family was estimated at upward of 2 thaler per week. Many were attempting to exist below this minimum.[39]

The working class of Germany was thus faced with genuine grievances but with a system of work and

[37] For a description of guild ethos and guild customs, see Stadelmann and Fischer, *Bildungswelt*, ch. 2, "Das Ethos des Handwerkerstandes"; also Rudolf Wissell, *Des alten Handwerks-Recht und Gewohnheit*, Berlin, 1929, 2 vols.

[38] Horror stories abound: one mother in Vienna was reported to have cooked her dead baby and served it to her starving children. At the same time the Viennese press reported a dinner for the wealthy with strawberries imported from Italy at £1 apiece. C. Edmund Maurice, *The Revolutionary Movement of 1848-9 in Italy, Austria-Hungary and Germany*, London, 1887, p. 210.

[39] Ernst Dronke, *Berlin*, Berlin, 1953 (first published in 1846), pp. 229ff.; Born, *Erinnerungen*, pp. 123-124; Hermann Meyer, *1848, Studien zur Geschichte der deutschen Revolution*, Darmstadt, 1949, p. 80; Wilhelm Friedensburg, *Stephan Born und die Organisationsbestrebungen der Berliner Arbeiterschaft bis zum Berliner Arbeiterkongress*, Leipzig, 1923, p. 5.

organization in the various trades which hampered any efforts at improvement. It was the artisan far more than the factory worker that was hurt by this system. Moreover the guild structure was in part a bar against efforts at self-improvement. The master stood in a semipatriarchal relationship to his journeymen and apprentices and it was considered almost a sign of ingratitude for the latter to complain against his regime.[40] This spirit of servitude extended to the state and went back to the days of Frederick the Great and Joseph II. Indeed the workers looked primarily to the state to regulate their position, to maintain the old trades and guilds. Yet the state, as the Prussian industrial ordinance of 1845 indicated, was increasingly unable or unwilling to do this.

Such was the position of the workers when faced with the economic crisis of the mid-1840s. The potato famine of 1845 was followed by grain failures of 1846 and 1847. By the middle of the latter year the price of wheat in the Rhineland was 250 per cent higher than it had been in 1845; rye was up by 300 per cent and potatoes by 425 per cent.[41] Wages did not keep pace with prices but remained roughly constant. State aid, though immediately sought by the workers, was slow in coming. When it came it consisted mainly in the alteration of tariffs in favor of imports and the prohibition of the exportation of foodstuffs, together with such questionably beneficial measures as the publication of recipes for baking bread from grass and the holding of public barbecues to encourage the eating of horsemeat. The bad harvest of 1847 coincided with a considerable financial and trade crisis which began in England and spread throughout the

[40] Born, *Erinnerungen*, p. 124.
[41] Oscar J. Hammen, "Economic and Social Factors in the Prussian Rhineland in 1848," *American Historical Review*, vol. 54 (1949), pp. 828-830.

continent. From August 1847 through January 1848 some 245 firms and 12 banks failed in Germany alone.[42] To high prices and low wages was added the threat, and often the reality, of unemployment.

The workers responded with a flood of petitions for government protection, with increased interest in the workers' associations and at least the slogans of socialism, and with a readiness for revolution.

[42] Max Wirth, *Geschichte der Handelskrisen*, Frankfurt am Main, 1858, p. 457.

CHAPTER 2

SOCIALIST THEORIES AND
WORKERS' CLUBS

THE DISCONTENT of the German workers in the mid-nineteenth century first broke into open revolt in Silesia in 1844. Some 5,000 weavers in the neighborhood of Peterswaldau and Langenbielau rose in protest against near starvation and the increased use of machines, burning shops and the houses of the more prosperous master weavers and the entrepreneurs or middlemen who hired out the work. They were joined by masons, carpenters and other artisans in the area; the rebellion set off a series of strikes in Breslau, the chief city of Silesia, and in Berlin itself among the workers in the calico factories and on the new railroads. The rebellion was brutally suppressed.[1]

The rising of 1844 and the subsequent strikes marked the beginning of a period of increasing unrest among the workers; the threat of working-class violence was one of the realities of Germany in the mid-1840s. There had been isolated examples of workers' riots before, especially from the 1790s when the journeymen of Berlin and Breslau, especially the tailors, returned from their *Wanderjahre* in revolutionary France to lead revolts

---

[1] Strict censorship was imposed in Silesia at the time, and accurate information, as opposed to the dramatized legend embodied in Gerhart Hauptmann's play, is hard to come by; but see two recent articles, Friedrich May, "Der Weberaufstand 1844," in Leo Stern, ed., *Archivalische Forschungen zur Geschichte der deutschen Arbeiterbewegung*, Berlin, 1954, pp. 123-127, and Kurt Koszyk, "Der Schlesische Weberaufstand von 1844 nach Berichten der 'Mannheimer Abendzeitung,'" *Jahrbuch der Schlesischen Friedrich-Wilhelms-Universität zu Breslau*, vol. 7 (1962), pp. 224-232.

against the master craftsmen.[2] In the 1830s there were instances of rioting and machine breaking, particularly in the Prussian Rhineland. But mostly the workers confined themselves to legal means of protest, petitioning for redress of their wrongs. In 1841, for example, the handicraft workers of Cologne sent an address to the newly crowned Frederick William IV, from whom so much was hoped by so many, urging him, "from the wisdom of his majesty," to remove the threat of poverty which went with trade freedom, to restore and support the guild system. The petitioners also requested the establishment of industrial libraries so that they could increase their knowledge of new techniques, a request symptomatic of the nonrevolutionary goals of many of the workers.[3]

After 1844 this mood of quiescence was broken. Many still placed reliance on legal means and self-help, a reliance which was to show itself even in the revolutionary years in the flood of petitions and the drive for organization. At the same time workers' demands were increasingly accompanied by workers' demonstrations and riots, provoked by the rising price of bread and the growing threat of unemployment. The workers of Leipzig paraded through the streets of that town in 1845, again calling for state action to fix wages and prevent competition. In 1846 there were strikes for higher pay among the railway workers in various parts of Prussia and a further attempt at machine-breaking among the Silesian weavers. In the spring of 1847 there were hunger demonstrations in several cities, including the so-called "potato revolution" in Berlin. These riots were perhaps

[2] Eduard Bernstein, *Die Schneiderbewegung in Deutschland, Ihre Organization und Kämpfe,* Berlin, 1913, vol. 1, p. 68.

[3] Wilhelm Eduard Biermann, *Karl Georg Winkelblech (Karl Marlo), Seine Leben und sein Werk,* Leipzig, 1909, vol. 2, pp. 39-41.

purely economic in character, devoid of any political content, the blind reaction of working men to forces beyond their control or understanding. Yet before 1844 they were all but unknown.[4]

The question was one of outlets: what form would this unrest take, could it be harnessed to political agitation? This was to be the central problem of 1848.

*

The history of the pre-March period offered little comfort to those who sought to build a revolution on working-class unrest. Radical and socialist theories were much discussed, but mainly among the intellectual, and middle-class, Young Hegelians; working-class understanding of these theories was minimal, working-class support was marginal.

Nonetheless socialist ideas were to color the revolutions of 1848. Socialist slogans were to be adopted by many, though their goals were often remote from those advocated by the socialists themselves; they were to be feared by many more. The debates among the German intellectuals about the "social question" and the implications of the new philosophy and the ways in which the issues of these debates filtered down to the workers remain a part of the pre-March period essential for understanding events which followed the outbreak of revolution in March of 1848.

The accession of Frederick William IV to the Prussian throne in 1840 was an occasion for renewed hope to those who longed for national revival and reform; a number of apparently liberal appointments, coupled with a relaxation of censorship, temporary though it proved to be, gave impetus to a series of publications which attempted to assess the condition of Germany

[4] Adler, *Geschichte der Arbeiterbewegung*, p. 136.

and supply remedies for it.[5] Much of the writing was purely political; much more was on abstruse philosophical or theological issues. But the "social question," the beginnings of the industrial revolution and the plight of the artisans were also taken up. Newspapers appeared such as the *Rheinische Zeitung*, published in Cologne under the editorship of the young Karl Marx and with backing from liberal businessmen, the *Gesellschaftsspiegel*, edited by Moses Hess in Elberfeld (1844-1846), and the *Westfälische Dampfboot* (originally the *Weserdampfboot*), edited by Otto Lüning and Karl Grün in Bielefeld from 1843 to 1846. To these newspapers were added books which raised the "social question" such as Lorenz von Stein's *Socialism and Communism in Contemporary France*, published in 1842, and Friedrich Engels' *The Condition of the Working Class in England in 1844*, published in Leipzig in 1845. The latter work, whatever its limitations as a description of English conditions, provides, with its vision of an impoverished and oppressed industrial proletariat, an accurate key to what many Germans thought to be the inevitable results of industrialization.

Such were the more famous examples of the means by which the "social question" was brought to the German consciousness in the 1840s.[6] One should note,

[5] As the *Verbrüderung* was later to note (Oct. 31, 1848): "When Frederick William IV mounted the throne of his father, who rested in God, people then believed that, with the old king, the old state was also buried and that in the new purple was a new dawn."

[6] There is not space here to cite more examples of the flood of materials, books, articles and pamphlets which took up German social problems in the mid-1840s. For the literature produced in just one of these years, see Kurt Koszyk, "Die Bedeutung des Jahres 1845 für den Sozialismus in Deutschland," *Annali dell' Instituto Giangiacomo Feltrinelli*, Anno Sesto, 1963, pp. 510-520; a useful and extensive bibliography may be found in Paul Mombert, "Aus der Literatur über die soziale Frage und die

however, that German socialism was not just a trans-
planted French growth nor the agitation simply a vi-
carious response to the English industrial revolution;
many of its roots were indigenous. Indeed such relatively
respectable and even conservative figures as Fichte, von
Baader and Metternich himself espoused a sort of socialism. On the left the variety of socialisms which were
presented at this time was much greater than the
later categories of Marx and the Marxists would indicate.
The criticisms of Hegelian idealism, the influx of French
socialist thought and in particular the development of
the ideas of Karl Marx down to the *Communist Manifesto* of 1848 have of course been traced in great detail.[7]
It is worth noting, however, that it was not obvious, at
least in the 1840s, that Marx was to be the most important thinker of his time and country; though the Young
Hegelians, the "true socialists" and the Utopians are
now chiefly remembered as the early, and defeated,
opponents of Marx, it would be wrong to assume that
they were without effect at the time. Moreover, the
dialectic by which Marx arrived at his doctrines, his
adaptation of the concept of alienation which he found
in Hegel and Feuerbach to a purely or at least largely
economic analysis, was a more gradual and more tortuous
process than was once thought.

In many of these early writers whom Marx attacked,
particularly in the group of "true socialists," Hess, Grün,
Lüning, Semmig and others, one finds a number of
elements calculated to appeal to the German workers

Arbeiterbewegung in Deutschland in der ersten Hälfte des 19.
Jahrhunderts," *Archiv für die Geschichte des Sozialismus und der
Arbeiterbewegung*, vol. 9 (1921), pp. 169-236.
    [7] See Sidney Hook, *From Hegel to Marx, Studies in the In-
tellectual Development of Karl Marx*, New York, 1936; Robert
Tucker, *Philosophy and Myth in Karl Marx*, Cambridge, 1961;
George Lichtheim, *Marxism, An Historical and Critical Study*,
London, 1961.

of the 1840s. The emphasis on organization and association, the belief that industrialization and its attendant evils could be by-passed or avoided altogether, were to be key elements in the demands of the German workers after March 1848. Marx was probably right in claiming in the *Manifesto* that "true socialism" aimed at preserving the remnants of the petty bourgeoisie from proletarization; but this was also the aim, however divided they might have been about means, of the bulk of the German workers and artisans of 1848.[8]

The appeal of this sort of socialism can also be seen in the career of Wilhelm Weitling, who was for a time a serious challenge to Marx's leadership of the socialist movement and who was also—a rare thing among the socialists of the time—himself a worker.[9] Born in 1808, the illegitimate son of a German serving girl and a French noncommissioned officer stationed with the occupying troops in Magdeburg, Weitling was apprenticed at an early age to a tailor. He spent his *Wanderjahre,* beginning in 1826, first in Germany and later, when he failed to advance to the rank of master, abroad.

It was in Paris in 1836 that Weitling first became acquainted with socialist doctrines. Working there and in the early 1840s in Switzerland with the League of the Just, one of a number of groups of exiled German

[8] For the "true socialists'" emphasis on organization and association, see Hook, *From Hegel to Marx,* p. 198; Kurt Koszyk, "Das 'Dampfboot' und der Rhedaer Kreis," *Dortmunder Beiträge zur Zeitungsforschung,* vol. 2 (1958), p. 10. Marx's attack appears in the *Manifesto,* Karl Marx, Friedrich Engels, *Selected Works,* Moscow, 1951, vol. 1, p. 56.

[9] See Carl Wittke, *The Utopian Communist, A Biography of Wilhelm Weitling, Nineteenth Century Reformer,* Baton Rouge, 1950. Weitling was to be hailed by the Nazis as the true representative of German socialists; blond, blue-eyed and "Teutonic" (in spite of his French father), he was contrasted by historians with the "Jewish socialism" of 1848 as represented by Marx and Stephan Born. (Kurt H. Neumann, *Die jüdische Verfälschung des Sozialismus in der Revolution von 1848,* Berlin, 1939.)

workers, Weitling produced in three works, *Humanity as It Is and Ought To Be* (1838), called by Heine "the catechism of the German communists," *The Guarantees of Harmony and Freedom* (1842) and *The Gospel of the Poor Sinner* (1843), his own version of socialism. Weitling's position belonged to the Christian communist tradition; moral precepts were exalted even when organized religion was attacked. He protested against economic injustice from the point of view of the artisan and called for the development of a moral society based on co-operation and handicraft.[10]

Weitling's attacks on established religion led to his arrest in 1843 and his expulsion from Switzerland in 1844. Expelled in turn from Prussia, Weitling spent some time in London and Brussels before leaving in 1846 for the United States. There he passed the remainder of his life with the exception of an ineffectual visit, during the revolution, to Germany, where the former hero of the German workers found himself ignored by all.

While in London Weitling met with the local German Workers' Union, a remnant of the old League of the Just led by Joseph Moll and Karl Schapper, and through them he was put in touch with Karl Marx in Brussels. There, on the eve of Weitling's departure for the United States, a showdown took place between Weitling and Marx which was partly a struggle for the control of the

[10] Weitling even tried to convert children to his version of Christian socialism, writing such nursery rhymes as the following:

> Ich bin ein kleiner Kommunist
> Und frage nichts nach Geld
> Da unser Meister Jesu Christ
> Davon ja auch nichts hält.

Freely translated this reads: "I am a little communist / And never ask for money / For our lord and master Jesus Christ / Also did not have any." (Quoted by Hermann Buddensieg, *Wilhelm Weitling und der frühe deutsche Sozialismus*, Heidelberg, 1934, p. 60.)

exiled German workers' groups and partly a debate on the nature of socialist theory and the workers' movement.[11] Marx objected to Weitling's socialism as being based on idealist morals rather than on scientific materialism. Weitling was outvoted and Marx became the unchallenged leader of the Brussels group. Yet Weitling's theories remained of far greater appeal to the German workers than those of Marx; moral precepts and the preservation of the artisans were far more characteristic of the German workers' movement of the 1840s than was the abstruse reasoning of scientific socialism.

Marx thus gained control of the Communist League formed from the remaining branches of the League of the Just; in argument the ignorant and romantic artisan was never a match for him. At the League's convention in London in November of 1847, Marx together with Engels was asked to produce a statement of the group's purposes and program. The result was the *Communist Manifesto,* published in London in February of 1848, a few weeks before the outbreak of the revolution. The economic and social situation of Europe was analyzed in a suitable "scientific" manner; the rival socialist creeds of the Utopians, the "true socialists" and others were dismissed; the call for revolution was sounded. The attention of communists was directed particularly to Germany because that country was held to be, more than any other, ripe for revolution, if only a bourgeois one, and "because," Marx and Engels seemed clearly to believe, "the bourgeois revolution in Germany will be but the prelude to an immediately following proletarian revolution." [12]

Both socialism and communism, in spite of Marx's efforts to define them, remained vague and general terms

[11] See Wittke, *Utopian Communist,* pp. 105-123.
[12] Marx, Engels, *Selected Works,* vol. 1, p. 61.

throughout 1848, referring to almost any doctrine which held out some means of solution to the "social question" or some alleviation of social distress. Engels' later assertion that "socialism was, in 1847, a middle-class movement, Communism a working-class movement" [13] had no basis either in contemporary class structure or contemporary usage. In official and bourgeois circles anyone concerned with social problems was regarded as a socialist or communist. A dictionary published in 1848 defined "communism" as "a new French word nearly synonymous with agrarianism, socialism and radicalism," [14] and in 1849 the Austrian general Windischgrätz referred to his brother-in-law, Felix von und zu Schwarzenberg, the then prime minister of the Austrian Empire, as a "communist" because he refused to restore the privileges of the landowning nobility. Workers' groups often thought in similarly vague terms. After the revolution one paper offered the following definition of "socialism": "What one calls socialist is the destruction of *all* limits which stand in the way of the universal right to the enjoyment of *all* the goods of life, of *free work*." Listed as "socialist" measures were universal suffrage, freedom of the press, the right of assembly— a radical but not specifically socialist program.[15] The symbols and slogans of the socialists were often taken up, "emancipation of the working class" and "organization of work" were advocated, but the meaning they

[13] From the preface to the 1888 English edition of the *Manifesto*, Marx, Engels, *Selected Works*, vol. 1, p. 27.

[14] A. E. Bestor, "The Evolution of the Socialist Vocabulary," *Journal of the History of Ideas*, vol. 9 (1948), p. 263.

[15] *Verbrüderung*, Aug. 3, 1849. Another paper from the revolutionary period, admittedly hostile to such goals, lumped "radicalism, communism, separatism, fanaticism and popery" together as synonomous terms and went on to puzzle over the fact that all contemporary evils ended up in a mishmash (*ein Mus*) of ideologies. (*Die Geissel, Tageblatt aller Tageblätter*, June 6, 1849.)

were given was determined not by the socialist writers but by the condition of the German workers.

✿

The history of the artisans' clubs and workers' organizations during the pre-March period shows a continuing flirtation with such radical ideas but also a continued emphasis on the solid, traditional values and interests of the guilds and the handicraft workers.

Only two instances of a possible "communist conspiracy" were brought to light before 1848, and this in spite of considerable zeal on the part of the police to unearth plots even where they did not exist. Indeed even the two instances which were discovered seem to have been exaggerated out of all proportion both by the horrified governments at the time and by admiring communist historians in more recent years.

In Warmbrunn in Silesia a "conspiracy" was revealed at the beginning of 1845; it was said to aim at the overthrow of the state and the establishment of a society based on equality. Some four artisans were sentenced to short terms in prison (they were released in 1847), and the leader, a master cabinetmaker named Wurm, was condemned to death, a sentence later commuted to life imprisonment. Wurm was included in the general amnesty of March 19, 1848, and allowed to return to Warmbrunn. In spite of the vaguely socialist content of Wurm's program, the conspiracy seems to have been totally devoid of contact with the other socialist thinkers or groups.[16]

The police discovered a small group of communist reading cells in Berlin late in 1846. It had been organized by two journeymen, a tailor, Christian Mentel (or

[16] Georg Becker, "Franz Wurm und die sogenannte 'Warmbrunner Verschwörung' im Jahre 1848," Stern, ed., *Archivalische Forschungen*, pp. 129ff.

Mäntel), and a shoemaker, August Hätzel. Mentel had been to Paris during his *Wanderjahre* and there had met Weitling and joined the League of the Just. Returning to Berlin in 1845, he tried to organize groups to study the new doctrines and joined the Journeymen's Union with this end in mind. He attracted Hätzel and a few others to the cause, but in general he had little success. The workers were apathetic and uninterested; some at least regarded Mentel as a police spy.[17] The arrest of Mentel and Hätzel in December 1846 put a sudden stop to a movement which was probably dying anyway of natural causes. Hätzel was acquitted in July 1847 for lack of evidence, and Mentel, though found guilty, was released since he had already served six months in prison.

There were communist reading and study groups similar to the one in Berlin in other cities in Germany; indeed police reports warned of as many as fifty of these.[18] Most were organized by workers who had traveled abroad during their period as journeymen and had been in contact with the various branches of the old League of the Just, which had dispersed from Paris after its implication in the Blanquist conspiracy of 1839.

Part of the League had collected in Switzerland around Weitling, who was attempting to organize a consumers' cooperative association and to spread communist propaganda. Weitling's efforts made little headway. The Germans in Switzerland seemed more interested in the Young Germany group which was affiliated to Mazzini's

[17] Eduard Bernstein, *Die Geschichte der Berliner Arbeiterbewegung,* Berlin, 1907-1910, vol. 1, p. 6.

[18] Wermuth and Stieber, *Die Communisten-Verschwörungen des neunzehnten Jahrhunderts,* Berlin, 1853-1854, vol. 1, pp. 54-55. The authors had access to the official records of the Prussian police and give much useful information. At the same time they seem to have been sort of proto-McCarthys, seeing a communist under every bed and behind every bush, so that there is a good deal of exaggeration in their reports.

Young Europe movement. Or they turned to such curious leaders as the "Prophet" Albrecht, who called for reform based on the Bible and "the reestablishment of the Kingdom of Zion," or George Kuhlmann, who also regarded himself as a prophet, wore his hair and beard long and preached on "the New World or the Proclamation of the Rule of the Spirit on Earth." [19] These figures represented the lunatic fringe of the pre-March movement; yet to many of the workers their doctrines probably seemed no less practical than the Utopian socialism of Weitling or even the "scientific socialism" of Marx.

Another, probably larger, part of the League of the Just moved to London, where under the leadership of Moll and Schapper the group began to reorganize itself in the mid-1840s. A third group grew up in Brussels, where they were joined by Marx after the banning of the *German-French Yearbooks* which he had been editing in Paris in 1844 with Arnold Ruge. It was this group that Marx wrenched from the possible control of Weitling. The way was thus left clear for the foundation of a new and revised group, the Communist League, which was formed out of the union of the London and Brussels organizations. The new Communist League adopted a set of statutes at the same congress which instructed Marx and Engels to draw up their manifesto. The first of these statutes read: "The purpose of the League is the overthrow of the bourgeoisie, the establishment of the rule of the proletariat, the abolition of the old civil society which rests on the opposition of classes and the founding of a new society without classes and without private property." [20] Such was Marx's strategy in the period before the actual outbreak of revolution.

[19] Adler, *Geschichte der Arbeiterbewegung*, pp. 37, 66-68.
[20] Wermuth, Stieber, *Die Communisten-Verschworungen*, vol. 1, pp. 239ff.

Yet it is very doubtful if this sort of socialist organization attracted much support among the workers themselves. The communist groups in Germany were probably
uninterested in the reforms made by Marx and the
London group; they remained loyal to the older Utopian
theories, or perhaps unable to distinguish between them
and the newer sort, accepting any theory without a great
deal of care as to its precise meaning or implications.
Even outside of Germany, in Paris, where Engels himself
was trying to organize the German workers' colony and
to gain support for the new doctrine, few converts were
made. Engels wrote to Marx in January of 1848: "Here
the League makes miserable progress. Such sleepy-
headedness and petty jealousy among the lads I've never
seen. Weitlingism and Proudhonism are really the most
complete expression of the condition of these asses and
nothing can be done about it. Some are aging louts, the
others rising petty bourgeoisie." [21]

✻

The socialist and communist intellectuals were not the
only group bidding for the support of the workers in
the years before 1848. Following the weavers' revolt
of 1844 and frightened by it, the governments of the

[21] Karl Marx, Friedrich Engels, *Historische-Kritishche Gesamtausgabe*, pt. 3, vol. 1, *Der Briefwechsel zwischen Marx und
Engels, 1844-1853*, Berlin, 1929, p. 92. Another aspect of Marx's
position which failed to appeal to the German workers and
artisans was his assault on conventional morality and such bourgeois institutions as marriage. In this respect the workers were as
bourgeois as the more prosperous members of the middle class.
Engels lamented in 1848, according to one contemporary source
(Gustav Scheidtmann, *Der Communismus und das Proletariat*,
Leipzig, 1848, p. 53), that the communist attempt to emancipate
women had produced only "a couple of confused questions, a
few blue-stockings, some hysteria, a good portion of German family quarrels (*ein guter Theil deutschen Familienjammer*)—not
even one bastard has come out of it!" This was perhaps a measure
of the failure of the socialist movement.

various German states made some attempt to placate the workers and to allow them to organize for their own benefit.

The officially sanctioned Central Union for the Well-Being of the Working Classes was established in Berlin in October of 1844. It was supported by the bourgeoisie and the industrialists and even received royal patronage from Frederick William, who offered the Union a gift of 15,000 thaler. The Union aimed at promoting working-class self-help and hoped for a large working-class membership; its program was to consist of the establishment of local and district unions which would encourage thrift by setting up and operating savings banks and would attempt to educate the workers through lectures and the distribution of pamphlets. Some provision for aid to the sick and needy was also envisaged.

The scheme was only a modified success. Several local branches were set up; the Stettin union even created an employment bureau to cope with the crisis of 1847.[22] But little of practical value was accomplished before the revolutions of March of 1848. The Berlin union never actually got under way; a debate on the statutes to be adopted by the Berlin group was called for November 24, 1844, and was used by middle-class intellectuals as the occasion for a discussion of the abstract issues of democracy and freedom. The meeting, described by Bruno Bauer as "a true burgher parliament," was closed by the police.[23] The king's offer of money was never taken up: the Central Union could find no way to use it in the pre-March period!

[22] *Mittheilungen des Centralvereins für das Wohl der arbeitenden Klassen,* Aug. 15, 1849.

[23] Bruno Bauer, *Die bürgerliche Revolution in Deutschland seit dem Anfang der deutsch katholischen Bewegung bis zur Gegenwart,* Berlin, 1849, p. 83. For another description of this meeting, see Dronke, *Berlin,* pp. 283ff.

There were also several groups organized by the workers themselves which achieved a fair amount of official toleration, provided they did not go too far politically. The most important of these was the Berlin Artisans' Union which was set up in 1844 in premises in the Sophienstrasse as the successor to a former temperance society. The aim of the Artisans' Union, as stated in its statutes, was "to further the popular development of the spiritual, moral, social, industrial and civil life of the workers through teaching and action." [24] The club held lectures and discussion periods for its members, which included in 1846 some 94 master craftsmen and 1,984 journeymen.[25] Its leader during the first years was the radical printer Julius Berends. A similar institution was the Berlin Journeymen's Union, which overlapped in aims and possibly in membership with the Artisans' Union. The journeymen had "a large, friendly" room in the Johannisstrasse and their meetings were much given to singing and the reading of the efforts of worker-poets.[26] Neither club attracted the poorest among Berlin's workers; they appealed rather to the better-off and better-educated handicraftsmen who sought intelligent conversation and convivial surroundings.

The movement to organize workers' clubs spread throughout Germany. Sometimes they professed serious aims; in Hamburg there was the Educational Society for the Improvement of the Working Class, which was founded in December of 1844 and had five hundred members by the end of 1847, most of them, as in the Berlin clubs, skilled craftsmen. Elsewhere the ostensible purposes of the clubs were more frivolous, as in the revived Gymnastic Union in Frankfurt or the workers' Singing Union in Breslau or the club in Altona called

[24] Friedensburg, *Stephan Born*, p. 22.
[25] Friedensburg, *Stephan Born*, p. 27.
[26] Dronke, *Berlin*, pp. 292-293.

simply the *Feierabend Verein*. Only in Austria was the government so strict as to suppress all such attempts to form workers' organizations in the pre-March period, a restriction which may account for the failure of Austrian workers to support an all-German workers' organization after the March Days.[27]

The clubs, whatever their declared purpose, served to develop a spirit of unity among the working-class members, a sense of common cause which was to carry over into the revolution. They provided an alternative to the declining master-dominated guilds. Moreover, in discussions with the more traveled members, many workers came through the clubs to be aware of the growing body of socialist theory. Specific attempts to use the clubs to form "communist cells" were generally unsuccessful, but at the same time the attempt to keep the clubs apolitical, to prevent the discussion of controversial topics, also failed. The clubs were, in the words of one of their members, "a school for growing revolutionaries." [28] They produced a degree of class consciousness which, though not always corresponding to the actual social and economic situation in Germany, was to prepare the workers and artisans to defend and promote the interests of their "class." Thus a congress of these clubs held at Wiesbaden in September 1847 adopted the following "Address to German Handicraft Workers": "Men from the proletariat, artisans, who go through Germany with a beggar's staff, oppressed, whipped by the police. . . . You are the best part of the people; raise your head. It is an honor to wear rags

[27] Heinrich Laufenberg, *Geschichte der Arbeiterbewegung in Hamburg, Altona und Umgegend*, Hamburg, 1911, vol. 1, pp. 99ff.; Adler, *Geschichte der Arbeiterbewegung*, p. 127.

[28] Born, *Erinnerungen*, p. 23. Of the influence of socialism on the Artisans' Union, Born comments that "the general opinion leaned toward socialism," but it was of the vaguest sort (p. 30).

and to be a proletarian. Make yourselves worthy of this honor and, when the time comes, attack!" [29]

*

The link between the socialist thinkers and the communist groups abroad on the one hand and the artisan clubs in Germany on the other was provided by the wandering journeymen who set out to travel from town to town, learning their trades. Many of these sought out the revolutionary centers of the time, hoping to learn something of the new theories as well. Paris, for example, where the German workers "sang, drank and talked politics, the socialist note dominating the conversations," [30] must be ranked as one of the larger "German" cities; the German colony numbered some 80,000 to 85,000.[31] Switzerland with its Young Germany group and its workers' clubs ranked second as an attraction for the traveling worker. The German Federal Diet in 1835 passed a law, an ineffectual one, forbidding journeymen to travel to "those countries and places in which associations and meetings exist openly aiming at endangering and destroying public order." [32]

Such journeymen as Weitling, who, once exposed to socialism, propagated his own Christian-Utopian version abroad, and Mentel, who returned to try unsuccessfully to interest the workers of Berlin, are examples of this link. But perhaps the most typical of these traveling handicraftsmen of the pre-March period, and certainly the most significant for the history of the workers' movement after the March revolutions, was the Berlin compositor Stephan Born.

[29] Valentin, *Frankfurt am Main*, pp. 278-279.
[30] Born, *Erinnerungen*, p. 38.
[31] Wittke, *Utopian Communist*, p. 19.
[32] Wermuth, Stieber, *Die Communisten-Verschwörungen*, vol. 1, p. 136.

Born came from a lower-middle-class family in the small town of Lissa in Posen, where he was born on December 28, 1824. His father was Meyer Buttermilch, a Jew whose profession was listed in the town records as that of *Makler*—a middleman or broker.[33] The name Buttermilch was soon dropped by the family in order to avoid the legal and social disabilities attached to being a Jew in Germany. They were at first relatively prosperous. Born received the beginnings of *Gymnasium* education and was encouraged to use the local library; his elder brother was sent to university in Berlin. The family later hit upon hard times; the father died and Born was sent first to live with a poor uncle and then, in 1840, to Berlin as an apprentice to the printing trade.

In Berlin Born quickly learned the skills required of an apprentice printer and compositor; indeed he later estimated that it took him two years to absorb all the necessary techniques, though guild regulations forced him to remain an apprentice for five.[34] His spare time he devoted to acquiring knowledge; he attended lectures at the university during the lunch hour, read voraciously, wrote a novel and theater criticism, some of which was published.

Upon becoming a journeyman in 1845 he joined the Artisans' Union and became an active member, participating in its discussions and singing in its choir. Through contacts made at the Artisans' Union, especially through the printer Julius Berends, he was introduced to some of the "intellectuals" of Berlin, the writers and artists who frequented such restaurants as the Café d'Artistes. There he met the poet Hoffman von Fallersleben, the author of "Deutschland über Alles," and the group of Young Hegelians centered around Bruno Bauer who

[33] Friedensburg, *Stephan Born*, contains the best account of Born's early life.
[34] Born, *Erinnerungen*, p. 13.

called themselves "the Free Ones." He also wrote a short pamphlet (eighteen pages) which was published by Wigand in Leipzig, entitled *The Union for the Improvement of the Working Classes and the Opinion of the People* and signed "by an artisan." The pamphlet denounced economic injustice and claimed that cooperation with the middle classes was useless, that reform must come from the workers themselves through "the development of the pure humanity which rests in the breasts of the proletariat."

In the middle of 1846, after a farewell concert given by the choir of the Artisans' Union, Born set out on his *Wanderjahre,* going first to Leipzig to visit such radicals as his publisher Wigand and Robert Blum. From there he moved on to Paris, arriving at the end of 1846. Born soon plunged into the socialist discussions among the German workers' colony; he met Engels and was persuaded to join the Communist League which was then in the process of being reformed. He even went on a proselytizing mission for the League to Lyons and Switzerland, where he hoped to persuade the groups which Weitling had formed to join the League. In Switzerland he also published a pamphlet, *Heinzen's State, A Critique by Stephan,* attacking the Utopian socialist Karl Heinzen, which was praised by Engels as "the first [work] written by a worker which does not take a moral approach but seeks to trace the connection between the political struggles of the present and the struggles of various classes." [35] Finally Born journeyed at the end of 1847 to Brussels where he met Marx, whom he found to be pleasant and helpful. [36] Engels had indeed already written Marx of Born's impending arrival and possible usefulness. "Just coach him a bit," Engels

[35] Marx, Engels, *Gesamtausgabe,* pt. 1, vol. 6, *Werke und Schriften von Mai 1846 bis März 1848,* Berlin, 1932, p. 267.
[36] Born, *Erinnerungen,* p. 67.

advised. "The fellow is ripe for our affairs and will even give us good service in London if he's prepared a little." [37] Born was employed as a compositor and writer for the *Deutsche-Brüsseler Zeitung* which Marx was editing at that time.

Born was not, however, as "ripe" for the communists as Engels thought. Indeed, few fellow workers in the Communist League, Born later recorded, were actually convinced of the possibility of communism; they joined partly from moral or even semireligious motives and partly from the hope of improvement of the material conditions of their lives, but in any case "without a great deal of hard thought." [38] Marx he found tolerable, but Engels seemed egotistic; to Born and his fellow workers he represented the "rich bourgeois' son" with his weekly remittance from his father. Moreover, even while writing the pamphlet Engels praised so highly, Born began to have doubts about the materialist doctrines he was preaching. Far more important to him was the need for working-class solidarity and self-help.[39] He was to pursue these goals in Germany after the outbreak of revolution.

❋

Born was still in Brussels, working for Marx's paper, at the end of February 1848, when the news arrived of the Paris revolution. Reports of the riots of the twenty-second and the fall of the Guizot ministry came quickly, but then there was a break in the news; trains were delayed at Valenciennes near the Belgium border. A crowd of German workers with Born among them, but almost no Belgians, gathered at the station to await the next train. Finally one came through: [40]

[37] Marx, Engels, *Gesamtausgabe*, pt. 3, vol. 1, pp. 83-84.
[38] Born, *Erinnerungen*, pp. 44-46.
[39] Born, *Erinnerungen*, pp. 48-49, 64-65.
[40] Born, *Erinnerungen*, p. 77.

Before it had completely stopped, the driver sprang down and cried with a ringing voice: *Le drapeau rouge flotte sur la tour de Valenciennes, la république est proclammée.*

Vive la république! resounded from our midst as from one voice.

That night the German workers in Brussels celebrated the beginning of the revolution, singing, drinking and crowding the middle-class customers from the cafés.

SECTION II
BARRICADES,
MEETINGS AND CLUBS
SPRING OF 1848

CHAPTER 3

THE MARCH DAYS

THE NEWS of the French revolution of February spread throughout Germany, rousing as much excitement there as it had among the exiled workers in Brussels. As meeting followed meeting and concession followed concession, a feeling of achievement, a mixture of euphoria and enthusiasm, swept across Germany. The mood of the March Days was summed up by the Russian revolutionary Bakunin, who visited Germany soon after the outbreak of revolution: [1]

> It seemed as if the entire world was turned upside down. The improbable became commonplace, the impossible possible; the possible and the commonplace however had become senseless. In a word: people found themselves in such a state of mind that if someone had said, "God has been driven from heaven and a republic has been proclaimed there," everyone would have believed it and no one would have been surprised.

To call the events of March 1848 a German "revolution" has seemed to some an exaggeration. Only in Vienna and Berlin were barricades erected and shots exchanged. Elsewhere violence was rare: a few factories were attacked and a few machines broken in the Ruhr and in Silesia by handicraft workers fearing competition; a few castles were destroyed and their records of taxes and rents burnt by peasants in the southwest. Yet all felt that a revolution had taken place, though some were uneasy about its unreal nature. Rudolf Gneist, one of

[1] *Michael Bakunins Beichte aus der Peter-Pauls-Festung an Zar Nikolaus I*, ed. Kurt Kersten, Berlin, 1926, p. 20.

the legislating German professors who have been so scorned by later historians, wrote in 1849 with a mixture of pride and despair of the disarray of the revolutionary forces, of the lack of organized force behind the revolution: "a revolution in this sense, in which the element of the fists plays only a subordinate role, is possible only in Germany with its predominantly idealistic spirit; its danger lies less in the renewal of the barricades than in the vagueness and haste of the ideals themselves." [2] Men were aware in 1848 of the problems of organization and revolution, of the need and failure to channel the social forces behind the revolution.

Enthusiasm, the feeling that a revolution had in fact occurred and that the old order in fact was overthrown, remained as the chief product of the March Days; the *Märzschwärmerei* affected all Germans from Frederick William of Prussia, who volunteered to place himself at the head of the "German nation," to the artisans and peasants who saw in the revolution a chance to improve their lot. The liberal concessions made by the various states in the March Days added to this sense of enthusiasm: the promise of constitutions, the summoning of diets or assemblies and the holding of elections, the end of censorship and the promise of freedom of the press—all stimulated discussion and debate, stirring support for the revolution. The enthusiasm worked on two levels, the political-national level and the social-economic level. Bruno Bauer noted in 1849 that: [3]

[2] Rudolf Gneist, *Berliner Zustände: Politischen Skizzen aus der Zeit vom 18. März 1848 bis 18. März 1849*, Berlin, 1849, p. 8. "We are," he said, in a shrewd assessment of the Germans of 1848, "theoretically overripe, practically as inexperienced as children. Hence that boldness of system next to complete inability of execution and lack of courage and endurance in action." (p. 128.) The thesis that 1848 was a revolution of intellectuals dates back to the revolution itself.

[3] Bauer, *Die bürgerliche Revolution*, p. 3.

The German movement which had been aroused by the French revolution of February fell from the beginning into two parts, namely the social movement and the national movement; these were essentially separated from each other and therefore worked against each other. The social movement was an affair of the great mass of the working people; in contrast, the national movement comprised mainly the so-called third estate or bourgeoisie.

The liberal demands and the concessions of March did however refer at least indirectly and sometimes directly to the "social question" which underlay the meetings and riots. Often among the liberal demands for a constitution and responsible government were such items as the abolition of all privilege, progressive taxation on incomes, universal education and the protection of labor against capital.[4]

It was in the meetings and riots which provoked the concessions of the March Days that the working-class movement showed itself. It was not the bourgeoisie but the "common man," the masses, or more specifically the workers and artisans of the cities, who manned the barricades and fought in the streets, who provided the

[4] See, for example, the March demands cited by Tim Klein, ed., *Der Vorkampf deutscher Einheit und Freiheit, Erinnerungen, Urkunden, Berichte, Briefe,* Ebenhausen bei München, 1914, pp. 115-116. Typical also was the proclamation issued on Mar. 11 by that paradigm of petty princes, Henry LXXII of Reuss-Lobenstein-Ebersdorf. (*Berliner Zeitungs Halle,* March 22, 1848.) All of the usual demands were granted: constitutional government, freedom of the press, trial by jury, the foundation and arming of a civil guard. In addition Henry promised to abolish all remaining feudal dues and to lower taxes on salt and beer. Finally he expressed concern for the unemployed; he had no positive program, but relied on the good will of all; in particular he "expected the owners of factories to imitate my sacrifices and those of the landed estate and to do the utmost to procure bread for the poor." Such was Henry LXXII's solution to the "social question."

force, or threat of force, which, however disorganized, made 1848 a revolution in the eyes of contemporaries and hence of history.

✿

The news of the French revolution had an immediate impact on the economic situation in Germany. In Berlin the reports of events in Paris were slow to arrive; nothing definite was known by Saturday, the twenty-sixth of February, and rumors circulated freely over Sunday and Monday, when no papers appeared on account of the weekend holiday. Crowds gathered at the station to pick up the latest reports; accurate information was hard to come by.[5] The result was financial panic; prices on the Berlin stock exchange fell sharply. The same effect was reported elsewhere.[6] In Vienna, where the news from France arrived on the twenty-ninth, people flocked to the banks to remove their savings, and the cost of foodstuffs rose rapidly.[7]

The social-economic side of the revolution first showed itself however in the peasant risings which took place in southwest Germany during the last days of February and the early part of March. In the Odenwald and the Schwarzwald, areas of rural discontent since the Peasants War of the sixteenth century, the aims of the peasantry had little to do with the liberal demands of the middle classes or the republican program of such leaders as Struve and Hecker. The peasants were concerned with land rights and debts; in Württemberg, for example, nine hundred attacked the castle at Weiler, demanded destruction of the archives and refused to be put off with

[5] Adolff Wolff, *Berliner Revolutionschronik,* Berlin, 1849-1854, vol. 1, pp. 4-5.
[6] For example, see the report on Hamburg published in the *Berliner Zeitungs Halle,* Mar. 4, 1848.
[7] R. John Rath, *The Viennese Revolution of 1848,* Austin, Texas, 1957, p. 55.

the offer of the keys to the wine cellar: "We have not come," they declared, "to eat and to drink; we want nothing, nothing at all but to burn the records which force us into beggary and then we'll go to the king and tell him of our need and poverty." [8] The peasants also turned on local businessmen, traders and money lenders, most of whom were Jewish. Indeed the movement in Baden and the Rhenish Palatinate amounted to a general persecution of the Jews, who were forced to flee to the larger towns and seek the protection of the army.[9] Elsewhere the peasants demanded access to forests and the right to cart away dead wood to use as fuel. The peasants too were affected by the *Märzschwärmerei*. Rumors of a general redistribution of property were circulated and believed. The peasants of Nassau descended on Wiesbaden on the second of March, the date the redistribution was to take place, with sacks and carts in which they expected to take away their share.[10]

Related movements occurred in the towns of the southwest. On the day the news arrived from France the tailors of Heidelberg paraded through the streets, demanding protection for the tailors' guild and storming the shop of a Jewish clothing merchant who sold ready-made products.[11] Similar outbreaks occurred in Neckarbischofsheim, Breisgau and Mühlheim. In Rheinhesse there were attacks on Jews, on the Taunus railway then under construction and on improvements in the harbor works at Mainz. All along the Rhine there was hostility toward the increasing use of steam shipping.[12]

[8] Stadelmann, *Soziale und politische Geschichte,* p. 79.

[9] Klein, *Der Vorkampf,* p. 113.

[10] Valentin, *Geschichte der deutschen Revolution,* vol. 1, pp. 356-357.

[11] Ludwig Bamberger, *Erlebnisse aus der pfälzischen Erhebung im Mai und Juni, 1849,* Frankfurt, 1849, p. 27.

[12] Valentin, *Geschichte der deutschen Revolution,* vol. 1, pp. 356, 483.

The situation in the southwest was thus confused and chaotic, ripe for the republican *putsch* which Hecker and Struve were to attempt in April and ripe too for its failure. The social-economic demands of the area were deeply rooted but largely incoherent; they found their outlet chiefly in anti-Semitism. The interests of the workers and peasants were often in conflict and even came once to an open clash when armed countrymen descended upon Heidelberg in order to "relieve" the city dwellers of their "excess of wealth." [13] The workers of the southwest were to support the efforts to strengthen the guilds later in the year and to adhere for a time to the schemes of Karl Georg Winkelblech, who envisaged the extension of the guild system to all branches of economic activity and the participation of the guilds in government. But during the March Days these workers were inarticulate, unorganized, almost totally without leaders.

*

The strength of the workers and their drive toward organization and associations showed itself primarily in the cities: first during the March Days, in Cologne and above all Berlin; later throughout most of Germany.

Cologne, the chief city of the Prussian Rhineland, saw the first outbreak of revolution on Prussian soil in 1848 and the first instance of a proletarian movement which showed some degree of organization and influence from socialist theories.[14] The Cologne municipal council attempted to forestall popular action on March 3 by en-

[13] Stadelmann, *Soziale und politische Geschichte,* p. 85.
[14] Hans Stein, *Der Kölner Arbeiterverein* (1848/49), *Ein Beitrag zur Frühgeschichte des rheinischen Sozialismus,* Köln, 1921, pp. 26ff. The following account of the Cologne events is based largely on Stein's excellent and often neglected work. For a recent East German account of the Cologne workers' club in the revolution, see Gerhard Becker, *Karl Marx und Friedrich Engels in Köln, 1848-1849: Zur Geschichte des Kölner Arbeitervereins,* Berlin, 1963.

trusting the merchant Ludwig Camphausen with a petition to Frederick William IV calling for the usual liberal concessions: a United Diet for Prussia based on an extended franchise, the abolition of censorship, a federal constitution for Germany and so on. The council's meeting was interrupted by a crowd of workers. Led by the Jewish physician Andreas Gottschalk and two former lieutenants in the Prussian army, Friedrich Anneke and August von Willich, the crowd forced its way into the council chamber with a petition calling for universal suffrage and responsible government; complete freedom of press, speech and association; an end to the standing army and, instead, a civil guard under popularly elected officers; free education for all; and, finally, protection for labor and a guaranteed standard of living.[15] Gottschalk defended these demands "not in the name of the people—that name has been all too often misused by the privileged classes—. . . [but] in the name of that most worthy of all estates, which receives for the sweat of its labor nothing with which it can cover its nakedness or still its hunger." The council offered to "debate" the issues with Gottschalk alone, but when the crowd grew unruly, troops were summoned. A few shots were fired; no one was injured; the crowd dispersed. Gottschalk and Willich were arrested, not to be released till the twenty-first of the month, following the events in Berlin and a general amnesty.

The situation in Cologne grew more quiet. A civil guard, one of the demands of Gottschalk's crowd, was set up on the fourth of March, but this was for the protection of the propertied classes; no worker was admitted. The council stuck to its original moderate demands which it sent to the king on the tenth. On the fifteenth a delegation from the council left for Berlin

[15] The petition was printed in the *Berliner Zeitungs Halle,* Mar. 7, 1848.

to urge the Prussian king to place himself at the head of the national movement.

The eruption of the Cologne crowd remains the first instance of socialist-led action by the German workers in 1848; indeed the events were regarded at the time as "a movement of communists," though this was meant only in the vague sense that the leaders were not merely liberals or even democrats but claimed to speak for the working classes.[16] Gottschalk and his fellows were acquainted with and probably members of the Cologne branch of the Communist League. But it is doubtful whether they felt any allegiance to the League or any interest in the doctrines of Marx and Engels. The claim that the riots of March 3 were organized by the League seems to be totally without support.[17] Engels complained bitterly at the time of the ineffectual nature of the demonstration, particularly of the failure to provide the workers with weapons, and noted, in a letter to Marx, that "our old friends in Cologne seem to have held themselves back" and left the leadership to others.[18]

*

Berlin too was faced with mounting unrest among the workers from the first days of March. The Borsig works

[16] *Berliner Zeitungs Halle,* Mar. 15, 1848. The article went on to predict that the movement was over and that "the opponents of private property will be quiet now for a long time."

[17] Ernst Czobel, "Zur Geschichte des Kommunistenbundes, Die Kölner Bundesgemeinde vor der Revolution," *Archiv für die Geschichte des Sozialismus und der Arbeiterbewegung,* vol. 11 (1923-1925), pp. 299-335, and Karl Obermann, *Die deutsche Arbeiter in der Revolution von 1848,* pp. 111ff., show that Willich and Anneke were connected with the Cologne branch of the Communist League; from this they argue that the demonstration *must* have been planned by the league and known beforehand by Marx and Engels. There is no evidence for this. Yet the story is accepted by Valentin, *Geschichte der deutschen Revolution,* vol. 1, p. 416, and by Pinson, *Modern Germany,* p. 91.

[18] Marx, Engels, *Gesamtausgabe,* pt. 3, vol. 1, p. 94.

dismissed some four hundred men. Rumors that the remaining workers would soon be unemployed and that several other factories would close had to be denied in the press.[19] On March 1 the municipal government announced its intention of opening an employment bureau on March 6, one branch for men in the Rosstrasse and another for women in the Alexanderplatz.[20] When the bureau actually opened on the ninth it was totally incapable of dealing with the numbers that applied: six thousand to seven thousand on the first day in spite of the reluctance of many workers, especially qualified masters, to use such a procedure.[21] There were proposals to increase the number of public works projects, to encourage the construction of canals and highways; the municipal assembly voted to set up a commission to advise on the problem and invited masters, journeymen and factory workers to elect representatives. The middle-class press, fearing the example of Paris, carried on a campaign to quiet the workers; under the headline "Don't deceive yourselves," the conservative *Vossische Zeitung* warned the workers that jobs, food and low prices could be obtained only through the preservation of peace and order. In spite of such warnings, unrest increased.[22]

Public meetings were held from March 6 in the area north of the Tiergarten known as the Zelten. The product of one such meeting on March 10 was an address to the king calling for the formation of a ministry of labor which could mediate between the capitalists and usurers on the one hand and the oppressed workers on the other and thus achieve the "quick abolition of the poverty

[19] Wolff, *Berliner Revolutionschronik*, vol. 1, pp. 53-54.
[20] *Berliner Zeitungs Halle*, Mar. 1, 1848.
[21] Bernstein, *Geschichte der Berliner Arbeiterbewegung*, vol. 1, pp. 11-12.
[22] Wolff, *Berliner Revolutionschronik*, vol. 1, p. 55.

which is now so great and of the lack of work or any assurance as to the future which prevails among all workers." [23] The same address was reread on the thirteenth to a meeting of workers who defied the efforts of soldiers to disperse the crowd.[24]

Alarmed by such meetings, the head of police, von Minutoli, announced a ban on public meetings on March 14. On the same day the mayor and the city council issued a placard urging all citizens to follow "the way of law and order" in the certainty that all proper requests would be granted from "the fatherly wisdom of our king." On the fifteenth the city council had to deny rumors of the bankruptcy of the municipal savings banks, hoping in vain to forestall a rush to withdraw savings. On the sixteenth the city government called for the formation of a "protective commission" consisting of the respected citizens of each district, including especially the established master craftsmen and the chairman of the guilds.[25]

These measures of pacification and repression failed to achieve their purpose. The meetings continued; the petition for a ministry of labor was circulated; the danger of revolution increased. The news of the rising in Vienna reached Berlin on March 16, and some took this as a cue to set up barricades at crucial points. There seemed little purpose or direct political goal in the rioting of the workers. The movement was as yet without leadership. One journeyman, asked why he was throwing stones at the window of a minister in the Wilhelmstrasse,

[23] Wolff, *Berliner Revolutionschronik*, vol. 1, p. 58. This was the first "workers' address" to be printed in Berlin during the March Days.

[24] George Schirges, *Der Berliner Volks-Aufstand*, Hamburg, 1848, p. 23.

[25] *Plakate*, Ratsbibliothek, Berlin, portfolio 1.

replied: "In order that he might put his head out and see what the world looks like!" [26]

✱

An armed clash did not occur till the afternoon of the eighteenth of March. A crowd had gathered in the square before the Royal Palace to demand freedom of the press, a United Diet, withdrawal of the army and the arming of a civil guard. The members of the crowd were, an eyewitness noted,

> all well dressed and very respectable people. . . . Quite in the background at the corners of the streets leading into the Square, I saw working men and common people standing. A few came one by one to the front, and when they saw the cheerful faces around them, they said, "This sort of thing won't help us poor people at all!" [27]

Of the crowd's demands the king was willing to grant the first two; he said as much to the delegation from the Cologne municipal council which visited him on the morning of the eighteenth. But he was unwilling to place responsibility for security solely in the hands of a civil guard. The troops were ordered to clear the square, two shots were fired—by whom it was not clear [28]—and the cry went up, "To the barricades!"

Fighting flared up all over the city and continued into the night. In the construction and defense of the bar-

[26] From a description of the rioting on March in Louis Koch, *Berliner Witzhagel gefallen in der Barrikadennacht vom 18. und 19. März und Später*, Berlin, 1848.

[27] As quoted by J. G. Legge, *Rhyme and Revolution in Germany, A Study of German History, Life, Literature and Character, 1813-1850*, London, 1918, p. 284.

[28] For a discussion of the evidence on this point, see Valentin, *Geschichte der deutschen Revolution*, vol. 1, pp. 428ff.

ricades the workers participated more than any other group. Estimates of the number killed have varied. The official statistics of the Ministry of War listed 20 soldiers (including 3 officers) dead and 254 wounded, but this report may have minimized the losses of the army.[29] On the civilian side some claimed that there were as many as 1,500, many of whom were said to have been dumped into the Spree by the soldiers.[30] A more reliable account estimates that some 230 civilians were killed.[31] Of the corpses which were identified, some 88 per cent belonged to the working classes. The largest group of these were journeymen (approximately 40 per cent of the total killed), and most belonged to the skilled trades of one sort or another. The most common trade was that of carpenter (25 killed). Few masters died (5) and there was only a small number of factory workers in the list—3 machine builders from all the factories to the north of the city.[32] The machine-shop workers had to be summoned to join the revolution by a deputation of the students; some indeed did participate in the fighting but they were none too eager and all carefully collected their week's wages (the eighteenth was a Saturday) before leaving the works.[33]

On the nineteenth Frederick William, whose command to the troops throughout had been *"Nur nicht schiessen!"* (Only don't shoot!) ordered the withdrawal of the troops just when they were on the point of victory. He urged his "dear Berliners" in a proclamation to pre-

[29] Valentin, *Geschichte der deutschen Revolution,* vol. 1, pp. 444-445.

[30] *Die Locomotive,* Apr. 1, 1848.

[31] Wolff, *Berliner Revolutionschronik,* vol. 1, pp. 174-175.

[32] Schirges, *Berliner Volks-Aufstand,* pp. 72-73; Schirges' list is more complete but approximates in terms of types and trades represented the list published in the *Berliner Zeitungs Halle,* Mar. 25, 1848, three days after the funeral procession of Friedrichshain.

[33] Schirges, *Berliner Volks-Aufstand,* p. 49.

serve law and order and conceded the liberal demands of the crowd. A civil guard was set up and weapons issued, though workers, apart from the more reliable members of the Artisans' Union and a special corps of machine builders, were to be excluded from it. A crowd gathered in the forecourt of the palace and forced the king, wearing the German colors of black, red and gold, to do homage to those who had died in the fighting. It was not however an occasion of revolutionary defiance but one of religious awe; the crowd sang *"Jesu, meine Zuversicht,"* which became the hymn of the revolution.[34] On March 20 the municipal government announced that it would pay for the burial of the March dead and support their relations, a promise apparently not trusted since a group soon began to collect money for the needy families among them.[35]

The official burial took place on the twenty-second. Services were held in the Protestant and Catholic churches as well as the synagogues. The procession of coffins, followed by an estimated twenty thousand mourners, wound its way from the *Gendarmenkirche* in the center of the city past the royal palace, where Frederick William watched with bared head, toward the cemetery at Friedrichshain. Led by the mayor and the rector of the university, the procession included representatives of all the major guilds, each with the emblems and flags of his trade; there was also a delegation of factory workers, including a group of machinists accompanied by the manufacturer Borsig himself.[36]

The fighting in Berlin on March 18 and 19 marked a victory for the working classes and the "proletariat," but

[34] Wolff, *Berliner Revolutionschronik,* vol. 1, p. 248.

[35] *Plakate,* Ratsbibliothek, Berlin, portfolio 1.

[36] Hans Blum, *Die deutsche Revolution 1848/49,* Leipzig, 1898, p. 201; Valentin, *Geschichte der deutschen Revolution,* vol. 1, p. 454.

not—as has often been implied—the industrial proletariat. Artisans, above all journeymen, were responsible for the March Days.

*

Nor was it the liberal demands for which these workers fought; the formation of the new ministry under the liberal businessman Camphausen and the summoning of the United Diet were at best means to an end. Unemployment, high food prices and low wages were the chief concern of the fighters of the barricades, and if these concerns were not dealt with there would be danger of further violence. Yet the threat of violence and in particular the fear created by the withdrawal of the army from Berlin added to the economic difficulties. There was little confidence in the civil guard in spite of the gleam and glisten of their new uniforms. Many businessmen fled the city only to return with the troops at the end of the month.

Some among the lower classes realized the danger and advised caution. One worker wrote somewhat pretentiously in a letter to a newspaper of the "historical" role of the working classes: [37]

> Workers! The list of the dead and fallen is your historical proof that you knew how to fight and die for the freedom of your nation; workers, give historical proof in these days when the future is being born that you know how to work and live for the freedom of your nation. . . . Only if we all remain at work and demand no higher wages from those who employ us can these employers—now, when the condition of trade is at its worst—remain in a position to give us bread for our families.

Numerous editorials in the respectable press not surprisingly echoed these sentiments: the only way to

[37] *Berliner Zeitungs Halle,* Mar. 25, 1848.

improve conditions was to restore order. The magistrate of Berlin circulated a placard on the twenty-fourth of March calling on all to remember that the revolution had been made for all, that freedom had been obtained for all classes and was to be achieved only by constitutional means, that is, by the coming elections. He warned against "a split among the various classes," urged the workers to remain calm and expressed confidence that property owners would remember that the revolution "was also for our poorer brothers." [38]

Exhortations to unity were not successful; many noted a growing amount of class antagonism. "Already," wrote Robert Virchow, a young and democratically minded physician, on the twenty-fourth of March, "the reaction against the workers (the people) has begun among the burghers (the bourgeoisie). Already there is again talk of the 'mob,' already thought of how to split up political rights unequally among the different branches of the nation." [39] The atmosphere was one of tension and depression; Stephan Born, arriving in Berlin shortly after the eighteenth, noted a feeling sharply contrasted to that of Brussels and Paris which he had just left. In Paris there was exaltation over the February revolution lasting well into March; in Berlin "the smoke of battle had cleared quickly while people looked earnestly into it as if they feared the future." [40]

The middle classes did, however, try to organize more positive forms of action to relieve the condition of the workers both privately and through the government. Factory owners published announcements urging all that had left work at the time of the fighting to return, promising stable wages and regretting that these could

---

[38] *Plakate*, Ratsbibliothek, Berlin, portfolio 1.

[39] Quoted by Friedrich Meinecke, *1848, Eine Säkularbetrachtung*, Berlin, 1948, p. 20.

[40] Born, *Erinnerungen*, p. 116.

not be raised.[41] On the twenty-third a group of solid citizens formed a committee to collect money for bread for the poor; the announcement at a meeting in the Zelten on the following day that this group would provide six thousand loaves "produced a very acquiescent mood in the lower orders." [42] Another group of officials and manufacturers, including Borsig, set up a Society for Publicly Useful Constructions and issued with the approval of the authorities a list of public works; a number of buildings were to be constructed or repaired after the fighting, roads were to be improved and a canal built from Moabit to Spandau.[43] The government also agreed to stop production in the Spandau prison and in the royal artillery workshop and to turn the jobs thus done over to private workers, creating more work and removing a long-standing grievance. An announcement of the return of all securities from the state pawnshops was less quieting since private pawnbrokers were also besieged and the civil guard had to be called out.[44] On the twenty-fifth of March the municipal assembly formed a Deputation for the Consideration of the Well-Being of the Working Classes, which was to hold public hearings on all grievances and proposals. And on the twenty-seventh the king promised to set up a new Ministry for Trade, Industry and Public Works in the following month.

❋

The workers themselves began to meet in the latter part of March, at first in trade groups only and later in general meetings for all workers. By March 25 some nine of the older skilled trades had held such meetings,

---

[41] *Deutsche Arbeiter Zeitung,* Apr. 8, 1848.

[42] Wolff, *Berliner Revolutionschronik,* vol. 1, p. 410; also *Plakate,* Ratsbibliothek, Berlin, portfolio 1.

[43] *Berliner Zeitungs Halle,* Mar. 25, 1848.

[44] Wolff, *Berliner Revolutionschronik,* vol. 1, pp. 404-405.

including the bookbinders, the printers and the gold-smiths and silversmiths. The machine builders had also set up a committee to consult with the factory owners.[45] In these and the more general meetings the historian can see the goals which lay behind the March Days.

The first general workers' meeting occurred on Sunday, March 26, in the Exercierplatz near the Schönhausen Tor to the northeast of the city. Beginning at two in the afternoon and lasting till dusk, the meeting attracted an enormous crowd; some estimated as many as twenty thousand were present.[46] The assembly had been called by the Deputation for the Abolition of Need, a group consisting of several master craftsmen—a cigar maker, a calico printer, a dress maker—and a number of journey-men as well as the veterinary Urban. They aimed at conducting an orderly meeting, obtained official permission, started the program with three coldly received speeches by Berlin's representatives in the Landtag and restricted the following speeches to delegates chosen by specific groups of workers.

But these workers went beyond the limits which the organizing committee had envisaged, and the demands of the meeting soon got out of hand. They complained universally of low wages and the fear if not the fact of unemployment; they had little desire to carry the revolution further, but they demanded what they regarded as their due.[47] As one speaker, a tanner, awkwardly put it:

[45] Wolff, *Berliner Revolutionschronik*, vol. 1, pp. 413ff.; Quarck, *Erste deutsche Arbeiterbewegung*, p. 79.

[46] The account of the meeting of the twenty-sixth, unless other-wise stated, is taken from the reports in the *Berliner Zeitungs Halle*, Mar. 28-29, 1848, which included long extracts from the speeches delivered. The figure of 20,000 in attendance should be compared with more conservative estimates which varied from 6,000 to 10,000. (See Wolff, *Berliner Revolutionschronik*, vol. 1, p. 435.)

[47] One observer found the workers far more eloquent than the demagogues of the meetings in the Zelten: "Without many phrases

Our wish is fulfilled; we do not want to renew the bloodbath but we demand the fruit of our sweat. We work from five in the morning till seven in the evening. A reduction of the working time by two hours, a fixing of this time between six and six, and an increase in wages to four thaler weekly—that's not asking too much.

A reference to the gathered crowds as "the proletariat" was bitterly resented; the speaker, the journalist Zacharias, was shouted down and forced to retract the expression. Most admitted the genuine difficulties which faced the master craftsmen; one speaker was warmly applauded for declaring that "we wouldn't ruin our masters—we don't want that at all." The solution was seen in help from above, the establishment of a ministry of labor which would "guide" the masters and mediate between employers and employees. Such a ministry would find jobs for the unemployed, raise wages and lower hours, limit the employment of women and children and prevent the spread of machinery.

The meeting finally adopted a seven point program proposed by the journeyman goldsmith L. Bisky.[48] The

and with inelegant words they went straight to the matter at hand; through the simplicity of their speech they had a more shattering effect than all the rhetorical devices of the so-called democrats." Paul Boerner, *Erinnerungen eines Revolutionärs, Skizzen aus dem Jahre 1848*, Leipzig, 1920, vol. 2, pp. 73-74.

[48] Bisky was twenty-eight years old at the outbreak of the revolution. He came from Breslau but was active in the pre-March Artisans Union in Berlin. Along with Born he was to take the lead in the Berlin workers' movement of 1848, and after Born left for Leipzig, he served as head of the Berlin regional committee of the *Verbrüderung*. With Born in exile, Bisky acted as president of the *Verbrüderung* congress in Leipzig in February 1850, but soon left Germany himself, sailing from Hamburg for the United States on Apr. 8, 1850. See Frolinde Balser, *Sozial-Demokratie, 1848/49—1863, Die erste deutsche Arbeiterorganisation "Allgemeine deutsche Arbeiterverbrüderung" nach der Revolution*, Stuttgart, 1962, pp. 174-177.

demand for a ministry of labor to be elected in guild fashion by the workers and their masters was combined with other economic goals such as provision for injured workers and a number of liberal demands—for economies in government expenditure, for subordination of a reduced standing army to the civilian militia, for universal education. To these were added the radical political goals of universal suffrage and universal eligibility for office.[49]

These points were not accepted unanimously; the meeting split over the last two. Those who had summoned the meeting refused to accept the provision for universal suffrage though the majority of the crowd favored it. In the end two deputations went to the king on the twenty-ninth of March, the organizing committee and a new group which included Bisky and was elected by the meeting. The first was received by Frederick William with a declaration of his love for his people, which he petulantly declared to be greater than their love for him; the second was dismissed with the words: "Everything through the proper authorities."[50] The central demand for a ministry of labor had by this time already been granted, though not in the form envisaged by the meeting of the twenty-sixth.

More significant from the point of view of the workers' movement was the meeting which was held on the evening of March 29 at the Café d'Artistes. Here some 150 of the "more intelligent section of the workers" gathered under the chairmanship of J. C. Lüchow to consider the possibility of the formation of a central committee for the Berlin workers.[51] Lüchow, a tailor, had just published a pamphlet on *The Organization of Work*

[49] The demands were printed in the *Berliner Zeitungs Halle*, Mar. 31, 1848.

[50] *Berliner Zeitungs Halle*, Apr. 1, 1848; Quarck, *Erste deutsche Arbeiterbewegung*, p. 33.

[51] Wolff, *Berliner Revolutionschronik*, vol. 1, p. 486.

and Its Practicality in which he called for the formation of workers' clubs and advocated as well the erection by the government of "national workshops," which would provide not only work but food, beds, dining halls and recreation areas. Lüchow's proposals represented a combination of the ideas of such French writers as Fourier and Blanc with the organization and ideals of the guilds. Lüchow contrasted his position to the guild system only in that, as he argued, his chief concern was the "organization of workers" whereas the guilds aimed only at the "organization of work." [52]

The meeting, however, after a rousing opening speech from Lüchow in which he called for "a common front against reaction," settled down to a consideration of the more modest courses of possible action open to the workers. The suggestion of a campaign for higher wages was rejected as inopportune, as it had been at the meeting on the twenty-sixth. Hätzel, the shoemaker who had been arrested in 1846 as a "communist conspirator," expressed the moderate view: "The demand for a fixed increase in wages," he argued, "is at the present moment an unjustified demand; it means nothing less than ruining the masters and finally ourselves." [53] The major decision of the meeting at the Café d'Artistes was to form a provisional Central Workers Club in an attempt to implement Lüchow's ideas of organization. The chairman was the young compositor Stephan Born. A further meeting of the provisional Central Club was called for the sixth of April. In the meantime those present were to form smaller associations, either for a particular trade, using the old guild basis where possible, or for the

[52] Quarck, *Erste deutsche Arbeiterbewegung*, pp. 55-56; Friedensburg, *Stephan Born*, p. 61. The provision for dining halls was perhaps prophetic; Lüchow's son, August, emigrated to the United States in 1872 and, a decade later, founded a famous restaurant in New York.

[53] *Berliner Zeitungs Halle*, Mar. 31, 1848.

workers of a particular area. These smaller groups were to elect delegates to the next meeting of the Central Club. The attempt to organize the workers had begun.

＊

The situation in Berlin at the end of March presented a picture in many ways reassuring to those who feared further revolution. The economic position had improved slightly; the municipal Deputation for the Consideration of the Well-Being of the Working Classes was able to report on March 31 that almost all male laborers requesting work on the public projects had been employed.[54] Radical agitators seemed to have made little headway. The Württemberg ambassador in Berlin wrote that "the lower classes are less infected than elsewhere with socialist and communist doctrine." [55]

But the meetings of the twenty-sixth and the twenty-ninth revealed what were to be the characteristic goals of the workers' movement of 1848, in Berlin and throughout Germany: government aid and working-class organization. The petition for a ministry of labor was the first of many which the workers were to direct both to the governments of the individual states and later to the National Assembly in Frankfurt, calling for state regulation of the conditions of work and state aid to improve those conditions. The attempt to form a Central Workers' Club in Berlin was the first of many efforts at organizing workers' groups, first on a local basis, later in regional and even national associations. These goals were also evident in the demands presented by Gottschalk in Cologne on March 3. Both had their roots in the condition of the German workers in the pre-March period, in

[54] Ernst Kaeber, *Berlin, 1848,* Berlin, 1948, p. 140.
[55] Quoted by Valentin, *Geschichte der deutschen Revolution,* vol. 1, p. 418; see also Wolff, *Berliner Revolutionschronik,* vol. 1, p. 487.

the autocratic, paternalistic state and in the guild system. Both were to be expressed in 1848 with incredible naïveté and innocence. *Märzschwärmerei* led the workers to believe that at one blow they had achieved governments which would recognize their interests; under these governments and with their support the workers could proceed to the organization and improvement of their own affairs. One writer summed up the achievements of the March Days: "The Berlin revolution, the greatest deed of heroism yet performed by the working classes, together with other revolutions and transformations in Germany and in Europe, has in essence brought forth one world-historical fruit: political and social recognition of the working classes." [56] This was to a large extent wishful thinking, but it was widely believed; the revolution was a single, unique event. All that remained was the enjoyment of the "fruit" of the revolution. To the workers, political recognition meant government support; social recognition meant the right to organize, to form associations which would have the power and prestige once held by the guilds.

These two goals were both affected by the socialist doctrines of the pre-March period. Many of the leaders of the workers' groups—Born and Hätzel, Gottschalk and Willich—had been associated with the Communist League. The slogans they adopted were cast in terms used by the socialists; the call for association and the organization of work was derived from the "true socialists" and the French Utopians. But the goals themselves were of a more traditional, more limited and possibly more practical nature. "National Workshops" were translated into the demand for public works projects to relieve the immediate problem of unemployment; the "organization of work" became a campaign for the foundation of

[56] From the anonymous pamphlet, *Contre-Revolution in Berlin.*

workers' groups with specific aims, based on the old guild system but including unskilled labor and the new factory workers.

Yet where the socialists tried to state their case directly and win working-class support, they failed. In Leipzig, for example, the socialist writer Hermann Semmig attacked the liberal leaders of the revolution, putting forward a socialist program in a pamphlet entitled *Saxons! What Is Necessary and What Is Blum Doing?* published on March 12. A series of Saturday meetings for workers was arranged to consider the socialists' proposals. Here the pattern seen in Berlin was followed. At the first of these meetings, held on March 18 and attended by some two thousand people, the crowd supported the speech of a printer, Skrobek, who called for workers' clubs, particularly for journeymen, and the formation with government help of an insurance program for the sick and needy; Skrobek saw these measures as a way "to destroy the phantom of communism." "Not only this speaker," wrote one eyewitness, "but all the other workers who spoke after him declared themselves most decisively against communism and specifically urged also the putting down of fears through quiet, dignified behavior rather than allowing among these [the working] classes a violent mood hostile to the middle class." [57] At the second meeting on the twenty-fifth some five thousand workers endorsed the election of Blum to the *Vorparlament* about to convene in Frankfurt and adopted a petition to be presented to the Saxon government in Dresden, calling for the formation of a ministry of labor. The petition mentioned again the danger of socialism and hoped that this movement could be prevented from gaining ground in Germany.[58] Meanwhile, as in Berlin, a number of the more skilled among the

[57] *Zeitung für das deutsche Volk,* Mar. 23, 1848.
[58] *Zeitung für das deutsche Volk,* Mar. 27, 1848.

Leipzig workers—the metalworkers, carpenters, printers, tailors and shoemakers—had met to form trade groups.[59]

The workers' demands for government help and organization were often seen in direct opposition to socialism. In Munich one writer saw the campaign to organize the workers under official auspices as a solution to the problem of communism, a problem he probably exaggerated in order to gain support for the cause of the workers: "Communism and socialism are the specters which at present time go like a password of fear from mouth to mouth. A remedy can only be found through the organization of work; cannons and bayonets will not prevail against the upsurgence of the people." [60] The writer went on to argue that organization was possible only with government support and that "the necessary organization must occur through and for all of Germany: this is one of the most important tasks of the German Parliament which is greeted with joy and trust by all Germans."

At this point the German workers' movement merged into the national movement. But on the national level the same elements were present as in the individual states and cities: organization of the workers and support from the new governments and the leaders of the middle class were to be the results of the March Days; to these results all could look forward with "joy and trust." The specters of communism and socialism would quickly vanish.

[59] Lipinski, *Arbeiterbewegung in Leipzig,* vol. 1, p. 48; Curt Geyer, *Politischen Parteien und Verfassungskämpfe in Sachsen von der Märzrevolution bis zum Ausbruch des Maiaufstandes 1848/49,* Leipzig, 1914, pp. 58-59.

[60] *Betrachtungen eines deutschem Proletariers,* pp. 14-15. The pamphlet came out in March.

CHAPTER 4

ALTERNATIVES TO ORGANIZATION

GOVERNMENT ACTION

THE GOVERNMENTS of the German states were taken by surprise by the March Days; monarchs and ministers were uncertain how to respond. Many bowed before the revolutions, considering the demands of the liberals, the nationalists and even the workers, and flirting with the possibility of alliance with one or the other of these groups. Yet no final or permanent concessions were made; the threat of reaction lurked in even the most liberal or far-reaching declarations of the ruling classes. As one radical journalist wrote at the beginning of April 1848, the governments "are handling the revolution with kid gloves and thus obtain the double advantage of honoring the revolution as a lady with whom one would not dance without gloves and at the same time keeping their hands clean of the democratic dirt of the revolution." [1]

Most hesitant of all was the approach of the rulers toward the demands of the working class. Neither the monarchs and the aristocratic court circles nor the new liberal ministers nor those representatives of the national movement who met at Frankfurt to summon an all-German parliament had any clear idea of how they should meet the problem posed by the workers. The workers themselves hoped for much from the government; the question of when and whether these hopes would be fulfilled was an important one for the course of the revolution.

During the early months of 1848 the issue remained

[1] Friedrich Held in *Die Locomotive*, Apr. 1, 1848.

undecided; yet the very lack of decision on the part of the ruling classes forced the workers back on their own resources, still hoping for aid from the governments and above all from the Frankfurt Assembly, but turning more and more to their own leaders and the possibility of self-help through organization.

❋

Frederick William IV of Prussia attempted to place himself at the head of the German national movement in his declaration, "To My People and the German Nation," on March 21, 1848, announcing that "Prussia is merging into Germany." He held out to the masses a shimmering image of "our beautiful aggregate father-land blossoming through trade and industry." [2] Yet, as at the time of his coronation in 1840, he failed to assume the leadership of the movement he thus attracted to his person.[3] In doing so he rejected the advice of at least one of his ministers, who urged him to seek the support of the working classes.

The minister was Joseph Maria von Radowitz, later scorned by Bismarck as "the keeper of the wardrobe to the king's medieval fantasies." [4] Radowitz proposed a series of measures which were in fact similar to Bismarck's social-insurance legislation of the 1880s. In a memorandum sent from Vienna as early as March 16, 1848, Radowitz advised the king to gain influence over "the great mass of the discontented." In a further memorandum, submitted to the king on the twentieth of April, Radowitz argued that "one can and must seek to absorb the justifiable core of the socialist program into the

[2] *Plakate*, Ratsbibliothek, Berlin, portfolio 1.

[3] As early as March 28, 1848, Frederick William wrote to Camp-hausen explaining away his action in placing himself at the head of Germany as a purely temporary measure designed to deal with the current danger. Friedrich Wilhelm IV, *Briefwechsel mit L. Camphausen*, ed. Erich Brandenburg, Berlin, 1906, pp. 20-21.

[4] Bismarck, *Gedanken und Erinnerungen*, p. 82.

program of the monarchy." He envisaged the workers as forming a "mighty counter-weight" to the middle classes. The workers, he argued, were not interested in politics and the form of government; they were not committed to the republic. Rather they would be satisfied, and their loyalty won, through a series of economic measures: a progressive income tax, the regulation of relations between capital and labor, relief for the poor and the sick.[5]

Whether in fact Radowitz's program would have altered the course of the revolution will never be known; the plan was never seriously considered.[6] Frederick William at first listened to Radowitz, as he did to many others. But he was soon persuaded by the court circle, the Camarilla, that the schemes were impractical and against the interest of the monarchy. Radowitz, a western German and a Catholic, was a figure of suspicion to the Protestant Junkers who surrounded the king. Von Gerlach labeled the plan "communistic" and thought that it could only lead to the "effacement" of the monarchy.[7] The king was convinced and any hope of direct alliance between the Prussian throne and the social forces behind the revolution disappeared in the spring of 1848.

*

Yet the governments of the German states were much more preoccupied with the problems of the workers, with the danger of unemployment and famine, than is gener-

[5] Friedrich Meinecke, *Radowitz und die deutsche Revolution*, Berlin, 1913, pp. 72-78; Paul Hassel, *Joseph Maria von Radowitz*, Berlin, 1905, vol. 1, pp. 586-589.

[6] Valentin would seem to place considerable emphasis on the possibilities of Radowitz's plan; yet, if this was one of the "missed opportunities" so much lamented by German liberals, it was never a very great one. See Valentin, *Geschichte der deutschen Revolution*, vol. 2, p. 561.

[7] Leopold von Gerlach, *Denkwürdigkeiten aus dem Leben Leopold von Gerlachs Generals der Infantrie und General-Adjutanten König Friedrich Wilhelms IV*, Berlin, 1891, vol. 1, p. 153.

83

ally recognized. Indeed it may be argued that during these early months this was their main concern. "In Prussia," one early historian of the revolutions noted, "the condition of the working man had assumed a position of such paramount importance, during the period from April to August, as to obscure even the most pressing constitutional questions." [8] In Austria it was noted that "the mass of workers have no more respect at all for the military, and they despise the bourgeoisie whom they regard as their enemies"; action was needed to restore the confidence of the workers.[9]

The Prussian government had already made some attempt to alleviate the condition of the workers before the outbreak of revolution; these efforts were increased after the barricades had actually been erected. The various branches of the government issued a number of placards aimed at the workers. Typical of these was the declaration of the Berlin magistrate which appeared on the eighth of April, calling upon "our fellow citizens, in particular the guildsmen and workers," to maintain order, joining "with us in the great task of constructing a better state of affairs for our city and country." [10]

The government made more practical efforts to aid the workers as well. The Berlin labor exchange, for example, continued its efforts to find jobs for those without employment. The figure of some 7,000 seeking work had been reduced by nearly one third by the beginning of May.[11] Many of the jobless were employed on the public works projects, paving streets, repairing buildings, laying railway lines, constructing canals and tending the gardens in the cemetery at Friedrichshain where the March

[8] Maurice, *The Revolutionary Movement*, p. 402; cf. also Hammen, "Economic and Social Factors," pp. 837ff.

[9] *Wanderer*, May 9, 1848.

[10] *Berliner Zeitungs Halle*, Apr. 10, 1848.

[11] Friedensburg, *Stephan Born*, pp. 54-55.

dead were buried. A total of some 5,500 workers was employed on the various public projects in Berlin, 3,000 by the state and 2,500 by the municipal government at wages varying from 12.5 or 15 silbergroschen per day for unskilled labor to 25 silbergroschen per day for masons and carpenters.[12]

The public works projects were the Prussian counterpart to the National Workshops in Paris.[13] But they were never more than a temporary measure, generally regarded with contempt by the government and the workers alike. Little useful work was done; the Berlin workers treated them as a "comedy," loafed on the job and happily collected their wages.[14] The government hoped that the minimum of employment and wages offered would keep the workers off the streets and prevent the spread of revolution. Indeed for a time it was thought that the independent *Rehberger* (so-called after the sand hills to the northwest of Berlin which they had been set to level) and the canal workers might form the nucleus of a counterrevolutionary army to be used against the middle-class liberals.[15]

The projects soon got out of hand and had to be cut back. Early assurances by the Berlin magistrates that more work and higher wages would be forthcoming were dropped; piece rates were introduced and a means

[12] From the report of the minister for trade, von Patow, *Verhandlungen der Versammlung zur Vereinbarung der Preussischen Staats-Verfassung*, Berlin, 1848-1849, vol. 1, pp. 66-67; cf. also *Berliner Zeitungs Halle*, Apr. 16, 1848.

[13] So they were regarded by Boerner, *Erinnerungen*, vol. 1, p. 263; Born, *Erinnerungen*, p. 133.

[14] Born, *Erinnerungen*, p. 134.

[15] The suggestion is made by Bernstein, *Geschichte der Berliner Arbeiterbewegung*, vol. 1, p. 38. There is no direct evidence that a serious use of working-class troops was ever contemplated, though Frederick William and his ministers did use the threat of working-class revolt to intimidate the middle-class *Bürgerwehr*. See Friedrich Wilhelm IV, *Briefwechsel*, pp. 30-32.

test adopted to insure that only the neediest were hired.[16] Workers were sacked for disturbing the peace and severely reprimanded for their "ingratitude." [17] Work on the East Prussian railroad, the Ostbahn, was resumed at the beginning of the summer, and it was decided to send as many as possible of the unmarried men previously employed on the canals to work on the railroad. The Ostbahn had the advantage of getting the workers out of Berlin; it also permitted the payment of lower wages, justified by cheaper food and government housing.[18] The scheme was received with protests by many of the workers; rioting broke out on the twenty-eighth of June, and troops had to defend the leaders of the official union who had accepted the government's conditions but were themselves to stay in Berlin.[19]

It became increasingly obvious during the spring of 1848 that the government regarded the work projects as a special measure, adopted only in the face of mass unemployment and the March Days; the workers would have to look elsewhere for a solution to their problems.

*

There were also a number of private middle-class ventures which received the sanction of the government and aimed at improving the lot of the workers. The Central Union for the Well-Being of the Working Classes was revived on April 12, 1848, and use was at last found for the 15,000 thaler offered by Frederick William four years previously.[20] Local branches were set up in places as

[16] *Plakate*, Ratsbibliothek, Berlin, portfolios 1 and 2.

[17] *Berliner Zeitungs Halle*, May 30, 1848.

[18] *Kölnische Zeitung*, June 25, 1848; *Neue Rheinische Zeitung*, June 26, 1848.

[19] *Verhandlungen der Versammlung zur Vereinbarung der Preussischen Staats-Verfassung*, vol. 1, p. 330.

[20] *Mittheilungen des Centralvereins für das Wohl der arbeitenden Klassen*, Aug. 15, 1849.

far afield as Düsseldorf, Koblenz, Grüneberg and Frankfurt. But the Union soon became involved with the wider move to organize the workers and was taken out of middle-class hands. The Berlin branch, for example, became an adjunct of the workers' clubs. It supported the artisan movement, sent delegates to the workers' congresses, established savings and sickness insurance schemes. It was run by such working-class leaders as Bisky, Michaelis and David Born, the brother of Stephan.[21]

More in the pre-March tradition of "aid from above" was the allied organization of the Berlin Ladies' Union for the Abolition of Need among the Small Manufacturers and Artisans. The members included the wives of the manufacturer Borsig, the banker Mendelsohn and the police director Duncker. The list of contributors was headed by Her Royal Highness, the Princess of Prussia, who presented the club with a case of pearls and jewels.[22] Such groups distributed a certain amount of charity, but they offered no real hope for the workers unless they were absorbed into the workers' own organizations.

*

The most important and apparently far-reaching measure adopted by the Prussian government during the spring of 1848 was the creation on the seventeenth of April of the Ministry for Trade, Industry and Public Works. This satisfied, or seemed to satisfy, one of the major demands of the workers' meetings in Berlin immediately following the March revolution; the new ministry would, it was hoped, devote itself to the concerns of the workers. It was the "ministry of labor" for which so many of the workers' gatherings had called. According to the cabinet order which authorized its

[21] Friedensburg, *Stephan Born*, p. 56.
[22] *Berliner Zeitungs Halle*, May 4, 1848.

creation, the ministry would concern itself with "the care of the working and manufacturing classes of the urban as well as the rural population." [23]

But the new ministry achieved little of value or interest to the workers. The first minister, who occupied the post till the fall of the Camphausen ministry on June 25, was Erasmus von Patow. A liberal in the narrow, pre-March sense, von Patow had been concerned for years with questions of trade in the Prussian foreign ministry; he had traveled widely and was fitted by knowledge and experience as well as conviction to forward the commercial interests of Prussia in the new Germany and in the world at large.[24] He had little sympathy with the demands of the workers; they in turn complained that they had never even heard of him.[25]

Von Patow's chief attempt to deal directly with the workers was his scheme for the formation of local committees to discuss the relations between employers and workers, with a final central committee to meet with him to consider what steps could be taken. His interest seems to have been more in maintaining the flow of trade than in any substantial improvement of conditions.[26] The committee scheme was soon abandoned since too few local groups were formed to make it worth while.[27] Late in May he appointed a Dr. Grosse to ad-

[23] Quoted by Margret Tilmann, *Der Einfluss des Revolutionsjahres 1848 auf die preussische Gewerbe- und Sozialgesetzgebung* (*Die Notverordnung vom 9. Februar 1849*), Berlin, 1935, p. 23; cf. also Wolff, *Berliner Revolutionschronik*, vol. 2, pp. 169-170.

[24] Valentin, *Geschichte der deutschen Revolution*, vol. 2, p. 617, n. 17. Von Patow's successor as Minister of Trade, Karl August Milde, was the son of a Silesian calico and woolen goods manufacturer and was similarly unsympathetic to the demands of the workers.

[25] *Die Locomotive*, Apr. 23, 1848.

[26] *Berliner Zeitungs Halle*, May 11, 1848.

[27] Report of Moritz Veit to the Economic Committee of the Frankfurt Assembly, *Akten des volkswirtschaftlichen Ausschusses*, vol. 2; Tilmann, *Einfluss des Revolutionsjahres*, pp. 27-28.

minister a "workers' bank" to grant loans to needy artisans and small manufacturers, thus implementing a scheme set up by the United Diet a month and a half earlier.[28] This scheme also aimed at increasing trade with the hope that prosperity would ultimately filter down to the workers. Von Patow's attitude toward the public provision of jobs for the unemployed emerged clearly in his attempt to deal with the crowd which gathered in front of his house on the evening of the thirtieth of May protesting the reduction of work and the attempt to introduce piece rates on the public projects. Von Patow's first response was to summon the *Bürgerwehr*, which refused to intervene in what seemed a perfectly peaceful gathering. The workers rejected von Patow's offer of an outright gift of 20 thaler to each present, claiming that they were not beggars but "free men." The neediest among them accepted 10 silbergroschen, regarded by the workers as advance pay, by von Patow as charity. Misunderstanding between the two parties was complete.[29]

Instead of granting the workers' demands von Patow went ahead with his program of limiting the number of publicly employed workers in Berlin and cooperated in the scheme of getting the jobless to leave town for work on the Ostbahn. A special committee was formed as the result of the events of the thirtieth of May to consider ways of preserving order in the city. The committee, headed by von Puttkamer of the Ministry of the Interior and including representatives of the Berlin magistrate, the mayor, the city council, the police and the *Bürgerwehr*, issued a public declaration on June 1, 1848,

[28] *Zeitung für das deutsche Volk*, May 22, 1848; Wolff, *Berliner Revolutionschronik*, vol. 2, pp. 169-170.

[29] *Das Volk*, June 1, 1848; *Neue Rheinische Zeitung*, June 2, 1848; *Verhandlungen der Versammlung zur Veinbarung der Preussischen Staats-Verfassung*, vol. 1, pp. 66-67; Kaeber, *Berlin*, p. 141; Valentin, *Geschichte der deutschen Revolution*, vol. 2, pp. 49-50.

lamenting the unrest which disturbed the city and drove away those with property.[30] The forces of order were once more uniting in Berlin; the approach to the workers' problems had returned to the policy of empty appeals for peaceful behavior.

❋

Prussia was not alone in attempting to bring the power of the state to bear on the problems of the workers. In Vienna, for example, public works were set up, in the Prater, on the Donau canal and elsewhere, and similar problems were experienced: little work was done; higher wages were demanded; the gangs on the projects formed ready-made corps for street riots and further revolution. The matter came to a head with the riots of June 15, 1848. Dr. Fischhof, chairman of the revolutionary Security Committee, was forced to call out the National Guard to protect the city from the workers. Here too the interests of the workers were ignored by the government they had helped to establish.[31]

Elsewhere other measures were adopted. In Hanover the artisans forced the rescinding of the industrial law passed in 1847 which was to have opened all trades to free entry from July 1, 1848; instead the guild system was to be retained with some allowance for special concessions.[32] It was the first victory of the artisans in 1848; there were to be more. In Hesse-Darmstadt the finance ministry brought forward proposals for a tax on both personal and capital gains.[33] In the Duchy of Nassau a ministerial order set up a commission composed of representatives of the various industrial and agricultural

[30] *Plakate*, Ratsbibliothek, Berlin, portfolio 3.
[31] Rath, *The Viennese Revolution*, pp. 219-222.
[32] Hans Meusch, *Die Handwerkerbewegung von 1848/49, Vorgeschichte, Verlauf, Inhalt, Ergebnisse*, Eschwege, 1949, pp. 40-41.
[33] *Zeitung für das deutsche Volk*, June 15, 1848.

associations under a government official to seek ways of improving working conditions.[34]

The most comprehensive scheme adopted was that of the government of the Kingdom of Saxony, perhaps the most radical of any of the March ministries. A decree of the minister of the interior, Oberländer, on the third of April called for the formation of a workers' commission in Dresden to propose economic legislation. The commission met on the twenty-ninth of May; its members included the printer Skrobek, of the Leipzig workers' club. With 12,000 thaler voted by the Saxon Diet for expenses, the commission prepared a questionnaire with 384 items: these included such problems as the position of the master artisans within and without the guild system, journeymen and assistants, employers and workers in home industries, and the growing number of factories. The results of this questionnaire were to be tabulated by six subcommissions and submitted to the central commission later in the year.[35]

The Saxon workers' commission marked the first systematic attempt to find out just what problems were in fact plaguing the workers of 1848. Yet it produced no immediate results in terms of legislation. The workers still hoped for action from the government of the German states, but it became increasingly obvious that the "achievements" of the March revolution were inadequate, that the workers would have to organize in order to apply continual pressure to obtain such action.

*

The workers also hoped that their demands would be considered by the Pre-Parliament; again their demands

[34] Goldschmidt, *Die deutsche Handwerkerbewegung*, p. 19.
[35] *Zeitung für das deutsche Volk*, June 5, 1848; Veit's report, *Akten des volkswirtschaftlichen Ausschusses*, vol. 2; Lipinski, *Arbeiterbewegung in Leipzig*, vol. 1, pp. 174-175.

were neither openly rejected nor fulfilled. The Pre-Parliament met in Frankfurt am Main on March 30, 1848, amid general rejoicing throughout Germany. Its task was to make arrangements for a National Assembly which could draw up a constitution for all of Germany. This task was interpreted by von Gagern and the liberals of southwest Germany, the men of the Heidelberg Committee which had summoned the Pre-Parliament, as strictly political. But social and economic issues were implicit in even this limited aim, and the wider nature of the revolutions of 1848 became evident at the Pre-Parliament.

The official program of business drawn up for the Pre-Parliament by the Committee of Seven appointed by the Heidelberg group was attacked at the first regular session of the Pre-Parliament by Gustav von Struve, who offered instead a democratic one. The main aim of Struve's program was to force the meeting at least to discuss the possibility of a republic, but its fifteen points included such items as a progressive income and property tax, government aid to the needy and support for failing industries and trades, and a ministry of labor to "equalize" the relation between capital and labor.[36]

The program was rejected out of hand, without discussion, and led to the withdrawal of Struve from the Pre-Parliament and the abortive Hecker-Struve *putsch* in mid-April. The attempt by Hecker and Struve to proclaim a republic and support it by force of arms failed to attract much interest among the working classes. Radicals, ranging from Robert Blum to Friedrich Held, condemned the attempt as unjustified violence, a betrayal of

[36] G. A. U. Freyer, *Das Vorparlament zu Frankfurt a. M. im Jahre 1848*, Greifswald, 1913, pp. 36-42; Quarck, *Erste deutsche Arbeiterbewegung*, p. 67; Valentin, *Geschichte der deutschen Revolution*, vol. 1, pp. 472-473.

the revolution and the German people.[37] Their lead was followed by the workers who still hoped to gain their economic goals through organization and government action and had little desire to join in a struggle for what seemed to them to be the purely abstract issue of republican government.

The Pre-Parliament, which continued its business after the interruption of Struve, was unrepresentative and inefficient. Perhaps the most important issue with which it had to deal was that of the franchise law for the coming elections to the National Constituent Assembly. Yet this crucial issue was to a large extent avoided. The Pre-Parliament proposed that the vote be given to all adult male citizens with representation distributed at the ratio of one delegate for every fifty thousand inhabitants. In the final form of the law, though curiously not in the debates, it was stipulated that the vote could be limited to "independent" citizens; the law concluded that "each who can vote in his own land can vote in Germany." In other words, the question of the franchise was referred back to the individual states; there was to be no universal manhood suffrage in 1848. The franchise was so constructed in almost every state that the workers were prevented from exercising any major influence on the elections to the Frankfurt Parliament.[38]

Social issues did find expression in the Pre-Parliament in speeches of others than the extreme republicans such as Struve. Eisenstuck, an industrialist from Saxony and certainly no republican, agreed with a number of points in the republican program. He called the well-being of

[37] Klein, *Der Vorkampf*, p. 493; *Die Locomotive*, Apr. 23, 1848.
[38] Theodore S. Hamerow, "The Elections to the Frankfurt Parliament," *Journal of Modern History*, vol. 33 (1961), pp. 15-32; Veit Valentin, *Die erste deutsche Nationalversammlung, Eine geschichtliche Studie über die Frankfurter Paulskirche*, Munich, 1919, p. 4; *Frankfurt am Main*, p. 186.

the working classes "the true and great public question of the present" and proposed a ministry for the working classes, free elementary and technical education, an arbitration court to settle labor disputes, taxes favorable to the workers, including an income tax, a tax on capital and protective tariffs. The Baden democrat Venedy included in a declaration of basic rights a scheme for a credit bank to aid workers in paying off debts to masters and government support for clubs which would aid those unable to work.[39]

None of these proposals was passed; the assembly was too firmly committed to the doctrines of liberalism and believed too firmly in the panacea of an all-German constitution. In the words of one observer: "Liberalism rose up like four hundred marionettes on a single wire and there's an end of it: the social question was solved in their eyes." But the Pre-Parliament did find it necessary to adopt by a standing vote a measure indicating its "sympathy" with the working classes and its hopes for improvement in their condition.[40] And the proposals made in the Pre-Parliament were to come up again in the National Assembly. The problem of the German working classes remained a central and irrepressible issue of the revolutions of 1848.

❋

The Pre-Parliament, upon its adjournment on the third of April, elected a Committee of Fifty to carry on its business during the period of preparation for the elections to the National Assembly. Such democrats as Struve and Hecker were not included, though they were high up on the election list, Hecker coming fifty-first—

[39] Walter Schneider, *Wirtschafts- und Sozialpolitik im Frankfurter Parlament 1848/49*, Frankfurt am Main, 1923, p. 47; Valentin, *Geschichte der deutschen Revolution*, vol. 1, p. 479; Freyer, *Das Vorparlament*, pp. 134-135.
[40] Freyer, *Das Vorparlament*, pp. 108-109.

another cause of grievance on their part. The committee did contain, however, a number of radicals, including Robert Blum from Leipzig, Johann Jacoby from Königsberg and Jacob Venedy from Baden; all of these were interested in the workers' cause.[41] On their insistence, the Committee of Fifty appointed a special workers' commission under Blum to investigate conditions among the working classes and make recommendations to the National Assembly when it met. In its report, submitted to the Committee of Fifty on the eighth of May, the commission held that the poverty of the workers was caused by a flooded labor market, the result of overpopulation, and that low wages were necessary in this situation. The solution proposed was the limitation of competition, a task which the commission felt to lie in the province of the forthcoming National Assembly.[42]

The report played into the hands of those who advocated protective tariffs as well as those who regarded a strong guild system as necessary. It was not, however, widely publicized, appearing only in a Leipzig newspaper, presumably out of local interest in the activities of Robert Blum. But it set the tone of many of the proposals which were to be considered by the Economic Committee of the Frankfurt Assembly.

The elections to the National Assembly were scheduled for the first of May. The campaign for these elections and for the elections to the Prussian Assembly which took place at the same time marked, according to some historians, the separation between the working-class and the bourgeois revolutionary movement in 1848.[43] Yet the issue was probably not as clearly drawn as

---

[41] Freyer, *Das Vorparlament,* pp. 120-121.

[42] Obermann, *Die deutschen Arbeiter in der ersten bürgerlichen Revolution,* pp. 170-173.

[43] Bernstein, *Geschichte der Berliner Arbeiterbewegung,* vol. 1, p. 18.

these historians would indicate, in spite of the exclusion of most of the working class from the vote.

The result of the electoral law promulgated by the Pre-Parliament was the effective disenfranchisement of most of the working class. Property or tax qualifications or the requirement of birth or long residence excluded many, while some states—Hanover, Electoral Hesse and Württemberg—went so far as explicitly to remove workers and servants from the list of eligible voters. Also the method of election limited the choice of the workers; elections were often held in public or with numbered ballots so that it was known for whom a particular worker had voted. In all but four states there was a system of indirect election, a method which tended to eliminate the expression of extreme opinion. The mere cost of being a delegate to the Frankfurt Assembly (transportation and upkeep were not provided) excluded many from the campaign. Finally there was a tendency in most areas to select the more respectable candidates for this, the first all-German elected assembly, a tendency which arose out of a feeling of local pride as much as anything else. Born himself refused to run in Berlin because he thought he was not old enough. There were no organized parties and the election was solely for single "personalities," those who were important on a local level. This factor as much as anything else produced the results which won the Frankfurt Assembly the title, largely undeserved, of a "parliament of professors." [44]

The extent of working-class protest against the elections to the Frankfurt Assembly was not as great as might have been expected. Some of the workers' spokesmen expressed themselves content with the franchise laws. [45]

[44] Wilhelm Mommsen, *Grösse und Versagen des deutschen Bürgertums, Ein Beitrag zur Geschichte der Jahre 1848-1849,* Stuttgart, 1949, p. 75; Born, *Erinnerungen,* p. 132.

[45] *Die Locomotive,* April 6, 1848.

Born himself, and with him the great body of the Berlin workers, refused to participate in the protest campaign which the radical student Gustav Adolf Schlöffel tried to organize, staying away from the "great demonstration" against the electoral law planned for the twentieth of April.[46] The right to vote, where it did exist, was often left unexercised by the workers.[47] The workers still hoped that the Frankfurt Assembly, in spite of the limited basis on which it was chosen, would meet their demands. It was the conservatives who deplored the elections of the first of May; their attitude was summed up by Leopold von Gerlach, who declared that "no good can come from them; only after them." [48]

The lack of interest on the part of the workers was not based as yet on any realization of just how little they were to achieve from the Frankfurt Assembly; they still hoped for much and laboriously began to draft petitions which would instruct the National Assembly in the condition and needs of the workers. The acceptance of the electoral laws was based more on a conception of society which regarded the exclusion of the workers' estate from parliament as proper. The workers had little interest in political issues. Rather they hoped to form their own associations which would then represent the whole class in dealing with the government. They also placed their faith in the workers' congresses which met during the summer and were regarded by many of the workers as

[46] Max Lenz, *Geschichte der Königliches Friedrich-Wilhelms-Universität zu Berlin*, Halle, 1910-1918, vol. 2, ii; pp. 240-241; Franz Mehring, *Geschichte der deutschen Sozialdemokratie*, Stuttgart, 1922, vol. 2, pp. 90-91.

[47] It has been estimated that participation in the elections was everywhere below 50 per cent of those entitled to vote and often as low as 30 per cent; the workers appeared to be even less anxious to exercise their vote than did the middle classes. Hamerow, "Elections to the Frankfurt Parliament," pp. 27ff.; *Restoration, Revolution, Reaction*, pp. 123-124.

[48] Gerlach, *Denkwürdigkeiten*, vol. 1, pp. 155-156.

an auxiliary branch of the National Assembly, a parliament for workers which could deal with economic matters just as the middle-class assembly dealt with political issues.

Finally the workers were still subject to the excitement of the revolutionary events. Just as they believed in the magic of the barricades, in the fact that the revolution had been made once and for all, so they believed in the universal efficacy of parliaments and constitutions.[49] It was only later, in the course of the long and ultimately fruitless struggle for organization, that the workers came to realize how little had actually been won from the governments on the barricades.

[49] Cf. Veit Valentin's statement, "Die Zeit war ja so überaus parlaments- und verfassungsgläubig." *Geschichte der deutschen Revolution,* vol. 1, p. 482.

CHAPTER 5

ALTERNATIVES TO ORGANIZATION
—RADICAL LEADERS

THERE WAS no program inherent in the German revolution; the liberals, the radicals, the various groups of artisans and workers all had different aims and different hopes. The assumed unity of the March Days was bound to be short-lived; the revolution of March, according to one observer, "was a symptom, not a cause of the upheaval. . . . The motto, recognition of the revolution, had too many meanings and thus said nothing." [1] It remained to be seen whether the radical agitators would have any more success than the new ministries and the liberals of the Frankfurt Pre-Parliament in persuading the mass of workers to follow their lead, to accept their interpretation of what the revolution meant.

The March Days left the way open for putative popular leaders of all sorts to attempt to make names for themselves. With a single speech in the Zelten in Berlin or in the central square of one of the other German towns, with a satiric broadside or a serious article in one of the innumerable newspapers which appeared briefly at the book stalls, it was possible to gain a reputation and a following in the streets. The "apostles of the Zelten," the "sans-culottes in frock coats," were a common feature of the early days of the revolution. [2]

But the radicals and democrats were as much taken by surprise by the revolution as were the governments of the German states. Few had any clear program; few

[1] Gneist, *Berliner Zustände*, p. 8.
[2] *Deutsche Arbeiter Zeitung*, ed. Lubarsch and Bittkow, Apr. 22, 1848.

knew what strategy they should adopt. The appeal of such demagogues as the journalist Friedrich Held or the student Gustav Schlöffel was to "the people" and more specifically to "the workers." Even when they called for cooperation with the middle classes and stressed the importance of the preservation of law and order in any attempt at improving economic conditions, they still acknowledged the special demands and needs of the working classes. Their fame and their influence were often transitory; their programs were usually too vague to attract any lasting support. They were concerned almost solely with loyalty to the ideal of "the revolution" in the abstract without attempting to translate this into a practical program. They gave the appearance of being more radical than such advocates of working-class organization as Stephan Born, but this radicalism went with a lack of any specific goal.

The problem of the radical in the revolution faced not only such opportunists as Held and Schlöffel but the intellectual Karl Marx and his followers. Like Held and Schlöffel, Marx felt that little had been achieved by the March Days, that the real revolution, the revolution of the proletariat, lay ahead. The problem was to utilize the bourgeois revolution, to force it to its extremity and, at the same time, to prepare for the coming proletarian revolt. Following what he held to be the implications of his theoretical analysis of the development of history, Marx took his stand in the early months of the revolution with the radicals, criticizing the middle-class liberals but refusing to join with the working-class organizations which aimed at immediate improvement of the workers' lot. The problem was similar to that of the Bolsheviks in March of 1917: what was to be the role of a proletariat leader in a "bourgeois" revolution? Marx rejected in 1848 the solution which Lenin advocated in the April

Theses of 1917. To Marx there seemed in the spring of 1848, contrary to the predictions of the *Manifesto,* no immediate possibility of a transition to a second stage of the revolution placing power in the hands of the workers. Therefore he neglected the workers' attempts at organization, giving support instead to the radicals among the bourgeoisie.

Both Marx and the other middle-class radicals failed in the early days of the revolution to gain the allegiance of the working-class groups; without radical leadership and without support from the government, the workers turned to the only alternative that was left them—self-help through organization.

❋

The principal gathering place for crowds in Berlin in the days following the revolution and the center for radical agitation was the Zelten. An open park beyond the Brandenburger Tor, just to the north of the Tiergarten, it had once been occupied by tents (whence its name); it now contained cafés, concert halls, puppet shows and the other paraphernalia of popular amusement. Here the crowds assembled to hear speakers on political subjects after the victory of the eighteenth of March. The meetings in the Zelten "offered colorful, continually festive doings. Here streamed the laborers on the earth works in their strange attire; here the artisan kept himself in the background with a cool glass of Berliner *Weissbier,* and, along with the proletariat, students, journeymen and even a few curious soldiers in uniform swayed around the speakers' stand." [3]

A club was formed, the *Volksverein unter den Zelten,* with Max Schassler as organizer and Louis Lewissohn as

[3] Boerner, *Erinnerungen,* vol. 2, p. 71.

secretary. The real leaders of the club and the most frequent speakers were Friedrich Held and Gustav Schlöffel. It proved to be the most popular and influential of the lower-class clubs during the early days of the revolution, providing an outlet for the expression of working-class opinion similar to that which such organizations as the Constitutional Club and the Political Club offered the more radical of the Berlin burghers.[4]

The People's Club of the Zelten, though radical and even revolutionary in some of its pronouncements, was essentially conservative; that is, it supported the state and placed the preservation of order above all other goals. Indeed, like the demagogues who led it, the club was without any specific program; it merely provided a forum for the expression of opinion and was tolerated by the government on the theory that it prevented worse excesses.

But the club made more positive efforts at controlling the working classes, for it constantly and expressly discouraged any further outbreak of violence. Typical was the broadside which it issued on April 5, 1848, in which it denied most indignantly the rumor that the club advocated the plundering of shops or that any such opinion had been expressed at the meetings in the Zelten. Rather it called on the workers to preserve order: [5]

> Friends! As much as we all love freedom, so much we also love order, since only through order can work and a just wage be ours. We would be a single, fraternal people, with one standing for all and all for one, and each treating as an enemy those who act for themselves alone and permit deeds of violence against the property of the people, endangering our freedom.

[4] Bernstein, *Geschichte der Berliner Arbeiterbewegung*, vol. 1, pp. 20-21.
[5] *Plakate*, Ratsbibliothek, Berlin, portfolio 1.

The club went further than this and promised to join with the machine workers in a campaign to meet force with force in preventing the spread of robbery and destruction. The People's Club of the Zelten scarcely provided the workers with an organization through which they could gain their ends.

The leaders of the meetings in the Zelten, Held and Schlöffel, may be taken as typical of the radicals who sought there the allegiance of the Berlin workers.

*

Friedrich Wilhelm Alexander Held had been born in Silesia in 1813; educated in a military orphanage in Potsdam, he was commissioned as a second lieutenant in the army at eighteen. A rebel at an early age, he found that "this position harmonized so little with my view of freedom, the church and state that . . . I asked for my discharge at the end of the six year period of service"— or at least this was the reason which Held gave in his campaign biography when running for the Prussian Assembly in 1848.[6] From the army he turned to the stage, spending four years acting in minor companies, but during the increased interest in politics, the *Aufschwung* which followed the accession of Frederick William IV in 1840, Held was attracted to journalism and published a paper, *Die Locomotive*, which was sufficiently radical to land him in prison in 1845.

The revolution offered Held an ideal opportunity to make a name for himself. Striking in appearance, with red hair and a flowing beard, an able orator and a clever journalist with a gift for sharp phrases, he soon attracted a considerable following, mostly among the unskilled workers with a hard core of followers among the machine

[6] *Die Locomotive*, May 1, 1848. On Held, see Kurt Koszyk, "Das Bild des Demagogen im Berliner Tollen Jahr 1848," *Festschrift für Emil Dovifat*, Bremen, 1960, pp. 156-170.

builders.[7] But his influence should not be exaggerated. His popularity was short-lived, and the machine workers, although they made him an honorary member of their association, were perfectly capable of looking after their own affairs.

Held maintained a distant and somewhat sceptical attitude toward the revolution, which he styled a "childish prank" (*ein Bubenstreich*) and "a great blancmange." [8] In the first issue of the revived *Locomotive*, he wrote: [9]

> The specter of the revolution has passed through the *teutschen Gaue* (if one may talk black-red-gold) and tied together the shroud on the promises of 1815. From this unification new promises have in turn emerged, together with the firm promise that these promises are not to remain mere promises but are to become more than promises.—Such is the achievement up to now of the German revolutions, large and small.

Later in the same issue he corrected himself (Held was not above apparent inconsistencies in his position): there was one further achievement—the revolution had forced the Berlin chief of police to suspend the law which prohibited the smoking of tobacco out of doors.[10]

Held maintained that the achievements of the revolu-

[7] The historian should not confuse the two groups as Priscilla Robertson appears to do in *Revolutions of 1848, A Social History,* Princeton, 1952, pp. 132-133; they represent opposite positions in the social scale of jobs and had different and often conflicting economic demands, so that it would have taken a more forceful leader than Held to have held them together. Mrs. Robertson in general seems to exaggerate the position which Held occupied among the Berlin workers, putting his influence on a par with Born's (p. 131).

[8] *Die Locomotive,* Apr. 22, 1848.

[9] *Die Locomotive,* Apr. 1, 1848.

[10] Even this concession came as a great shock to some conservatives; see Gerlach, *Denkwürdigkeiten,* vol. 1, p. 154.

tion were at best limited because freedom itself was limited: [11]

> One must regard the individual human being not solely as an individual but as part of a whole, as a member of society, as a participant in the society of the state: there can be no talk of natural freedom just as there can be no talk of it among two or three billiard players. For . . . rules must intercede through the agreement of the players so that each sacrifices a portion of his natural freedom; and so we have limited or conditioned freedom, the freedom of the state.

On the other hand, the state should not, in Held's opinion, "hinder the citizen in the fulfillment of the natural purpose of his life, that is, existence. Thus arise the duty of the state to see to it that the citizen does not lack the public means of existence, namely, work."

The duty of the state to provide work for its citizens was a theme to which Held returned repeatedly. He advocated direct aid as well as the extension of the public works projects and a number of other schemes. In his address to the "men of work," published as a broadside on the eighth of April, Held identified himself with the workers and called on them to present their demands to the government in a peaceful fashion, preserving order:

> A man of labor speaks to you, a man who works with his head as you work with your hands for daily bread and the general welfare. . . . The great European revolution of the year 1848 is a social revolution, that is, one which aims at a basic cure for the evil under which the working classes lie ill.

[11] *Die Locomotive*, Apr. 4, 1848.

Held claimed to tolerate no half-remedies for the problem of the workers; he regarded the revival of the guilds, for example, as a waste of energy and felt that the only cure was the guarantee by the state of work and a living wage for all.[12]

Though the guarantee of the "right to work" remained the chief duty of the state, in Held's opinion, there were other remedial measures which the state could adopt. In his election platform for the campaign for the Prussian Assembly in May 1848, Held listed a number of other goals in addition to the provision of work. He claimed to be a democrat and stood for constitutional government, direct elections and freedom of the press, religion, speech and association. He called for free public education, for the abolition of the standing army, for the equal administration of law; he advocated progressive taxes on income and property and state aid to the sick and aged.[13] Elsewhere he called for systematic inflation in order to wipe out all accumulated wealth and propagated birth control to solve the problem of overpopulation and poverty. The rich, he maintained, had long practised birth control but hid this fact from the poor in an effort to sustain the supply of cheap labor.[14]

Held deplored the false issues, the distractions, which led the workers from their true interests. One of these distractions was the attempted revival of the guild system; another was the call to sporadic violence. But perhaps the most dangerous of the distracting issues was the demand for national unification. Held regarded this as a secondary goal which had to yield to the more imperative needs of the working classes. Perhaps alone among the Germans of the time he perceived the con-

[12] *Plakate,* Ratsbibliothek, Berlin, portfolio 1; also *Die Locomotive,* May 23, 1848.
[13] *Die Locomotive,* May 1, 1848.
[14] *Die Locomotive,* Apr. 7, June 10, 14, 1848.

tradiction inherent in Germany's national demands. "What it [the Prussian State] supports in Posen, it seeks to destroy in Schleswig, and what it demands in Schleswig, it seeks to repress in Posen." [15]

For many of these doctrines Held found little hearing among the working classes, while the more thoughtful of the middle classes, even those with radical pretensions, regarded him as a rabble rouser of the worst sort.[16] In vain did Held attempt to point out the difference between his position and that of mere anarchy.[17] The workers understood little of his program; they were not simply interested in the "right to work," but in the right to work under better conditions, with more pay, shorter hours and more security; many resented his attacks on the guilds. Held, though a shrewd critic of the revolution, had nothing to say about the practical methods by which the workers could attain these ends. As time went on, Held became convinced that he was the victim of slander, of a campaign to ignore or nullify his efforts. Against this he protested too much and soon gained the reputation, not altogether undeserved, for incorrigible vanity.[18]

Held's reputation waned rapidly and with it his interest in further agitation. From the end of July his articles in *Die Locomotive* became less frequent; he left it to others to carry on his work. In September he was discovered in an interview with a conservative leader at the house of a noted Berlin hostess; Held claimed that he had never been there, that the interview was a plot, that the conversation was perfectly innocent. No one really cared; indeed the exact nature of the com-

[15] *Die Locomotive,* Apr. 14, 1848.
[16] *Deutsche Arbeiter Zeitung,* ed. Lubarsch and Bittkow, Apr. 11, 1848; Gneist, *Berliner Zustände,* p. 88.
[17] *Die Locomotive,* May 20, 1848.
[18] *Die Locomotive,* May 18, June 8, 9, 1848; Boerner, *Erinnerungen,* vol. 2, p. 186.

promise involved was never clear.[19] By the end of 1848 Held was back at this old stand in the Zelten, but this time in the capacity of puppeteer. He published one last self-justification, protesting that his new work was quite as honorable as his old.[20] And indeed it may have been more to his liking, for pulling the strings on marionettes and saying their lines for them was in a sense what he had been trying to do all the time.

*

The career of Gustav Adolf Schlöffel as a revolutionary radical was much shorter than that of Held, yet in some ways it was more significant, for Schlöffel was perhaps the only open advocate of violent class warfare and the continuation of the revolution. As such he has been praised by recent communist writers, but he also earned the admiration of his fellow university students as one "motivated [by] one thought only, to help his poorer brothers, the proletarians, to raise them out of their pressing need." [21] He was the most prominent of a number of radical students who won and then lost the confidence of the workers in such university towns as Berlin, Vienna and Bonn; he was also the most radical. Yet his call for the "destruction of capital" received little support from the workers, and his campaign against the limited franchise failed.

Born in 1828, the son of a rich but radical Silesian manufacturer, Schlöffel was at university at the time of

---

[19] *Berliner Zeitungs Halle,* Sept. 20, 1848.

[20] *Die Locomotive,* Dec. 27, 1848.

[21] Boerner, *Erinnerungen,* vol. 1, p. 271. Boerner was also a student in Berlin at the time of the revolution. For recent communist comment on Schlöffel, see *Die Revolution in Deutschland 1848/49,* ed. F. W. Potjomkin and A. I. Molok, trans. from the Russian by Werner Meyer, Berlin, 1956, vol. 1, pp. 179, 183, 190ff.; also Obermann, *Die deutschen Arbeiter in der Revolution von 1848,* pp. 168ff.

the outbreak of the revolution, or rather between universities, for he had been expelled from Heidelberg in February of 1848 for distributing communist literature among the peasants of the Odenwald and had only just arrived in Berlin with the intention of matriculating.[22] He soon launched into the popular agitation in Berlin, speaking at public meetings and visiting the workers in their factories and shops. On the fifth of April he brought out, together with his fellow students Salis and Eduard Monecke, the first issue of a paper entitled *Der Volksfreund*, named after Marat's *Ami du Peuple* and dated "the Year One of Freedom." The paper was distributed free among the workers and was especially popular with the *Rehberger* and the canal builders.

In the first issue Schlöffel placed his allegiance firmly with the working classes: "*The People's Friend* . . . intends without limitation and without reserve to pursue only *one* goal and only *one* purpose in its discussions: the revolution of existing conditions *through* and *for* the people, . . . through and for the repressed and enslaved *working* classes." [23] Schlöffel deplored the current conditions in industry: "everywhere the lack of bread, everywhere overcrowding, competition, low wages, long hours of work, everywhere the same corroding, cancerous sore of our society: *the exploitation of the human power of work by capital.*" The usual remedies proposed were, in Schlöffel's opinion, insufficient; higher wages, shorter hours, minor concessions by employers—all these were merely adding "a new ring, if a golden one," to the chain which enslaved labor. The chain had to be cast off, the revolution continued: such was Schlöffel's position.[24]

Schlöffel joined with Born in the early attempts to

[22] Lenz, *Geschichte der Universität zu Berlin*, vol. 2, pt. 2, pp. 238-239; Kaeber, *Berlin*, p. 142.
[23] *Der Volksfreund*, Apr. 5, 1848.
[24] *Der Volksfreund*, Apr. 8, 1848.

organize the workers. But he was not content with Born's purely economic program; he attacked Born at a meeting on the sixth of April, calling for the complete destruction of capital and further revolution.[25] Later in the month the split between Born and Schlöffel widened over the issue of the franchise. Schlöffel wished to organize a mass demonstration against the franchise law and went ahead with this plan, delivering inflammatory speeches and hinting at possible violence, even when Born and the new Central Workers' Committee refused to cooperate. Sixty thousand were to march from the Alexanderplatz to the royal palace on the twentieth of April in protest against the limited suffrage; Schlöffel indicated in speeches before the event that violence would not be inappropriate.

The demonstration organized by Schlöffel was a failure. A mere one thousand to fifteen hundred turned up and the procession was canceled. On the following day Schlöffel was arrested for an article published in the *Volksfreund* the day before the demonstration, attacking the king, referring to the minister Camphausen as a Barrabas for whom the Christ of democracy was to be sacrificed and calling on the Prussians to emulate the example of Hecker and Struve in Baden.[26]

Schlöffel was tried on May 11, 1848, and sentenced to six months in prison. At his trial he expressed his disillusion with the German revolution. He had soon discovered, he said, "that the pendulum of the people as it oscillated in those days in Berlin was already seized with the last quivering which goes before stillness. Yes, the Germans want *stillness*; they want no revolution of the

[25] *Berliner Zeitungs Halle*, Apr. 8, 1848.
[26] *Der Volksfreund*, Apr. 19, 1848; Mehring, *Geschichte der deutschen Sozialdemokratie*, vol. 2, pp. 90-91; Bernstein, *Geschichte der Berliner Arbeiterbewegung*, vol. 1, pp. 38-39; Lenz, *Geschichte der Universität zu Berlin*, vol. 2, pt. 2, pp. 240-241.

people and no independent movement. The Germans are indolent, very indolent." [27] Three weeks before the end of his sentence Schlöffel escaped from the prison at Magdeburg. He joined the Hungarian revolutionary army, but returned to Germany in the spring of 1849 to participate in the rising in the Rhenish Palatinate and Baden. He was killed fighting at Waghäusel on June 21, 1849.

✻

The failure of such radicals as Held and Schlöffel to attract the working classes in Berlin was repeated by Karl Marx and his communist colleagues in Cologne. Like Held and Schlöffel, Marx regarded the revolution of March as insufficient. Like them, he sought to criticize the middle-class liberals and encourage more radical elements through the medium of a newspaper. Like them, he ignored the more practical efforts of the workers to organize and gain immediate improvements. But there was a further difficulty which Marx faced; he had been, before the revolution, the leader of a revolutionary party and the author of a theory of history and revolution. The events of 1848 thus presented him with the problem of fitting his theory to the facts of the revolution and establishing the role of the Communist Party; both these factors forced him into a position which alienated him from the workers of 1848.

On April 1, 1848, the Communist Party of Germany

[27] *Schlöffels des jüngeren Pressprocess verhandelt vor dem Kammergericht in Berlin*, Berlin, 1848, p. 3. Schlöffel went on to point out that the Germans seemed to prefer the goals of nationalism to that of freedom: "Alle deutschen Professoren schnupperten an den Grenzen Deutschlands herum, und wo sie uns da ein früher deutsch gewesenes Dorf unter fremder Herrschaft herausforschen konnten, wurden mit alle Urkunden der Universitäten der erweiterte Rechtsspruch der vaterländischen Herrscher begründet, und die erlorschenen Sympathien zu einem nationalem Wechselfieber aufgefrischt."

issued, from Paris, a seventeen-point manifesto which began with the familiar motto, "Proletarians of all countries, unite!" The manifesto was signed by a committee which included Karl Marx, Friedrich Engels, Karl Schapper, Heinrich Bauer, Joseph Moll and Wilhelm Wolff.[28] After signing the manifesto, the members of the committee left Paris for various parts of Germany where they were to further the proletarian revolution in the name of the Communist League.

The manifesto itself was in many ways a moderate document; it was markedly different from the policy outlined in the *Communist Manifesto* which Marx and Engels had written for the Communist League during the preceding winter. Of the ten points which Marx and Engels put forward as constituting a model communist program in the earlier document, only four were included among the seventeen points of the first of April.[29] These were the demands for a state banking system, the nationalization of transport, the introduction of a progressive income tax and the provision of free education. Two other points of the *Manifesto* were included, though in a modified form: the right of inheritance was to be "limited" rather than "abolished" and the lands of the feudal princes, and not all lands, were to go to the state.

This last change suggests the general tenor of the program of the first of April. For it was an attempt—and probably a rather unsuccessful attempt, since the program was soon discarded—to deal with the particular conditions of the revolution in Germany; it was a plan

[28] Copies of the manifesto were published in the *Berliner Zeitungs Halle,* Apr. 5, 1848, and in the *Zeitung für das deutsche Volk,* Apr. 9, 1848.

[29] Cf. the copy of the *Manifesto* in Marx, Engels, *Selected Works,* vol. 1, pp. 50-51.

of action for communists in what Marx insisted was a purely "bourgeois" revolution. Of such doctrines as the equal liability of all to labor and the extension of state industry there was no mention. Instead the program aimed at abolishing the remains of feudalism and the effects of particularism, at achieving the unification of Germany under a republican government. There was little mention of the workers; they were to be granted political rights but the only economic measure of interest to the workers contained in the program of the first of April was point sixteen, which called for national workshops to guarantee the right to work. The program was indistinguishable from the republican demands which Struve presented to the Pre-Parliament.

This program was not a mere extension of the *Manifesto*, an attempt to translate its general proposals into a particular plan for the German situation as some Marxist writers have maintained.[30] Nor does it seem likely that the *Manifesto*, though admittedly aimed at all Europe, had not been designed to deal with Germany as well.[31] The truth is that Marx, in spite of the *Manifesto* and its predictions, was as surprised by the outbreak of revolution as were the other radicals, that from the beginning of the revolution and indeed throughout 1848 and 1849, he improvised a program—sometimes bril-

[30] Potjomkin, Molok, *Die Revolution in Deutschland,* vol. 1, pp. 248ff.; Obermann, *Die deutschen Arbeiter in der Revolution von 1848,* p. 83. Earlier writers on the subject were less anxious to prove Marx's consistency and omniscience and seem to have accepted the fact that the April program marked a change in tactics at least and probably of strategy as well; see Quarck, *Erste deutsche Arbeiterbewegung,* p. 52, and Mehring, *Geschichte der deutschen Sozialdemokratie,* vol. 2, pp. 101-102. One writer has argued that even the April program was far better adapted to the French situation than to the German: August Cornu, *Karl Marx et la révolution de 1848,* Paris, 1948, p. 13.

[31] See Marx, Engels, *Selected Works,* vol. 1, p. 61.

liantly, sometimes with less success—which was by no means a consistent whole.

*

Marx was in Brussels at the end of February 1848. On the second of March the Belgian government announced the expulsion of all social revolutionaries from the country; Marx was arrested on the fourth and forced to leave. In the meantime he had received an invitation to Paris from Flocon on behalf of the provisional government of the Second Republic.[32] He had also managed to hold a meeting of the Brussels committee of the Communist League, which was at this stage also the Central Committee since the London body had disbanded at the outbreak of the revolution and passed control to Brussels. At this meeting it was decided to move the Central Committee once again, this time to Paris, the center of the revolution, and at the same time to give Marx "complete discretionary power for the central direction of the affairs of the League." [33] Marx was thus in full control of the Communist League in the early days of the German revolution.

In Paris Marx rejected the efforts of Herwegh, Bornstedt and others to organize a German legion to invade Baden; he regarded this sort of "black-red-gold" patriotism as extremely foolish.[34] Instead, Marx concentrated on the reorganization of the Communist League, which was achieved at the meetings of March 8 and 9.[35]

[32] Potjomkin, Molok, *Die Revolution in Deutschland,* vol. 1, p. 246.

[33] The decisions of the meeting, which was held on March 3, are given in Wermuth and Stieber, *Die Communisten-Verschwörungen,* vol. 1, pp. 65-66.

[34] Marx, Engels, *Gesamtausgabe,* pt. 3, vol. 1, p. 97.

[35] The minutes of these meetings are given in Karl Marx, Friedrich Engels, *Historische-Kritische Gesamtausgabe,* pt. 1, vol. 7, *Werke und Schriften von März bis Dezember 1848,* Moscow, 1935, pp. 588-589.

A German workers' club was set up in Paris under the presidency first of Heinrich Bauer and later of Moses Hess.

But the majority of the workers and agitators gathered around Marx returned to Germany. Born left for Berlin in the middle of March. The others waited till the manifesto of the first of April had been drawn up and then they too departed, taking copies of the manifesto with them.[36] Wilhelm Wolff went to Breslau, Carl Schapper to Wiesbaden, Engels to Elberfeld and Barmen and Marx himself to Cologne. There Marx intended to found a newspaper, which, from the center of Germany's most industrialized area, could lead the working classes in support of the bourgeois revolution and the further-ance of the proletarian one.[37]

*

Once in Cologne Marx ran into difficulties. The work-ers proved to be far less "advanced" than he had hoped. Though the nearby Ruhr contained some industrialized areas, Cologne itself was a city of small craftsmen much like the rest of Germany, and one local problem, the use of steamboats on the Rhine, had already created so much unemployment that there was considerable resent-ment against any sort of mechanization. Moreover, there

[36] In spite of this propaganda campaign, the program of the party did not become well known. As far as I can tell, it was published in two papers only, one in Berlin and one in Brunswick (see above). Engels later regarded it as fortunate that the pro-gram was so little known; wider knowledge would have undercut his efforts to recruit backers for the *Neue Rheinische Zeitung;* cf. Engels' letter to Marx, Apr. 25, 1848, Marx, Engels, *Gesamtaus-gabe,* pt. 3, vol. 1, p. 100.

[37] Cologne also had the advantages of being familiar to Marx and Engels and being under the *Code Napoléon,* not the Prussian *Landrecht,* and thus less troubled by censorship than the *Residenz-stadt,* Berlin. Marx, Engels, *Selected Works,* vol. 2, p. 300.

was already in Cologne a well-developed workers' movement, the leaders of which were hostile to Marx.[38]

Gottschalk, the leader of the March third rising, was released from prison on the twenty-first of March. He wrote to Moses Hess on the twenty-sixth, urging him to persuade Marx and Engels to go elsewhere and suggesting that they run for the National Assembly from Trier and Barmen respectively.[39] Gottschalk feared that Marx and Engels had little comprehension of or sympathy for the immediate difficulties of the Cologne workers. The theories of the *Manifesto* and of "scientific socialism" he regarded as ill-adapted to the artisans, the journeymen and small master craftsmen and the unskilled day laborers of Cologne. His own socialism was based on direct "sympathy and human love" rather than an abstract analysis of society; it was derived from the pre-March Utopians.[40]

Gottschalk therefore proceeded with his own plans to organize a workers' association in Cologne. On April 6 he published in the *Kölnische Zeitung* an advertisement calling for the formation of a "democratic-socialist" club.[41] A meeting was subsequently held on April 13 in a pub in the Mühlengasse and attended by about three hundred workers and artisans. Gottschalk spoke, asserting that "the social relations of rich and poor, of work and wage, etc., involve the political formation of a country just as political freedom makes possible the end of misery." With this in view he proposed the formation of a "socialist" club, which was named the Workers' Union;

[38] The point is often missed; Quarck, for example, assumes that the Cologne workers were immediately under Marx's control and makes no mention of Gottschalk. *Erste deutsche Arbeiter bewegung,* p. 64.

[39] Czobel, "Zur Geschichte des Kommunistenbundes," p. 326.

[40] Gustav Mayer, *Friedrich Engels, Eine Biographie,* Haag, 1934, vol. 1, pp. 296-297.

[41] Stein, *Der Kölner Arbeiterverein,* p. 35.

alternative titles such as "democratic-socialist club" and "people's club" were rejected. Gottschalk was elected president of this club and a committee was chosen consisting of representatives of twenty-eight handicraft trades together with factory workers and machine builders. It was decided to publish a newspaper and to petition the city officials to improve work conditions.[42]

On the fourteenth of April the Cologne Workers' Union sent a letter to Camphausen, the Prussian prime minister, expressing the mistrust of the workers toward the government, calling for a reduction in taxes on food stuffs and essential goods and for direct financial aid to the artisans and workers. The Workers' Union attacked the belief that indirect aid given to failing businesses would eventually filter down to the workers. "We say to you, the working class has no time to lose—it's hungry!" [43] On the same day the Cologne workers wrote the workers' association in Mainz, endorsing working-class solidarity in the common struggle for "guarantees of the rights and the interests of the workers."

Gottschalk and the Workers' Union considered the political achievements of the revolution inadequate. Direct economic aid from the government and regulation of industry were necessary, according to Gottschalk, and his position was endorsed by, among other such meetings, a gathering of tailors and dressmakers on the sixteenth of April.[44] Gottschalk's agitation was instrumental in persuading the municipal government to set up public works in April, paying 11 silbergroschen for a twelve hour day spent rebuilding the Rhine banks, clearing lots and repairing streets. In May the Workers' Union adopted

[42] *Zeitung des Arbeiter-Vereins zu Köln,* Apr. 23, 1848.
[43] *Zeitung des Arbeiter-Vereins zu Köln,* Apr. 23, 1848.
[44] The tailors complained in particular of the plight of the married journeyman whose advance to the rank of master was blocked and who had to support a family on a small wage. *Zeitung des Arbeiter-Vereins zu Köln,* May 14, 1848.

117

Gottschalk's proposal for the establishment of elected arbitration courts to settle labor disputes and attempted to convince the municipal council of its feasibility.[45]

The Workers' Union proved a considerable success. The workers of Cologne joined in large numbers. By the end of April a membership of over four thousand was reported; by mid-June the number was between six thousand and seven thousand. At the meeting on May 15, the club was reorganized to include six local affiliated groups which could accommodate the growing numbers. Moreover, in addition to Gottschalk's group there was a second, far less active association for workers in Cologne, the Club for Employers and Employees, led by the young barrister Hermann Becker. This group advocated cooperation between the two classes, viewed their common privation as the chief problem and called for government aid through a ministry of labor.[46]

❋

Marx was not therefore the leader of the chief working-class groups in Cologne, at least during the early months of the revolution. When he arrived in Cologne in mid-April, Gottschalk's organization was already under way. Marx was still, to be sure, head of the Communist League, which in theory had representatives throughout Germany. But communication between these representatives was lax and much of the League's organization gradually disappeared. As Born wrote to Marx from Berlin in May: "The League has dissolved—it is everywhere and nowhere." [47] It was the success of the revolution in 1848 which caused the dissolution of the

[45] Stein, *Der Kölner Arbeiterverein*, pp. 39-43, 82.

[46] *Zeitung des Arbeiter-Vereins zu Köln*, April 27, June 16, 1848; Stein, *Der Kölner Arbeiterverein*, pp. 34, 37.

[47] The letter, dated May 11, 1848, is quoted at length by Franz Mehring in an article included in Karl Marx, *Enthüllungen über den Kommunistenprozess zu Köln*, Berlin, 1952, pp. 160-161.

118

League and not the defeat of the revolution in 1849 as was later maintained.[48] "The League had no other than a propagandistic purpose. It therefore dissolved during the political revolution of 1848. What use was a secret league as soon as the right of association and the freedom of the press were acknowledged as the basic rights of the nation?" [49]

After the defeat of the revolution, Marx and Engels came to regard the dissolution of the League as a mistake and dissociated themselves from it.[50] In fact they seem to have supported this policy during the spring of 1848. The League did not just dissolve of its own accord: it *was* dissolved by Marx, who, since the third of March, had had dictatorial powers over the League. The Cologne group of the League was in existence as late as May of 1848.[51] But sometime that spring Marx used his power to dissolve the League, ignoring the strenuous objections of Karl Schapper and Joseph Moll. As a member of the Cologne branch later testified, "Marx considered the continued existence of the League to be superfluous." [52] In doing so he may have been merely

[48] See the address of the Central Authority of the (revived) League in Marx, *Enthüllungen*, p. 137.

[49] Born, *Erinnerungen*, p. 48.

[50] Marx, Engels, *Selected Works*, vol. 1, pp. 98-99.

[51] The minutes of the meeting of the Cologne branch of the League for May 11, 1848, are given in Marx, Engels, *Gesamtausgabe*, pt. 1, vol. 7, p. 592; thus Nicolaevsky's assertion that the League was dissolved as early as April must be rejected. See Boris Nicolaevsky, "Towards a History of 'the Communist League' 1847-52," *International Review of Social History*, vol. 1 (1956), p. 235. The rest of the article, however, is most useful.

[52] P. G. Röser, quoted in Otto Mänchen-Helfen, Boris Nikolajewsky, *Karl und Jenny Marx, Ein Lebensweg*, Berlin, 1933, p. 151. Marx's action makes nonsense of some of the extreme claims made for the League; see, for example, Karl Obermann, *Zur Geschichte des Bundes der Kommunisten 1849 bis 1852*, Berlin, 1955, p. 7: "Alles, was gross und bedeutend ist in der Geschichte der deutschen Arbeiterbewegung, geht vom Bund der Kommunisten aus." Obermann claims to be using Röser's testimony

bowing to circumstances, but the fact remains that he acquiesced in making final the disbanding of the communist organization. The League was started again by Moll and others in London in the autumn of 1848, but during most of the revolutionary period Marx ignored its existence.

*

Marx's efforts in the spring of 1848 were concentrated not on revolutionary societies, and certainly not on working-class organizations, but on the arrangements for the publishing of the *Neue Rheinische Zeitung*. The democrats of Cologne had already made preparations for a newspaper when Marx arrived on the tenth of April. Marx, however, soon assumed the lead and became editor in chief of the new paper; Heinrich Bürgers of the democratic group was admitted to the editorial board, but had little influence and published only one article.[53] Money for the paper came from various radical bourgeois groups in Cologne and elsewhere. Marx became a leading figure in the Cologne Democratic Union partly with a view to making contacts useful to the paper. Engels attempted to raise funds in his home town of Barmen and in Elberfeld. He wrote to Marx on the twenty-fifth of April, complaining of the difficulties he encountered:

> We can count on damned few shares from this place. Blank, to whom I had written earlier on the subject and who is still the best of all, has become a bourgeois in practice; the others still more so, since they are established and have come into collision with the

for the first time, ignoring the fact that Mänchen-Helfen and Nicolajewsky had not only used it but quoted it at length twenty-three years previously. Obermann also ignores the issue of whether and how the League was dissolved in 1848.

[53] Bürgers' article appeared in the second number of the newspaper; see Marx, Engels, *Selected Works*, vol. 1, p. 299.

workers. Everyone shies away from discussion of social questions like the plague; they call it agitation.

For the workers Engels had almost as little use: "The workers are beginning to stir themselves a little, still in a very rough fashion, but powerfully. They have immediately joined in coalitions. It is precisely that which stands in our way." Finally he concluded that the program of the first of April was ill-adapted to the situation in Germany: "If a single copy of our seventeen points were distributed here, everything here would be lost for us." [54]

The first edition of the *Neue Rheinische Zeitung* was dated June 1, 1848, though it in fact appeared on May 31. The paper was subtitled "An Organ of Democracy," a label which indicated the basic allegiance and position it took. Under Marx was an editorial committee consisting of Friedrich Engels, Wilhelm Wolff, Georg Weerth, Ferdinand Wolff, Ernst Dronke and Heinrich Bürgers; Bürgers soon dropped out and the committee was later joined by Ferdinand Freiligrath. Quarterly subscriptions to the paper were 1 thaler, 15 silbergroschen in Cologne and 2 thaler, 3 silbergroschen, 9 pfennig in the rest of Prussia, as much, that is, as the weekly wage of some of the poorer workers. [55]

The paper concentrated on the reporting and analysis of political events, centering on Germany but including items from the rest of Europe and even from America. Quotations were given at regular intervals from the stock exchanges in Berlin, Frankfurt, Cologne, Amsterdam, Rotterdam and Paris, a curious feature to find in a communist paper. On the other hand there was little

[54] Marx, Engels, *Gesamtausgabe,* pt. 3, vol. 1, pp. 99-100.
[55] Cf. the price of the *Neue Kölnische Zeitung für Bürger, Bauer und Soldaten,* which appeared in the autumn of 1848. It was issued six times a week like the *Neue Rheinische Zeitung* and claimed as well to appeal to the workers; the quarterly subscription was 22.5 silbergroschen. Marx's paper was expensive.

attempt to cover "working-class" news; riots were occasionally reported, but the wage movement and the strikes it entailed were largely untouched, and no significant mention was made of the various attempts during the coming months to set up a national workers' organization. The two main points of the political program of the *Neue Rheinische Zeitung*, as Engels later described it, were "a single, indivisible, democratic German republic and war with Russia," points scarcely designed to appeal to workers interested in higher wages and the preservation of their jobs.[56] The closest the paper came to advocating a direct revolutionary measure was in the autumn of 1848 when it joined with the left of the Prussian National Assembly in opposing the payment of taxes. To call the *Neue Rheinische Zeitung*, as Lenin did, "the best and unsurpassed organ of the revolutionary proletariat," seems a considerable exaggeration.[57]

The lengthy analyses of the revolutionary situation and capitalist economics which Marx published were scarcely designed to attract the working-class reader. Even Engels complained that Marx spent too long over his analytic essays and showed too little concern for journalistic deadlines.[58] Abstract and difficult to understand, Marx's articles were seldom read and had little effect among the working classes. As one worker commented: "The music in them is pitched too high for us; we cannot whistle it." [59]

The *Neue Rheinische Zeitung* was soon criticized in the paper of the Cologne Workers' Union which Gottschalk

[56] Marx, Engels, *Selected Works*, vol. 2, p. 300.

[57] Cf. also August Cornu's statement, "*La Nouvelle Gazette rhenane* fut le seule journal en Allemagne et même en Europe, à l'exception du Nothern [sic] Star qui prit ouvertment et fièrement la défense du proletariat." *Karl Marx et la révolution de 1848*, p. 27.

[58] Quarck, *Erste deutsche Arbeiterbewegung*, p. 233.

[59] *Deutsche Zeitung*, Aug. 18, 1848.

edited: "The world is full of contradictions. The *Neue Rheinische Zeitung* advertises itself as an 'organ of democracy' when it is in the hands of confirmed aristocrats, indeed the most dangerous of all, the aristocrats of money." [60] The article went on to attack the labor policy of the paper, accusing the publisher, Clouth, of attempting to lower wages or substitute piece rates.[61] In addition Clouth had refused to have any dealing with the local printers' association in Cologne, had attempted to force his printers to sign a document promising not to strike and had finally resorted to hiring workers from out of town. Needless to say, the dispute between the *Neue Rheinische Zeitung* and the printers' union was not discussed in its own columns and has been ignored by historians since 1848.

The picture of Marx presented by a detailed study of events in Cologne is far different from that usually offered. Marx remained above the fray; uncertain of the outcome of the revolution, he chose the role of commentator only. He dissolved the Communist League and ignored the efforts of Gottschalk and the various trade groups in Cologne to better the lot of the workers. Like the other middle-class radicals, he had nothing to do with the wider movement, led by Born and others, to form an all-German workers' organization. Yet it was into this movement that such revolutionary force as the workers had in 1848 was channeled.

[60] *Zeitung des Arbeiter-Vereins zu Köln*, June 11, 1848.

[61] Clouth claimed in reply that he had merely refused a wage rise and had offered piece rates as an alternative. *Zeitung des Arbeiter-Vereins zu Köln*, June 18, 1848.

CHAPTER 6

THE BEGINNINGS OF ORGANI-
ZATION

ON APRIL 6, 1848, the right of free association was decreed throughout Prussia. The decree only recognized what had in fact been inevitable since the eighteenth of March, but its effect was explosive. It gave official sanction to the formation of clubs, societies and associations of all sorts; it paved the way for the attempt to improve the workers' lot through organization.

Before the proclamation of the right of free association only two clubs had been formed in Berlin, the Political Club on the twenty-first of March and the Constitutional Club on the twenty-eighth; both of these were composed of middle-class liberals, and neither appealed to or interested the workers and artisans who had fought on the barricades and attended the endless street meetings. Now at last a way was open to them for action; some positive use for the "achievements" of the revolution had appeared. "Organization," "association," the formation of self-help societies became the order of the day. "Opposed to demonstrations of force, the intelligent workers had found above all in organization of their class in the form of narrower or wider associations the means not only to improve the external condition of the workers but also to promote their independent political and social development." [1] The *Vereinsmensch* [2] was a feature of the time; his attitude, as satirized later in the year in

[1] Wolff, *Berliner Revolutionschronik*, vol. 2, p. 133; cf. also pp. 338ff.

[2] The "union man" or "association man," or perhaps even the "organization man."

one of the popular papers, was that associations provided a panacea for all the ills of the workers: [3]

> When one person cannot perform a task through his own power, bring in two who can easily support each other, and where two are too few, perhaps four will suffice, and so forth. Thus in recent times arose the associations—associations for all possible and impossible purposes. . . . Indeed a man can be from the first seconds of his existence to the funeral bier, and even beyond, the subject of innumerable association activities.

To deal with the almost bewildering variety of clubs and societies, newspapers soon had to publish special columns of "association news." [4] "March clubs," the product of the revolution, grew up everywhere.

There were complaints that the workers used their newly won freedom of association for purely selfish ends, that they regarded the revolution simply as a means and an excuse for self-seeking demands for half the work and twice the pay, for protection through guild regulations, tariffs and government regulations, that they demanded "unconditional equal rights without regard to duties and burdens." [5] Certainly there is a naïveté about the workers in Germany after the revolution, about the petitions they drew up and the organizations they formed, which suggests that they were not thinking beyond their immediate needs, that they viewed the state and their new rights of organization as designed solely for their immediate benefit. But this was perhaps natural for men

---

[3] *Die Barrikaden,* Sept. 15, 1848: there follows the mock biography of one Traugott Leberecht Treumund Fürchtegott Pietsche who lived under the morally sapping "cradle-to-grave" protection of the associations.

[4] The *Berliner Zeitungs Halle,* for example, published such a column from May 15.

[5] Gneist, *Berliner Zustände,* pp. 84-85.

whose economic position was as desperate and as degraded as was that of the mass of the German workers.

Many of the workers did in fact seek to moderate their demands, cooperating with the efforts of the government. This was partly out of public spirit, a genuine concern for peace and order; partly, perhaps, out of a general tendency toward obedience and submissiveness; and partly out of the purely selfish motive that some degree of stability was necessary for a revival of trade and the return of prosperous conditions. "Money," ran a popular saying of the time, "is a mouse: if it hears a noise, it will creep away, but just hold still and it will soon come again." [6] The workers were as aware of the truth of this adage as the most prosperous middle-class businessman.

Several workers' groups took care to publish statements asserting their loyalty to the state and their interest in the common good. The People's Club of the Zelten, for example, printed such a declaration early in April. An appeal of the workers in the various machine building factories, published on the seventeenth of April, assured the middle classes of their peaceful intentions.[7] On the specific issue of wage demands, some at least of the workers' leaders advised caution. The *Deutsche Arbeiter Zeitung*, in an article of the eleventh of April entitled "More Wages and Less Work!" concluded that even justifiable demands were neither politic nor feasible under present conditions.

The workers, in spite of the limitations placed upon

[6] Wolff, *Berliner Revolutionschronik*, vol. 3, p. 40.

[7] "If we had wanted plunder, we could already have seized it undisturbed and unpunished weeks ago when the richest of the country, who have gradually deserted, were still among us. We could have made ourselves masters of your wealth and your property; we had the power to do so." (Quoted by Valentin, *Geschichte der deutschen Revolution*, vol. 2, p. 617, n. 17.) It was perhaps not the most tactful way of reassuring a nervous bourgeoisie.

their actions and in spite of the urgings both by members of their own group and by others to remain quiet, were determined to seize the advantage which the revolution and the decree of the sixth of April offered them. Spontaneous and sporadic working-class action was not enough. There were to be sure innumerable outbreaks in which the workers attempted to gain some specific, limited goal. The processions on April 17 and 18 were such affairs; the workers went the rounds of the Berlin bakers to check whether they were cheating on the weight of bread loaves.[8] But the workers wanted more than this; they wanted to organize. The meetings of different trade groups which began in March spread to many cities and to almost every trade. Even the barbers met and decided, not unreasonably in view of the difficulty of the operation, that no one should be allowed to cut his own hair.[9] More than this, the drive to organize spread beyond the trade groups to the unskilled and untrained laborers, to the mass of the "proletariat."

In all this the workers were not in fact thinking solely in material terms in the drive for organization. Far more, the artisans, the small master craftsmen and the journeymen who were beginning to despair of their chance to rise in the world, and the factory workers, facing for the first time the mechanization of modern industry, were concerned with their status, their position in society, even, in a sense, with their dignity as human beings. To the conservative von Gerlach, perhaps the most shocking demand of the revolution was that of the workers to be called by the formal "*Sie*" rather than the informal "*Du*."[10] Yet the workers were quite as serious

[8] Kaeber, *Berlin*, p. 147; Bernstein, *Geschichte der Berliner Arbeiterbewegung*, vol. 1, p. 42.

[9] *Deutsche Arbeiter Zeitung*, ed. Lubarsch and Bittkow, Apr. 16, 1848.

[10] Gerlach, *Denkwürdigkeiten*, vol. 1, p. 154.

about this as they were about their more material aims of higher wages and shorter hours.

In this may be seen as well the difference between the actual workers' movement of 1848 and the movement that had been envisaged by the communist theorists before the revolution—and written about by them afterward in spite of what really happened. The pre-March communists and socialists had hoped that all workers, indeed all men, would address each other as "*Du*"; the workers of 1848 demanded to be called "*Sie.*"

This chapter will consider three aspects of the drive for organization in the spring of the year of revolutions: the wage movement, which was the first attempt to achieve specific ends by organized labor in Germany; the growth of workers' organizations in the towns, particularly the formation of the Central Committee of Workers in Berlin, headed by Stephan Born; and finally the growing demand for some form of all-German workers' organization.

*

The general move for higher wages was perhaps the most prominent feature of the immediate post-March period. Specific improvements in wages and hours were the first aim of the newly formed trade and workers' groups. A wave of strikes and threatened strikes spread from group to group, first in Berlin and then throughout the German Federation. Some of these were more or less spontaneous and unorganized; others, particularly the printers' and compositors' strike in Berlin at the end of April, were well organized and carried out with an efficiency quite surprising for the time, particularly considering the "backward" condition of the German workers. The wage movement, since it paid off in immediate results, was one of the most important aspects of the activities of the German workers in 1848; its initial success accounts to some extent for the later quiescence and patience of the German workers toward both local government and the National Assembly in Frankfurt. A small but substantial gain was made, conditions in fact improved and the workers felt they could afford to wait for the more distant goals which required government cooperation.

The first of the Berlin strikes broke out on the fifth of April among the calico workers in the factory of Goldschmidt in the Köpnickerstrasse. The unskilled workers— or rather a group of them, for three hundred remained at work in the factory during the strike—demanded higher wages, shorter hours and limitations on the use of machinery. The management gave in to these demands, avoiding violence but setting off a further strike by the skilled calico printers who also demanded less work.[11]

On the evening of the same day there were demonstrations among the journeymen tailors against the ready-made clothes shops, demonstrations with an anti-Semitic tinge since most of the shop owners, so it was believed, were Jews. On the eighth of April a committee of the journeymen presented a series of demands to the master tailors, calling for a twelve-hour day and a six-day week with regular fixed wages. The masters were to undertake to cut work by no more than one quarter during the slack periods, to employ no females and to join with the journeymen in a trade union which could seek aid from the state. A strike followed, ending in a compromise solution on the eighteenth of April with substantial wage gains for the journeymen.[12]

[11] *Berliner Zeitungs Halle,* Apr. 7, 1848; Wolff, *Berliner Revolutionschronik,* vol. 2, p. 113; Adler, *Geschichte der Arbeiterbewegung,* p. 159.
[12] *Plakate,* Ratsbibliothek, Berlin, portfolio 11; *Berliner Zeitungs Halle,* Apr. 7, 1848; *Deutsche Arbeiter Zeitung,* ed. Lubarsch and Bittkow, Apr. 8, 1848; Bernstein, *Schneiderbewegung,* vol. 1, pp. 73-74.

From the tailors and the calico printers on the fifth of April the wave of strikes spread throughout the city from trade to trade. Demands for higher wages and shorter hours were made by the goldsmiths, the locksmiths, the carpenters, the masons, the cabinetmakers, weavers, serge and silk makers, potters and iron workers in the machine-building factories. In general these groups demanded a minimum wage of between 3 and 4 thaler per week and a reduction in work from 12 and in some cases 14 hours per day to 10.[13]

Strike action was in some instances taken against the municipal authorities. The masons and carpenters employed by the city went on strike on the fourteenth of April and were able to get the city to agree to a daily wage of 25 silbergroschen or 5 thaler per week.[14] A more interesting case, symptomatic also of the rifts within the working class, was that of the *Rehberger* who were engaged in clearing the land beyond the Oranienburger Tor. They demanded that the day laborers employed on the canal from Moabit to Charlottenburg cease piece work and receive a fixed wage as desired by the majority of the Berlin workers. The *Rehberger* marched in procession into Berlin, joined in a street fight against the canal workers and "persuaded" the latter to give up piece rates.[15]

In the majority of cases, however, the strikes were conducted by the journeymen against the master crafts-men in their trade, men who were often little better off than the strikers themselves and unable to acquiesce to demands which were too high. The spirit of the strikers was friendly; there was little or no violence. When their demands were granted, the workers would march in

[13] Wolff, *Berliner Revolutionschronik,* vol. 2, pp. 153-157; *Kölnische Zeitung,* May 7, 1848; Kaeber, *Berlin,* p. 148.

[14] *Berliner Zeitungs Halle,* Apr. 16, 1848.

[15] Wolff, *Berliner Revolutionschronik,* vol. 2, p. 114.

procession through the streets, often with a band and flags, stopping in front of their employers' houses to cheer them for their generosity.[16] Such processions often developed into an excuse for a country outing and a drinking bout, as with the celebration of the machine builders, and miscellaneous other workers who joined them, on the eleventh of April.[17] The picture is scarcely that of a conscious working class in the grip of the class struggle, deeply embittered against their employers, but rather one of a group which is concerned for its economic situation without seeing itself, as indeed it was not, marked off from the rest of society by any insuperable class barrier.

*

The most highly organized strike in Berlin in the period was that of the book printers and compositors, a strike in many ways different from the haphazard affairs in other trades. The journeymen printers met in early April to consider what they might reasonably demand. Under the leadership of Stephan Born, newly returned from his travels abroad and his work with Marx, they decided to wait till the end of the month before presenting their demands in the hope of achieving greater unity.

The basic terms for which the printers were to strike were settled at their first meeting on the eighth of April: the minimum weekly wage was to be raised from 3 thaler, 20 silbergroschen, to 5 thaler, and the amount of work was to be lowered from twelve to ten hours per day.[18] The wage demand, an increase of nearly 50 per

[16] Lenz, *Geschichte der Universität zu Berlin*, vol. 2, pt. 2, p. 238.

[17] *Berliner Zeitungs Halle*, Apr. 14, 1848.

[18] The *Comite der Berliner Buchdruckergehülfe* claimed the figures to be average, though it admitted that some received considrably higher wages—notably the employees of the *Berliner Zeitungs Halle*, who got 6 thaler per week (though for a seven-day week and a 14-16 hour day). *Plakate*, Ratsbibliothek, Berlin, portfolio 2.

cent, would place the printers among the highest paid workers in Berlin, the equal of those in the machine factories. In addition the printers in a meeting on the twenty-fourth of April, just before the strike was to take place, asked for 3 silbergroschen per hour for Sundays and night work and for time spent waiting for a manuscript. They also demanded a limitation on the use of mechanical presses.[19]

The strike was scheduled to start on the twenty-eighth of April.[20] Born, as leader of the printers, entered into negotiations with the various printing firms, with the *Handelsmeister* Pieper and even with the Minister for Trade and Industry, von Patow, and the court printer, von Decker, but no settlement was reached. A meeting of the printers on the twenty-seventh determined to go forward with the plan in spite of opposition from many quarters. There was dark talk of "workers' despotism," and even such liberal organs as the *Berliner Zeitungs Halle* held it a mistake to strike just before the elections, scheduled for the first of May, and limit the chance for publicity and public discussion. There was the fear that the success of the printers would set off a series of wage claims without limit. The "workers' friend," Friedrich Held, condemned the printers' demands as excessive.[21]

In spite of opposition the strike was effective. The vast majority of the six hundred journeymen printers in Berlin and most of the apprentices came out. Newspapers were reduced to a single sheet or even half a sheet and some

[19] *Berliner Zeitungs Halle*, Apr. 12, 1848; *Zeitung für das deutsche Volk*, Apr. 26, 1848; the workers' objections to mechanical presses can be seen from their German name, *Schnellpressen*.

[20] Born's own account of the strike may be found in his *Erinnerungen*, pp. 125-130. There is also an account given in the placard published by the *Comite der Berliner Buchdruckergehülfe* on May 1, 1848, *Plakate*, Ratsbibliothek, Berlin, portfolio 2.

[21] *Berliner Zeitungs Halle*, Apr. 30, 1848; *Die Locomotive*, Apr. 29, 1848; *Kölnische Zeitung*, May 2, 1848; Wolff, *Berliner Revolutionschronik*, vol. 2, p. 320.

failed to appear altogether.[22] The strike weapon was sufficient to force the magistrate to intervene, promising a settlement by the first of June. This, together with an assurance from the employers not to punish those who had gone on strike, persuaded the printers to return to their jobs. Work was to start again on the first of May.

But the strike was not over. Word got out that the employers, led by one of their number, Sittenfeld, planned to give the returning workers a "yellow dog" contract to sign, denouncing the strike and promising not to resume. Born gained knowledge of this plan on April 30 and called the workers out again, scheduling a mass meeting in the Zelten on the evening of May 1. Once more the magistrates were forced to intervene. The employers promised to drop the proposed document; order was restored and the printers at last returned to work, apparently victorious in their struggle.

When the first of June came, the print-shop owners, in spite of the efforts of the city authorities, still refused to grant the workers' demands, offering only a small proportion of the requested wage increase. The workers rejected this offer, continuing at the old rates, for, by this time, the Berlin printers had established contact with the print-shop workers in other parts of Germany. A congress was to be held at Mainz and there were plans for a strike throughout the German states. In view of these plans, the Berlin workers decided to wait rather than strike again on their own.[23]

✼

While Berlin was the scene of the most concentrated and organized wage movement in Germany in the spring of 1848, there were similar demands and similar strikes

[22] *Kölnische Zeitung*, May 2, 1848; also Born's article on the strike in the *Berliner Zeitungs Halle*, May 12, 1848.
[23] *Das Volk*, June 1, 1848.

elsewhere, particularly when the news of the successes in Berlin became known.

Not all, however, were dependent on the Berlin example. In Leipzig the printers met as early as the third of April to demand higher wages, the ten-hour day, limitations on the use of the machine press and the establishment of an arbitration court consisting of three employers, three compositors and three printers. The Leipzig printers, unlike their Berlin colleagues, were not willing to carry the issue to the point of a strike; there was some disagreement between the masters and the journeymen on this, but the opinion of the more conservative masters prevailed. The journeymen's wage demands were provisionally accepted, but the workers had to promise to submit the whole issue to the Saxon ministry for trade when it was formed.[24]

The most successful of the printers' strikes were in Dresden and Breslau; the agreement of the Breslau printers, which went beyond the Berlin demands in several respects, was then adopted by the printers in some thirty-nine other towns in Silesia.[25] Elsewhere the printers met with less success. In Hamburg, for example, the same demands were presented as in Berlin—the ten-hour day, a weekly wage of five thaler and limitations on the use of the machine press; the employers rejected these demands on the twenty-first of May, and the Hamburg-Altona journeymen printers' committee had to turn for aid to the forthcoming all-German printers' congress in the hope that a strike might be organized throughout the country.[26] The demands made by the printers in Vienna were more modest in respect of wages

[24] *Zeitung für das deutsche Volk*, Apr. 12, 1848; Quarck, *Erste deutsche Arbeiterbewegung*, pp. 81-82.

[25] Quarck, *Erste deutsche Arbeiterbewegung*, p. 82; *Das Volk*, June 1, 1848.

[26] Laufenberg, *Geschichte der Arbeiterbewegung in Hamburg*, vol. 1, pp. 122-124.

(7-8 florins per week), but far more extensive in their limitations on such things as the employment of females, the number of apprentices and the use of the mechanical press.[27]

In some places the municipal authorities or the masters broke the power of the strikers. When the Munich shoe-makers went on strike at the end of May, the chief of police threatened to expel those who failed either to return to work or to report voluntarily at the police station for their traveling papers. In Frankfurt the master masons dismissed those journeymen who took the initia-tive in submitting a petition to the Frankfurt Senate calling for a wage increase and a limitation of the hours of work; the Senate failed to respond to the petition and supported the masters.[28] But the hope of success remained.

*

The wage movement, limited though it was in scope and achievement, pointed the way to what appeared to many of the workers the chief necessity of the time: organization. Only through organization and collective action did it seem possible to put through the demands of the workers and to prevent the onrush of competition and industry from swallowing the mass of them into the "proletariat." Some degree of organization had of course been involved in the strikes, but this was only on a local and trade basis, even in the most successful of these, the Berlin printers' strike. The spring of 1848 saw the be-ginnings of a labor movement embracing all trades on a city level and the demand for such an organization on the national level. The best known of these city move-

[27] *Die Constitution, Tagblatt für constitutionalles Volksleben und Belehrung,* Apr. 12, 1848, gives the program drawn up by a committee elected by 464 workers in some 18 printshops in Vienna.
[28] *Neue Rheinische Zeitung,* June 4, 1848; Quarck, *Erste deutsche Arbeiterbewegung,* p. 102.

ments was in Berlin, led again by Stephan Born, who had managed the Berlin printers' strike. But there were similar if smaller groups throughout Germany, and it was from these other groups that the demand for all-German workers' congresses first came.

These groups operated under different conditions and sought different things. Some were based on trade organizations while others sought to include all workers, unskilled laborers as well as trained handicraft workers. Some wished to preserve the guild system and the rights and position of the master artisans while others demanded freedom of trade. Some relied solely on working-class self-help while others saw the salvation of the workers in the action of governments, particularly the new German government which was to be established at Frankfurt.

The story of the German workers' movement in 1848 is to a large extent the story of the unsuccessful attempt to reconcile these differences.

❋

The public meetings at the end of March in Berlin, held in the Zelten and elsewhere, led to the demand for a central workers' organization which would include all trades throughout the city. Such an organization would be able to bring greater pressure to bear on the municipal authorities as well as the Prussian government to improve the condition of the workers. It could unite the workers in a concerted effort to help themselves.

On the fourth of April the Workers' Union issued a notice of a meeting to form such an organization to be held on the evening of the sixth of April in the Maas'-chen Locale, a pub at No. 62 Sebastianstrasse. The notice, deploring the fact that nothing had been done "from our midst" to meet the generally recognized need of the workers, called for deputations of workers to form a central committee "which would be concerned to further the interests of the workers through constant activity." The announcement was signed by Engelhardt, Fromm, Lüchow, Müller and Michaelis—all "workers" and in fact all members of the committee which was at the same time organizing the strike of journeymen tailors.[29]

The meeting which was convened on the sixth of April proved to be the first in a series which was necessary before the workers could unite on a program and statutes for the new committee; others were held on the eleventh and the nineteenth of April.[30] These were all weekdays; the meetings were held indoors in the evenings and attracted the more serious, sober-minded and articulate among the Berlin workers and artisans. They differed markedly in character from the great outdoor rallies which had been held in the Zelten on Saturdays in the weeks following the eighteenth of March. Even so the majority of moderate workers had to defend themselves against extremists of both the left and the right.

At the first of these meetings, on April 6, Stephan Born was elected president. His opening address tried to set a moderate tone: he called upon the workers to "learn now what their rights are, so that they will not be tricked out of the fruits of the revolution." [31] He attacked those who thought that street riots were enough or who

[29] *Berliner Zeitungs Halle,* Apr. 5, 1848.

[30] Born, in his memoirs, telescoped the three meetings into one, on April 6, and ignored the considerable controversy which went into the formation of the Central Committee. He also claimed that, from the beginning, the main purpose of the committee was the preparation for an all-German workers' congress. (Born, *Erinnerungen,* p. 162; also p. 143.) As far as can be seen from contemporary sources, this was not so. The Central Committee was formed in the first place to meet the needs of the workers in Berlin for some coordinating body. Only later in the spring, after the demand arose elsewhere, did Born and the Central Committee turn their efforts to the summoning of a congress. Indeed the committee appeared at first to be cool to such a proposal. (*Das Volk,* May 25, 1848.)

[31] From the account of the meeting in the *Berliner Zeitungs Halle,* Apr. 8, 1848.

plotted the destruction of machinery. The task of the meeting, he said, was to search for some unifying plan. A second speaker, Michaelis, criticized the meeting of March 26 and the Deputation for the Abolition of Need as "unauthorized" and "incompetent." Petitions, he maintained, were useless; political activity was necessary: "Political consciousness belongs to our daily bread." The commission was attacked by another worker but tempers remained cool until the speech of Schlöffel, a student and the editor of the *Volksfreund.*

Schlöffel claimed to speak for the unskilled day laborers. He was intentionally provocative, promising to "astound" his hearers. He declared that all that had been done and all that had been proposed was in vain; higher wages and shorter hours were useless—they would only cause a rise in prices. From this he launched into a discourse on the national economy which failed to hold his audience's attention.[32] But he soon became less abstract and indeed caused a stir with an assault on "capitalism":

> We must destroy capital! We must unite as brothers! We must clear away the bayonets! (Many cries of bravo) Those with property don't want to work; that's why they are now carrying muskets! (Bravo) They'd rather let themselves be repressed by the despots than fraternize with the workers. Yes, we must overthrow the power of the moneybags, we must work against the noble people who are now arousing the countryside to the point of fanaticism.

With this speech the meeting broke into disorder. After considerable effort Born was able to regain control. He

[32] The *Berliner Zeitungs Halle* noted that his audience seemed far from astounded, calling out several times during the earlier portion of the speech, "We've heard that already!" (*Schon da gewesen!*)

138

urged quiet and advised against overhaste: "Revolutions cannot be consummated in a day."

But though the meeting disbanded peacefully and Schlöffel's influence with the workers was soon found to be negligible, the initial purpose of the meeting was not achieved. A further meeting was called for the eleventh; to this meeting only elected representatives of the various trades were allowed to come. It was hoped thus to avoid the extreme and violent radicalism which Schlöffel represented and which ran contrary to the ideal of organization pursued by Born and his group.

At the meeting on the eleventh of April the debate centered on the disagreement between Born and Lette, the middle-class president of the Deputation for the Abolition of Need, on the necessity of a purely working-class organization.[33] Born opened the meeting with an address in which he argued that for historical reasons in Germany

> the bourgeoisie and the proletariat, capital and labor, do not yet oppose each other so sharply as in France and England; there two sharply differentiated parties regard each other, eye to eye, in cold blood and armed for battle. In Germany this opposition is not yet completely present, since in the first place manufacturers still offer us a friendly hand by way of mediation and in the second place because the workers are not yet organized; they do not regard themselves as a party.

This led to the, for Born, inevitable conclusion: "We must not demand the impossible as single individuals

[33] The account of the meeting is taken from the *Berliner Zeitungs Halle*, Apr. 13, 1848. It is interesting to note that the East German historian Karl Obermann ignores the fact that Born attacks the right as well as the left in his account of the meeting. (*Die deutschen Arbeiter in der Revolution von 1848*, pp. 171-172.)

from single individuals. We do not want senseless destruction of capital, but we do want to improve our condition in general. Therefore we must organize."

On this theme Born opened the debate. Again he met with opposition, this time not from the left but from the right in the person of President Lette, who proposed cooperation with the employers and capitalists and the formation of a trade council which would include workers, masters and manufacturers. The main aim, he claimed, was for Germany to achieve dominance in world markets. Born was as hostile to this notion as he had been to Schlöffel's call for violence, and led by him, Bisky, Goldschmidt, Michaelis and others all rejected Lette's proposal and came out for a purely working-class group. An attempt by Schlöffel to exclude guild members from the forthcoming organization met with no response from the others present.

A Central Committee of Workers was thereupon elected, consisting of twenty-eight members, one for each of the various trades that had sent representatives to the meeting. An inner council of five was also selected to draft statutes for the organization and to present these at a meeting on the nineteenth of April. Born was elected president of the Committee by acclamation.

Meanwhile there were other bids for the allegiance of the workers. A meeting was called for the ninth of April before the Schönhauser Tor by the Deputation for the Abolition of Need. But the ineffectiveness of this group had lost the support of the workers. Bisky took the chair and there was a general demand for the resignation of the veterinary Urban, President Lette and the others of the Deputation. Charges were made that the Deputation was plotting the return of the troops and that it had been involved in an attempt to bribe some workers to attack the "Jews" of the Political Club. Instead the meeting called for a workers' organization and supported the plan to elect delegates to the meeting on the eleventh.[34] On the sixteenth a small public meeting of workers took place with Schlöffel in the chair. There was much talk about the need for a united workers' organization, presumably independent from the Central Committee. Little was done apart from appointing a committee to draw up proposals for a sickness and death insurance scheme and these schemes were later subsumed under the work of the Central Committee.[35]

A further and final meeting on the nineteenth received and accepted the proposed statutes drawn up by the committee elected on the eleventh. The Central Committee for Workers had come into being.

*

The statutes of the Berlin Central Committee were in four parts.[36] The first dealt with the formation of workers' committees in general and was designed to serve as a model for such groups throughout Germany. The committees were to consist of the elected representatives of the various trade groups and workers' societies in a town, and these were defined in the broadest sense possible to include everyone from the unskilled day laborer to the schoolteacher as well as the skilled artisans. These committees were to hold regular meetings, to investigate the needs and abuses of workers in their districts, to choose a governing board, consisting of a chairman, vice-chairman, two secretaries, a treasurer and two overseers of funds, to send written reports to the central committee

[34] *Plakate*, Ratsbibliothek, Berlin, portfolio 1; *Deutsche Arbeiter Zeitung*, ed. Lubarsch and Bittkow, Apr. 8, 1848; *Berliner Zeitungs Halle*, Apr. 12, 1848.

[35] *Berliner Zeitungs Halle*, Apr. 20, 1848.

[36] The statutes were printed in the *Berliner Zeitungs Halle* on April 23, 1848, and in *Das Volk*, the organ of the Central Committee, on June 15, 1848, under the title of "Statutes for the Organization of Workers."

and to elect delegates to an annual general meeting of workers' committees.

The second section of the statutes dealt with the Central Committee which was to have its residence in Berlin and was to be selected by the various workers of that city. The duties of the Central Committee were to secure the interests of the workers among themselves and with the state, to instigate and carry out all measures which the general interest of the workers required. A special section of the Committee was to look after the affairs of the guilds. The Central Committee was responsible to a general assembly of workers to which was devoted the third section of the statutes. The general assembly was to meet once a year in Berlin, though it could be called more frequently if the Central Committee felt that special circumstances warranted; it was to receive a report from the Central Committee and elect its members.

The fourth and final section of the statutes consisted of a number of general rules: all meetings of the workers' committees were to be public, though only deputies would have the right to vote; all officers of the committees were to be elected annually and, with the exception of the treasurer, could stand for reelection; everyone who participated had to agree to submit to the decisions of the majority.

The first officers of the Central Committee, also elected at the meeting on the nineteenth, were Born, the delegate for the printers, as chairman; Bisky, delegate for the goldsmiths, as vice-chairman; Dr. Wöniger, delegate for the office clerks, and Michaelis, delegate for the tailors, as secretaries; Dr. Ries, delegate for the workers in the state mint, appropriately as treasurer; Dr. Waldeck, delegate for the Polytechnic Society, and Lüchow, delegate for the tailors, as overseers of the funds. Born was from the first the leader and dominant force on the committee; the presence of the three "doctors" contributed little to the group beyond a vague air of respectability. The committee remained predominantly working class in character.

The Central Committee met regularly in Berlin at No. 62 Sebastianstrasse, first twice a week on Wednesdays and Saturdays, and then once a week on Thursdays.[37] Its activities were published at first through the *Deutsche Arbeiter Zeitung*, the organ of the old Artisans' Union, as well as in articles which Born wrote for the *Berliner Zeitungs Halle*. But Born regarded this arrangement as unsatisfactory; he characterized the *Deutsche Arbeiter Zeitung* in a letter to Marx as "a trumpet into which everyone can blow." [38] Having joined the editorial committee of the *Arbeiter Zeitung* at the time of the founding of the Central Committee, Born resigned from it and decided to found a paper which would be exclusively the organ of the Central Committee.

The paper was to be entitled "The People"—*Das Volk*. An invitation for subscriptions was issued in the middle of May, a trial number was brought out on May 28 and the paper appeared regularly from the first of June with three issues a week. Born alone was responsible for the writing and editing of the paper.[39] Its tone, according to one historian, was "somewhat dry and pedagogical" [40] and its format was of the crudest and simplest sort, a series of quarto pages with articles printed in double columns. Yet it gave coverage to the activities and organizations of the workers throughout Germany—and was in fact the only paper to give such coverage. In it were to be found the underlying assumptions and beliefs of the workers' movement or at least that part of the

[37] *Das Volk*, June 10, 1848.
[38] The letter was dated May 11; it is quoted in Marx, *Enthüllungen*, pp. 160-161.
[39] Born, *Erinnerungen*, p. 120.
[40] Quarck, *Erste deutsche Arbeiterbewegung*, p. 89.

movement which followed the leadership of Stephan Born.

Das Volk defended the proposals of the Central Committee, citing examples not only from Germany but from such foreign writers as Louis Blanc and Proudhon and from such experiments as the Swiss-German attempts at communal production. The paper was by no means opposed to industrial progress but urged the need for government regulation to limit the human cost of change. The core of its policy was the demand for state action to "guarantee work." [41] It abhorred violence but prophesied bloodshed if the state did not fulfill this demand.[42] It realized that the greatest source of conservative support lay in the peasantry and the country districts and that industrialization was in fact a means of combating reaction.[43]

The tone of the paper was to some extent international. It proclaimed the brotherhood of all workers and rejected international boundaries as without significance for the working class. It included news of the Paris workers and the English Chartist movement. At the time of the June rising of the Paris workers the paper called for the support of their fellows everywhere: "We have the right to take sides for our oppressed brothers, be they German, French or English; no differences of language, no territorial boundary separates the workers. They all have only one interest; liberation from the chains of the rule of money; they all have only *one* oppressor." [44]

Nor did the paper in fact confine itself to the working classes. The demands which it printed on the tenth of June were made in the name of "manufacturers, small masters and workers." The paper published much that

[41] *Das Volk,* July 7, 8, 1848.
[42] *Das Volk,* July 18, 1848.
[43] *Das Volk,* June 8, 1848.
[44] *Das Volk,* June 4, 1848.

was of interest to the skilled craftsman rather than to the unskilled day laborer or "proletarian." One article dealt with the protection of inventions and the problem of German patent laws, drawing the obvious conclusion that there was need for national legislation.[45] Yet this was scarcely a concern of the mass of exploited workers.

Indeed, as its name suggested, *Das Volk* sought to forward the concerns of "the people." It was the belief of Born and the Central Committee that the interests of the workers and of the whole community coincided in many respects: [46]

> "*Das Volk*", so I explained in its first number, had the purpose on the one hand of supporting the middle classes against the aristocracy in the struggle against the still erect institutions of the middle ages and the powers of "God's grace," and on the other hand of assisting the small manufacturer as well as the worker against the power of capital and of always striving, where it did any good, to gain for the people by fighting some still withheld political right in order that they might have the means to achieve more quickly social freedom and an independent existence.

The paper described itself as a "social-political" journal; it was scarcely revolutionary in either content or intent.

*

In *Das Volk* Born sought to elaborate the policy of moderation and working-class self-help that had been outlined in the statutes of the Central Committee. Perhaps the clearest and most concise statement of this approach came in an essay which Born published, in the name of the workers, together with the statutes in

[45] *Das Volk*, July 13, 1848.
[46] Born, *Erinnerungen*, pp. 144-145. See also the article in the first issue of *Das Volk* entitled "Was Wir Wollen," May 25, 1848.

the Berlin newspapers on April 23.[47] Basically it was a plea for the recognition of the rights and even the existence of the working class by the rest of society and at the same time a call to the workers to unite for their own good.

Believe us, we aim neither too high nor too low; it is true that we now stand on the threshold of development from which no force on earth can any longer throw us back; the collapse of the police state and its guardianship has also given us, the children of need and privation, our majority: *we are taking our affairs into our own hands and no one is to snatch them from us again. . . .*

If we want to persuade people that we exist as a workers' class, as a power in the state, that everyone of us declares himself a member of this class and takes an active part in it, then the *organization of the workers* becomes for us the first necessity; it is our first task.

The essay noted with bitterness the contempt in which the workers were held by the middle classes of Germany, the reluctance to regard the workers "as an historical movement, . . . as a class in society which carried through its own development." Since the revolution, Born noted, the contempt was still there, but the indifference had changed to fear, fear which was largely unjustified since the maintenance of order was necessary for the prosperity of all groups in society, for the workers as well as the middle classes.

We know very well that we could get into imminent danger with any unintelligent attempt at a new revolution, would lose all that we have already achieved and would put Germany into a state of anarchy in which

[47] Printed in the *Berliner Zeitungs Halle* for Apr. 23, 1848.

we know not who would come to power. At this point our interests and the interests of the capitalists meet; we both want peace, we both must want it.

Part of the problem was, of course, that the working class still did not exist as a unified, homogeneous body:

> . . . there are still in our fatherland in no sense two sharply separated classes of people; there are capitalists and workers, but in these groups still other elements are significant—elements which belong neither to the one nor the other of these two classes and which continue to maintain a significant independence. . . . There are to be sure workers, poor, oppressed and burdened, but still no working *class*. From such a people a revolution cannot originate.

Born explained this in terms of "historical development" and the differing position of Germany, France and England. At the same time he argued that there was a sufficient unity of purpose and needs between the various groups of workers to form some sort of organization. Included in those to which Born appealed were not only the workers and journeymen, but also

> the great number of small masters who are being stifled through the competition of large capital, the farmer whose small allotment no longer suffices to feed himself and his family, the teacher who instructs our children, and the girl who sits behind the embroidery frame or the machine—to us belongs everyone whose industry and efforts are being outbid by the might of capital and who must perish in free competition.

Finally Born asserted that the remedy for the misery and privation which these groups suffered lay not with the charity of individuals but with the duty of the state to enable all to acquire the means to live. This, the

147

activity of the state in helping the working classes, was to be the great achievement of the revolution. The elaboration of specific proposals for state action remained as one of the chief tasks of the workers' organizations, and such proposals were soon to be drawn up by the Central Committee and printed and discussed at length in *Das Volk.*

A great deal of Born's Marxist training was evident in this essay. The concern for the "historical development" of the working class; the belief that it was not yet "fully developed," as if such a class were bound to arise; above all, the assertion that the present, underdeveloped class could not be the source of a revolution—all these ideas were derived from Marx. But Born differed sharply with the position that Marx himself maintained at the time. For Born, the organization of the workers, the development of self-help societies, the attempt to get the state to look after the interests of the workers and to legislate against the ill-effects of competition and industrialization—all of these were possible, indeed necessary. To Marx they were useless.

This is the origin of the "quarrel" between Marx and Born. They did indeed part company in the course of 1848, though the separation seems to have been gradual, brought about by the force of circumstances rather than by any actual or conscious split. It was only afterward that Marx, and more particularly Engels, in writing about the revolutions of 1848 assaulted Born's policy as unwise, impractical and disloyal to the communist cause.[48] But during the spring at least Born remained in fairly close contact with Marx; he even became the Berlin correspondent for the *Neue Rheinische Zeitung* when it ap-

[48] See in particular Engels' comments on Born's activities in his essay, "On the History of the Communist League," Marx, Engels, *Selected Works,* vol. 2, pp. 318-319.

peared at the beginning of June, sending it some of the same material he published in *Das Volk*.[49]

Born, too, later came to regard his activities as a rejection of Marxism. In part Born was provoked by Engels' attacks; he always claimed that Engels was responsible for his break with Marx. In his memoirs Born denied emphatically that there was anything in his policy during 1848 and 1849 that was reactionary, that there was a single line in *Das Volk*, or in the later newspaper *Die Verbrüderung*, which "showed a reactionary economic tendency." [50] At the same time he admitted that the experience he had in the course of the revolution, "in the stream of public and political life," had convinced him that communism was a mistaken creed: [51]

> For me all communist thoughts were at once washed away; they had nothing to do with the demands of the present. . . . I would have been laughed at or pitied if I had declared myself a communist. That was no longer open to me! How could distant centuries concern me when every hour offered me urgent tasks and work in full.

The Marxist analysis of history appeared to Born to be inapplicable. The concept of class, class warfare, the increasing misery of the proletariat, the successive crises and ultimate collapse of capitalism seemed to Born to be too remote from the actual situation. Misery there was to be sure, but the collapse of capitalism seemed unlikely and the problem was rather to control its growth, to preserve if possible some of the status and position of the

---

[49] Born, *Erinnerungen*, p. 123; see also Born's letter to Marx of May 11, 1848, as evidence of their continued association. (Marx, *Enthüllungen*, pp. 160-161.)

[50] Born, *Erinnerungen*, p. 146.

[51] Born, *Erinnerungen*, p. 122.

artisans rather than to aid the middle classes in the hope of their eventual downfall: [52]

> The phrase, "the antithesis of classes," had then, measured by the actual conditions of Germany, scarcely any justification. If one accepts a few industries, the machine builders, the printers and one or two others, there were to be sure employers and employees but the master was as a rule nothing more than a former journeyman. There were two age levels, not two classes. . . . Predominant in the cities of Germany in 1848—with the exception of a few points in the Rhineland—were the petty bourgeoisie, which were made up of artisans and shopkeepers and formed the broad middle class.

In this situation the goal of equality as preached by the communists seemed to Born to be entirely irrelevant if not undesirable. The main aim had to be to organize the workers, to provide for some immediate way of meeting their needs, through wage negotiations, through such measures as funds for the sick and invalid, for widows and for traveling journeymen, and through petitioning the government to preserve the position of the skilled artisans and their guilds against the advance of "capitalism." [53] Again and again Born asserted in his memoirs that this policy was the necessary result of the pressures of the time and the need for immediate and efficacious action; such problems had not been faced by Marx and Engels.[54]

Born thus took a position which in fact owed little to Marxist theory and nothing to the actual activities of Marx and Engels in 1848. There was as far as is known

[52] Born, *Erinnerungen*, pp. 136-137.
[53] Born, *Erinnerungen*, pp. 48, 120-121.
[54] Born, *Erinnerungen*, pp. 148, 150-151.

no actual "split" during the period of the revolution.[55] But there was a definite parting of the ways: Born became preoccupied with the workers' movement till forced to flee the country after the unsuccessful rising in Dresden in May of 1849 while Marx and Engels continued their general commentary on events through the medium of the *Neue Rheinische Zeitung,* ignoring the workers' movement, until they too were forced to leave and turned once more to the clandestine activities of the Communist League. To argue that Born remained in fact "loyal to Marxist theory and practice" throughout 1848 [56] is to ignore not only Born's later testimony but the sort of activity in which he engaged during the year of revolutions as well. On the other hand, to simplify Born's position and to disregard the many practical efforts he made toward bettering the lot of the workers—the formation of an all-German workers' organization as well as the various funds that were set up to aid the workers and the beginning of consumers' and producers' cooperatives—to write all this off simply because it did not have the blessing of the two Cologne journalists,[57] is to reject as invalid any effort to relieve the real misery with which the workers were faced.

Born, more than anyone else in 1848, saw the true position of the workers, caught at a moment when hand and household industries were giving way to machines and mass production. He did not reject, as many did, the new methods and techniques, but he saw the necessity of self-help and aid from the state if the workers were to avoid the misery which went in the wake of this vast change. This problem, the human cost of industrializa-

[55] Some historians talk as if there were such a split, though they cite no evidence. See, for example, Kaeber, *Berlin,* p. 158.

[56] As does Quarck, *Erste deutsche Arbeiterbewegung,* p. 55.

[57] As does, to a large extent, Karl Obermann, *Die deutschen Arbeiter in der Revolution von 1848,* pp. 173, 177ff.

tion, is one which certainly had not been solved in the course of the English industrial revolution; it remains today. That Born failed to solve it in a few years of turbulent German history when there were many other issues to occupy his mind and the public's attention is scarcely surprising. That he made an attempt, and to some extent a successful one, deserves recognition.[58]

❋

The movement to organize the workers was by no means confined to Berlin and the efforts of Born. The workers of Cologne soon founded a club and even began printing a newspaper. Similar groups were to be found in Breslau, in Leipzig, in Frankfurt, in Mainz, in Gotha, in Hamburg, indeed throughout the German Federation.[59] Each of these associations drew up a set of statutes, a list of purposes and demands or a constitution of some sort, attempting to establish on paper the exact nature of their organization much in the manner of the men of the *Paulskirche* who were to draw up the con-

[58] Not surprisingly, the first writer to praise Born for what he was, or at least to come close to it, was the revisionist socialist Eduard Bernstein (*Geschichte der Berliner Arbeiterbewegung*, vol. 1, pp. 55, 58). But then Bernstein was perhaps more concerned to point out the similarities between Born's position and his own, to trace the origins of the revisionist position, than he was to chart the course of events in 1848. And even he regarded Born as being in a way a more accurate interpreter of the "teachings of Marx" than was Marx himself. Writers of the Nazi period condemned Born both as an adherent of Marx and as an advocate of gradualist methods for the achievement of socialism. (Werner Koeppen, *Die Anfänge der Arbeiter- und Gesellenbewegung in Franken (1830-1852), Eine Studie zur Geschichte des politischen Sozialismus*, Erlangen, 1935, p. 56; Neumann, *Die jüdische Verfälschung*, p. 59.)

[59] There was even an *Arbeiterverein* set up by Wilhelm Weitling in Philadelphia in the United States in the spring of 1848 which hailed the German revolution as the beginning of the "social emancipation" of the workers. It continued in existence till the end of the century. Wittke, *Utopian Communist*, pp. 122-123.

stitution of the new German state.[60] Paper constitutions, often without any basis in reality, were a mark of 1848.

The workers' associations were on the whole extremely mild in their stated objects. Typical statutes took as their purpose "the general and moral education" of the workers or the "encouragement of a sense for everything that is beautiful and noble" [61]—not the most practical of aims and not the most revolutionary. The activities of these clubs were to consist of lectures and discussion groups, singing sections, a reading room where the latest newspapers could be seen. There was some mention of political issues, of "the realization of the basis of popular sovereignty" and the acquisition of political rights for all citizens.[62] But little was envisaged in the way of direct action. The Educational Union for Workers in Stuttgart regarded as its purpose: "To obtain a general and moral education for the workers and to bring the workers with all legal means into the full enjoyment of all civil rights; also to represent and further in general the material and spiritual interests of the workers most forcibly." The Workers' Union in Kassel limited itself to "the furthering of the spiritual and moral well-being of the working class and the spreading of a basic recognition of its situation": any other or more specific interest—"as such"—could be pursued by the club only on a vote of two thirds of its members.

More radical elements tended to come from outside the working class. Perhaps the most extreme of the workers' clubs was the group in Breslau; there the workers' union expressly rejected the "liberal" label and described itself as "socialist." The leader of this group was

[60] The Bundesarchiv in Frankfurt has a collection of the statutes of a dozen of the workers' clubs founded after the March Days.

[61] Statutes of the *Bildungsverein für Arbeiter* in Stuttgart, the *Arbeiterverein* in Esslingen and the *Bildungsverein für Arbeiter* in Hamburg.

[62] Statutes of the workers' *Demokratische Verein* in Mainz; also those of the *Arbeiterverein* in Esslingen.

no worker but the elderly and eccentric professor of botany Nees von Esenbeck, and the group worked closely with the middle-class Democratic Club of Breslau.[63] In Kassel the chemist Karl Georg Winkelblech failed altogether in the early months of the revolution to get the Workers' Union to support his particular brand of guild socialism and had to set up his own Democratic-Social Union.[64] Radical leadership easily led to a clash with the local authorities. Even in Frankfurt the National Assembly was unable or unwilling to protect the local group. The workers' club there had developed out of a pre-March gymnastic society and Frankfurt soon became a center for the organizational efforts of the workers in southwest Germany, ranking with such other cities as Berlin, Breslau, Leipzig and Hamburg. It was led by two republicans, Eduard Pelz and Christian Esselen, who sought to use the workers as a source of demagogic power. Since both came from outside the city (Pelz from Silesia and Esselen from Westphalia), the city authorities were able to order their expulsion on May 24. A workers' demonstration outside the *Paulskirche* on May 25 and protests by a number of speakers within had no effect.[65]

The moderate model was followed even by the most industrialized of the workers. The purpose of the Union of Machine Builders in Berlin, as stated in their statutes, was twofold: first, the "education of its members in scientific, social and political affairs through the holding

[63] Adler, *Geschichte der Arbeiterbewegung*, p. 163. Adler had access to the papers of von Esenbeck.

[64] Biermann, *Winkelblech*, vol. 1, pp. 296, 368ff. Winkelblech, a lecturer in chemistry at the Industrial School in Kassel, was to become the leader of an important section of the German workers' associations, a rival later in the year to the leadership of Born.

[65] *Kölnische Zeitung*, May 29, 1848; *Neue Rheinische Zeitung*, June 1, 1848; Valentin, *Frankfurt am Main*, p. 283; Quarck, *Erste deutsche Arbeiterbewegung*, pp. 104, 119; and "Die erste Frankfurter Arbeiterzeitung," *Archiv für die Geschichte des Sozialismus und der Arbeiterbewegung*, vol. 11 (1923), pp. 122ff.

of scientific lectures and discussions and through the founding of a library"; and second, the material well-being of its members which it was to pursue through contact with the general workers' movement, through the establishment of a committee to negotiate with factory owners and through various cooperative enter-prises—a fund for those who were unemployed or sick, a gun factory where those who were without jobs could find work. Membership was limited to workers in the various machine-construction factories (though outsiders could be elected after special nomination) and dues were 2.5 silbergroschen per month. The club was also to found and run a newspaper, the *Vereinblatt der Maschinenbauer zu Berlin*. And there was to be a club choir for those who enjoyed singing.

The Machine Workers' Union, far from presenting a new departure from the traditional culture of the German artisans, thus became a bulwark of it. It was typical, though probably better organized and better financed than many of the other associations of skilled artisans. There was no sense of class hostility to the employers and industrialists; in fact, as the history of the machine workers in 1848 shows, they were on exceptionally good terms with their employers. Nor did the club regard itself as an instrument of the revolution. When in mid-April a placard appeared in the name of the machine workers denouncing the government and calling for the arming of the workers, the Machine Workers' Union immediately issued a broadside of its own, asserting its members' devotion to the cause of order.[66]

✻

In many cities the guild and trade structure of the workers' movement dominated the drive to organization. In Leipzig, for example, the guilds formed the basis of

[66] *Plakate*, Ratsbibliothek, Berlin, portfolio 1; *Die Locomotive*, Apr. 20, 1848; Wolff, *Berliner Revolutionschronik*, vol. 2, p. 162.

the workers' association and revealed the split between journeymen and masters. The Leipzig journeyman's club was formed in April under the chairmanship of the journeyman-locksmith Friedrich Hempel.[67] The club met informally at a pub, the Goldene Hahn, but did manage to set up a newspaper which served as a center for the news of the workers' movement in Saxony. The Leipzig Journeymen's Union was the first to hold a regional conference for delegates from the workers' clubs in the area. The conference met on the twenty-ninth of May and was attended by representatives of the workers in Dresden, Chemnitz and Potschapel in addition to the members from Leipzig. Such conferences paved the way for the attempt to form a national workers' organization.

There were also attempts by the masters of the guilds to organize and to prevent either the government, the new nonguild industrialists or the journeymen from seizing too much power. The master craftsmen of Leipzig ignored the efforts of the journeymen of the city to organize. Instead the guilds of Leipzig issued on the twenty-second of April an open letter "to all members of the German guilds as well as all citizens and heads of families." The Leipzig letter was a classic statement of the advantages of the guild system and thus marked the opening of the guild movement in 1848.

The letter began with a description of the current state of decline in which the guilds found themselves; it was feared that the destruction of the artisans, the "middle class," would lead to communism. An equation was made between the support of the guilds and the support of the state, between guild loyalty and patriotism. The destruction of the guild system was viewed as the source of the breakup of marriage and the family, of the whole structure of German society. The training

[67] Lipinski, *Arbeiterbewegung in Leipzig*, vol. 1, pp. 49, 54ff.

of the apprentice and the journeyman, it was held, was a training not only in a trade but in citizenship as well. The letter rejected the pernicious "French" principle of free trade and demanded a universal requirement of guild membership as the basis of all legislation and government action. Finally there was an attack on the "emancipation of the Jews," the "greatest enemy" to the guild system and the lower middle class.[68]

Similarly 391 master artisans, representing some 36 different crafts in the city of Bonn, drew up a petition on the sixteenth of April which was presented on the nineteenth to the Prussian minister Camphausen. In an address to "Our Brothers in Handwork" which accompanied the petition, the master craftsmen attacked with great vigor the policy of freedom of trade, "an ideal which only brings misery in practice," and called for a revision of the 1845 industrial ordinance in favor of the guilds. They also called for state arbitration courts to settle disputes between masters and journeymen. There were to be no masters under the age of twenty-five; no master could have more than one apprentice; no master could qualify in or practice more than one trade; the use of steam machines was to be limited; the state was to set up industrial halls as market places for local produce and to make loans to artisans. The Bonn petition served as a pattern for a number of others—from Gotha, Magdeburg, Karlsruhe, Offenbach and elsewhere—which were also sent to Camphausen.[69]

In Offenbach am Main in Hesse the assembled guild masters demanded the continuation of guild regulations, particularly the masters' examination and the age limita-

[68] Biermann, *Winkelblech*, vol. 2, pp. 32-37; Goldschmidt, *Die deutsche Handwerkerbewegung*, p. 25.
[69] Biermann, *Winkelblech*, vol. 2, pp. 42-44; Meusch, *Die Handwerkerbewegung*, p. 35; Goldschmidt, *Die deutsche Handwerkerbewegung*, pp. 24-25.

tions. In Gotha the leaders of the established guilds issued a statement as early as the thirteenth of April in the *Gotha Zeitung;* they defended the guild system and called for its preservation at all costs. They declared that they "would rather a thousand times renounce the achievements of recent days than give up their well-won institutions, founded in history and proved in use." [70]

The demands of the workers and the conflicts between them, particularly the conflicts inherent in the guild structure, could lead just as easily to reaction as to further revolution.

❀

Finally there were also in the spring of 1848 moves to hold congresses of working-class groups from all parts of Germany and to achieve some sort of all-German organization for the movement. The first of these attempts was made by a single trade. The journeymen printers of Heidelberg issued a call on the sixteenth of April for a national organization of the printing trade workers and invited groups from seven other south German towns to meet at Riesenstein near Heidelberg on the twenty-third of April, Easter Sunday. This meeting in turn invited printers from all Germany to a national conference to be held in Mainz on Whitsunday, the eleventh of June.[71]

From Gotha also a call was issued on the sixth of May for an all-German workers' congress, but it was directed only at the master artisans of the guilds. The revolution, so argued the masters of Gotha, had assured the freedom and unity of the German states; but there was a danger that things might go too far and that old and necessary institutions might be swept aside in the new race for freedom; this would endanger the material

---

[70] Biermann, *Winkelblech,* vol. 2, pp. 37-38; Friedrich Weidner, *Gotha in der Bewegung von 1848,* Gotha, 1908, p. 158.
[71] Quarck, *Erste deutsche Arbeiterbewegung,* p. 133.

existence of thousands. The Frankfurt Assembly was held competent to deal with political problems but not with economic ones. To consider the economic problems of Germany, delegations of master artisans were invited to attend a congress to be held in Gotha.[72]

But the final demand for a congress, and the first one to be realized, came from north Germany. Again, it was largely confined to guild workers. The demand for the congress arose during May among the independent masters of Lauenburg and Bremen but was soon taken up by the Educational Club for Masters in Hamburg. The congress was called for the beginning of June.[73] A representative of the Hamburg group, Martens, carried the news of this move to Berlin and attempted to persuade the Berlin Central Committee, perhaps the largest and certainly the most influential workers' group in Germany at the time, to join the Hamburg Congress. The proposal was discussed at a meeting of the Central Committee on the twentieth of May, and there seems to have been some hesitation on the part of the Committee about sending a representative, perhaps out of the fear of spreading their efforts too thin.[74]

The Hamburg Congress was, however, held in June with representatives of the Berlin group in attendance. It was an inconclusive affair, but it was the first of a series of workers' congresses which were held in Germany during the summer of 1848 in an attempt to achieve some sort of national organization for the workers' interests. Some of these congresses were supplementary; more were rivals, claiming for themselves the sole right to speak for the German workers. Some were dominated by the master artisans, some by the journey-

[72] Biermann, *Winkelblech*, vol. 2, p. 38; Meusch, *Die Handwerkerbewegung*, p. 35.
[73] Biermann, *Winkelblech*, vol. 2, p. 49.
[74] *Das Volk*, May 25, 1848.

men and some sought to organize all the workers no matter what their position. All attempted to influence the National Assembly in Frankfurt and the governments of the various German states to accept their point of view. Some even hoped to form the prototype of a "social chamber" which would act in conjunction with the National Assembly, deciding economic issues as the Frankfurt Assembly decided political ones.

With the summoning of the Hamburg Congress the workers' movement of 1848 entered a new phase, the period of the rival congresses.

SECTION III
THE RIVAL CONGRESSES
—SUMMER OF 1848

CHAPTER 7

THE ARTISAN CONGRESSES
AND THE GUILD MOVEMENT

THE FRENCH workers, and with them the more radical elements of the French revolution, were defeated in Paris in the June Days. Many have since assumed that the June Days marked the defeat of the revolution and the workers throughout Europe.[1] But the June Days were regarded by the German workers less as a defeat than as a spur to further action. To be sure, the *Neue Rheinische Zeitung* announced the beginning of the reaction in its article on the fighting in Paris, declaring that "this second act of the French revolution marks the beginning of the European tragedy."[2] But to the majority of workers, the defeat of their French colleagues was either a matter of indifference or a sign of the irrepressible nature of the working-class demands.[3] In any case, the attention of Germany was occupied during the summer of 1848 not by the approach of reaction but by the beginning of the debates of the Frankfurt Assembly; at the same time, the workers were involved in the debates,

[1] This view was accepted by a number of nineteenth century German historians; see, for example, A. Bernstein, *Revolutions- und Reaktionsgeschichte Preussens und Deutschlands von den Märztagen bis zur neuesten Zeit,* Berlin, 1882, vol. 1, p. 181. It may also be found in such generally shrewd modern reinterpretations as Sir Lewis Namier's *Revolution of the Intellectuals,* pp. 11, 23, or Professor Hamerow's *Restoration, Revolution, Reaction,* p. 117.

[2] *Neue Rheinische Zeitung,* June 27, 1848.

[3] Born, in *Das Volk,* June 29, 1848, took the latter view. In Cologne, Gottschalk used the opportunity to urge his working-class followers to work—without "excesses"—for a workers' republic. Stein, *Der Kölner Arbeiterverein,* p. 55.

equally important to them, of the series of rival working-class congresses.

*

The artisans were the largest segment in the German working classes before the revolution; the artisans were the leading element in the crowds which fought the revolution and manned the barricades. It is therefore hardly surprising that the workers' congress held during the summer after the revolution were all dominated by artisans, by skilled craftsmen and the masters and journeymen of the guilds. This is true of the first of the congresses which met in Hamburg on the second of June and of all the subsequent gatherings, both those in Frankfurt and those in Berlin. It is also true of the various trade groups which held congresses and attempted to form trade organizations throughout Germany—the printers, the tailors and the cigar makers.

Yet different strands may be traced within the groups of workers' congresses. In the first place the congresses varied in origin and geographical representation. The Hamburg Congress—or "Pre-Congress" as it came to be called, in imitation of the Pre-Parliament which summoned the National Assembly at Frankfurt—found that it could not accomplish the work it set out to do, since the delegates who arrived in Hamburg came on the whole from a fairly narrow area in north Germany and were insufficiently representative of the whole Federation to form an all-German workers' group. A further congress was therefore called for Frankfurt. It met toward the end of July and continued on into August; it represented mainly the masters of the guilds and sought to preserve their interests. Because of the dominance of the masters in the first Frankfurt Artisans' Congress a second group split off from it, the Journeymen's Congress which also met in Frankfurt during August and the first

164

part of September. Naturally enough, the two Frankfurt congresses, that of the masters and that of the journeymen, were dominated by the delegates from southwest Germany.

A second series of congresses was held in Berlin, the first in June, called by the old Artisans' Union and the second in August called by the Central Committee for Workers after it became obvious that the artisans' congresses had not answered the need for the national organization of the workers. And, in addition to these congresses, there was a series of trade congresses, held in various cities—Mainz, Frankfurt and Berlin—but often dominated by the delegates from Berlin.

The congresses also differed in the programs they advocated. Some relied more on government help than others; some sought the preservation of existing institutions. Others hoped to stem the tide of industrialization. And still others hoped to organize the workers' into new forms of self-help, cooperative production, the establishment of funds for the support of traveling journeymen as well as for the unemployed or those too old or sick to work. All these various schemes and plans appeared in some form in the programs advocated by the various congresses. All sought some form of organization or association; all began with the existing institutions; all hoped to protect the workers to some extent and in some fashion from the encroachment of industrial techniques and the abandonment of the old skilled handicraft trades. These elements are common to all the groups, since they were formed, indeed they had to be formed, from the artisans.

Nonetheless the various congresses may be divided into two groups according to the attitude which they adopted toward the guild system and the rights of the masters. Certainly no significant body of workers in Germany at the time advocated complete freedom of trade and the destruction of all requirements of skill and

165

group membership. The continuance of the guilds was assumed by all.[4] Some hoped to increase the power, prestige and scope of the guilds, to raise entrance and examination requirements and to preserve at all costs the rights and privileges of the limited group of master artisans who ran the guilds. On the other hand, many wanted a reform of guild regulations which would allow greater mobility, increasing the rights of the journeymen, adding to their position and opening to them a reasonable chance of rising to the rank of master. Moreover this second group hoped that the workers' organization might be expanded to include all trades, both those that were under guild discipline and those outside.

Not unnaturally these two groups within the congresses appealed to different segments of the working class outside the number actually represented at the meetings. The first group sought the support of guild members only, and in particular the support of those who were well off under the guild system, the master artisans. The second group of congresses was aimed at the mass of workers; they included guild members, and in particular the journeymen, but they aimed more widely than this, hoping to instigate a movement with broad support, including all workers in Germany.

The first group of congresses, the artisan congresses which supported in all their rigor the system of the medieval guilds, will be dealt with in the present chapter. This group includes the first two congresses to meet: the Hamburg Pre-Congress and the first Berlin Workers'

[4] The only area in the country where the workers came out solidly for trade freedom, as revealed in the petitions to the National Assembly in Frankfurt, was the Rhenish Palatinate, but the workers there were subject to special conditions. Guild restrictions had been largely removed by the French under Napoleon only to be restored in a highly rigid form by the Bavarian government to which the territory was entrusted after the Congress of Vienna.

166

Congress which met in June. But the main statement of the guild movement in 1848 was to be found in the proceedings of the often neglected Frankfurt Artisans' Congress, which represented the masters of the guilds, and it is to this congress that the body of the chapter will be devoted. The next chapter will deal with the other group of congresses, those which sought to represent all workers and which constituted in effect an attack on the old established guilds. Both the Berlin Congress of German Workers, which met in August and is perhaps the best known of the 1848 workers' conferences,[5] and the lesser known but equally important Journeymen's Congress, which was held in Frankfurt, come into this second chapter. To this group also belong a number of the special trade congresses which encouraged the journeymen to demand higher wages and better conditions from their masters.

The description of the rival congresses must also include the work of what was in a sense the most important congress of them all, the National Assembly in Frankfurt. To be sure, the workers were not directly represented in the Frankfurt Parliament. But the Assembly did concern itself from the beginning with economic problems and the condition of the workers; the Economic Committee was second only to the constitutional committee in importance and activity. Moreover the first German parliament was a focus of attention for the workers; the Frankfurt Assembly, it was hoped, would fulfill not only the desires of the middle-class liberals who ran it but also the urgent demands of the mass of people. With this end in view the workers of Germany unleashed a storm of petitions upon the delegates; not only the congresses but many smaller groups sought to

---

[5] It is the only one of the congresses mentioned by Koppel Pinson, for example, who calls it, with questionable justification, "the first all-German workers' congress." *Modern Germany*, p. 86.

influence the work of the Frankfurt Parliament. It is from these petitions that perhaps the clearest picture of the condition and desires of the workers of 1848 emerges. The final chapter of this section (Chapter 9) will discuss the Frankfurt Assembly and the workers' demands.

❖

The first of the artisan congresses, the Hamburg Pre-Congress, met from the second to the fourth of June, a weekend; this was followed by a two-day session of a committee appointed to draw up an address to the Frankfurt Assembly.[6] The official title of the congress was the Assembly of Delegates of the North German Handicraft and Industrial Class. It was attended by two hundred of these delegates, chosen by a variety of local workers' and artisans' clubs. There were representatives from Berlin, elected by the Artisans' Union but including the follower of Born, the goldsmith Bisky, and from a number of other cities: Bremen, Hanover, Kassel and Hamburg; indeed the delegation from Hamburg was so large that its votes were restricted. But the vast majority of the delegates were from the smaller towns and the minor states of north Germany: Oldenburg, Holstein, Brunswick and the two Mecklenburgs. They represented the independent artisans and master craftsmen with a few journeymen as well. They were committed to a man to the preservation of the guilds.[7]

---

[6] The proceedings of the congress were printed: *Verhandlungen der ersten Abgeordneten-Versammlung des norddeutschen Handwerker- und Gewerbestandes zu Hamburg, den 2.–6. Juni 1848*, Hamburg, 1848. There are also accounts of the congress in Biermann, *Winkelblech*, vol. 2, pp. 49-50; Goldschmidt, *Die deutsche Handwerkerbewegung*, pp. 27-29; Meusch, *Die Handwerkerbewegung*, pp. 37-38; and Hamerow, *Restoration, Revolution, Reaction*, pp. 143-144.

[7] The organ of the Berlin Central Committee, *Das Volk*, attacked the delegates to the congress as "the fanatical defenders of the medieval guilds." June 10, 1848.

On the first day of the congress, Wischmann, a delegate from Bremen, was elected president; in an address he traced the conflict between the guilds and the principle of trade freedom over the past century. He admitted the dangers of the guild system, that the skilled worker might become the servant of the rich master and lose independence, but saw the dangers of the introduction of trade freedom as far greater and far more certain. Wischmann went on to propose consideration of various measures for guild regulations, for the establishment of arbitration courts and for state support of the workers.[8]

On the second day of the congress the tide turned against such discussion of specific measures. The court bookbinder from Brunswick, Selencka, proposed that the congress apply itself only to general issues, that it postpone any more detailed argument till a body which was more representative of all Germany could be summoned.

Hence arose the plan for the All-German Artisans' Congress to be held in Frankfurt in July. The Hamburg Pre-Congress confined itself to a declaration condemning economic liberalism and calling on the Frankfurt Assembly to include the abolition of trade freedom, in so far as it existed, as part of the fundamental law of the new German nation. These proposals were ultimately drafted into the final address drawn up on the fifth and sixth of June by a committee of seventeen and sent to the National Assembly to Frankfurt.

The Hamburg Pre-Congress was perhaps frightened into this position and into summoning the further congress in Frankfurt by the realization of the deep gulf which separated the interests of the more prosperous masters from the mass of journeymen and workers. The

[8] The speech was reported in the *Neue Rheinische Zeitung*, June 6, 1848; it was one of the few reports of the workers' congresses to appear in that paper throughout the summer of 1848.

169

delegate from Berlin, Bisky, upheld the position of the journeymen; his speech was innocent enough, a plea for the dignity of work and workers' education, but it contained a favorable reference to some of the effects of trade freedom. It was enough to throw the delegates into confusion.[9]

The congress also rejected the comprehensive proposals of the delegate from Kassel, the chemistry instructor Winkelblech. Going beyond mere condemnation of trade freedom, Winkelblech pointed to the changing position of the journeyman whose advancement was blocked and who was in many cases reduced to the rank of the ordinary worker. Drastic remedies were necessary, Winkelblech argued, to prevent the methods of modern industry from undermining entirely the guild system. He called for a vast range of special legislation and the summoning of a second "national assembly," a "social chamber" which would be competent to legislate in this field. The guilds themselves were to be adapted to deal with the new conditions and expanded to include all types of industry. Winkelblech hoped thus to avoid the destruction of the lower middle class and the creation of a mass proletariat out of the former artisan class, which he regarded as the chief result of industrialization in England and France.

These proposals were too radical and too far reaching for the timid masters who had met in Hamburg. Winkelblech's advice was rejected; indeed the whole position of the journeymen was left untouched. Winkelblech himself was ultimately to split with the guild movement at the Artisans' Congress in Frankfurt and to join the Journeymen's Congress.

In the meantime, the Hamburg Pre-Congress con-

[9] The speech was printed in full in *Das Volk*, June 10, 1848; see also Mehring, *Geschichte der deutschen Sozialdemokratie*, vol. 2, p. 78.

tented itself with the declaration it had drawn up for the Frankfurt Assembly, with a denunciation of trade freedom—the only point on which all, journeymen and masters alike, could agree—and with preparations for the Congress in Frankfurt which was to be held in six weeks' time. The various local guilds and industrial associations were to elect delegates to this second congress in proportion to the number of representatives already sent to the National Assembly in Frankfurt; the congress was to represent the handicraft and industrial class of the entire nation.

*

The fatal split between the interests of the masters and the journeymen, as well as the difference between the demands of the guilds and those of the workers as a whole which revealed itself in the Hamburg Pre-Congress in June may also be seen in a number of other regional congresses of workers and artisans held during that month. On June 13 a meeting of handicraft workers took place in Gotha, summoned by the masters of that city and including delegates from the guilds in a number of neighboring towns. It was a respectable affair; indeed much of the artisan movement at the time was accepted by the better elements in society as a natural product of the revolution and the liberal measures that had been adopted. The Duke of Coburg himself was in attendance. The main demands of the meeting were for the abolition of monopolies created by patents and for the reestablishment of the guilds.[10]

A similar meeting took place on June 18 in the Odeon in Leipzig, attended by representatives of the workers' clubs throughout the kingdom of Saxony. Some forty-two delegates came from thirteen different towns. The meeting endorsed the formation of workers' clubs as the only

[10] *Berliner Zeitungs Halle,* June 29, 1848.

171

means of forwarding the interests of the workers, elected
a committee consisting of a chairman, Tirnstein from
Dresden, a vice-chairman, Hampel from Leipzig, and a
secretary, Skrobek from Leipzig, and designated the
Leipziger Arbeiter Zeitung as the official organ of the
Saxon workers' clubs.[11]

The Saxon Congress of Workers' Clubs went further
in its demands than did either the assembly in Gotha or
the Pre-Congress in Hamburg, but it still fought shy of
any open declaration of the opposition of interests between the various groups within the workers' movement.
It called on the state to protect the products of German
handicraft through tariffs which "equalized" the competition offered by factory production, both foreign and
domestic. It endorsed many of the conventional "liberal"
demands found in most of the manifestos of 1848. But
the Saxon Congress went beyond these items with requests which heralded in many ways the demands of
the workers' movement as it developed later in the year.
The program of the congress called for the establishment
of state supported hospitals for the ill, old and incapacitated; state support to journeymen during their *Wanderjahre*; arbitration courts to settle disputes between workers and their employers; state stores to sell excess produce; credit banks to grant loans to failing industries;
legislation for maximum hours and minimum wages; lien
laws to insure that workers received what was their due.
Finally the congress called for a state ministry which
would devote itself exclusively to the "workers question."

The artisans of the Prussian province of Silesia held a
congress on the nineteenth of June which was perhaps
the most guild-dominated of all these early regional
congresses.[12] The congress met in Breslau and drew up a

[11] Lipinski, *Arbeiterverein in Leipzig*, vol. 1, pp. 50-52.
[12] Biermann, *Winkelblech*, vol. 2, p. 77; Meusch, *Die Handwerkerbewegung*, p. 41.

full scale plan for the organization of work and the revival of the guilds. The congress called for an end of the industrial ordinances of 1810 and 1845 and the re-establishment of the guilds on a new basis with a simpler series of tests for the various ranks and a greater amount of self-control. In addition to trade guilds the artisans, both masters and journeymen, were to form local industrial guilds, which were in turn to elect district and provincial guild committees. The artisans were also to elect directly a handicraft chamber for the province—a proposal similar to Winkelblech's idea of a "social chamber"—and the legislative body together with the provincial guild committee was to form a ministry which would administer all economic measures. The Silesian Congress also went further than the Hamburg meeting had been willing to do on the issue of granting journeymen equal rights with masters and on expediting the rise of the former to the rank of the latter.

The final and in some ways the most important of the preparatory congresses was held in Berlin on the eighteenth and nineteenth of June, attracting some thirty-three delegates from ninety-five different artisans' clubs.[13] The congress had been summoned by the conservative Artisans' Union; it was, however, supported by the Central Committee as well in the hope that it might counteract what it considered to be the failure of

[13] *Berliner Zeitungs Halle,* June 20, 1848. The proceedings of the June Congress in Berlin were never published; however, the report in the *Zeitungs Halle* was of more than average length, and the meetings were discussed in *Das Volk,* June 20, 22, 1848. There was also a brief mention of the congress in the *Neue Rheinische Zeitung;* this was the last of the summer congresses to which Marx's paper paid any attention—all the later and more important ones were ignored. There are also accounts of the congress in Biermann, *Winkelbloch,* vol. 2, pp. 73-74; Adler, *Geschichte der Arbeiterbewegung,* p. 166; Quarck, *Erste deutsche Arbeiterbewegung,* p. 151; Friedensburg, *Stephan Born,* p. 92.

the Hamburg assembly.[14] The declared purpose of the meeting was "the propagation of insight, morality and a sense of brotherhood among the artisans."

The cities represented, in addition to Berlin, included Hamburg, Altona, Kiel, Halle, Stettin and Breslau. There was also a delegate from Saxony who claimed to speak for the artisans in fifty-two towns. Finally there were delegates from the smaller towns within Prussia and the enclave states of northeast Germany. There were no representatives from Bavaria or the southwest and none, significantly, from the Prussian Rhineland. Letters expressing interest in the proceedings came from workers' groups in a number of other cities; the artisans of Brandenburg wrote that they wished to attend but feared possible police action against them.

The congress lasted a scant two days. Again the divergence of interests of the various groups within the working class was evident; again the delegates present were often unable to agree on any positive program. Like the Hamburg Congress, the Berlin meeting also drafted a brief address to the Frankfurt Assembly. The Berlin address in fact had more in common with the radical proposals of the Saxon and Silesian congresses than with those of the Hamburg group; it asserted that the core of the nation, the class of workers and artisans, demanded as their inalienable right the guarantee of work and a living wage by the state; there was also to be free instruction and education, free care of invalids and similar benefits.

The Berlin congress also mapped out a "program of activity" for workers' and artisans' clubs. This consisted simply of a general statement that these clubs existed "to further the contemporary development of the spirit-

[14] *Das Volk*, June 10, 1848; Bisky left the Hamburg meeting before it was finished in order to participate in the preparation for the Berlin congress. Biermann, *Winkelblech*, vol. 2, p. 60.

ual, moral, industrial and political life of the worker through lesson and deed." Beyond this statement however nothing was proposed, and *Das Volk* commented that the program seemed "scarcely important enough" to discuss.

The Berlin Congress, again following the example of the Hamburg meeting, appointed a committee which was to make arrangements for a further assembly of delegates from the workers' clubs to be held in August; the new committee was to attempt to attract representatives from the whole of Germany. The committee was to have considerable influence on the development of the 1848 workers' movement. It consisted of a number of the more radical members of the Prussian Assembly, then meeting in Berlin, including Waldeck and the Breslau botanist Nees von Esenbeck, and a number of the leaders of the Berlin workers' movement, notably Brill, Bisky, the machine builder Krause and Stephan Born. The purpose of the second Berlin Congress was not to be confined to narrow limits; it was to take into consideration the whole "social question."

The document which this committee issued on June 26, 1848, summoning the All German Workers' Congress to Berlin for August 26 marked the beginning of the broader workers' movement and the attack on the more narrow conception of the handicraft guilds which will be discussed in the next chapter.

But the preparatory congresses held during June of 1848 showed clearly that the movement which had begun with such high hopes after the March Days was already sliding into a state where the common concerns of the workers were overshadowed by the differences which separated them. The congresses had all failed to come to any specific conclusions or to adopt any detailed policy. Even the Hamburg meeting, where there was perhaps the greatest unity of opinion, had failed to

175

do anything more specific than call for the abolition of free trade, where it existed, a demand which was echoed in one form or another by the other groups. Beyond this and a few proposals for state action, there was nothing on which the groups could agree, except of course the general statement of policy for workers' clubs drawn up at the Berlin meeting. But that, as Born's paper declared, was scarcely worth discussing.

The elaboration of a working-class program had to wait for further discussion, which the congresses summoned to Frankfurt and Berlin were to provide. But this discussion had in turn to wait upon a willingness to face the issues which divided the masters and better-paid artisans from the journeymen and mass of workers.

This division was first brought into the open at the Frankfurt Congress of Artisans which had been summoned for the end of July.

*

The Frankfurt Artisans' Congress, the First German Handworker and Industrial Congress as it was called, began to assemble on July 14, 1848. The opening session was held the following day in the *Römer*, the ancient coronation hall of the Holy Roman Emperors in the main square of Frankfurt, just around the corner from the *Paulskirche* where the National Assembly was meeting. There the discussions continued till the eighteenth of August, dealing in thirty-one sessions with the major problems which confronted the artisans. By the time the congress closed, the split between the more substantial artisans and the mass of workers, particularly the journeymen of the guilds, had become evident; reconciliation of the conflicting interests seemed impossible.

The congress got off to a slow start. Only fifty delegates were present in mid-July. By the end of the month, sixty were gathered and others were gradually arriving; it was expected that the total would come to well over a hundred.[15] In particular the delegates from southern Germany were late in arriving and many did not appear till toward the end of the congress.[16]

The master butcher from Frankfurt, Johannes Martin May, was elected president at a preliminary meeting on the fourteenth of July. May had been chairman of the Frankfurt commission which had made the local arrangements. He declared in his acceptance speech that "the elections to the Industrial Congress were as legitimate as those to the National Assembly itself" and protested against the continuation of discussions of a future German industrial ordinance which did not take into consideration the opinion of the congress, a protest which was greeted with cheers by the assembled delegates.[17]

But the legitimacy of the election of some of the delegates was in fact open to question. The Hamburg Pre-Congress had failed to issue any clear instructions about the election of delegates; most areas had interpreted the call for "free" elections as applying only to the masters of the guilds. But this practice was not followed uniformly. Some were afraid that the congress would arouse hostility against its decisions and provoke the charge that it was not sufficiently representative.[18] Few were concerned about the absence of industrialists and factory owners, for they, it was felt, were already represented in the National Assembly.[19] But it was an open question whether the artisans themselves were

[15] *Kölnische Zeitung,* July 23, 1848.

[16] Meusch, *Die Handwerkerbewegung,* p. 43.

[17] *Verhandlungen des ersten deutschen Handwerker- und Gewerbekongresses, gehalten zu Frankfurt am Main, vom 14. Juli bis 18. August 1848,* ed. G. Schirges, Darmstadt, 1848, p. 1.

[18] See the speech of the delegate Reintle at the session on July 15, 1848, *Verhandlungen des ersten deutschen Handwerker- und Gewerbekongresses,* p. 3.

[19] For this reason the interests of the factory owners were expressly excluded from the address to the National Assembly drawn up by the Artisans' Congress. *Verhandlungen des ersten deutschen Handwerker- und Gewerbekongresses,* pp. 10-11.

sufficiently represented. The workers' clubs of Koblenz, for example, had chosen not one of their own number but a student to represent their interests.[20] Others seemed to be "official" delegates from the town governments and unrepresentative of the mass of workers.[21]

The most pressing problem which the Frankfurt Artisans' Congress faced, a problem which occupied the first week or so of its deliberations, was the question of whether or not journeymen and their representatives could be admitted to the proceedings. The instinct of the leaders of the congress was to avoid the issue when it first came up at the meeting on the eighteenth of July. The delegate from Koblenz and the delegate from Leipzig who were the first to apply for admission were not in fact journeymen themselves but students, and on this ground May hoped to put off discussion.[22] But this was not good enough for most of the delegates. One of the first speakers declared flatly that there could be no question of even considering the issue: journeymen as such simply could not be admitted.[23] Another suggested that they should tell the delegates of the journeymen that they should "go quietly home and await written news, consoled in the expectation that the masters would look after their interests." After all, one speaker added, the masters were all old journeymen themselves.

The journeymen delegates pressed their demands, however, and the credentials committee was instructed

[20] The mandate for Herr Lorenz Enders, Cand. Phil., who was elected at a meeting of the Koblenz *Arbeiter-Gesellen-Verein* and the *Allgemeine Arbeiterverein* on July 11, 1848, may be found in the *Akten des Handwerker-Kongresses.*

[21] The municipal representatives and magistrate of Magdeburg were persuaded to pay for the town's delegates to the Frankfurt Artisans' Congress. *Kölnische Zeitung,* July 23, 1848.

[22] Session of July 18, 1848, *Verhandlungen des ersten deutschen Handwerker- und Gewerbekongresses,* p. 20.

[23] Speech by Herr Todt, *Verhandlungen des ersten deutschen Handwerker- und Gewerbekongresses,* p. 19.

to consider the issue. The committee reported back to the general assembly of the congress on the following day, the nineteenth of July, presenting what it held to be a compromise solution. The journeymen's delegates were to be admitted to the proceedings, but they were to be observers with the right to join in debate only on issues which the congress as a whole felt concerned the journeymen. No votes were to be given to the journeymen under any circumstances.[24] Even this compromise was too much for many of the master artisans. The journeymen, it was argued, were not independent; they had no idea of the responsibilities of a master and head of a family; they stood in a son-father relationship toward the masters; and to destroy this would be to attack the core of the guild system. On the other hand, the journeymen were recognized as allies of the masters in the struggle against capital; their support was sought, though only within the limits of the guild system and the compromise proposal of the committee.[25] Finally, on the twenty-second of July it was decided to accept the proposal of the credentials committee: journeymen were to be admitted, without voting rights and with only limited rights of debate. But the number of such delegates was to be restricted to ten.[26]

The debates over the issue of the admission of journeymen to the congress may serve as an illustration of the desperation into which the artisans had been driven. The main motive behind the intransigence of the masters was, as a contemporary account commented, the desire on the part of the masters to preserve their rank and position, their social superiority over the journey-

[24] *Verhandlungen des ersten deutschen Handwerker- und Gewerbekongresses,* p. 20.
[25] *Verhandlungen des ersten deutschen Handwerker- und Gewerbekongresses,* pp. 21-23.
[26] *Verhandlungen des ersten deutschen Handwerker- und Gewerbekongresses,* pp. 43-47.

men, rather than any direct material or economic issue.[27]

The compromise was not a success. The journeymen organized a congress of their own in which their interests could be directly represented. On the fourth of August the ten journeymen delegates admitted to the sessions of the Artisans' Congress in the *Römer* resigned their seats in order to attend the Journeymen's Congress. With this resignation the Artisans' Congress dropped all pretence of representing the interests of the journeymen. The Committee on the Affairs of the Journeymen which had been set up was dissolved; there was no further attempt to consider their interests.[28]

The Artisans' Congress received a protest from the Workers' Club in Heidelberg, drawn up on the ninth of August, complaining against the exclusion of the journeymen.[29]

> The Industrial Class of Germany has met and has straight away left the ground of justice in that it has left unconsidered the largest part of the industrial class, the assistants, the true workers, and shut them out of the elections. No one in Germany up to now has done this. If our masters claim that they have other interests to consider and to represent than us, the workers, then they themselves announce the gulf which they would open between us and them and no just man will blame the working class if it unites throughout Germany and seeks to defend itself against the self-confessed concerns of the German masters.

Such threats were ignored by the master artisans.

❋

The Artisans' Congress was thus left free to consider the interests and demands of the guilds and the master

[27] *Deutsche Reichs-Zeitung,* Aug. 8, 1848.
[28] *Verhandlungen des ersten deutschen Handwerker- und Gewerbekongresses,* pp. 139, 143.
[29] *Akten des Handwerker-Kongresses.*

artisans who were represented and who had expressed their needs to the congress in a host of petitions and memorials which had been drawn up by the various local groups and sent to Frankfurt.[30] The congress set itself three main tasks: to assess and debate the proposals contained in these petitions, to draft on the basis of the petitions an industrial ordinance for the whole of Germany and to persuade the Economic Committee of the Frankfurt Assembly to adopt the proposals of the congress.[31]

The delegates to the Artisans' Congress viewed the revolution as the work of the class which they represented and as an opportunity to further the interests of that class and to remove it from the state of economic decline into which it had fallen. A petition drawn up by the Union of Handicraft Masters in Bielefeld on the ninth of June and forwarded to the congress expressed this clearly: [32]

If any class in society, if any estate, is preeminently called upon to intervene decisively in the history of the state, then it is the artisan class. In it rests the actual power of the cities; it is the core of the state.

[30] The *Akten des Handwerker-Kongresses*, which were presented to the Stadtarchiv in Frankfurt am Main by the president of the congress, Martin May, include two portfolios containing more than 200 of these petitions. These represent perhaps half the actual number of petitions sent to the congress, since they are arranged alphabetically by place of origin and run only from A to K.

[31] As reported in the *Kölnische Zeitung*, July 22, 1848. The *Kölnische Zeitung* characterized the proceedings as "a large slice of the Middle Ages drawn up in the old *Römer*" and claimed that the chief difficulty lay in the fact that the delegates believed that there were two distinct groups, artisans and industrialists, where in fact there was only one—the middle class, to which the workers and journeymen were opposed. This was in many ways a shrewd comment on the Artisans' Congress, but it overestimates the clarity with which class lines could be drawn in the Germany of 1848.

[32] *Akten des Handwerker-Kongresses.*

It is called to end the great schism which separates the propertyless from the property owners; mediating the opposition between overpowering riches and hopeless poverty, it stands between them, the scales of justice in its hand. . . . Recent times have wounded the artisans deeply; the limitless freedom of industry, the production of handicraft goods in factories, the superior power of capital which enslaves the artisan, threaten to destroy the position which the artisans have held up to now and to make them into a proletariat, will-less tools in the hands of the capitalists.

The causes of the decline of the handicraft trades were discussed in petition after petition against the introduction of free entry into trade. The Industrial Club in Aub in Lower Franconia in Bavaria wrote that trade freedom would "bury the morality and well-being of this class; to be sure some could survive but thousands would be destroyed." Some groups—the butchers of Danzig, for example, and the artisans of Jena—cited the Prussian example, seeing in the industrial ordinance of 1845, and the measure of trade freedom which it introduced, the cause of the suffering of the workers. "We would refer briefly," wrote the group in Jena, "to the example of Prussia, which has called forth so great a number of proletarians through the freedom of trade that in fact the Prussian state does not now know how it is to satisfy them even slightly." The butchers' guild in the same city traced a connection between the condition of the workers and the outbreak of revolution:

The recent political events which have broken out over all Europe so unexpectedly and so surprisingly and have suddenly placed all existing relationships in question and have radically changed them so that the end is still not in sight must without doubt be con-

182

nected with the already existing prevalence of the proletariat.

One speaker at the congress estimated that "a third of the population is now without bread as a consequence of trade freedom" and another went so far as to make specific the equation between the revolution and trade freedom: "Without trade freedom, there would have been no barricades." [33]

The main solution was seen in the revival of the guilds, whose glories were extolled by many.[34] A number of abuses of guild regulations were cited; one speaker pointed out that masters often took between twenty and thirty apprentices and a petition from the carpenters of Halle noted an example in that town of a master having thirty-two apprentices.[35] Apprentices, it was argued, should be limited to two under each master. Other petitions dealt with the position of journeymen and the need to maintain the custom of the *Wanderjahre* as an essential part of the training and education of the artisan. One petition even saw in the institution a way of keeping down the size of the population; traveling journeymen, it argued, were far less likely to marry and have children.[36]

There were also attacks on what were considered to be contraventions of the guild system—household produc-

[33] *Verhandlungen des ersten deutschen Handwerker- und Gewerbekongresses,* p. 7; *Akten des Handwerker-Kongresses;* cf. also Biermann, *Winkelblech,* vol. 2, p. 134; Goldschmidt, *Die deutschen Handwerkerbewegung,* p. 33.

[34] See, for example, the pamphlet, printed in Hamburg and addressed to the Frankfurt Artisans' Congress, cited in Biermann, *Winkelblech,* vol. 2, pp. 80-81.

[35] *Verhandlungen des ersten deutschen Handwerker- und Gewerbekongresses,* p. 64; *Akten des Handwerker-Kongresses.*

[36] Petition of the butchers of Danzig, *Akten des Handwerker-Kongresses.* The married journeymen, the petition noted, soon "fell back into the class of workers" and weakened the strength of the handicraft guilds.

tion, state factories and the like. The practice of estate owners in Pomerania of using their agricultural laborers to manufacture goods was condemned. There was an attack on rural production in general and an attempt to confine all handicraft work to the towns; at least, it was argued, all rural workers must be members of the city guilds unless their trade was directly involved in agriculture.[37] And of course the whole new system of factories came in for abuse. When the question of the limitation of factory production and the taxation of factories and large industries in favor of the small handicraft producer came up before the congress, it was voted on without discussion; no need was felt to defend such obviously necessary measures.[38]

Other local issues were brought forward; the members of the *Zollverein* outside Prussia argued that the ordinance of 1845 had to be revamped in the interests of all Germany, as well, of course, for the protection of the artisans within Prussia. Considerable time was spent in discussing the differences in real property rights between northern and southern Germany.[39]

Finally the artisans held the state, both the individual members of the German Federation and the new national government which the Frankfurt Parliament was in the process of creating, responsible for the interests of the artisans, for protecting them from the ravages of open competition. After all, it was argued, the preservation of the handicraft trades was in the interests of the whole country; the guilds were necessary not only

[37] *Verhandlungen des ersten deutschen Handwerker- und Gewerbekongresses*, pp. 72-75.

[38] *Verhandlungen des ersten deutschen Handwerker- und Gewerbekongresses*, pp. 95-96.

[39] *Verhandlungen des ersten deutschen Handwerker- und Gewerbekongresses*, pp. 67-70. The *Kölnische Zeitung*, July 28, 1848, cited this debate as an example of the narrow interests and general uselessness of the members of the Artisans' Congress.

economically but as the center of the German social structure. The cabinetmakers' guild of Köpenick adopted a petition to the Artisans' Congress on the seventh of July in which it was stated that: [40]

It is recognized by all sides and in all European states, with the possible exception of Russia, Sweden and Norway, where completely different social conditions prevail, and it therefore needs no further proof, that the industrial situation of the class of artisans is at the present so dismal that an improvement of the same must not only be sought for the preservation of this class, which is necessary to every state, but for the preservation of the state itself.

From this it followed that the state must be expected to participate in the effort to revive the guilds and support the artisans. Several specific proposals were discussed. For example, some delegates called for state supported industrial halls which would sell the produce of the artisans and, it was hoped, put the handicraft trades on an equal footing with factory production.[41] In any case the congress expected the National Assembly to endorse the industrial ordinance proposed by the master artisans. To this ordinance the congress devoted most of its time.

In the debates on the ordinance at the Artisans' Congress, three different parties were apparent to a contemporary observer.[42] First there was a small group of "liberals" who came mainly from the Rhineland and from the Palatinate in particular; this group accepted the possibility of freedom of trade and hoped to be able to compete on this basis. The "liberals," however, were of but minor importance in the proceedings of the congress; they found no support among the mass of members. The

[40] *Akten des Handwerker-Kongresses.*
[41] *Deutsche Reichs-Zeitung*, Aug. 6, 1848.
[42] *Kölnische Zeitung*, Aug. 7, 1848.

second and by far the largest group was that of the city artisans and guild masters; these were described as the "old monopolists." They came mainly from north Germany, but were joined on most issues by the delegates from Bavaria. They wanted a restoration of the guild system pure and simple, with state legislation to protect the guild and limit the growing use of machinery and the spread of the factory system.

Finally there was on the left of the congress a small group described as "the progressive, social party." This faction was led by Winkelblech, who was elected as a delegate for Kassel late in July and consequently did not arrive in Frankfurt till the proceedings were well under way.[43] His main efforts at the congress were devoted to an attempt to reconcile the interests of the masters and the journeymen and to undo the damage caused by the exclusion of the latter.[44] But, as in Hamburg, he also endeavored to put through proposals for a social chamber and a federated system of guilds. These ideas were expressed in a minority petition which Winkelblech submitted to the National Assembly; they were also to form the basis of the demands of the Journeymen's Congress. Winkelblech had some influential support for his views; among the nineteen signatures

[43] Winkelblech did not speak in the debates of the congress till Aug. 7, *Verhandlungen des ersten deutschen Handwerker- und Gewerbekongresses*, p. 148; cf. Biermann, *Winkelblech*, vol. 2, p. 91.

[44] Biermann, *Winkelblech*, vol. 2, p. 118, quotes a letter from the president of the congress, Martin May, praising Winkelblech's efforts at reconciliation. See also Winkelblech's speech at the final session of the Artisans' Congress, *Verhandlungen des ersten deutschen Handwerker- und Gewerbekongresses*, p. 257, in which he deplored the split between the congresses of the masters and the journeymen: "The interests of the workers and the middle classes in Germany," he declared somewhat optimistically, "coincide completely, and only through the close cooperation of both parts is the fight against capital to be waged with success."

to his petition were the president of the congress, Martin May, and its secretary, Georg Schirges. A few other radicals showed up but were even less influential than Winkelblech.[45]

The majority of the master craftsmen who dominated the congress had no interest in utopian schemes such as Winkelblech's; the old guild system, buttressed by the new German state, was enough for them.

✳

Nonetheless the program which the Artisans' Congress adopted was an extensive and all-embracing attempt to restore the power of the guilds; indeed it sought to raise the guilds to a position they had never in fact held.[46] All handicraft and skilled trades were to be organized on a guild basis; the old guilds were to be retained and incorporated into the new system, but new ones were to be formed to include trades not previously organized. When there were fewer than twelve workers practicing a particular craft in a given city, then combined guilds could be formed to include the various small trades. Each guild was to be run by a committee, elected by the masters, which would settle all disputes within the guild. In addition the guild committees in a given city would elect an industrial council which would deal with municipal problems and establish an industrial court to judge interguild disputes.

[45] *Akten des volkswirtschaftlichen Ausschusses,* vol. 21, i.
[46] The program, *Entwurf einer allgemeinen Handwerks- und Gewerbe-Ordnung, berathen und beschlossen von dem deutschen Handwerker- und Gewerbe-Congress zu Frankfurt am Main vom 15. Juli bis 15. August 1848,* was printed by Volkhart, delegate to the congress from Schwaben and Neuberg in Bavaria, at Augsburg in the autumn of 1848. Summaries of its contents may be found in Meusch, *Die Handwerkerbewegung,* pp. 69-76; Goldschmidt, *Die deutschen Handwerkerbewegung,* pp. 33-37; Hamerow, *Restoration, Revolution, Reaction,* pp. 145-146.

There were also to be legislative bodies, industrial chambers, in each state within the German confederation, elected by the municipal industrial councils. Above these was to be an all-German industrial chamber which would work in cooperation with the Ministry of Labor and would legislate in all areas affecting the economic interests of the artisans. Thus it was proposed that a whole structure of guild institutions be set up, a sort of "corporate state," parallel to the political institutions of Germany, which would control the economy in favor of the handicraft trades and the guilds.[47]

The program of the Artisans' Congress also included a number of proposals for the organization of the guilds which would preserve the traditional pattern of apprentices, journeymen and masters and would maintain the rights of the masters. Tests for the various ranks conducted by the masters were to be continued and made uniform throughout Germany. Apprentices had to serve between three and five years; journeymen had to travel for three years and could not marry; masters had to be at least twenty-five years old, could practice only one trade and could acquire no more than two apprentices. Trades had to be carried out in the cities; there were to be no public works, no household production; factories were to be limited by taxation.

The state was required to look after the interests of the handicraft workers in a variety of ways. There were to be progressive income and property taxes and protective tariffs. The income from these was to be used for loans to the artisans, for funds for the sick and incapacitated as well as the widows of artisans. There were to be handicraft schools financed by the state; all

[47] The idea was to find a twentieth century reflection in the provision of the Weimar Constitution (article 165, paragraphs 3 and 4) for a National Economic Council as a sort of economic parliament.

188

education was to be free. The journeymen, too, were to be helped financially during their required *Wanderjahre*. Weights, measures and coinage were to be made uniform throughout Germany. Aid was to be given to the unemployed and help in finding a job.

The industrial code of the Artisans' Congress was indeed extreme; it represented, in the words of the preamble, a "last, dying protest against freedom of trade." It was for these measures that the master artisan had fought the revolution.

And it was in the hope of their fulfillment that the master artisans turned to the Frankfurt Assembly. Indeed the relations of the Artisans' Congress to the National Assembly were closer than any of the other workers' congresses held during the summer of 1848. The members of the Artisans' Congress considered themselves to be in a way a subsidiary branch of the Frankfurt Parliament, an "alternative parliament" which would deal with economic issues.[48] When the Artisans' Congress was announced, it was held that its main task would be to supply the Economic Committee of the National Assembly with the information and informed opinion necessary to its task.[49] The first official act of the congress was to adopt an address of loyalty to the National Assembly, expressing its unanimous opposition to free trade and offering its services to the Economic Committee in the drafting of an industrial law. The address noted that the industrial class "was scarcely represented in the lap" of the National Assembly and hoped that its deliberations and advice could make up for this.[50] The industrial regu-

[48] The name *Gegenparlament* was often given to the Artisans' Congress. Tilmann, *Einfluss des Revolutionsjahres*, p. 15.

[49] *Berliner Zeitungs Halle*, June 27, 1848.

[50] *Verhandlungen des ersten deutschen Handwerker- und Gewerbekongresses*, p. 6; cf. Meusch, *Die Handwerkerbewegung*, p. 44.

lations which the congress proposed were presented to the National Assembly with a second address on the fifteenth of August, praising the men "of courage and intelligence" who had been elected to the National Assembly, eschewing "the bloody path of force" but drawing quite explicitly the connection between revolution and the present plight of the artisans.[51]

The Frankfurt Assembly for its part listened to the demands of the Artisans' Congress politely and with interest. The president of the National Assembly, Heinrich von Gagern himself, received May and the delegation which presented the first address and assured them that the deliberations of the National Assembly were "in no way of a threatening character to the interests of the industrial class and the artisans."[52] The Economic Committee made every effort to consult with the members of the congress and consider their demands. But the problem of the German working class was wider and more varied than the master craftsmen of the Artisans' Congress were aware or were willing to admit and the National Parliament had to take into consideration a number of groups less well-off than the master artisans.[53]

✻

The proceedings of the Artisans' Congress did reveal, in the words of the introduction to the published debates, "the complaints and the burdens of the people, the bared

[51] The address is quoted in full by Biermann, *Winkelblech,* vol. 2, pp. 110-111.

[52] *Berliner Zeitungs Halle,* July 26, 1848.

[53] The artisans held a banquet for the members of the Economic Committee in Frankfurt on Aug. 5, 1848; the food at this banquet was so lavish, according to one contemporary source, that it might well have persuaded the members of the Economic Committee that the artisans were very well off indeed. *Kölnische Zeitung,* Aug. 9, 1848.

wounds of the nation." [54] But the program adopted was confined to the narrow interests of the guilds and the master craftsmen. Here perhaps was one of the "lost opportunities" of 1848. For the congress did present the possibility of uniting the more respectable elements of the working classes: "This Congress, the first of its sort—for Germany is once again in this ahead of all other countries—can be of the greatest importance if it takes the trouble not to split its powers and not to waste its noble time with useless phrases as so often happens in such deliberating assemblies." [55]

But the time was wasted and the forces were split. The Artisans' Congress failed to persuade the Frankfurt Assembly of the wisdom of its demands; it failed to unite the rest of the working class in its support, rejecting the representatives of the journeymen and refusing to adapt the old guilds to new conditions. A number of other and opposing movements grew up among the workers and journeymen; these too held congresses and claimed to speak for the whole of Germany.

[54] *Verhandlungen des ersten deutschen Handwerker- und Gewerbekongresses,* p. iii.
[55] *Berliner Zeitungs Halle,* July 19, 1848.

CHAPTER 8

THE WORKERS' CONGRESSES

AND THE

ATTACK ON THE GUILDS

"STILL, MY brothers, let's not deceive ourselves; no one wants to unite with us. That was only anxiety for their money bags on the part of these philistines. They respect us far too little to meet us in the negotiations." [1] So wrote the Hanover journeyman-printer Stegen on July 27, 1848, in an article headed, "A Few Words about the Union of Workers and Employers." Such a union, he held, was impossible. This had been proved by the refusal of the Frankfurt Artisans' Congress to admit journeymen on an equal basis with the masters. It could also be seen in the reaction of the master printers and printshop owners to the demands of the printers which had been drawn up at a printers' congress in Mainz in June and for which the printers were about to strike.

The guilds, and much of what they stood for, were rejected by Stegen; he even talked in modern terms of "workers" and "employers" rather than journeymen and masters.

Stegen's view of the isolation of the workers, their need to act for themselves, was shared by many in 1848. The strikes in the spring of the year had marked a break with the old guild pattern; the journeymen had revolted against the rule of the masters. The same tendency was

[1] *Das Volk*, Aug. 9, 1848. Stegen, a republican and the founder of the Hanover workers' club, was perhaps embittered; he had just been released, after five weeks in prison, for lack of evidence. *Berliner Zeitungs Halle*, Aug. 2, 1848.

continued during the period of the rival congresses, the summer of 1848. There were a number of trades in which the journeymen and ordinary workmen sought to improve their lot. In particular, the printers, the tailors and the cigar makers held national congresses and set up national organizations; the first of these groups organized a nationwide strike at the beginning of August, the first such strike to take place in Germany. All three organizations marked a break with the traditional guild form, centered on the master craftsman; they represent the beginning of modern trade unions in Germany.

An attack on the guilds was implicit in the two congresses of "workers" which were held during the summer of 1848 as well, the Journeymen's Congress in Frankfurt and the All-German Workers' Congress in Berlin. Both groups sought to organize all the workers in Germany, including all trades and all ranks within the various trades. Both included in their proposals measures which would change the traditional structure of the guilds. Free trade and the unregulated growth of the factory system were as abhorrent to the supporters of these two groups as to the members of the Frankfurt Artisans' Congress, but there was a greater attempt to adapt to the new techniques and a wider realization of their implications.

The workers' congresses differed from those discussed in the last chapter in another important respect. The masters of the Artisans' Congress had simply petitioned the Frankfurt Assembly for the enactment of the proposals which they considered necessary; and after drawing up their petition they disbanded, content for the time with the existing guilds. Indeed their whole program, even its more extreme elements such as the setting up of a social or industrial chamber which could legislate in economic matters, was based firmly on the guild system; also it was closely tied to the state—hence the reliance on the Frankfurt Assembly.

The workers' congresses, however, sought to set up separate organizations, organizations which were distinct from and often in opposition to the traditional guilds, organizations which would represent the workers as a special group, apart from the rest of society. They were based, however weakly, on a growing consciousness of the existence of a "working class." In this respect the workers' movement of 1848 marked a sharp break from the various journeymen's movements and isolated wage demands which had flourished spasmodically at least since the time of the first French revolution. The influence of the English industrial revolution and the influx of socialist thought had begun to be felt in the activities of the working class. The workers' congresses were in effect an attack on the guilds.

✻

The first National Assembly of Book Printers took place in the hall of the palace of the electoral prince at Mainz from the eleventh to the fourteenth of June, 1848. It was attended almost entirely by journeymen and ignored by the masters and printshop owners, who refused to recognize its legitimacy, to send delegates or to negotiate on the basis of the demands which were drawn up. The meeting was attended by 41 delegates, representing some 12,000 journeymen printers in 141 cities in Germany.[2]

[2] A list of delegates is given in *Beschlüsse der ersten National-Buchdrucker-Versammlung zu Mainz am 11., 12., 13. und 14. Juni 1848*, Flensburg, 1898, pp. 21ff. *Das Volk*, June 27, 1848, emphasized the fact that the Mainz Printers' Congress was an organization of *Gehülfe*, though nine or ten representatives of the masters were admitted as "observers"; see also Willi Krahl, *Der Verband der deutschen Buchdrucker, Fünfzig Jahre deutscher gewerkschaftlicher Arbeit mit einer Vorgeschichte*, Berlin, 1916, suppl. to vol. 1, pp. 3-10.

The delegates viewed the congress as being a direct result of the revolution and the spirit of the March Days, "so warm, so cordial, so stirring to the beating heart"; one delegate spoke of "the shadow of doubt [which] had disappeared before the sun of unity." [3] Like the other activities of the workers in 1848, the printers' congress was an attempt to realize the goals for which the revolution had been fought.[4]

The printers' congress issued three documents as a result of its deliberations: an address to the owners of the printing shops and establishments, an address to the National Assembly in Frankfurt and the basic statutes for the German National Bookprinters' Union. All three of these documents emphasized the growing feeling of isolation on the part of the workers in the printing industry. The journeymen hoped that the master printers and owners would join with them in seeking the fulfillment of their demands, that the National Assembly would aid them, but they felt that the only real hope was through their own organization and activity. Thus the principal proposals which the printers made were to be sought in a strike, scheduled to begin on the first of August in all parts of Germany.

In the address to the employers the printers identified their own needs with those of all the workers of Germany. They viewed themselves only as the "most intelligent of the working classes"; their own demands were

[3] *Beschlüsse der ersten National-Buchdrucker-Versammlung*, p. 6.

[4] It is, however, interesting to note that a proposal made for the congress before it actually met, that it adopt a resolution against the printing of anything that had been censored, was ignored; it was not to be found in the *Beschlüsse* of the congress. See *Das Volk*, June 6, 1848; Born, who presumably wrote the article in which this appeared, felt that such a resolution should be the first act of the congress. But the printers themselves were interested in more immediate and material concerns.

195

in fact the demands of all workers, the goals of the revolution: [5]

> Since the glorious days of the month of March, . . . the class which has been particularly oppressed in this century, the working class, has risen against the repression of capital; the just balance between capital and working power is the cry which resounds everywhere, in the north and the south, the east and the west of Germany. . . . It is not alone political freedom which the worker has had so painfully to do without; how much mightier is his cry for bread and shelter. It is a question not alone of his political existence but far more of his material existence.

The printers pointed to a number of abuses of the guild system and to the growing threat of machine printing. These evils, it was hoped, could be solved by joint action and the Mainz Congress called upon the employers to unite with the workers in seeking a remedy. August first was the deadline for such a solution. The hope that workers would be joined by the employers was, of course, in vain; that it should be expressed at all, and with apparent sincerity, is symptomatic of the lack of experience of the printers and the atmosphere of the months following the March Days. They were soon to learn better.

The same innocence can be found in the address to the National Assembly.[6] The Mainz Congress called attention to the changing conditions of the printing trade and the changed position of the masters within it: "We have seen the well-being of the masters increase from year to year . . . [while] our own future became ever

[5] *Beschlüsse der ersten National-Buchdrucker-Versammlung*, pp. 3-5.

[6] *Akten des volkswirtschaftlichen Ausschusses*, vol. 12; *Beschlüsse der ersten National-Buchdrucker-Versammlung*, pp. 7-13.

darker." Nonetheless the printers relied on the enforcement of guild regulations to stave off the impending disaster; they put great faith in the willingness of the Frankfurt Assembly to aid them in this. A ministry of labor elected by the workers and their masters, government control of working conditions and limitations on machines, government support for the guilds and for sickness funds for workers—these represented the workers' "share" of the newly won rights of the German people. Finally, the printers called upon the Frankfurt Assembly to recognize the competence of the working class to regulate its own conditions.

These general demands were followed by a list of specific conditions which the printers were seeking for their own trade. Work was to be limited to ten hours per day, with a prohibition against Sunday, holiday or night work except on exceptional occasions when such work was to receive higher pay. Wages were also to be fixed at a minimum level of 8 florins or 4 thaler, 17 neugroschen per week, except in cases where room and board were furnished, when wages were to begin at half the ordinary rate. Wages had to be paid at least once every two weeks in cash. The number of apprentices was to be limited and their period of apprenticeship fixed at five years. Such machines as were already in use could continue, but new machines were to be installed only when there was no danger of putting printers out of work. All these issues were to be under the jurisdiction of arbitration courts which were also to administer the examinations for the ranks of journeyman and master; the arbitration courts were to have seven members, of whom four would be journeymen and only three masters.

These were the terms on which the printers proposed to strike on the first of August, should they not receive the cooperation of their masters. In order to facilitate the strike and in order to form a more permanent organization, the Mainz Congress issued as its final act the statutes of the German National Bookprinters' Union which was set up at the congress. Once again there was an elaborate list of regulations for an organization whose possible existence was questionable. There were to be "head" associations in all towns with forty or more printers and "branch" associations in towns with fewer printers. The associations were to elect delegates to an annual conference of the National Union to be held at Whitsuntide; the conference in turn was to choose a twelve member national committee. Members of the Union would have to pay dues, attend all meetings, subject to fines, and work only under the conditions of wages and hours set forth by the National Union. There was to be a series of funds for various club purposes, for the sick, the invalid, the widows of printers. The National Union was to publish a newspaper called *Der Gutenberg.*[7]

*

In spite of the faults of the printers' congress, the vagueness of its proposals and the failure to draw clear lines of interest, the congress was hailed as a great success.[8] The Mainz Congress represented the first attempt on a national level of the workers to improve their own lot and to achieve demands which ran contrary to the interest of the employers.

[7] The organization of the printers in 1848 never got as far as proposed at Mainz; no "head" or "branch" associations were formed and the strike was carried out merely by a series of loosely organized *ad hoc* journeymen's committees, Krahl, *Verband der deutschen Buchdrucher,* suppl. to vol. 1, pp. 9-10.

[8] Born wrote in *Das Volk,* June 27, 1848: "The first association of German workers had succeeded and we have the bookprinters to thank for this. May this achievement serve as a glowing proof to all those who doubt the unity of the workers that a strong will and a sufficient power of action know how to make the seemingly impossible possible."

198

The lines of economic interest were drawn more clearly at the beginning of August when the printers went on strike for the program of the Mainz Congress and the recognition of the new National Bookprinters' Union. The strike was ultimately a failure; conditions had improved since April, labor was more easily obtained and the city governments less ready to force the employers into some sort of settlement for the sake of law and order. Nonetheless the nationwide strike of the printers remains a significant event, the first such strike in a single trade to occur in Germany.

Attempts at negotiations before the outbreak of the strike were all failures. A meeting in Leipzig in mid-July of printshop owners from many parts of Germany voted that "under no circumstances" would they negotiate on the basis of the Mainz demands. In Berlin an arbitration commission of "trusted men" was established; the owners were often willing to grant high wage demands provided all discussion took place "without reference to the Mainz demands." On this issue the negotiations foundered.[9]

The area of disagreement thus lay not in the actual wage demands, but in the recognition of the right to organize and the right to strike.[10] Once the strike had begun this became the only issue involved.[11] As Born

[9] *Berliner Zeitungs Halle,* July 2, 7, 15, 1848; *Deutsche Reichs-Zeitung,* July 22, 1848; *Neue Rheinische Zeitung,* July 21, 1848.

[10] Born wrote on the eve of the strike (*Das Volk,* July 29, 1848): "The great question which at this moment stirs the souls of all German printers is not so much the question of whether there will be a rise in wages or not as whether the workers, whether one class of society, has the right to order its affairs by itself. . . . It is time to begin a new organization on some other basis than that of free competition and this new basis is that of association."

[11] *Kölnische Zeitung,* Aug. 4, 1848. After all, the printers pointed out, they were only following the profit motive and they could scarcely be criticized by the capitalists for doing so. *Das Volk,* Aug. 2, 1848.

asserted in a broadside issued by the Committee of the Berlin Bookprinters on the tenth of August in an effort to present their case to the public and in particular to their fellow workers: [12]

No one can deny us the right to sell our working strength as expensively as possible, just as no one can forbid the capitalists to sell their wares at the best prices. . . . However we have not gone on strike for the sake of the few pennies which will accrue to us and which still cannot make our lot a happy one; we have gone on strike because our right to unite with our German brothers in common demands has been contested, because not one point has been accepted of the decisions taken by the Mainz Congress. . . .

We want to see whether or not we can maintain for ourselves the right of every citizen in the country to remain free to sell his wares at his own discretion or whether we workers are slaves who *must* take what anyone *wants* to give them for their work.

We want further to discover whether or not we workers can claim for ourselves the right of every citizen to join in association or whether we may be forced to compete singly against each other, mutually destroying each other.

In spite of the urgent issues which Born and others saw, the strike was not a success. *Das Volk* reported that, on the first day of the strike, work had completely ceased in the Berlin printing plants. But this seems to be an exaggeration and, whatever initial success was gained, was soon lost again as the strike wore on.[13] Most of the large papers were stopped at first, both the conservative

[12] *Plakate,* Ratsbibliothek, Berlin, portfolio 5.

[13] *Das Volk,* Aug. 2, 1848. Quarck states that only 400 printers, that is, some two thirds of the Berlin working force, came out on strike; *Erste deutsche Arbeiterbewegung,* p. 155.

Vossische Zeitung and *Neue Preussische Zeitung* and the radical *Berliner Zeitungs Halle,* but by the beginning of the second week of the strike the majority of them had found ways of appearing, if only in reduced form.[14] The strike dragged on throughout most of the month; though a few owners gave in to the Mainz demands, most resisted.[15]

The last of the strikers in Berlin finally returned to work on August 24; the journeymen agreed to join the masters in a joint "corporation." The revolt against the traditional organization of the printing trade had failed. Some one hundred printers were left without jobs when the strike was over. A committee of the Berlin printshop owners called upon the chief of police to charge the strikers with infringement of the provision against strikes in the industrial ordinance of 1845, claiming that the right of association did not cover such action.[16]

Elsewhere the strike was scarcely more effective. There were some local successes in Breslau, Munich, Freiburg and Weimar, but in the majority of places the strike failed, notably in Hamburg, where the printers remained out for seven weeks. Most important of all there was no strike in Leipzig, the center of the German printing trade. Many of the shop owners were able to buy off the printers with wage increases, avoiding any recognition, even in form, of the Mainz demands and the Printers' Union. Where violence did occur, as in the

[14] *Neue Rheinische Zeitung,* Aug. 7, 1848. The conservatives imported printers from out of town; the *Zeitungs Halle* was printed for a time in the printshop belonging to the Central Committee of Workers, so necessary did it seem to have a favorable newspaper out on the stands. *Berliner Zeitungs Halle,* Aug. 8, 1848; *Das Volk,* Aug. 9, 1848; Friedensburg, *Stephan Born,* p. 96.

[15] Declaration of the strike committee, Aug. 10, 1848, *Plakate,* Ratsbibliothek, Berlin, portfolio 5.

[16] *Kölnische Zeitung,* Aug. 20, 27, 1848; Quarck, *Erste deutsche Arbeiterbewegung,* p. 156.

attack on a printing plant in Erfurt on August 27, the military was soon called out to restore order.[17]

A second congress of the printers from most parts of Germany took place in Frankfurt on August 27-28, but the delegates were selected from the "corporations" of masters and journeymen, workers and shop owners. A leader of the Berlin strike, Spiegel, did show up, but he was allowed to attend only as an observer and that with much protest. The meeting elected a new central committee for the printers, headed by a journeyman, Karl Fröhlich, and the printers' paper, *Der Gutenberg*, continued to appear from Berlin. But the spirit of the printers had been tamed and the old master-journeyman relation restored. The printers drew away from the rest of the workers' movement, particularly from the section led by Stephan Born, himself a printer. There were no more strikes.[18]

The Mainz Congress and the printers' strike remain however one of the most important efforts of the workers of 1848 to achieve their demands; the right of association and the right to strike had been asserted, the need for organization was clear. Though the strike was a failure, as indeed was the entire workers' movement of that year as well as the revolutions themselves, the experience was not soon forgotten.

❋

In addition to the organizational efforts of the printers there were two further trade groups which held congresses during the summer of 1848 and attempted to form

[17] *Neue Rheinische Zeitung*, Sept. 2, 1848; Adler, *Geschichte der Arbeiterbewegung*, p. 192; Quarck, *Erste deutsche Arbeiterbewegung*, p. 138.

[18] *Berliner Zeitungs Halle*, Sept. 3, 1848; Adler, *Geschichte der Arbeiterbewegung*, p. 193.

nationwide unions. The first of these was the tailors', which met in Frankfurt from July 20 to July 25, at the same time as both the Artisans' and the Journeymen's congresses. The Tailors' Congress was attended by 89 delegates from 143 cities. Its proceedings and the addresses the tailors directed to the Artisans' Congress and the National Assembly reflected the fact that the tailors' trade was already affected by machine methods as well as by large-scale production and distribution and the growing number of ready-made clothes shops. There was not even any discussion of free trade; the president of the congress assumed all were against it. The tailors called for the elimination of clothing storehouses, the limitation of the right of finishing garments to hand tailors who had been trained by the tailors' guilds, the prohibition of tailoring work in prison and military establishments and the maintenance of the guild monopoly. They also requested state funds to aid poor tailors.[19]

The last of the trade groups to hold a congress was the cigar-making industry; the cigar makers met in Berlin in September 1848 and decided to set up a League of Cigar Workers throughout Germany.[20] The League was to include local and regional associations under a national president; the president would also issue a newspaper, *Concordia,* devoted to workers' affairs in general and the interests of the cigar makers in particular. The first

[19] *Akten des volkswirtschaftlichen Ausschusses,* vol. 21, i; Biermann, *Winkelblech,* vol. 2, pp. 119-121; Meusch, *Die Handwerkerbewegung,* pp. 54-55.

[20] *Concordia,* Mar. 10, Apr. 21, 28, 1849, gives an account of the proceedings of the congress. The dates given for the congress are September 25-29, 1848; Adler, *Geschichte der Arbeiterbewegung,* p. 194, and Quarck, *Erste deutsche Arbeiterbewegung,* p. 177, state that the cigar makers met at the same time as the All-German Workers' Congress, that is, at the end of August and the beginning of September, but they cite no evidence.

president was the Berlin cigar maker, Franz Wenzel Kohlweck.[21] The cigar makers called for the fixing of minimum wages and standard prices for cigars throughout Germany, for the standardization of the periods of apprenticeship and journeyman, for arbitration and a law against the employment of children.

The cigar industry was in many ways a difficult one to organize, for much of the production was still carried on in the houses of the cigar makers themselves. Nonetheless the demand for organization was widespread. The cigar makers of Heidelberg and Mannheim called for a national assembly of cigar makers at the same time that the group led by Kohlweck was meeting in Berlin.[22] This second congress never took place, for the southwest joined in the national organization and Kohlweck soon had over sixty cities represented in his group.

*

The cigar makers were eventually to be drawn into the movement for an organization which would embrace all workers throughout Germany. There were two congresses in the summer of 1848 which sought to set up such an organization.

The first meeting which claimed to represent and speak for all the workers, masters and journeymen, guild members and ordinary laborers, was that organized in Frankfurt at the end of July by the journeymen excluded from the Artisans' Congress by the master craftsmen. Though largely composed of delegates of the journeymen of the guilds of southwest Germany, the group came to call itself the "General German Workers' Con-

[21] Like Born and many of the other leaders of the workers in 1848, Kohlweck was a young man; he was born in 1822. Wermuth, Stieber, *Die Communisten-Verschwörungen*, vol. 2, p. 67.

[22] Walter Frisch, *Organisationsbestrebung der Arbeiter in der deutschen Tabakindustrie*, Leipzig, 1905, p. 11.

gress." The Journeymen's Congress is perhaps the most neglected of all the workers' meetings of the summer of 1848.[23] Yet it is in many ways the most typical and the most representative; it expressed the frustration and hopelessness of the less fortunate guild workers unmixed with the socialist doctrines which had been imported to Berlin by Stephan Born.

The Journeymen's Congress met in Frankfurt from July 20 to September 20, disbanding in the wake of the riots against the National Assembly itself. Its history falls into two periods; during the first few weeks it confined itself almost exclusively to the interests of the members of the guilds and to an attack on the proposals issued by the masters of the Artisans' Congress. Afterward the Journeymen's Congress occupied itself with the interests of the working class in a wider sense, attempting to adapt or modify the traditional guild organization to meet the needs of an increasingly large and unskilled body of workers. By the end of August and the beginning of September a far larger and more representative number of delegates had arrived and gave more justification to the claim of the journeymen to be a "general German workers" group. Even so the delegates to the congress remained heavily weighted toward the southwest of Germany.

[23] This neglect is partly due to the lack of sources. The proceedings of the congress were never published; however, its proposals were printed together with a brief account of the origins of the congress: *Entwurf zu den Vorlagen für den volkswirtschaftlichen Ausschuss bearbeitet von den Mitgliedern des hiesigen Gesellen-Congresses*, Frankfurt am Main, Aug. 3, 1848. The *Beschlüsse*, which were published at the end of the congress as well as a memorandum on the proposals of the Artisans' Congress, are quoted in full in Biermann, *Winkelblech*, vol. 2, pp. 441-474. Biermann gives a fairly full account of the Journeymen's Congress, though he is inclined to exaggerate the role played by Winkelblech (see, for example, pp. 271-272). Cf. also Goldschmidt, *Die deutsche Handwerkerbewegung*, pp. 45-48; Meusch *Die Handwerkerbewegung*, pp. 80-86.

The decision of the Artisans' Congress not to admit the journeymen delegates did not come as a surprise; even before the opening of the proceedings in the *Römer* there had been a general apprehension on the part of the journeymen that their interests would be ignored by the masters.[24] On the twentieth of July, after the Artisans' Congress had been in session a mere five days, it became clear that the masters would refuse to allow the journeymen to voice their interests or to vote for them, and the journeymen who had arrived as delegates formed a congress of their own. During this early stage of the journeymen's congress it was decided simply to appoint a committee of ten who would publish a supplement to the proposals of the Artisans' Congress. The report of this committee appeared on the third of August. At the same time the journeymen endorsed the social recommendations of the minority of the Artisans' Congress led by Winkelblech.[25]

Together with the report of the third of August the Journeymen's Congress issued a call for more delegates, who were to be elected by journeymen's and workers' associations throughout Germany. It was only at this point that the congress came to the decision that it should represent all workers and should change its name from the Journeymen's Congress to the General German Workers' Congress.[26] The decision to expand the congress

[24] See the letter in *Das Volk,* July 15, 1848, from the journeymen of Altona, who feared that the masters alone would return to a "dead, hollow form" of organization and called for a new "guild constitution, recognizing the equality of all producers and covering all professions."

[25] *Entwurf des hiesigen Gesellen-Congresses; Kölnische Zeitung,* July 25, 1848; *Akten des volkswirtschaftlichen Ausschusses,* vol. 21, i.

[26] The *Beschlüsse* which were published by the congress after it had disbanded on Sept. 20, 1848, attempted to give the impression that the unity of the workers and the journeymen had been realized all the time and that the congress from the beginning

to include all workers, both within and without the guilds, was taken partly in response to outside pressure. The committee of the Workers' Association of Frankfurt issued a letter "To the Workers' and Journeymen's Associations of Germany" on July 22, 1848, urging a more widely based assembly. The letter was published in August by Born, who announced that he had written to the Frankfurt group in hope that it would abandon its own plans and join the congress which had been summoned to Berlin to set up an all-German workers' organization.[27]

Thus the idea of forming a workers' organization separate from the guild system was introduced into the Frankfurt Workers' Congress only after the proceedings were under way. It arose from the search for an alternative to the old guilds.

The decisions of the Journeymen's Congress remained closely tied to the guild system; they constituted an attack on the guilds from within, seeking to substitute a greater degree of democratic control for the oligarchic rule of the masters and attempting in particular to raise the position of the journeymen. The decisions of the Journeymen's Congress may be divided into two parts: those which were in the main a reply to the proposals of the Artisans' Congress, and which included but went considerably beyond the "social" measures of the minority of the master artisans; and secondly those which dealt with the establishment of a general German workers' association.

The first of these groups of proposals was aimed at the

was a workers' organization; see Biermann, *Winkelblech*, vol. 2, p. 442. But the *Entwurf*, published on Aug. 3, suggests that this was not so, that the congress originally intended to confine itself to the interests of the guilds and the quarrels of the journeymen with the masters.

[27] *Das Volk*, Aug. 7, 1848.

Frankfurt Parliament. The journeymen stated in the introduction to their proposals that they too rejected as disastrous the experiments in free trade, but that a return to the guild system with all its restrictions and injustices and monopolies would be equally dangerous. Rather they had a number of modifications to make in the guild organization proposed by the masters which would put the journeymen on a level equal with the masters. The old guilds should be abolished and new ones set up covering all industries and fields of commerce, including factories. In addition to the official guilds, voluntary associations of journeymen and workmen should be permitted to forward specific class goals, deal with local conditions and set up funds to aid the needy among their number. These voluntary associations would also help finance the *Wanderjahre* of the journeymen. The journeymen also agreed in general with the need for courts of arbitration, local and national industrial councils and an industrial or "social" chamber in the national legislature, but they warned against the danger of too much centralization. They demanded that all such bodies, together with a national ministry of labor, represent by direct election the journeymen of the guilds as well as the masters.

On the operation of the guild system the Journeymen's Congress also had a number of points to make. Apprentices were to be at least fifteen years old, and not merely fourteen; the length of apprenticeship was to be between two and three years only. Journeymen were not to be required to travel, since many of them were married; they were to be considered as full members of the guilds with equal voting and committee rights with the masters. The restrictions on the practicing of more than one trade were to be enforced with even greater severity than envisaged by the masters. The twelve hour

208

day, including two meal breaks, was to be required by law and there were to be minimum wage standards. Journeymen were to be free to move and accept employment throughout the German Federation and even to take up work in factories.

Government aid was also expected. The state was to be responsible for the enforcement of all regulations, above all for the maintenance of equality between the journeymen and the masters in the guilds. In addition the government was to help the workers through the establishment of industrial halls to sell excess produce, the bulk purchasing of raw materials, and the establishment of people's banks in order to arrange loans to needy workers. There were also to be national funds for the sick, the old, the widowed and, more importantly, the unemployed. All forms of "involuntary poverty" were to be abolished. Of the new constitution being drawn up in Frankfurt the journeymen demanded equal and universal suffrage, state financed education both for children and adults, including trade and agricultural schools as well as an extension of the university system, the abolition of internal tariffs and external tariffs which would favor raw materials and block the importation of manufactured goods. The government of the new German state, and all the member states as well, would be required to cease production in state-owned factories and on state farms in order not to compete with the produce of guild members. But on the other hand, the government was to be encouraged to buy or build railways, canals and mines. There were to be progressive income and property taxes and a number of other measures such as premiums on certain exports and financial aid in the purchasing of land in America to help relieve the problem of overpopulation.

The proposals of the Journeymen's Congress were thus

the most comprehensive that had been made by any of the workers' groups in 1848. They went far beyond the modest measures of the Artisans' Congress, though they shared with this latter group the emphasis on the guild basis of organization. At the same time they embodied a large number of welfare measures which, if adopted, would have made the new German government the first example of the "welfare state."

Moreover the Journeymen's Congress went beyond its rival in Frankfurt by proposing an organization which would be devoted exclusively to the interests of the "working class." The decisions of the Journeymen's Congress hailed the right of free association as the "greatest achievement of the revolution" and called for the formation of an association to include all workers: [28]

> We have come to terms not only on the goals which must be achieved but on the means for their achievement and have recognized that both the defenders of free trade and the communists are on the wrong path. Only in a contemporary guild constitution, which is completely different from earlier ones and which is based on the rights of all citizens, that is, a constitution of federated guilds, is our remedy to be sought and found.

The slogan "federated guilds" was the work of Winkelblech and represented the core of a system which he was to elaborate at great length in the 1850s.[29] Winkelblech was on the committee appointed to draft the provisions of this section of the conclusions of the

[28] Biermann, *Winkelblech*, vol. 2, pp. 444-445.
[29] See Karl Marlo (pseudonym for Karl Georg Winkelblech), *Untersuchungen über die Organisation der Arbeit oder System der Weltökonomie*, 3 vols., Kassel, 1850-1859. Winkelblech's idea of federated guilds has certain similarities to the "guild socialism" of S. G. Hobson and G. D. H. Cole, though Winkelblech himself had no direct influence on the English movement.

congress along with the tailor Arnold and a mason, Ritter.[30] His influence however seems to have contributed little to the actual provisions for the new association.

Beyond the slogan, the plan for organization was similar to many drawn up in 1848; it was notable chiefly in that it tied itself to the guilds, in this case the voluntary guilds of workers and journeymen provided for in the proposals submitted to the Frankfurt Assembly. The federated guilds or associations were to investigate social conditions and to seek means of improving them; they were to further the education of the workers in general and their "spiritual development" in particular. The associations were to avoid politics and confine themselves to social and class interests. Membership was to be open to all over eighteen who adhered to the goals of "the elevation of the working classes and restoration of the middle class"; thus not only workers but artists, scholars, merchants and manufacturers were to be admitted.[31] There was to be a series of local and district clubs, with some twenty-six district centers designated to cover all of Germany. Over these was a central committee which would summon annual meetings and publish an association newspaper.[32] The first central committee was elected and consisted of two cabinet makers, Müller and Linke, and a printer, Franz.

The congress even adopted a flag as the banner of the new workers' movement: both the red of communism and the black-red-gold of German nationalism, which the congress associated with the monopolies of the old guilds, were rejected in favor of a green banner, decorated with an oak wreath, a rising sun, the clasped hands of brotherhood and the initials ADFV (*Allgemeine*

---

[30] Biermann, *Winkelblech*, vol. 2, p. 443.
[31] Biermann, *Winkelblech*, vol. 2, p. 449.
[32] As far as is known, the paper never appeared.

deutsche Föderalisten-Verein).[33] Thus equipped with the symbols if not the substance of organization, the congress disbanded.

✻

The journeymen of the Frankfurt Congress had refused the invitation from Born in Berlin to join the congress which had been called to meet in Berlin at the end of August. They did however send one of their number, Koch, to attend this congress, which marked the second major attempt in 1848 to form a workers' organization embracing all parts of Germany.

The demand for a congress in Berlin arose out of the failure of the Berlin Artisans' Congress in June, discussed in the last chapter. A number of the delegates regarded the congress as unsatisfactory, since it represented only a small portion of Germany and a small section of the working classes. Moreover the artisans had fought shy of any discussion of the "social question," confining themselves rather narrowly to the interests of the guilds. A committee was formed consisting of Friedrich Crüger of the Königsberg Workers' Union, C. Bühring of the Hamburg Workers' Union, F. E. Steinhauer of the Education Union for Workers in Hamburg, Ernst Krause, A. Lucht and Eichel of the Berlin Machine Builders, and Stephan Born of the Central Committee for Workers in Berlin. The committee issued on the twenty-sixth of June a "Summons to the Working Classes of Germany to a Workers' Parliament to be held in Berlin from the twentieth to the twenty-sixth of August." [34]

[33] Biermann, *Winkelblech*, vol. 2, p. 453.

[34] The "Summons" was published in *Das Volk*, June 27, 1848, in the *Berliner Zeitungs Halle*, June 29, 1848, and in the *Kölnische Zeitung*, July 1, 1848; it seems to have been more widely publicized than the announcements of most of the other workers' congresses. A letter was even sent to associations of workers abroad, in Switzerland, Paris, Brussels and London, calling on them to send delegates to the congress. None came, though

The Berlin Workers' Congress was, according to the "Summons," to make up for the deficiencies of the other "more or less" local congresses already held. The delegates were to be elected from "all cities, factories and agricultural districts" in Germany and were to form a "general workers' parliament" which would "have as its sole purpose the expression of the material interest of the working classes" and would aim at the adoption of "a social people's charter of Germany." The echo of the British Chartist movement was conscious, but the political demands of the Charter of Lovett and O'Connor found no place in the program outlined in the "Summons." Measures for consideration were to include the guarantee of work to all, state support for independent workers' associations, state care of the sick and helpless, public education, progressive income and inheritance taxes and the abolition of all sales taxes as well as feudal dues on agriculture, legal limits on hours of work and the establishment of ministers of labor (elected by the workers themselves) in all the German states. The summoning committee thus proposed a comprehensive survey of social legislation, backed by the organization of the working class. But by August there was a marked shift in emphasis.

The Berlin Workers' Congress did not actually get under way until the twenty-third of August, three days later than scheduled. The meetings took place in the premises of the Berlin Central Committee in the Sebastianstrasse and lasted till the third of September. The congress was attended by thirty-five delegates representing the central committees for workers in Berlin, Leipzig and Hamburg and twenty-six workers' associations in twenty-four other cities in addition to the

Weitling did make a brief appearance, claiming to represent the German workers of North America, as he had at the Frankfurt Artisans' Congress.

213

Frankfurt Journeymen's Congress. There were also five observers and nine other workers' clubs who wrote expressing their interest in the congress. The largest number of delegates came from Berlin; seven were elected by the Central Committee, two by the machine builders and one by the chairmakers. There were three delegates from Breslau and four from Hamburg, but the rest came from a widely scattered group of places. However, although there were delegates from Crefeld, Bielefeld and Munich as well as Koch from Frankfurt, the Rhineland and the southwest of Germany were poorly represented, while northeastern Germany held an easy majority of the delegates.[35] The hope of the organizers of the congress for a meeting which would represent all Germany was not fulfilled; the Berlin Congress remained as much a regional affair as those which met in Frankfurt.

By the time the Berlin Congress began, the failure of the printers' strike and the limited achievements of the Frankfurt congresses had modified the aims of the leaders of the Berlin group, forcing them away from too great a reliance on state action and into a greater concern for working-class self-help. Crüger, who had taken the initiative in summoning the congress, was ill.[36] The leadership fell to Born and the members of the Berlin Central Committee.

The official president of the Berlin Workers' Congress was Professor Nees von Esenbeck, a delegate from Breslau to the Prussian National Assembly and representative at the Workers' Congress of the Breslau Workers' Club. Nees von Esenbeck had expressed considerable interest in the cause of workers' organization during the summer of 1848, but he was discouraged by the

<hr />

[35] See the list of delegates in *Beschlüsse des Arbeiter-Kongresses zu Berlin, vom 23. August bis 3. September 1848*, Berlin, 1848, p. 26; also Quarck, *Erste deutsche Arbeiterbewegung*, p. 157; Adler, *Geschichte der Arbeiterbewegung*, p. 168.

[36] *Illustrierte Zeitung*, Oct. 7, 1848.

example of the Frankfurt congresses and regarded as unlikely the possibility of a truly representative workers' movement, unattached to the guilds.[37] Von Esenbeck failed to attend a number of the meetings, and Stephan Born, who was vice-president, took charge. The other officers of the congress were Bisky from Berlin and Schwenniger from Hamm, both of whom served as stenographers for the meetings, and Fellner, also from Berlin, who was secretary.

The Berlin Congress considered its task to be, in part, the correction of false impressions created by earlier workers' meetings; it announced in an address, "To the German Workers," published at the end of August that it had been called "in opposition to the Masters' Congress."[38] "For the masters," it was claimed, "the workers were in fact never considered as citizens but only as ciphers in the population lists."[39] The members of the

[37] See the letter from Nees von Esenbeck written on July 30, 1848, from Berlin to Eduard Lasker, publisher in 1848 of a newspaper, *Der Sozialist,* in Breslau and leader of the left wing of the National Liberals after 1871, quoted by Paul Wentzcke, "Bibliographische Beiträge zur Geschichte des deutschen Sozialismus in der Bewegung von 1848," *Archiv für die Geschichte der Sozialismus und der Arbeiterbewegung,* vol. 11 (1923), pp. 209-210. Von Esenbeck was a distinguished botanist, famous for his work with mushrooms and professor since 1830 at Breslau. Born in 1776, he was attracted late in life to radical causes. In 1845 he published a tract in favor of the emancipation of women and free love. He was to be deprived of his chair and pension in 1851, at the age of 75, on charges of "concubinage." The charges were probably false, but they give some idea of the man's vigor. He died in 1858. Biermann, *Winkelblech,* vol. 2, pp. 248-253.

[38] *Beschlüsse des Arbeiter-Kongresses zu Berlin,* p. 25. The address was also published in the *Berliner Zeitungs Halle,* Sept. 8, 1848, as "a sign that, no matter how split Germany may be, the workers of Germany are still united." The advertisement which the Berlin District Committee circulated on Sept. 7, 1848, for the sale of the *Beschlüsse* of the congress dealt mainly with the limitations of the Masters' Congress in Frankfurt. *Plakate,* Ratsbibliothek, Berlin, portfolio 5.

[39] From the manifesto of the congress to the Frankfurt Assembly, *Beschlüsse des Arbeiter-Kongresses zu Berlin,* p. 5.

congress were opposed to the restoration of unlimited powers to the guilds. Though there was a provision for the continuation of the guilds in the program drawn up in Berlin as a necessary buffer against undue competition, the guilds were not to dominate the economy and were to be subject to democratic control by both masters and journeymen.[40]

The provisions of the Berlin Congress were all written in terms of the "workers" in general with no special mention of different groups within the working class. One observer held this to be the great achievement of the Berlin Congress: [41]

> This resolute program ought to have the effect in particular of producing as pure a representation of workers as possible and of holding off the remains of the medieval ghost of caste, the defenders of the dying obligatory guilds who have swaggered at the Frankfurt Industrial Congress to the amusement of all enlightened workers.

The Berlin Workers' Congress differed on a number of points from the Frankfurt Journeymen's Congress as well. Guilds still formed the core of the system envisaged by the journeymen; their program was based on a reformed and expanded guild system which the Berlin group was unwilling to accept. There was also a marked disagreement at the first session of the Berlin Congress over the proposals of Koch, the delegate from the journeymen, who called for an endorsement of the demand of the Frankfurt congress for a regularly elected workers' parliament to meet along with the Frankfurt Assembly.[42] The Berlin Congress refused to be rushed into any decision and postponed discussion. In the end Koch's pro-

[40] *Beschlüsse des Arbeiter-Kongresses zu Berlin,* p. 16.
[41] *Illustrierte Zeitung,* Oct. 7, 1848.
[42] *Das Volk,* Aug. 26, 1848.

posal was by and large accepted, though with certain reservations, since the social parliament was to be elected by all workers and not just by guild and trade groups and was to meet together with the National Assembly.[43] But the congress refused to rely on the good will of the Frankfurt Parliament; the workers would also have to organize themselves.

The need for workers' organization and self-help was the chief concern of the Berlin Congress.[44] The largest section of the decisions of the congress was given to elaborating the statutes for the formation of such an organization.[45] The form of the organization, which was to be called the *Verbrüderung*, the "Brotherhood," was similar to that outlined in the statutes of the Berlin Central Committee for Workers in April. There were to be local committees which would attach themselves to the district committees located in twenty-six cities throughout Germany, including, incidently, two in Austria (Vienna and Linz), one in Bohemia (Prague) and one in Moravia (Brno).[46] The Berlin Central Committee was to become one of these district committees.[47] The district committees were to hold annual meetings and to elect delegates to an annual general assembly of the organization. All branches of the *Verbrüderung* were to be subject to majority rule.

The general assembly in turn was to elect a Central

[43] *Beschlüsse des Arbeiter-Kongresses zu Berlin,* pp. 20-21; *Illustrierte Zeitung,* Oct. 7, 1848.

[44] See Born's article in *Verbrüderung,* Jan. 2, 1849.

[45] *Beschlüsse des Arbeiter-Kongresses zu Berlin,* pp. 7-15; this should be compared to the relatively short space devoted to "*Hülfe des Staates,*" pp. 15-17.

[46] The committees were never established in the Austrian cities; the *Verbrüderung* was *klein-deutsch* by default.

[47] The Berlin Committee remained the most active of the district committees, though its functions were reduced in one respect at least: *Das Volk* ceased to appear after the issue of Aug. 29, 1848.

Committee of the *Verbrüderung*. The first Central Committee, chosen at the close of the Berlin Congress, included Georg Kick, the delegate for the Central Association for the Kingdom of Saxony in Leipzig, Franz Schwenniger, a surveyor from Essen who was the delegate for the Artisans' and Workers' Union in Hamm, and Stephan Born. The duties of the Central Committee were to look after the interests of the workers in general and, in particular, to seek to spread the organization and to publish a newspaper, to be called *Die Verbrüderung*. The committee was to reside in Leipzig.

The program of the Berlin Congress also called for a large number of self-help measures on the part of the workers. The workers' associations within the *Verbrüderung* were to set up employment bureaus to find work for the unemployed and to settle disputes; they were to establish credit banks and funds for the sick and needy among them. Also the associations, both the local groups and the national organization, were to acquire land and housing and to run cooperatives for producers and consumers. In this program for self-help and cooperative enterprise, the Berlin Congress and the *Verbrüderung* pioneered in Germany.

The Berlin Congress also adopted an address to the National Assembly, though this formed a less important part of their program than did the addresses of the two congresses in Frankfurt and indeed those adopted by almost every other workers' group, large or small, that met in 1848. The delegates in Berlin contented themselves with an expression of their loyalty: "We, the workers, are by nature the supporters of quiet and order. . . . We extend our hands to our fellow citizens and the makers of our laws." [48] The demands of help from the state were kept to a minimum. The congress called for

[48] *Beschlüsse des Arbeiter-Kongresses zu Berlin,* p. 6.

universal manhood suffrage and condemned in particular the franchise laws of Bavaria, Saxony and Mecklenburg, which specifically excluded workers. The delegates devoted a whole section of their conclusions to the outline of a system of universal public education, including industrial schools for adults. They also called for the equal liability of all for taxes. There were a number of other provisions—lien laws to protect the workers, progressive income tax and the abolition of indirect taxes and internal tariffs, free entry of raw materials, the ten hour day, the abolition of prison production and house-to-house trading, the extension of the time limit on patent rights, as well as a social parliament elected by the workers. But the Berlin Congress did not set great store by these demands; many were sceptical of their realization.

The chief demand which the Berlin Congress made of the Frankfurt Assembly was that it should recognize the legality of the workers' associations. Beyond this it was hoped that the workers could help themselves.

A case in point was the regulation of the guilds. Here the proposals of the Berlin Congress were much more modest than any hitherto discussed. Guilds were admitted to be necessary to protect certain industries from undue competition, and, where this was the case, state control of tests was necessary. But there was no question of widening the guild system to include all workers and all trades. Many of the Berlin group agreed with the provisions of the Frankfurt Journeymen's Congress, particularly those which gave the journeymen a voice equal to the masters' in the management of the guild. Some members of the congresses at least proposed major modifications of the guild system even in those areas where it existed. Seven delegates voted both against the master's examination, since they thought it made the

219

Meisterrecht a monopoly, and against the limitation of the number of apprentices; such leading figures in the congress as Born, Bisky, Schwenniger and Kick were among this minority.[49]

The decisions of the Berlin Congress were in many ways similar to those of the journeymen in Frankfurt; both were the product of artisans and handicraft workers and did little to reflect the needs of the mass of unskilled labor, of the growing "proletariat." The Berlin Congress, partly from the influence of Born and the more industrialized condition of Berlin, did indeed claim to speak for the "workers" as a whole and sought to organize all groups in the working class, but the *Verbrüderung* which it set up remained largely confined to the skilled workers and eventually amalgamated with the southwest German organization which had been founded by Winkelblech and others at the Frankfurt Journeymen's Congress.

The handicraft character of the Berlin Congress can be seen from the description of the public meeting which was called on September third at the close of the congress.[50] A crowd of some seven thousand or eight thousand turned out to celebrate the occasion. There were several speeches, all in "the happiest and most inspired mood," dealing with the "brotherly unity" and "togetherness" (*Gemeinsamkeit*) of the working classes. And there were indeed a few factory workers there, mostly the elite of the machine-building groups. But the scene was dominated by the processions of the skilled trades, each headed by the banner or flag of its craft. None of the flags, according to the report, was a red one.

[49] *Beschlüsse des Arbeiter-Kongresses zu Berlin,* p. 20.
[50] *Illustrierte Zeitung,* Oct. 7, 1848.

CHAPTER 9

THE FRANKFURT ASSEMBLY
AND THE WORKERS' DEMANDS

THE GERMAN WORKERS looked to the Frankfurt Assembly as well as to their own congresses for a solution to the problems with which they were confronted in 1848.

Just as the bourgeois leaders of the revolution hoped to set up in Frankfurt a government which would fulfill the requirements of the national and liberal demands, so the mass of artisans and handicraftsmen there sought redress for the wrongs of the economic system and the establishment of a legal fortress from which they could fight off the onslaught of competition and the assault of the factory system on the handicraft trades. The petition which came from the artisans of Crefeld on June 9, 1848, was typical in its fears, its hope and its reliance on the National Assembly of the memorials drawn up by the workers throughout Germany: [1]

> Exalted Assembly! The undersigned 193 artisans, citizens of Crefeld (Rhine Province), have arrived at the sad conviction that without any blame of their own their class is daily in a worse condition. They ascribe this not only to temporarily unfavorable events but chiefly to the laws of the state and indeed in particular to unlimited freedom of trade as well as inadequate protection of German products against foreign competition. Convinced that the Exalted Assembly will regard it as one of its deserving tasks to act against the increasing impoverishment of the artisan class, which was once without doubt a stalwart

[1] *Akten des volkswirtschaftlichen Ausschusses,* vol. 17.

mainstay of the state and can still be an adequate protection, the undersigned venture to present to the Exalted Assembly the following as the points which appear most significant. . . .

The Crefeld craftsmen then listed a series of measures, the enforcement of guild regulations, the provision of financial aid, the maintenance of protective tariffs—variations on the proposals which were to be discussed by the workers' congresses. The petition was like many others both in its content and its form; its language was at once awkward and overwritten, its mood both truculent and sycophantic.[2]

Such petitions were the most common expression of the demands of the workers in 1848. They were sent to Frankfurt not only from the congresses but from local guilds and workers' meetings held in cities, towns and villages throughout Germany. There was a certain naïveté about them, a sense of self-importance, a self-centered approach toward economic problems and the function of the new government. The chief concern of the Frankfurt Assembly, it was assumed, should be the affairs of the guildsmen of Crefeld or Eschwege or Schmalkalden. The petitions and proposals were, in Schmoller's words, "amazing products of shortsightedness,"[3] yet they expressed better than anything else the goals for which the artisans had joined the revolution.

The real puzzle is why the workers thought there was any hope of achieving their goals from the Frankfurt Assembly, that much maligned "parliament of profes-

[2] Biermann, *Winkelblech*, vol. 2, p. 82, comments on the "kleinbürgerliche Stil," highblown, verbose and exaggerated, in which most of the pamphlets and petitions of the artisans' movement were written.

[3] *Geschichte der deutschen Kleingewerbe*, p. 85; cf. Mommsen, *Grösse und Versagen*, p. 157.

sors" whose narrow middle-class basis and general im-
competence seemed obvious to such disparate observers
as Marx and Bismarck.

The present chapter will seek a solution to this puzzle,
endeavoring to trace the relation between the workers
and the Frankfurt Assembly during the summer months
of 1848, from the opening of the Assembly in May to the
workers' riots which followed the acceptance of the
Truce of Malmoe in mid-September, and to analyze the
demands which were submitted by the workers to the
Assembly in petition after petition throughout 1848. It
will also seek in part the answer to a larger question
about the revolutions: why did the German people greet
the National Assembly of 1848 like "a Goddess of
Liberty," only to let it perish a year later, in the famous
phrase of the Spanish diplomat, Donoso Cortes, "like a
prostitute in a tavern"?

*

The 330 delegates who gathered in Frankfurt on
May 18, 1848, for the opening ceremonies of the National
Assembly, proceeding amid a flurry of black-red-gold
banners from the Emperor's Hall in the *Römer* across
the Römerberg and through the Neue Krämer to the
north door of the *Paulskirche,* were representative almost exclusively of the middle class. Though the number of delegates increased (an average of 400 to 500
were present at any given time and a total of 831 were
listed during the whole course of the Assembly), the
class composition remained the same. This narrow representation was, of course, hardly surprising in view of
the limited franchise under which the parliament was
elected, though few perhaps expected the results of the
elections to be quite so extreme.

Four master artisans and one peasant were the only representatives of the lower orders in the *Paulskirche*; there were no workers.[4]

The members of the Frankfurt Assembly were not however the impractical intellectuals they have often been depicted as being. Its familiar title, "the parliament of professors," is inaccurate, fostered by its enemies to the right and left.[5] Recent studies have pointed out that though the majority of the members were recruited from the *akademische Mittelstand*, the educated middle classes, the actual number of professors and teachers was fairly small.[6] While it is true that the majority of the delegates had been to university or some sort of *Hochschule*, this scarcely qualifies them for the adjective "intellectual." Rather the parliament represented men of affairs; judges, lawyers and civil servants were the most typical among the professions represented, accounting for some 370 of the members. There were also 140 engaged in economic activity of some sort, including 60 gentlemen farmers and over 50 in trade and industry.[7]

[4] The peasant Minkus from Silesia was a remarkable person, scarcely typical of his class; the artisans, alas, were. Valentin, *Geschichte der deutschen Revolution,* vol. 2, p. 11. The class composition of the Frankfurt Assembly was not lost upon the workers of the time. See *Das Volk,* July 22, 1848, which published a table showing the class origins of the delegates. A number of petitions to the Frankfurt Assembly regretted its narrow class composition and the absence of artisans and workers; for example, the petition of the tradesmen of Fulda in Electoral Hesse, *Akten des volkswirtschaftlichen Ausschusses,* vol. 12.

[5] But the title has been accepted by a number of its friends as well; Valentin claims that some 569 of its members were "*Akademiker,*" which is at the least misleading, and the same figure is repeated by Koppel Pinson who concludes that the delegates were "primarily theoreticians rather than practical politicians." Valentin, *Geschichte der deutschen Revolution,* vol. 2, p. 12; Pinson, *Modern Germany,* pp. 95-96.

[6] There were some 50 professors and 60 school teachers.

[7] See Stadelmann, *Soziale und politische Geschichte,* pp. 117-118; Gerhard Schilfert, *Sieg und Niederlage des demokratischen*

The Frankfurt Assembly was not, as it has often been characterized, an abnormality; it was in its composition a typical product of *Biedermeier* Germany; as such it bore considerable resemblance to other parliaments of the time.[8]

The task of the delegates to Frankfurt was to form a government for a new Germany. In attempting this they made a number of mistakes, including the ultimate one of failure. Few of the delegates had experience in parliamentary methods; but then no one could have had such experience in the Germany of 1848. All delegates placed great emphasis on legal form, as, one should note, did the workers' movement with its endless statutes and proposals for economic legislation. But the task of a constitutional convention is to draw up a constitution. The delegates were interested primarily and rightly in political issues, and this was as true of those on the democratic left as of the body of delegates.[9] Yet the economic problems of the new Germany were not ignored.[10]

*

Wahlrechts in der deutschen Revolution 1848/49, Berlin, 1952, pp. 402-405; Karl Demeter, "Die Soziale Schichtung des deutschen Parlamentes seit 1848: Ein Spiegelbild der Strukturwandlung des Volkes," *Vierteljahreschrift für Sozial- und Wirtschaftsgeschichte*, vol. 39 (1952), pp. 6-22; Hamerow, *Restoration, Revolution, Reaction*, pp. 124-125.

[8] The charge of Marx and Engels, that the Frankfurt Parliament was "a body so abnormal . . . that history will, most likely, never afford a pendant to it," would appear to be wishful thinking. *Revolution and Counter-Revolution*, p. 52.

[9] A Democratic Congress was held in Frankfurt in June and a Democratic Central Committee was set up, but the Congress failed to deal with any economic or social issues. (*Kölnische Zeitung*, June 14, 1848.) The composition of the "left" in the Assembly was not markedly different from the composition of the body as a whole. Schilfert, *Sieg und Niederlage*, p. 406.

[10] Nineteenth century German liberals were in general far more concerned with social problems, and their solutions were far more subtle, than was once thought: see Donald G. Rohr, *The Origins of Social Liberalism in Germany*, Chicago, 1963.

The task of considering the petitions which the workers of Germany drew up laboriously in meeting after meeting and wrote out in careful, neat handwriting fell largely to the Economic Committee of the Frankfurt Assembly, or more exactly, the Committee for the Relations of Workers, Industry and Trade.

The formation of an economic committee was first proposed as early as the second session of the Frankfurt Parliament, that is, on May 19, 1848. The original proposal was for a commission of fifteen members which would "in an appropriate fashion, namely through the mediation of the officials concerned, the examination of witnesses, etc., collect information about the conditions of industry and work in Germany." [11] On the recommendation of the president of the Assembly, von Gagern, the proposal was provisionally accepted. When it was discussed again, however, on the twenty-fourth of May, the scheme was expanded to a committee of thirty members who were to "make the question of the working class and everything in connection with it, namely, the proposals in relation to the conditions of trade and industry, the subject of their expert opinion and their proposals to the National Assembly." [12] Only two other committees were considered of equal importance and were discussed at the time: the Committee for the Planning of the Constitution and the Committee for Priority Questions. All other committees were to wait upon full organization of the Assembly. [13]

The importance which the members of the Frankfurt

[11] *Stenographischer Bericht über die Verhandlungen der deutschen constituirenden Nationalversammlung zu Frankfurt am Main*, ed. Franz Wigard, Frankfurt am Main, 1848-1849, vol. 1, pp. 27-28.

[12] *Stenographischer Bericht*, vol. 1, p. 71.

[13] There were eventually some 25 committees appointed by the Assembly. *Verzeichnisse der Abgeorgneten der Frankfurter National Versammlung*, Frankfurt am Main, 1848-1849.

Assembly did in fact attach to economic questions and to the work of the Economic Committee emerged from the debates on these proposals. There was no opposition to such a committee, merely some question as to its scope. But its immediate necessity was granted by all. One delegate saw the task of the National Assembly as being threefold: "We have to face current events. . . . Secondly we must make a constitution for all Germany and thirdly [we must] solve the social question." [14] The appointment of the three proposed committees would take care of all three tasks. Another delegate pointed to the immense influx of petitions which represented the chief popular support of the Assembly. "When we survey them, however," he commented, "then we find that they deal in essence with only two questions: with the constitutional task and with the social pacification of the fatherland." The proposed committee was accepted without a roll-call vote.

The attitude of the Frankfurt Assembly toward economic problems can also be seen in the speech with which Friedrich von Rönne, the chairman of the Economic Committee, presented the first report of the committee to the Assembly on the third of June: [15]

Recent times have brought us much that is great and magnificent, but they have also demanded sacrifices. Trade and industry are crippled and thousands of hands, eager for work, are now unemployed. Relief may be expected only from the establishment of trust. . . . It is up to us, however, to contribute to the establishment of trust with all our powers. . . . The people have sent us here in order to erect a new political building; but this building ought to be founded

[14] *Stenographischer Bericht,* vol. 1, pp. 69-70.
[15] *Stenographischer Bericht,* vol. 1, p. 195.

on the solid ground of improved material and social conditions.

It was, in von Rönne's opinion, the duty of the National Assembly to enable the German nation to reap the fruits of the revolution, to provide the people with law and order, active industry, "above all, remunerative work." This the Frankfurt Assembly could do by promoting national unity and security, internal free trade and the attraction of capital. "The solid ground of improved material and social conditions" was considered by most of the delegates to be as integral a part of the task of the National Assembly as was the erection of a super-structure of basic rights and the national constitution upon it.

The thirty members of the Economic Committee who were elected on the twenty-fifth of May and the various replacements who entered the committee after resignations during the course of the Frankfurt Parliament reflected the composition of the Assembly as a whole, though with a greater emphasis on trade and commerce. Of the thirty-eight delegates who served at one time or another on the Economic Committee, twelve were directly involved in commerce or manufacturing, eight were in government or the civil service, six in law and three were estate owners. There were six professors or teachers on the Economic Committee, but many of these had a special interest in the work of the committee, just as a number of the lawyers and civil servants had specialized in commercial law and administration. Wilhelm Stahl from Erlangen, for example, was a professor of law interested in economics, while Moritz Mohl, a public accountant from Stuttgart, held a doctorate in political science and wrote widely on economic matters. Professor Bruno Hildebrand from Marburg had been to England to study the development of the Industrial

Revolution there, and Hlubek from Graz was a professor of agriculture. In geographical origin they corresponded almost exactly to the distribution in the larger body: ten came from Prussia, six from Austria, five from Bavaria and the rest were divided among the smaller states.[16]

The members of the committee also seem to have been spread fairly evenly among the various party factions. A good solid group of the more influential members belonged to the right-center, Adolf Lette, Carl Mathy and Gustav Mevissen among them.[17] But others, Bruno Hildebrand, Johannes Fallati and Hermann, were members of the *Würtemberger Hof* or the other groups on the left-center and Moritz Mohl, Carl Degenkolb and the Saxon factory owner Bernhard Eisenstuck were regarded as members of the left. For every advocate of free trade on the committee, such as the Hamburg merchant Ernst Merk, there were several who followed the lead of Hildebrand and Eisenstuck in endeavoring to find some way of protecting the interests of the workers from the ravages of competition. It is a mistake to regard the Economic Committee as an instrument of the right, the tool of "capitalists" and free traders.[18]

[16] The figures are compiled from the various editions of the *Verzeichnisse der Abgeordneten* and from the *Wohnungsliste der Mitglieder der constituirenden Nationalversammlung*, Frankfurt am Main, 1848. Valentin says mistakenly that "nearly half" the members of the Economic Committee were professors. *Geschichte der deutschen Revolution*, vol. 2, p. 318. There is a useful list of "Abgeordnete und Beobachter" with biographical and bibliographical information compiled by Wolfgang Klötzer in Paul Wentzcke, *Ideale und Irrtümer des ersten deutschen Parlaments* (*1848-1849*), Heidelberg, 1959, pp. 275-307.

[17] All three were members of the "Casino" faction which is usually ranked on the right. Mathy and Mevissen have also been called "social liberals" on account of their interest in social and economic problems: see Rohr, *Origins of Social Liberalism*, pp. 117-118, 139-147.

[18] Quarck, *Erste deutsche Arbeiterbewegung*, p. 246.

Indeed, the fault which a number of later historians, among them Veit Valentin, have attributed to the Economic Committee is that of overactivity, of trying to do too much. The committee was indeed one of the most active and diligent among the various subdivisions of the National Assembly. It held frequent meetings, collected information, even started a library of books on economic issues [19] and presented an imposing number of bills and amendments to the National Assembly. Yet, it is charged, the committee overplayed its role. It attempted to become a sort of special parliament on its own, designed to deal with social and economic issues; it felt itself in competition with the constitutional committee and wanted to solve all the problems of the new Germany through economic means. The Economic Committee, Valentin argues, suffered "from the widest spread sickness of the time, the feeling of sovereignty"; it was a distraction from the main tasks of the National Assembly.[20]

But this attack on the Economic Committee is as misplaced as the charges of the left wing; it ignores the real need for economic legislation and the insistent demands of the workers and artisans who had made the revolution. The failure of the Economic Committee, like the failure of the Frankfurt Assembly itself, was due to a more complex series of causes.

*

The officers of the Economic Committee, elected at its first meeting, were Friedrich von Rönne (Berlin),

[19] Merk gave the committee his collection of books on trade and industry at the beginning of the committee's sessions, and this gift formed the nucleus of the library. *Akten des volkswirtschaftlichen Ausschusses,* vol. 10.

[20] Valentin, *Geschichte der deutschen Revolution,* vol. 2, pp. 15, 317-318.

first president; Karl von Bruck (Trieste), second president; Bernhard Eisenstuck (Chemnitz), secretary.[21] In October, when von Rönne resigned the chairmanship in order to become the first ambassador of the new central government to the United States, Eisenstuck moved up to the office of first president.[22]

In its early meetings the Economic Committee debated the scope of its own competence; its work, the members believed, should include all aspects of the government's relation to economic matters, both proposed or possible legislation and the rules and practices governing the administration of the central government. The committee divided into seven subcommittees to deal with the various areas of economic legislation: Agriculture and Forestry; Industry and Mining; Trade, Shipping and Tariffs; Internal Communications, Postal Services, Railways, Canals and Tolls; Money, Credit and Banking; Currency, Measures and Weights; and finally General Workers' Conditions and Emigration, which included questions of rights of residence and the freedom of movement within Germany. This last committee, the seventh subcommittee of the Economic Committee, was the one which concerned itself with workers' affairs most directly; it was also, under the chairmanship of Professor Bruno Hildebrand, the largest subcommittee, with fifteen members as opposed to an average of six or seven members on the other subcommittees. Finally the larger questions of the elaboration of an industrial ordinance for all Germany, which would include regulations about the freedom of trade and the guild system, were reserved for the whole committee.[23] On the third of June the

21 *Stenographischer Bericht*, vol. 1, p. 195.
22 *Stenographischer Bericht*, vol. 4, p. 2617.
23 *Akten des volkswirtschaftlichen Ausschusses*, vol. 10. This volume contains the minutes of the proceedings of the Economic Committee; the subcommittees were set up at the second session on May 26, 1848.

National Assembly granted the Economic Committee the right to call witnesses and collect information from officials.[24]

There was initially some discussion as to whether the sessions of the Economic Committee should be held in public or private. Bally, a delegate from Silesia, argued that the hearings of the committee should be held before all who wished to attend, serving as a sounding board for public opinion and a means of publicizing the interest which the Assembly took in the lower classes. Bally and his supporters hoped thus to undermine the activities of the agitators operating among the workers. The proposal was rejected both by the members of the committee itself on the grounds that their work was far better done in private and only the results made known through the legislation proposed to the National Assembly, and by the Assembly, which defeated the measure with a large majority on the thirteenth of July.[25]

The rejection of public meetings was perhaps the first mistake of the Economic Committee, the first departure from the demands of the workers for a forum in which their wrongs could be heard and their needs met. Up to that point it appeared that the Economic Committee and the Frankfurt Assembly might form the basis for the solution for which the workers had been hoping. After that, disillusion began to set in.

The disillusionment of the workers was gradual; it occurred throughout 1848 and was not complete till 1849. Nor was it the result of any conscious policy on the part of the members of the Frankfurt Assembly; it

[24] *Stenographischer Bericht,* vol. 1, p. 196.

[25] *Akten des volkswirtschaftlichen Ausschusses,* vol. 2, report of von Hermann on Bally's proposals, presented to the Economic Committee on July 17, 1848; *Stenographischer Bericht,* vol. 2, pp. 999-1001.

stemmed rather from a continual failure of communication between the two groups.

This may be seen from the story of the relations of the Economic Committee to the various workers' congresses, particularly those which met in Frankfurt during the summer of 1848. The Frankfurt Assembly was cordial enough to the workers' congresses; von Gagern received Martin May, and the delegation from the Artisans' Congress and the members of the Economic Committee dined with the Frankfurt Artisans' Club and the Artisans' Congress. But the Economic Committee was unwilling to go much further than this. The committee received the petition of the Artisans' Congress with interest, and one member, Lette, even suggested that the committee should send a delegation to the congress to observe and report on its proceedings; but even Lette admitted that the Economic Committee must maintain its independence and impartiality and that the *Geschäftsordnung* prohibited any further contact.[26]

In the end it was decided that the Artisans' Congress should be allowed to send a delegation to a session of the Economic Committee.[27] The visit of the delegation from this congress took place on the fifth of August; it was received with a friendly address by the chairman of the committee, von Rönne, who was however careful to point out that the two groups did in fact have different "spheres" of competence and interest. The artisans, in turn, expressed their unanimous opposition to freedom of trade. There followed a close discussion of the details of the program of the Artisans' Congress with the members of the Economic Committee asking questions about guild regulations, the plan for industrial councils and an

[26] *Akten des volkswirtschaftlichen Ausschusses,* vol. 10, minutes for the session of July 20, 1848.
[27] *Kölnishche Zeitung,* Aug. 2, 1848.

industrial chamber. The meeting between the two groups was inconclusive and was not repeated.[28]

The Artisans' Congress closed in the conviction that the Economic Committee and the Frankfurt Assembly would fulfill its program. The president of the congress, Martin May, declared in his final speech that "the Exalted Assembly which, summoned through the trust of the German people, is now occupied with the foundation of their rights and freedoms cannot reject the unanimous demands of the German artisan class which we are about to present to them. In this firm conviction I conclude this congress." [29] May's assumption of unanimity on the part of the artisans was certainly mistaken; his confidence in the Frankfurt Assembly was probably misplaced.

The Economic Committee also received the petitions of the Journeymen's Congress and issued a similar invitation for the congress members to visit a session of the Economic Committee. At one time it was thought possible to have delegates from the two congresses to a single session, but it was decided for reasons of tact to arrange separate meetings with the two groups.[30] One member of the committee, the young manufacturer from Kassel, Philip Schwarzenberg, acted as the special spokesman for the demands of the Journeymen's Congress and the minority of the Artisans' Congress.[31] In general the Economic Committee encouraged the jour-

[28] *Akten des volkswirtschaftlichen Ausschusses,* vol. 10, minutes for the session of Aug. 5, 1848.

[29] Quoted by Biermann, *Winkelblech,* vol. 2, p. 110.

[30] *Akten des volkswirtschaftlichen Ausschusses,* vol. 10, minutes for the session of Aug. 4, 1848. As far as can be seen from the minutes of the Economic Committee, the journeymen, unlike the masters, never took up the invitation.

[31] *Akten des volkswirtschaftlichen Ausschusses,* vol. 21, i; the petitions were presented directly to the Economic Committee by Schwarzenberg.

neymen to present their own view and to argue the case against the masters' demands.[32]

The Economic Committee made an attempt to represent no single interest but to balance the demands of the various groups throughout Germany. Hence the members could not show too great partiality to any one of the workers' congresses.

Moreover the committee had another source of knowledge of the opinions and demands of the workers, the petitions which were sent to Frankfurt from all parts of the German Federation. During the course of the Frankfurt Assembly, from May 1848 to June 1849, 9,319 petitions were submitted, according to the running catalogue which was printed in the proceedings of the Assembly.[33] Of these approximately one fifth (1,831) dealt with economic conditions. But a number of other petitions were sent directly to the Economic Committee or to individual members, so that the total number of petitions on economic matters must have been considerably higher. When a member of the committee, Moritz Veit, drew up a report of the petitions dealing with workers' affairs and proposals for an industrial ordinance in the autumn of 1848, the Economic Committee had already received over two thousand petitions from various sources.[34] Though the influx of petitions on economic subjects undoubtedly tapered off during the autumn and winter—

[32] Valentin holds the Economic Committee in part responsible for the decision of the journeymen to hold a separate congress. *Frankfurt am Main*, p. 305.

[33] The last entry is for June 16, 1849. *Stenographischer Bericht*, vol. 9, p. 6886.

[34] Veit's report was presented to the committee at the beginning of December, *Akten des volkswirtschaftlichen Ausschusses*, vol. 10, minutes for the session of Dec. 8, 1848. The report, in a somewhat revised version, was included with the draft proposals for an industrial ordinance submitted to the National Assembly on Feb. 26, 1849, *Akten des volkswirtschaftlichen Ausschusses*, vol. 2.

indeed the majority was submitted during the summer months of 1848—the fact remains that the National Assembly and the Economic Committee received a very large number indeed of these documents of the workers' movement.

The petitions varied greatly in form and character. Some were printed; most were copied out laboriously by hand. Some represented a series of demands worked out by the local artisans while others contained merely a short introduction followed by a copy of the proposals of one or the other of the various workers' congresses. The signatures ranged from elegant scrolls to illegible scrawls and the halting marks of those unused to writing. Some were signed by the few leading artisans in a village or district; others showed signs of having gone the rounds of family groups. Still others were signed by larger numbers; several hundred names were not uncommon and some were supported by considerably higher figures. Thirteen thousand signers were claimed for a petition from Saxony, and another from Saxony and Württemberg "concerning the protection and promotion of national work, submitted to Frankfurt am Main by the committee of the All-German Association for the Protection of National Work," was signed by 120,502 workers, representing with their families a group of 602,510 persons.[35]

Veit, in his report, considered a sampling of 545 petitions which had been submitted to the Economic Committee during the summer of 1848 on the subject of trade freedom and the regulation of work. By far the largest group of these came from Prussia; Bavaria accounted for another 103, Saxony for 52 and Hanover for 59. The rest were divided among the smaller states,

[35] *Stenographischer Bericht*, vol. 8, p. 5704; *Akten des volkswirtschaftlichen Ausschusses*, vol. 2, Veit's report.

with some of the smallest submitting quite sizable numbers. Of these 22 came from Mecklenberg-Schwerin and 18 from Schleswig-Holstein. Austria on the other hand submitted only 9 petitions on workers' conditions and the regulation of work.

Veit divided the petitions into a number of different categories; there were 131 petitions in opposition to free trade and 54, mainly from the Berlin Palatinate, in its favor. But a number of the other categories overlapped with the opposition to freedom of trade—those calling for an industrial ordinance for example—so that the impression is that of almost universal opposition to the removal of all restrictions to the practising of the various trades. The second largest group of petitions was that in favor of the proposals of the Artisans' Congress; these numbered 102 as opposed to a bare 2 against the masters' demands noted by Veit.[36] It was on the basis of these figures that Veit summarized the demands of the workers.

The attitude with which Veit approached the petitions and the demands of the artisans was stated in the first paragraph of his report. Since it is typical of the approach of the Economic Committee as a whole (the report was endorsed by the committee) and indeed of the Frankfurt Parliament, it is worth quoting in full: [37]

The political movement of the March Days is so closely connected with the social grievances which have so long checked unnaturally the drive toward organic unification, peculiar to the German, that we have seen, already in the first days after the revolution, the tradesmen coming together in the larger cities of

[36] The petitions are summarized statistically on pp. 1-17 of Veit's report, *Akten des volkswirtschaftlichen Ausschusses*, vol. 2.
[37] Veit's report, p. 17, *Akten des volkswirtschaftlichen Ausschusses*, vol. 2.

the Fatherland in order to deliberate about their common interests. The warm breeze of freedom, which, in those parts of the country where the guild constitution had remained intact, had begun already to melt its rigid forms, awoke in the areas of trade freedom the memory of the old associative circles in which the German burgher class had grown great and had come to honor. At the same time it was felt with remarkable uniformity that unlimited freedom of trade corresponded to the republic just as the old guild system did to absolutism and that the intermediate state of a constitutional monarchy should be sought. Thus the establishment of a new constitution for the German artisans and industrial class became a goal of all wishes, an industrial order which avoided equally the exclusiveness of privilege and the unbridled anarchy of laissez-faire; the drafting of such an ordinance is viewed by the core of the industrial classes as one of the most important tasks of the National Assembly.

The National Assembly, then, was not unaware of the insistent demands of the workers of Germany; but as interpreted by Veit a certain metamorphosis had taken place in the workers' demands. The connection between the revolution and the social grievance of the German people was seen, the opposition to freedom of trade was clear, though the various positions within the working class, ranging from support of the guilds in their extreme form to the growing demand for associations or trade unions which would include all workers were sloughed over. But concerns which to the workers were primarily economic were translated into political terms; the social movement was seen as but an adjunct of the political drive for unification, "peculiar to the German," and the neat, all too neat equation was made between the various alternatives of government and the various forms of guild organization. Guild restoration was linked, not altogether inaccurately, with absolutism, but the further argument which connected freedom of trade with republicanism and the compromise of a modified guild order with a constitutional monarchy was too pat. Moreover the whole analysis failed to note, though it perhaps reflected, the growing fear of the workers and the proletariat, the growing amount of unclear but nonetheless real class antagonism.

The demands of the workers were changed in Veit's report into the political concerns of the middle-class delegates to the Frankfurt Assembly. The demands themselves dealt with much more immediate and material matters.

The most frequently recurring theme in the petitions which were received on economic matters from the workers and artisans of Germany was the almost universal opposition to freedom of trade, opposition to any measures which would open up the German markets either to competition from foreign produce or to the competition of free labor and the products of factories and machines. The question of freedom of trade, both in relation to tariffs and more particularly in relation to the regulations which governed the practising of the various trades within Germany, was perhaps the central issue in the revolution for the workers.

Such support as there was for trade freedom came almost entirely from one area, the Rhenish Palatinate; the restoration of guild regulations there by the Bavarian government in 1815, after a period of trade freedom under the French, had caused considerable hardship. Elsewhere the only supporters of freedom of trade were to be found among the merchant class; the artisans themselves would have none of it. Petitions came, for example, from the merchants in Breslau and Berlin who attacked the narrow interests of the workers and "the lower orders" and called for greater freedom in trade.[38]

But these were exceptions. To most of the artisans only those who failed to have the interests of the mass of the workers at heart could support the doctrine of freedom of trade. In the words of the tradesmen of Karlsruhe: [39]

Only theoreticians who do not know the internal conditions of industry and its needs, only people who find nourishment in unlimited freedom for their own flightiness without thinking of the future, only speculators and the aristocrats of money who snatch some advantage for themselves out of the frivolity and need of others, speak with scorn of a legal order in industry and praise unlimited trade freedom as a means to higher development, as a source of well being; while the professional with insight, supported by experience and instructed by facts, finds and sees in the unlimited freedom of trade the decline of the middle class, the disproportionate increase of the proletariat and the almost exorbitant burden of supporting the poor in the community which arise from this.

The opposition to freedom of trade was meant in two senses. In the first place it was intended in the ordinary sense: the government must raise tariff barriers in order to protect German industry from foreign competition. The superiority of French and English industry was feared and some protection was called for against the increasing use of machines in other countries. "German industry," wrote the Citizens' Association in Lallenberg in Saxony, "has not yet reached the high point of the

[38] *Akten des volkswirtschaftlichen Ausschusses,* vol. 17.
[39] *Akten des volkswirtschaftlichen Ausschusses,* vol. 12.

French and English; therefore we consider not free trade but suitable protective tariffs to be according to the German interest." [40] The merchants of Lübeck and Hamburg were willing to sign a petition calling for protection against foreign capital though they would not extend this to opposition to domestic freedom of trade.[41]

But the attack on freedom of trade within Germany, particularly on the extension of the right to practise a trade to those who had not gone through the guild system and had not been trained as masters, was far more important to most of the artisans who petitioned the National Assembly. This was the ultimate danger, the one most feared by the artisans. A rumor that manufacturing and commercial interests were flooding the Assembly with petitions in favor of freedom of trade was enough to set off a second round of protests from the artisans in August and September.[42]

The decay of the handicraft trades and the rise of the proletariat was another theme which ran through the body of petitions considered by the Economic Committee. A few workers complained of abuses which had always existed,[43] but the majority regarded the plight of the artisan as of but recent origin. Many spoke of a golden age which was being destroyed by the advent of machines and factories. "Previously, when machines and factories were still in their childhood, Germany's artisan class was well off, it was happy and contented, held firmly to justice and law, to prince and Father-

---

[40] *Akten des volkswirtschaftlichen Ausschusses,* vol. 5.

[41] *Akten des volkswirtschaftlichen Ausschusses,* vol. 17.

[42] Petition of the artisans and tradesmen of Giessen in the Grand Duchy of Hesse, *Akten des volkswirtschaftlichen Ausschusses,* vol. 12; Veit's report, vol. 2.

[43] The Berlin chimney sweeps, for example, petitioned against "von Alter noch bestehenden Missbräuche," *Akten des volkswirtschaftlichen Ausschusses,* vol. 20.

land." [44] Petition after petition referred to the need for the "raising of the so deeply sunk artisan class." [45]

The great fear of the artisans was that they would be reduced to the position of ordinary, unskilled workers, to the ranks of the proletariat. One petition referred to "the scare-word of modern times—proletarian." [46] The workers, it was acknowledged, were in the main "members of sick branches of the artisan class," but the healthy parts had to be preserved.[47] Trade freedom had led in but a few years to the growth of this proletariat, hitherto unknown in Germany; only the abolition of trade freedom could lead to the limitation of this class.[48] Some of the petitions, of course, came from the lower ranks among the workers and these were less marked by a fear of deterioration in conditions; yet even the lowest of the groups which petitioned the Frankfurt Assembly felt the fear of an increase in the mass of unskilled labor.[49]

A further danger was seen in the rise of the proletariat, apart from the threat to the more respectable artisans and the decline in standards of living. The proletariat, it was held, would be the prey of agitators and intriguers of all sorts who would use the misery and poverty of the masses to gain support for their theories.

[44] Petitions of the guild chairmen in Eschwege in Electoral Hesse, *Akten des volkswirtschaftlichen Ausschusses,* vol. 12.

[45] Petition of the artisans of Simmern in Prussia, *Akten des volkswirtschaftlichen Ausschusses,* vol. 17; cf. also the petitions of the masters of the district of Schmalkalden, vol. 12; the tradesmen of Karlsruhe, vol. 12; the handicraft masters of Bielefeld, vol. 17.

[46] Petition from Halberstadt in Prussian Silesia, *Akten des volkswirtschaftlichen Ausschusses,* vol. 17.

[47] Petition of the guildsmen in Eschwege in Electoral Hesse, *Akten des volkswirtschaftlichen Ausschusses,* vol. 12.

[48] Petition from the artisans of the Heidelberg and the surrounding area, *Akten des volkswirtschaftlichen Ausschusses,* vol. 12.

[49] Petition of the workers of Mannheim, *Akten des volkswirtschaftlichen Ausschusses,* vol. 12; petition of various journeymen in Frankfurt am Main, vol. 21, i.

Anarchy, socialism and communism would follow. It was up to the Frankfurt Assembly to prevent such evils by preserving the rights and status of the artisans. Trade freedom, indeed freedom in general, wrote the industrial committee of Kassel, "without measure, goal or limit, is arbitrary; it leads in religion to atheism and the abolition of the bond of the church, in politics to the destruction of the state and anarchy, in social life to the ruin of civil society and communism." [50] Yet to others the attack on freedom of trade itself contained the seeds of socialism. Merchants in Berlin, Hamburg, Lübeck and elsewhere subscribed to a petition which pointed out that the workers had "merely to strike from the theory of the limitation of trade the unessential adjective 'foreign' and their socialist theory was ready." [51]

Yet the Economic Committee noted only one petition which it regarded as tarred with the socialist brush and favorable to the various doctrines which it included under the label—the address drawn up by the Berlin Workers' Congress at the end of August. Even here the committee found no specific doctrine and no positive proposal reflecting the "socialist" influence of such leaders as Born. It was alarmed rather by the mere fact that the Berlin congress spoke of the exploitation of the workers in wider terms than were usual, offering a general theory of repression linked to the historical development of the European economy. [52]

Those who were looking for signs of a socialist revolution among the working classes of 1848 found little to support their case or feed their fears in the petitions of the workers. The workers hoped to gain things, quite specific things, from the revolution, but they were

[50] *Akten des volkswirtschaftlichen Ausschusses,* vol. 12.
[51] *Akten des volkswirtschaftlichen Ausschusses,* vol. 17, ii.
[52] Veit's report, p. 19, *Akten des volkswirtschaftlichen Ausschusses,* vol. 2.

scarcely revolutionaries and certainly not communist ones. "The German people," declared the tradesmen of Stralsund in Pomerania reassuringly, "disdain the bloody path of force and take the long and troublesome road of law and order." [53]

The examples of France and England were often cited by the petitioners. Those who discussed foreign trade feared most the competition of the factories and machines of these two countries. The impoverishment of the working classes and the growth of these classes was seen as a direct result of trade freedom and the factory system in England and France. Only America, among the countries with trade freedom, had a prosperous artisan class, noted one petition, but that was due to special political conditions and the abundance of natural resources.[54] But another lesson was to be drawn from the French example as well: overwhelmed by the proletariat, the French had, during the revolution, turned to regulation and the attempt to provide work through the government. The result was the June Days, which were taken by many as a lesson for Germany. The working class had to be supported by legislation, but it had to be allowed to organize its own affairs; the artisans hoped to avoid the mistakes of National Workshops and a central, all-powerful ministry of labor as in the Luxembourg. Industrial councils which would allow for local participation and self-government by the artisans were to be substituted for the dangerous experiments of the French.[55]

The internal enemies against whom the artisans called

[53] *Akten des volkswirtschaftlichen Ausschusses,* vol. 20.

[54] Petition of the artisans of Heidelberg, *Akten des volkswirtschaftlichen Ausschusses,* vol. 12.

[55] Petition of the tradesmen of the Grand Duchy of Hesse, *Akten des volkswirtschaftlichen Ausschusses,* vol. 12; petition from the merchant Kopisch of Breslau, vol. 17.

for action were variously described as capitalists, manufacturers, machine owners, theoreticians, money men and even "immature young people who have scarcely run away from their lessons when they want to found a family hearth." [56] Of these the capitalists were the enemies whom the artisans took most seriously. The capitalists destroyed the rights of the individual and made the artisans into mere slaves and subjects. The craftsmen of Hamm in Westphalia spoke of their fears of "harmful freedom and the competition of capital" and claimed that "capital has gobbled up the small but beneficent industry." [57] Capital and the "money powers" were responsible for the increasing proletarization of the artisans. The "money man" was held to be a danger to the entire "fatherland"; [58]

he alone knows no boundary to his avarice and has the magic agency to suck up completely all the blood of the poor, and so it happens that money accumulates in his hands until it becomes a power dangerous to the state. This is no dream; recent history substantiates it with horrible evidence.

Some wrote in emotional, almost hysterical tones of the growing power of the capitalists. Others called more calmly for laws equalizing the power of capital and labor.[59]

The restoration and support of the guild system was held by most of the petitioners in one form or another to be necessary for the preservation of the artisan class.

[56] Petition of the Industrial Committee in Kassel, *Akten des volkswirtschaftlichen Ausschusses*, vol. 12.

[57] *Akten des volkswirtschaftlichen Ausschusses*, vol. 17.

[58] Petition from the tradesmen of Schleiz, Tanna, Lobenstein, Ebersdorf, Saalburg and Reichenfels in the duchies of Reuss, *Akten des volkswirtschaftlichen Ausschusses*, vol. 22, i.

[59] Petition of the Frankfurt tailors, shoemakers and cabinetmakers, *Akten des volkswirtschaftlichen Ausschusses*, vol. 21, i.

The training program offered by the guilds, the preservation of the system of apprentice instruction, the *Wanderjahre* of the journeyman, the tests for the rights of practising a trade as a master were all included in most of the proposals presented by the artisans. Some realized the limitations of the guild system, arguing that it should be applied in those trades only that could not be self-taught and that freedom of trade could be granted to trades which could be learned without instruction.[60] Others argued for loopholes in the guild system to benefit their own particular group.[61] But most stuck by some form of the guild system. Guilds were defended as a necessary means of training workers, as a way of maintaining standards in finished products, as the central prop of German society and the defender of morality.

But the core of the argument was always the self-interest of the artisans, the preservation of their rank and livelihood against the onrush of competition. The old journeymen of Stolp in Further Pomerania wrote to the National Assembly defending the limitation of one apprentice to every master, "because," they argued, "even on this basis so many apprentices will join the troop of tradesmen that half the journeymen as well as some masters will have to seize the beggar's staff and become daily wage earners." The journeymen went on to calculate that if a master practised his trade from the age of thirty to the age of sixty and had some three or four apprentices at a time, he would have produced by the time he was fifty and still in the trade fifteen to twenty competitors who might indeed drive him out of

[60] Petition of the tradesmen of Mainz, *Akten des volkswirtschaftlichen Ausschusses,* vol. 12.

[61] Petition of the pedlars of Titmaringenhausen in Westphalia, *Akten des volkswirtschaftlichen Ausschusses,* vol. 17.

business.[62] For all these reasons the maintenance of the guilds was held to be necessary.

But the form which the guilds should take and the legislation with which the National Assembly should back them was by no means a matter of universal agreement among the various petitioners. Some artisans—indeed to judge from Veit's report, the majority—seemed to favor the proposals of the Artisans' Congress which met in Frankfurt. But the bitter quarrels between the various groups of artisans were reflected in the petitions sent to the National Assembly. The tradesmen of Mannheim, for example, attacked the masters' proposals as "laughable, . . . breathing the spirit of the crassest guild obligations," and called for state administration of the guilds in the interests of all the workers in them. The denial of the right to work independently till the age of twenty-five was a limitation on the rights of German citizens over the age of twenty-one; masters' privileges should be made attainable from that age.[63] The exclusion of the journeymen by the masters was held to be a piece of barefaced cynicism.[64]

Nonetheless all were agreed that the Frankfurt Assembly had to do something to support the artisans and workers of Germany. "We do not want to demand any privileges," wrote the tradesmen of the duchies of Reuss, "and we will solemnly guard ourselves against this reproach; we want only to *live* and that is no privilege."[65] And the tradesmen of the Grand Duchy of Hesse attempted to present with moderation the point of view

[62] *Akten des volkswirtschaftlichen Ausschusses,* vol. 20.

[63] Petition of the workers of Mannheim, *Akten des volkswirtschaftlichen Ausschusses,* vol. 12.

[64] Petition of various journeymen in Frankfurt am Main, *Akten des volkswirtschaftlichen Ausschusses,* vol. 21, i.

[65] *Akten des volkswirtschaftlichen Ausschusses,* vol. 22, i.

of the majority of the artisans, modest, far from revolutionary or socialist, yet urgent and insistent: [66]

> We want no unlimited freedom of trade, we do not want capital in the hands of an egotist to become a fearful scourge of the artisans. We do not want to abolish the difference between *rich* and *poor,* but we also do not want money to rule over the work of head and hand. We do not want to banish machines, we do not want to banish factories; but we do want mechanical power to serve the whole artisan class and not single individuals. We do not want a ministry of labor but we do want an industrial council. We want no French National Workshops, we want no national retail stores, we want no equality of wages; but we do want everyone to move freely and to receive a wage according to the measure of his ability, his intelligence and his efforts.

❋

Such was the multitude of requests with which the National Assembly and its Economic Committee were faced. There was no clear-cut program which emerged from them, but there was a consistent demand for some sort of legislation which would favor the artisans and workers and prevent further deterioration of their position.

Yet, though the Economic Committee met regularly and discussed and analyzed the demands of the workers, there was little chance during the early months of the Frankfurt Assembly to debate in public session the issues which directly concerned the workers. The National Assembly was occupied with the debates on the Basic Rights of the German citizens, and these offered few opportunities, at least as construed by the middle-class members of the Frankfurt Parliament, to consider the

[66] *Akten des volkswirtschaftlichen Ausschusses,* vol. 12.

demands of the workers. The Economic Committee was not inactive; altogether it brought some forty amendments to the proposed basic rights during the course of the debate.[67] But few of these would have been of interest to the workers.

The chief economic concern of many in the Frankfurt Assembly and in the Economic Committee as well was the external issue of free trade, the question of whether to protect the products of Germany through tariff barriers or to allow the free importation of foreign goods. This was coupled with proposals for the internal unification of the new German state, abolition of such tolls and customs as had not been removed by the *Zollverein,* and the provision for a system of equal weights and measures and a common currency.[68] Amendments by the Economic Committee often strengthened the proposals for economic unification.[69]

The issues of whether the national economic unit thus created would have high or low tariffs was, however, far less easy to decide and indeed was never resolved. The majority of the Economic Committee, headed by the two men who served as chairmen, von Rönne and Eisenstuck, was in favor of high protective tariffs. The only man to come out openly for free trade on the committee was the Hamburg merchant Merk. The minister for trade, Arnold Duckwitz, appointed under the regent, the Archduke Johann of Austria, on August 5, 1848, was a Bremen businessman and sympathized both with the needs for protective tariffs and the demands of the trading ports of the north for free trade; he sought a

[67] Valentin, *Geschichte der deutschen Revolution,* vol. 2, p. 131.

[68] Blum, *Die deutsche Revolution,* pp. 468ff.; Hamerow, *Restoration, Revolution, Reaction,* pp. 133ff.

[69] See the *Verbesserungs-Anträge des Ausschusses für Volkswirtschaft zu dem Entwurfe des Verfassungs-Ausschusses über die Befugnisse der Reichsgewalt,* Frankfurt am Main, 1848.

compromise between them.[70] But such a compromise was not easy to achieve, and the political issues of revolution, the national and constitutional demands of the middle classes, cut across the economic ones. When the subject of tariffs was debated in the Economic Committee it was argued that any decision would have to wait on a solution of the problem of the inclusion or exclusion of Austria, the question of big or little Germany.[71]

All these matters, though evidence of the zeal of the Economic Committee, were scarcely of any direct interest to the workers. The actual demands of the many working-class petitioners were dealt with by the Assembly itself during the early months of its meetings only in the most hasty and tangential fashion. On the twentieth of June a delegate of the extreme left, Reisinger, proposed that a "ministry of the proletarians" be established in all German states or, at the very least, that each state set up a commission to study statistically the condition of the working classes and report on possible remedies. The proposal was turned over to the Economic Committee, where it was relegated to the more general study of proposals for an industrial ordinance and never saw the light of day.[72] A proposal submitted to the National Assembly in May by the workers of Reichenbach in the Palatinate for the relief of the poor in the working classes through public works to be controlled by the workers was put off several times. In August it was admitted that the petition raised general issues which the National Assembly should discuss and a report was called for from the Economic Committee. But though the report, prepared by Osterrath and leaving

[70] Valentin, *Geschichte der deutschen Revolution,* vol. 2, p. 320; Hamerow, *Resoration, Revolution, Reaction,* p. 135.

[71] *Akten des volkswirtschaftlichen Ausschusses,* vol. 10, minutes for the meeting of Oct. 24, 1848.

[72] Valentin, *Geschichte der deutschen Revolution,* vol. 2, p. 101.

the matter to the individual states, was ready within a matter of days, the petition did not come up again in the National Assembly till the end of January.[73]

The only subject which touched directly the interests of the working class and which came up for debate during the early months of the Frankfurt Parliament was the question of emigration rights. The workers were concerned because of the growing economic pressure which caused many to leave Germany, particularly to go to America; it also was of importance for the guild system, since the *Wanderjahre* of the journeymen often took the young artisan out of Germany even though he had no intention of remaining abroad. The petitions of the workers often included references to the right of free movement and emigration and section 6 of the proposed basic rights dealt with this.

The first proposal to be brought forward by the seventh subcommittee appointed to deal with workers' affairs was for the extension of the rights of citizens to Germans living abroad; this was offered as an amendment to the simple guarantee of the right of emigration by the Economic Committee in the National Assembly on the twentieth of July.[74] The amendment was presented as a necessary guarantee of good faith to the working classes and a partial solution to the problem of overpopulation and the excessive size of the working force. Indeed it was even argued that the government should subsidize the emigration of those workers who wished to leave the country.

But even such measures, mild though they were and remote from the central problems and demands of the

[73] *Stenographischer Bericht,* vol. 2, p. 1415, vol. 7, pp. 4921-4922; *Akten des volkswirtschaftlichen Ausschusses,* vol. 2.

[74] *Akten des volkswirtschaftlichen Ausschusses,* vol. 10, minutes for the session of June 13, 1848; *Stenographischer Bericht,* vol. 2, pp. 1055ff.

workers though they seemed, were rejected. One positive achievement did, however, emerge from the debate. The National Assembly, convinced of the need for a more rigorous consideration of the needs of the workers, decided by 224 to 193 on the following day to instruct the Economic Committee to draw up a proposal for a general industrial ordinance which would regulate the affairs of the guilds and the workers. However, an amendment by Moritz Veit which directed that this ordinance be prepared by the time of the second reading of the Basic Rights was passed by only a narrow margin, 244 to 242. It could hardly be argued that the National Assembly was showing excessive interest in the condition of the workers.[75]

❖

Thus the question of the industrial ordinance, the regulation of the conditions of work, was left for a later stage in the proceedings of the National Assembly. Similarly several other issues which came close to the workers' concerns, the debate on section 30 of the Basic Rights which guaranteed the right of free association essential to the new workers' organizations, and the whole question of the franchise in the new German state, were left until well into 1849 before being taken up in the Frankfurt Parliament. But by that time conditions had changed.

"It was painful to note," commented one observer of the National Assembly and the German revolutions, "how little the Frankfurt Assembly had a real existence for the people." [76] And it is certainly true that the mass of the workers had little knowledge of the actual proceedings of that body. But it should be evident from what has been discussed above, particularly from the

[75] *Stenographischer Bericht,* vol. 2, pp. 1076-1077, 1082.
[76] Gneist, *Berliner Zustände,* p. 83.

petitions, that the Frankfurt Assembly was an important feature of the revolutionary scene as it appeared to the mass of workers; they had indeed high hopes for what they could achieve through that body. But they had little real knowledge of what the National Assembly had itself set out to do. The ineffectualness of the National Assembly in dealing with the demands of the masses became obvious only gradually. Paradoxically it was not until the autumn and winter of 1848 and 1849, when in fact the National Assembly did turn to some of the demands of the workers, that the mass of artisans and laborers came to feel their isolation from the rest of Germany.

And if the Frankfurt Assembly failed at first to have a real existence in the minds of the workers, but only a fantasy one, the delegates to the Assembly themselves appeared to be cut off from the realities of the German situation outside the debating floor of the *Paulskirche.* Reaction, the suppression of some of the leaders of the popular revolt, was gaining ground during the summer of 1848. To many outside the Frankfurt Assembly, the tide seemed to have turned in September of 1848 when the Truce of Malmoe was accepted by that body. From then on, the workers were on their own.

The reaction in Germany did not set in with the drama of an event such as the June Days; it came only gradually. No point in time, no single event, can be called the defeat of the revolution and the beginning of reaction.

As in the Frankfurt Assembly, there were still signs of progress throughout Germany during the summer of 1848, indeed some more encouraging than those visible in the national body. The Prussian National Assembly was in many ways more radical than the parliament in Frankfurt. In spite of the fact that it had rejected Berends' resolution on the ninth of June calling for the "recognition of the revolution" and that it was regarded by many as a detraction from the essential work of unification being done in Frankfurt, it still appeared to workers a far more likely source of aid than the national body. For one thing, the Prussian Assembly was more truly representative of the population, containing some twenty-eight artisans—though lawyers, judges and officials still formed the largest group.[77] The Prussian Assembly was the object of a series of petitions similar to those received by the Frankfurt body; by the middle of August six thousand of these had been received.[78] Quite early on the Prussian Assembly set up a committee to deal with economic demands, the Special Commission of the National Assembly on Trade and Industry with Special Reference to the Condition of the Working Classes. Only a few noticed that the elections to this commission were fixed so that members of the left wing of the Assembly, interested in the workers, were excluded.[79]

Elsewhere there were at least token gestures in favor of the working classes. In Austria the minister Schwarzer set up a Provisional Central Committee for the Employment of the Workers at the beginning of August.[80] In Saxony the fifteen-member workers' commission began its sessions at the end of May under the Minister for the Interior, Oberländer, with the intention of collecting information for the drafting of laws to improve the condition of the working class.[81] One state at least, liberal Baden, actually went so far as to adopt a progressive income tax, though it was of exceedingly modest propor-

[77] Tilman, *Einfluss des Revolutionsjahres*, p. 32.
[78] A report and summary of the contents of these petitions may be found in *Verhandlungen der Versammlung zur Vereinbarung der Preussischen Staats-Verfassung*, vol. 2, pp. 13-19.
[79] See the article by Nees von Esenbeck in the *Berliner Zeitungs Halle*, July 6, 1848.
[80] *Neue Rheinische Zeitung*, Aug. 9, 1848.
[81] *Zeitung für das deutsche Volk*, June 5, 1848.

tions.[82] Yet all these measures were more symptoms of promises of better things to come than actual achievements.

There was in fact a general improvement of conditions in the summer of 1848. A hurricane swept away the early crops in Silesia at the end of June,[83] but the summer was a good one and the prospects for the autumn harvests were excellent. At the same time years of starvation left many of the people weak and one of the last of the great plagues, a cholera epidemic, got under way in the middle of the summer. By the middle of August there were reports of cholera reducing considerably the revolutionary zeal of many of the workers.[84]

Moreover, it was noticed by some that the "March achievements," the results of the spring of 1848, were superficial at best. The mechanism of reaction still lay at hand; the governments had only to recover their nerve to set it once again in operation. At the end of July a list was drawn up of the post-1815 laws which were still on the Prussian law books and could be used against any attempt at further revolution, or indeed any effort to consolidate what had been thought to be the gains of the March one. It remained illegal to seek a solution to the social question through voluntary exile or through urging others to emigrate; it was illegal to join clubs or political associations; it was illegal to give speeches with political content or to carry banners other than the national (i.e. Prussian) flag at public meetings; and finally it was illegal to seek to raise wages by going on strike.[85]

[82] *Grossherzoglich Badisches Regierungs-Blatt,* July 29, 1848. The tax ranged from .5 per cent on incomes under 500 florins to all of 3 per cent on incomes over 5,000 florins.
[83] *Neue Rheinische Zeitung,* June 27, 1848.
[84] *Deutsche Zeitung,* Aug. 18, 1848.
[85] *Die Locomotive,* July 22, 1848.

The early months of the Frankfurt Assembly and the period of the rival workers' congresses were also accompanied by the sporadic and spontaneous outbreaks among the workers which had characterized the earlier period of the revolution. Bands of working-class marauders, it was reported, were lurking in the forests in Mecklenburg-Schwerin, raiding the local estates, demanding ransoms ranging up to 13,000 thaler, burning houses, destroying furniture and opening wine cellars. Near Wiesbaden the inhabitants cut down five hundred trees in the state forests in protest against waiting so long for an answer to their demands; it was feared that their example would be followed elsewhere in southwest Germany. In Baden sabotage of the railroads was so common that the railway lines were placed under public protection. Meetings of the workers from all the local villages in an area were held in Electoral Hesse in June and in Bavaria in August and September to call upon the Frankfurt Assembly to fulfill the demands of the workers.[86]

The cities were even more unsettled than the countryside. In Breslau there were processions and mock serenades (*Katzemusiken*) against the officials, so that the city government had to call upon the Workers' Association to attempt to control the rioters. In Sachsenhausen across the Main from Frankfurt there were similar serenades in July against a baker who overcharged on bread, so that the civil guard had to be called out, and in Munich in the same month there were riots because the price of beer was raised. In Neuss and Crefeld in the Rhineland the civil troops had to prevent rioting among the unemployed and those demanding higher wages. In Berlin the civil guard joined with the workers in

[86] *Neue Rheinische Zeitung*, June 7, 9, July 18, Sept. 6, 1848; *Grossherzoglich Badisches Regierungs-Blatt*, Sept. 25, 1848; Brunner, *Politische Bewegungen in Nürnberg*, pp. 75-77.

attacking the troops of the twenty-fourth regiment after the latter had insulted a passing woman. Rival factions among the workers quarreled; when in August a group of democratic organizers was assaulted by a workers' mob in Charlottenburg, with the police and the *Bürgerwehr* looking complacently on, the prodemocratic workers inside Berlin replied with a demonstration in front of the house of the minister Auerswald.[87]

Riots occurred with the smallest excuse or without one at all; they often adopted a political slogan or were occasioned by the rumor, however unfounded, of a political change, but they were basically the sign of widespread economic discontent. The threat of revolutionary violence was still present; organization was lacking. As one paper noted: [88]

> The unrest among the workers still will not abate. Almost daily great brawls take place among the workers themselves; these usually have a bloody end and the introduction of armed force is not infrequently made necessary. . . . With even the slightest unrest among the workers it is immediately rumored among the easily excited population of Berlin: Today the republic will be proclaimed! . . . As far as we are in a position to have a look at the activities of the parties, we must declare this alarm to be a mere fear of ghosts.

❉

Ghosts or not, the activities and the leaders of the working classes were increasingly restricted by the police and the governments. The leaders of the working classes and the delegates to the rival working-class congresses

[87] *Neue Rheinische Zeitung*, July 13, 17, 18, 30, Aug. 1, Sept. 6, 1848; *Das Volk*, July 15, 1848; *Illustrierte Zeitung*, Sept. 16, 1848; Valentin, *Frankfurt am Main*, pp. 300-301.

[88] *Deutsche Reichs-Zeitung*, July 4, 1848.

were subject to persecution and arrest. The first to be arrested was the Hanover printer Stegen, at the end of June, following his return from the congress of printers in Mainz.[89] At the beginning of July the leaders of the Cologne Workers' Association, Gottschalk and Anneke, and Julius Wolff, the chairman of the Düsseldorf People's Club, were seized by the police and kept in prison for some six months till they were brought to trial.[90] The Cologne arrests had important consequences for the workers' movement, for they meant that the followers of Marx and finally Marx himself took over the leadership of the Cologne Workers' Association; the latter group became much less active in the economic sphere and turned exclusively to politics, much to the disgust of many of its members.[91] In the south of Germany, in Württemberg, Baden and Bavaria, democratic clubs, and, under this rubric, a number of the workers' associations were banned in July and August.[92] In Berlin public meetings were prohibited unless specific police permission was obtained, and the regulation was enforced in spite of the uproar and the accusations of betrayal of the revolution which arose. Three men were fined 5 thaler each for speaking at an unauthorized meeting,

[89] *Neue Rheinische Zeitung,* July 2, Aug. 6, 1848.

[90] *Neue Rheinische Zeitung,* July 4, 5, 10, 1848; *Das Volk,* July 8, 1848.

[91] The growing disillusion and disinterest of the Cologne workers as a result of the changed orientation of their club was described in an article on the "Arbeiterverein, Köln" in the *Deutsche Zeitung,* Aug. 18, 1848. The author believed that the arrest of Gottschalk had made a considerable difference to the situation among the workers in the Rhineland and that, had Gottschalk remained free, the workers would have pursued far more revolutionary goals than they did under Marx.

[92] *Berliner Zeitungs Halle,* July 19, 1848; *Grossherzoglich Badisches Regierungs-Blatt,* July 23, 1848; *Neue Rheinische Zeitung,* Aug. 24, 1848.

and the house of the president of the Artisans' Union was searched for evidence of subversive activities.[93]

Perhaps the most violent repression of the workers was the battle of the Prater in Vienna on the twenty-third of August. A protest against the reduction of wages in the public works projects was halted by force; 30 workers were killed and 282 injured. The workers were defeated; the radicals did nothing to help them.[94]

It looked in a way like the June Days all over again. Yet it was only in Vienna that this defeat occurred; the rest of Germany was largely unmoved and unaffected.

But it is against this background of sporadic outbursts and piecemeal repression that the outbreak in Frankfurt on the eighteenth of September must be seen. The choice before the Frankfurt Assembly seemed clear; either continue the war against Denmark for what the majority of Germans regarded as the rightfully German territory of Schleswig-Holstein or surrender to the Truce of Malmoe, dictated to the Frankfurt Assembly by the Prussian government and, to make the shame worse, to the Prussian government itself by England and Russia. This for many was the turning point of the revolution; here was decided the issue of whether or not the Frankfurt Assembly exercised any sort of sovereignty or held in its hands anything other than the appearance of power, a mere chimera which would fade before the

[93] *Kölnische Zeitung,* July 30, 1848; *Neue Rheinische Zeitung,* Sept. 3, 1848; *Plakate,* Ratsbibliothek, Berlin, portfolio 5. Perhaps the most celebrated German working-class leader to come to trial at this time was Ferdinand Lassalle. But Lassalle's days of leadership lay in the future; he was arrested in April 1848 on the charge, not of revolutionary activity, but of conspiring to steal the jewels of the Countess Sophie von Hatzfeld. Acquitted on Aug. 11, he did become a figure in the Düsseldorf workers' association in 1849 but did not gain national prominence till the 1860s. *Neue Rheinische Zeitung,* Aug. 6, 1848; *Deutsche Zeitung,* Aug. 15, 1848.

[94] Rath, *The Viennese Revolution,* p. 297.

259

demands of the individual German states. The Frankfurt Parliament accepted the truce on the sixteenth of September. The left wing of the Assembly, meeting at the *Deutscher Hof* that evening, refused to contest the decision and rejected outright the suggestion of a number of working-class speakers that they should resign and form the pre-parliament of a German republic.[95]

Once again the artisans and laborers came out in the streets and barricades were erected. The initiative in the riots of the eighteenth of September seems to have been taken by the radical and workers' associations in the Rhineland, particularly the Workers' Union of Frankfurt itself. The aims were complex; in part perhaps it was simply patriotism, in part an objection to Prussian dominance, in part an effort to force the left of the Assembly to accept an alliance with the popular radical associations. In any case the attempt failed. By the twentieth of September there were thirty-five dead on the side of the rioters and seventy-two among the armed forces, which successfully defended the *Paulskirche* and the action of the Assembly. To many this decided the issue; Marx wrote that the struggle in Frankfurt meant the overthrow of the political rule of the bourgeoisie. In the eyes of most of the radical democrats the usefulness of the National Assembly was destroyed.[96]

Similarly, in the view of the vast majority of the members of the Frankfurt Assembly, the popular movement and the barricades, which had after all brought them originally to power, were completely discredited. Von

[95] *Neue Rheinische Zeitung*, Sept. 19, 1848; Valentin, *Frankfurt am Main*, pp. 314-316.

[96] *Neue Rheinische Zeitung*, Sept. 21, 23, 1848; Lüders, *Die demokratische Bewegung*, p. 31; Valentin, *Geschichte der deutschen Revolution*, vol. 2, pp. 158ff.; Obermann, *Die deutschen Arbeiter in der Revolution von 1848*, pp. 301-306.

Gagern spoke in strong terms in the Assembly on the day following the fighting, condemning the murder of Lichnowsky and von Auerswald as "wanton and barbarous" and denouncing the rising as "a crime against freedom." [97] The speaker for the left, Venedy from Cologne, endorsed von Gagern's speech and hailed the repression of the riots as the "victory of the National Assembly." [98] The methods of revolution were condemned by the revolutionary assembly itself.

Yet just as the June Days in Paris and the August rising in Vienna had not marked the defeat of the workers' movement, so the September rising in Frankfurt did not mean the end of the efforts of the artisans and workers to gain from the revolution an improvement of their lot. Reports of the death of the workers' movement were greatly exaggerated. The period following the Frankfurt rising did see, however, a change in the orientation of the workers' associations toward greater self-reliance. The fall and winter of 1848-1849 saw the final disillusion of the workers with the Frankfurt Parliament, a consolidation of the workers' organizations set up at the summer congresses and an increased interest in workers' cooperatives and self-help.

[97] *Stenographischer Bericht,* vol. 3, p. 2185.
[98] *Stenographischer Bericht,* vol. 3, p. 2187.

SECTION IV

THE CLOSING OF THE RANKS

—AUTUMN, WINTER AND SPRING,

1848-1849

CHAPTER 10

THE DEMOCRATIC DEADLOCK

THE AUTUMN of 1848 and the following winter saw the sorting out of many of the parties and interests involved in the revolution, the drawing of a line between its supporters and opponents. Beginning with the September riots in Frankfurt, it became increasingly clear that the March achievements were lost, that the forces of reaction were once more in a position of control, if indeed they had ever been out of this position, that the revolution was a failure.

The effect of this realization upon the working-class movement was to produce greater unity of purpose and organization. Yet the path to such unity was by no means a straight one, though it was perhaps excessively narrow; the results were superficially unimpressive. When the call to revolution was heard again in May of 1849, the response was inadequate. Many of the workers came out once more to man the barricades; but many others failed to do so and the forces of the governments were more than equal to the task of repression.

Moreover, the mere fact of unification of the workers' movement had the effect of diminishing its strength. In the first place, a number of groups, the more prosperous artisans and those factory workers who were secure in their jobs, dropped out of the movement, dissociating themselves from the interests and organizations of the working class. The unskilled laborers, the mass of the proletariat and above all the journeymen and small master craftsmen of the declining hand trades were left. And second, those who were left turned increasingly to economic measures and away from politics, to specific schemes for working-class self-help such as illness and traveling funds and cooperative production organized through the *Verbrüderung* set up by Born, and away from political agitation. Finally, all faith and interest in the Frankfurt Assembly was lost.

The most immediate effect of what has been called "the September crisis" [1] was not upon the workers' movement, however, but upon the intellectual and middle-class democrats. A democratic congress met in Berlin in October and came out in support of revolution, particularly in support of the besieged revolutionaries in Vienna. In the following month the democrats joined in the antitax campaign which followed the dissolution of the Prussian National Assembly and the declaration of a state of siege in Berlin. Marx in particular, and the *Neue Rheinische Zeitung*, took the lead in advocating a mass refusal to pay taxes until the Prussian Assembly was recalled and its legislative sovereignty recognized.

Some historians have described this development as the beginning of a popular front.[2] But this is to reckon without the workers. Whatever the middle-class democrats may have done, the workers—partly out of choice and partly out of the exigencies of the situation—fell back on their own resources.

Rather the events of the autumn and winter of 1848-1849 mark what might be called the democratic deadlock. On the one hand the democrats failed to gain the support of the workers; indeed they lost what influence they had with the workers' associations, arousing little interest in the republican program they put forward. The antitax campaign was a failure and by the spring of 1849 even Karl Marx felt it necessary to resign

[1] Valentin, *Geschichte der deutschen Revolution,* vol. 2, pp. 95ff.

[2] Obermann, *Die deutschen Arbeiter in der ersten bürgerlichen Revolution,* pp. 227ff.

ostentatiously from the democratic movement and to proclaim, rather late in the day, that the true interests of the revolution lay with the working class.

On the other hand the democrats failed to exert any decisive influence on the middle class and the various legislative bodies which had been summoned as a result of the revolution; even less could they exert effective pressure on the governments of the German states. The one major success of the democrats in 1848, the decision of the Frankfurt Assembly to provide for universal manhood suffrage in the constitution of the new Germany, was the outcome of a series of compromises in the Assembly and was due to pressure from the Economic Committee as well as the vote of the democratic block in the Assembly. Moreover the provision for universal suffrage went down to defeat with the rest of the work of the Frankfurt Assembly when Frederick William of Prussia refused to accept the offered crown.

Without the support of either the workers or those in a position of power, unwilling or unable either to adopt a program which would appeal to the one or to force a compromise with the other, ignored from below and from above, the democratic movement of 1848 reached a complete standstill. This chapter will consider the role which the workers played in this development as a preliminary to the discussion of the growth of the workers' organizations which marked the real interest of the workers during the latter part of 1848 and the early months at least of 1849.

*

The September crisis, the acceptance of the Truce of Malmoe by the Frankfurt Assembly and the suppression of the riots which followed came as a great shock to the democrats. For them it marked the parting of the ways with the Frankfurt Assembly. In particular the democrats turned from the hope for national unification and sought to achieve their aims through a concerted effort within the individual states. They decided that freedom in the separate states was the first essential; unification could follow.[3] The call to the workers was for "Unity! Unity at any price! . . . Workers! Regard yourselves as the brothers of the burghers and reflect that one cannot exist without the other."[4] But the call went unheeded. At the same time the rising in Frankfurt was blamed on the democrats and the danger cry of "the red republic" was proclaimed on street placards.[5] The isolation of the democrats had begun.

In the Rhineland there was a general movement of protest against the action of the Frankfurt Assembly. Struve proclaimed a German republic for a second time at Lörrach in southern Baden, near Basel, on the twenty-first of September, and some of the populace seized the opportunity for plundering. But the attempt was abortive; the government declared a state of war on the twenty-sixth and the rebellion was soon stamped out.[6] Further down the Rhine, in Cologne, a congress of Rhineland democrats was summoned for the twenty-fourth of September.[7] On the twenty-fifth the organizer of the congress, Hermann Becker, was arrested together with two other democrats, Karl Schapper and Heinrich Bürgers; all three were allies of Marx. The arrests led to rioting among the workers, the erection of barricades and the declaration of a state of siege.[8] All clubs were for-

[3] Lüders, *Die demokratische Revolution,* pp. 36-39.
[4] *Die Locomotive,* Oct. 21, 1848.
[5] *Plakate,* Ratsbibliothek, Berlin, portfolio 6.
[6] *Grossherzoglich Badisches Regierungs-Blatt,* Sept. 26, 1848; Valentin, *Geschichte der deutschen Revolution,* vol. 2, pp. 177ff. The attempt was referred to satirically as the "*Struwelputsch.*"
[7] *Neue Rheinische Zeitung,* Sept. 8, 1848.
[8] *Neue Kölnische Zeitung,* Sept. 26, 27, 1848; the paper was issued by the editor's wife, Frau Anneke, after the declaration of the state of siege, under the title, *Frauen Zeitung.* Cf. Stein, *Der Kölner Arbeiterverein,* pp. 72-75.

bidden to meet; radical newspapers, including the *Neue Rheinische Zeitung* and the newspaper of the workers' union, were suspended; a number of radicals, among them Friedrich Engels, had to flee the city. The restrictions were suspended on the third of October and the affair passed over without any decisive action by either side. Both the moderate *Kölnische Zeitung* and the *Neue Rheinische Zeitung* agreed in describing the episode as a mere "carnival game" (*ein Fastnachtsspiel*).

But the fact remained that the workers had once again come to the barricades only to find that they lacked leaders and were soon put down by the government forces. The *Neue Rheinische Zeitung* did not help by declaring itself unable to decide "Who is the most comic, the workers who exerted themselves on the twenty-fifth of September in building barricades or the Cavaignac, who declared a state of siege in the most pious seriousness on the 26th?" [9]

❋

Two democratic or radical meetings were summoned to Berlin at the beginning of October 1848 and actually succeeded in meeting. The first was a "Counter-Parliament" (*Gegenparlament*), which was announced by a number of democratic delegates to Frankfurt on the fifth of October and was to meet on the twenty-seventh. The second was the Democratic Central Committee on the seventh of October and was to meet in Berlin on the twenty-sixth of that month.[10] Both were prompted by the truce of Malmoe and the September riots in Frankfurt. Both proposed to discuss in a general way the situation in Germany, though there was the

[9] *Neue Rheinische Zeitung*, Oct. 13, 1848.
[10] Lüders, *Die demokratische Bewegung*, p. 35. The first Democratic Congress had met in Frankfurt in June and established the Democratic Central Committee.

suggestion that the Counter-Parliament, as implied by its name, might set up a further all-German assembly to rival the one meeting in Frankfurt.[11] Both bodies became involved in the attempt to rouse support for the besieged revolutionaries in Vienna at the end of October.

And finally both bodies were swept aside by the popular movement in Berlin which culminated in the riots of October 31. A series of street episodes and fights led up to these riots during the month of October, and the role which the workers played in them, and the final failure of the workers to support the two democratic assemblies, marked the first major break between the workers' movement and the bourgeois democrats.

The most serious of these riots was the fight which broke out in the southern part of Berlin, toward the Köpenicker Fields, on the sixteenth of October. The Berlin magistrate had announced on the tenth of the month a curtailment of employment on the public works. Because of the increase of jobs available in private concerns and because of the shortening of daylight, the city and state officials had decided to limit the work on public projects to ten hours a day and to reduce the daily wage on these projects to 12.5 silbergroschen. The magistrate called the attention of the workers to the "great sacrifice" the state had been making in order to support them and hoped that they would repay this by behaving peacefully, offering no resistance to the forces of order.[12]

The workers rejected this injunction. On the twelfth of October they attacked and destroyed a steam machine which was being used to remove water from a canal bed before the winter set in. It was believed among the workers that the machine was to do work previously

[11] Lüders, *Die demokratische Bewegung*, pp. 48-50.
[12] *Plakate*, Ratsbibliothek, Berlin, portfolio 7.

done by hand, when in fact its purpose was to prepare the canal so that work could continue during the winter. A procession of workers protested to von Bonin, the Minister for Public Works, but he denied all knowledge of the machine and said that he could scarcely countermand an order he had never given.[13] It was only then that the workers actually destroyed the machine, left unguarded by a group of sympathetic soldiers. In retaliation for this act of destruction, the government announced on the following day that all workers involved would be dismissed and the work force reduced on public projects. Further reprisals were threatened against any future "excess."[14]

Unrepentant, the workers organized a "burial" procession for the destroyed machine on the sixteenth, complete with banners, a band and a red flag. The procession went the rounds of the public work sites and then wound its way into the city, where someone had the idea of cheering and serenading the detachment of the civil guard located at the *Exercierhaus*. Here trouble broke out. The guard, perhaps, it was suggested, out of excessive zeal and a desire to prove that the civil guard could be as firm as the regular army, declined to enter into the spirit of the workers, blocked the workers' way into the city and curtly ordered them to disperse and return to their work. When the workers refused and, according to some reports, began to throw stones, the civil guard opened fire on the procession, killing eleven workers. Barricades were erected throughout the city. Though no further fighting occurred, the situation was tense till the following day when a procession of workers appeared

[13] *Neue Kölnische Zeitung,* Oct. 17, 1848; *Verbrüderung,* Oct. 20, 1848; declaration of the canal workers, Oct. 18, 1848, *Plakate,* Ratsbibliothek, Berlin, portfolio 7.

[14] *Plakate,* Ratsbibliothek, Berlin, portfolio 7.

before the National Assembly and a conciliatory speech was given by Waldeck.[15]

The whole city was shocked by the episode. Some even compared it with the June Days in Paris.[16] Both the liberals and the democrats published disclaimers, denying that they had any connection with the affair and hinting that it was the work of *agents provocateurs* sent out by the reaction, a charge for which there seems to be no evidence. The commander of the *Bürgerwehr* issued a declaration of sympathy with the victims of the fighting and called for unity among the people. A funeral was held on the twentieth of October for those who fell on the sixteenth, with a grand procession, headed by a commission representing the citizens of Berlin and followed by the representatives of fifty clubs and trades, each with their flags, and a group of the veterans of the 1813-1814 war.[17]

Yet the riots of October 16 marked a real split in the popular movement in Berlin. The civil guard, which had been formed after the revolution and was regarded by many as the defender of the revolution, had turned on the workers. There had long been suspicions of a *Bürgerwehr* from which the lower orders were excluded; these suspicions seemed confirmed and justified by the events of the sixteenth. To many it was the beginning of the class war.[18]

[15] *Deutsche Zeitung*, Oct. 20, 1848; *Illustrierte Zeitung*, Nov. 11, 1848; announcement by the Chief of Police, *Plakate*, Ratsbibliothek, Berlin, portfolio 7; *Verhandlungen der Versammlung zur Vereinbarung der Preussischen Staats-Verfassung*, vol. 3, p. 58; Bernstein, *Revolutions- und Reaktionsgeschichte*, vol. 1, p. 200.

[16] *Der Urwähler*, Oct. 22, 1848; the paper, edited by Weitling, appeared for only five numbers in October and November of 1848.

[17] *Plakate*, Ratsbibliothek, Berlin, portfolio 7; *Verbrüderung*, Oct. 27, 1848; Lüders, *Die demokratische Bewegung*, pp. 65-66.

[18] A contemporary illustration of the fighting showed clearly the class difference between the two groups—the civil guard dressed entirely in the high hats and frock coats of the middle classes, the workers dressed in their rough clothes, spades and tools their only weapons. *Illustrierte Zeitung*, Nov. 11, 1848.

Fear of class struggle and civil war extended to the working class. One of the interesting results of the riots of the sixteenth was a declaration issued on the twenty-fourth of October by the Machine Workers' Union, deploring the spread of internal conflicts. The placard declared: [19]

> We, the Machine Workers, have decided openly and firmly as the unbreakable support of democratic progress: "At the outbreak of a new struggle between the civil guard and the workers, we shall place ourselves, *together and armed,* as the defensive and offensive guard of brotherly unity between the two fighting parties, and only over our corpses will the unhappy road to civil war continue."

In other words, the machine workers were refusing to support the cause of the mass of workers and placing themselves on the side of the forces of order. To be sure, they spoke of preventing a further struggle and of separating the workers from the civil guard, but when they attempted to intervene in accordance with this resolution in the events of October 31, they did so with disastrous results.

✻

By the end of October 1848 the two democratic assemblies, the "Counter-Parliament" and the Democratic Congress, had gathered in Berlin. The first of these bodies consisted of members of the democratic left of the various German legislative bodies, including the Frankfurt Assembly. The group's interest was exclusively political, its main action a motion calling upon the German people to support Vienna. There was no discussion of social or economic matters, and the assembly was rendered largely ineffective by the hostility be-

[19] *Plakate,* Ratsbibliothek, Berlin, portfolio 7.

tween the members of the Prussian and the Frankfurt parliaments.[20]

The Democratic Congress was a somewhat wider and more representative body. It was attended by some 230 delegates from 140 different cities, representing 260 clubs. The dominant group was from northeast Germany, particularly from Berlin. Both the democratic left of the various legislative assemblies who were also attending the Counter-Parliament and the "democracy of the streets," of the clubs and associations throughout Germany, were present. There were several representatives from the workers' associations. Four delegates came from the Berlin Workers' Union and three from the Union of Machine Builders in Berlin. In addition Stephan Born was present as the delegate from Leipzig and Nees von Esenbeck, who had presided over the Workers' Congress in August, was one of the delegates from Breslau. And Wilhelm Weitling was once again in Berlin, claiming to represent the German workers of New York.[21]

The debates of the Democratic Congress were largely taken up with discussion of the internal affairs of democratic organizations and a plan for a new central power.[22] As at the Counter-Parliament, the only concrete resolution

[20] Lüders, *Die demokratische Bewegung,* pp. 70-71, 81.

[21] Lüders, *Die demokratische Bewegung,* pp. 164-167, lists the delegates to the second Democratic Congress. Cf. Meyer, *1848,* p. 74; Quarck, *Erste deutsche Arbeiterbewegung,* pp. 180-181.

[22] The *Neue Kölnische Zeitung,* Nov. 3, 1848, commented, "the debates in the Democratic Congress are so unedifying that it is best if they are passed over into forgetfulness. The Congress offers in every way the picture of our constituent assemblies; many beautiful words, innumerable erroneous and impractical proposals, amendments and amendments to amendments, interpellations and cries of order squander precious time. Everything, however, that would lead to energetic action is put to one side." The democratic lawyer Temme, leader of the left in the Prussian Assembly, received a similar impression: he had, he declared, "never in a single half hour experienced so much nonsense and crudeness." Quoted by Klein, *Der Vorkampf,* p. 365.

adopted was a call to all Germans on the twenty-ninth to support Vienna; nothing more than this was attempted. The *Neue Rheinische Zeitung,* itself a supporter of the democratic movement during the first months of 1848, described the motion as "the howling pathos of a preacher" and commented simply *"C'est incroyable!"* [23]

Those who had hoped that the democrats might seek an alliance with the workers were disappointed. The delegates assumed smugly that "the poor artisans are our supporters." [24] They did nothing to gain this support. At the second session of the congress on October 27, Hermann Kriege, speaking for the Democratic Central Committee, stated that there was no "ideal proletariat" in Germany capable of carrying out a revolution and his opinion was accepted by the majority of the congress. Born gained no support for his view that only through the organization of the workers could a democratic Germany be achieved; the congress refused to support the *Verbrüderung* or to do anything more than adopt a resolution declaring its "lively interest" in the workers' associations. Weitling's proposal of equal pay for all was greeted with shouts of laughter. [25]

The "social question" was not considered till the final day of the congress, the thirtieth of October. By this time some forty delegates had left, convinced of the uselessness of the democratic movement. Those who had departed included Gottfried Kinkel, the radical professor from Bonn who had interested himself in the artisans' movement and who had been elected by the congress to head the committee to draw up its social program. Thus some sort of document had to be patched together in a hurry, and this task was entrusted to Friedrich

[23] Nov. 3, 1848.
[24] *Neue Kölnische Zeitung,* Oct. 31, 1848.
[25] Lüders, *Die demokratische Bewegung,* pp. 91-92, 152-156; Wittke, *Utopian Communist,* p. 131.

Beust, the delegate of the workers' association in Cologne.

The program which Beust brought forward was not surprisingly a crib, word for word, from the program issued from Paris on the first of April by the "Communist Party of Germany," though its origin was tactfully not mentioned to the democrats.[26] The measures listed by the communists were preceded by a general statement, which urged gradualism in the achievement of these goals and gave as guiding principles the equality of all men, the duty of all to work, the common right to property; private ownership was condemned as the basis of class war and the exploitation of the many by the few. It was indeed an extreme statement; yet its import was apparently lost on the remaining delegates at the congress. It was passed without debate and shelved by the central committee. No attempt was made to implement its principles or even to gain support for the program among the workers. Moreover the program was considerably weakened by the adoption of a resolution to the effect that all social measures and the solution to the social question must wait upon the achievement of the republic.[27]

The workers were unimpressed by the concern, or rather the lack of concern, in social issues and the problems of the working population exhibited at the Democratic Congress. Born in particular, although present at the meetings, attacked the work of the congress in his newspaper, the *Verbrüderung*. An article published shortly after the congress rejected the belief that democrats and workers were "natural allies," arguing that the debate on the social question at the congress showed the

[26] A copy of Beust's report is given in Lüders, *Die demokratische Bewegung*, pp. 160-162.

[27] Lüders, *Die demokratische Bewegung*, p. 88.

weakness of this position, that the majority of democrats regarded the social question as insoluble or at best to be postponed. A second article published by Born at the end of November, "On the Relation between Politics and the Social Question," dealt with the inadequacies of such an attitude. The Democratic Congress, according to Born, revealed that there were "two parties within the democratic camp, . . . the purely political and the social." Only from the latter could the workers hope for any help. In the meantime they had to seek measures by which they could help themselves and find leaders within their own ranks; little or nothing of good would come to the workers through alliance with the middle-class democrats.[28]

＊

Before Born published these words about the Democratic Congress, events in Berlin and Vienna had proved him right. On the afternoon of Sunday, October 29, a meeting was held to protest the siege of Vienna and to circulate a mass petition in favor of the defenders of the city. A crowd, estimated at between one thousand and five thousand, was addressed by various speakers including Arnold Ruge and a number of the other delegates to the Democratic Congress.[29] On the thirty-first Waldeck moved in the Prussian Assembly that the government use all possible means to aid the insurgents in Vienna. The motion was debated at length, with amendments from the right, which called merely for the protection of "the freedom and nationality of the German race," and from the left-center, which put the burden of action on the national authority in Frankfurt. Both Waldeck's proposal and that of the right were rejected; the motion of the left-center passed by a large

[28] *Verbrüderung*, Nov. 14, 21, 1848.
[29] Lüders, *Die demokratische Bewegung*, pp. 102ff.

majority. Responsibility and the necessity of action were avoided.

In the meantime an angry crowd gathered in front of the theater where the Prussian Assembly was meeting; a procession was organized by the democratic clubs of Berlin, though both the Democratic Congress and the Counter-Parliament remained aloof. By the time the debate ended, at ten in the evening, and the delegates had found their way out through the back exits of the building, the crowd, threatened by the civil guard, was roused to a considerable pitch of excitement. At this point, true to their promise of the twenty-fourth, the machine builders appeared upon the scene, marching behind a white flag, in an effort to separate the opposing forces. Their intention was mistaken, the militia fired upon the machine builders and dispersed the crowd. Order was gradually restored.[30]

The proclamations of the democratic congresses and the meetings in sympathy for Vienna were ineffectual; the rest of Germany stood quietly aside while that city succumbed on the first of November to the troops under Windischgrätz and Jellačić. Working-class districts were looted and many of the defenders of the city were shot; all workers' associations were dissolved and relief through the public works ceased. Yet the event which attracted the greatest attention in Germany was the death of a single man, Robert Blum, who had gone to the city as a member of a delegation from the Frankfurt Assembly and had participated in the defense. When Blum was executed by the Austrian authorities on the ninth of November, protest meetings were held throughout Germany. In Leipzig, where Blum had lived, the workers'

[30] Lüders, *Die demokratische Bewegung*, pp. 110ff., contains a detailed account of the events of the thirty-first based on a comparison of the newspaper sources.

club organized a memorial meeting on November 26 at which Born spoke and urged a strengthening of effort against the reaction and increased support for the workers' organizations. The motto which the *Verbrüderung* adopted for the occasion was, "Everything through Labor, Everything for Labor." [31]

In Prussia as well as Austria the conservatives and the government gained the upper hand during the month of November. The new ministry under Count Brandenburg, appointed on the second of the month, set out to break the forces of revolution. On the tenth the regular troops under General Wrangel returned to the city; the civil guard offered no protest. On the twelfth of November Wrangel declared a state of siege. The civil guard was disbanded; the right to hold public meeting was suspended, a curfew established and radical journals suppressed.[32] The Prussian Assembly protested, declaring all who obeyed to be traitors; former units of the civil guard, including the two special workers' corps of artisans and machine builders, joined in the protest, but with little effect.[33] The Assembly was moved from Berlin to provincial Brandenburg. Before leaving Berlin, it adopted, on the fifteenth of November, a resolution calling on all citizens to cease payment of taxes till its sovereignty was recognized. On the fifth of December the Assembly was dissolved and a constitution promulgated by decree of the king.

The events of the autumn of 1848 marked the defeat of the democratic movement; the slogans of the movement were to be heard again at the time of the risings in May and June of 1849 but they failed to arouse the

[31] *Verbrüderung*, Nov. 28, 1848; Born, *Erinnerungen*, pp. 186-187.

[32] *Neue Kölnische Zeitung*, Nov. 15, 1848.

[33] *Plakate*, Ratsbibliothek, Berlin, portfolio 8; *Neue Rheinische Zeitung*, Nov. 15, 1848.

enthusiasm which once had greeted them.[34] More importantly, the democrats ceased to attract support from the workers. Many democrats were arrested following the fall of Vienna and the dissolution of the Prussian Assembly.[35] The Central Committee of the Democrats left Berlin in the middle of December and took up residence in Cöthen, but its activities were limited and it had no effect on the course of events during 1849.

With the disappearance of the democrats from the scene a number of the symbols often connected with the workers' movement also went. The red flag, for example, was associated far more closely with the democrats and the demand for a republic in 1848 than it was with a revolutionary workers' movement; indeed, as noted in discussing the Journeymen's Congress, it was quite specifically rejected by the workers. After the attack on the democrats it appeared much less often and was soon outlawed by the police. Two youths were arrested in Berlin early in 1849 for carrying a red flag and were sentenced to eight days in prison. Their case was appealed, however, and their sentence revoked when it was proved that the flag had been rolled up and not unfurled; by this time they had already spent eight days in prison.[36] The episode can serve perhaps as a parable of the fate of the whole workers' movement of 1848.

Yet, strangely enough, the dissolution of the demo-

[34] One newspaper at that time contained advertisements for a "democratic cigar" and "a pure democratic Mosell wine"; *Neue Kölnische Zeitung,* June 24, 1849. There is no evidence that this increased the sales of the products thus described.

[35] It was even claimed that the government had offered rewards to soldiers who were able to provoke suspected democrats into insulting the crown or the army and thus provide a pretext for arrest. *Neue Rheinische Zeitung,* Dec. 6, 15, 16, 1848; Valentin, *Geschichte der deutschen Revolution,* vol. 2, pp. 294ff.

[36] *Neue Kölnische Zeitung,* Jan. 17, 1848.

cratic organizations had no immediate effect on the workers' associations, which were ignored at this stage by the governments. There was one exception, the machine builders' association in Berlin. The meetings of this group were forbidden during the state of siege and the ruling was so meekly accepted by the association that, when the crisis had passed, General Wrangel made a contribution to the illness fund of the machine builders in token of their good behavior. Toward the end of the year the machine builders decided voluntarily to disband their association, since they could not resolve various internal conflicts about the proper function of the club.[37] Thus the one workers' organization founded in 1848 and composed entirely of persons employed in factories was the first to disappear as reaction to the revolution set in. It was the artisans, the workers in the old handicraft trades, who continued the struggle in the face of opposition and the increasingly apparent defeat of the revolution rather than the workers in the new industries.

*

The figure who was perhaps most affected by the standstill in the democratic movement was Karl Marx. For Marx had based his whole strategy in 1848 on alliance with the middle-class democrats, ignoring the efforts by the workers in order to concentrate on this alliance. The *Neue Rheinische Zeitung* had declared itself to be "The Organ of Democracy" and had reported the activities of the middle-class democrats and the affairs of the two democratic congresses with far greater regularity than it had chronicled the workers' movement. Marx himself had been active in the democratic organization in the Rhineland. Now the alliance with the demo-

[37] *Neue Rheinische Zeitung,* Dec. 7, 1848; *Neue Kölnische Zeitung,* Dec. 22, 1848.

crats and the middle classes appeared useless, and Marx turned increasingly to the workers' groups.

Marx began to despair not only of the proletarian revolution, which he had once believed was imminent, but of the success of even the bourgeois revolution. In letters to Engels, who, having fled Cologne, was traveling in France and Switzerland, Marx complained of overwork and begged for articles for the *Neue Rheinische Zeitung* on almost any subject—the theories of Proudhon, the federal system of government in Switzerland, the Hungarian *Scheisse* (*sic*).[38] The paper blamed the middle classes for the triumph in Austria and Prussia of the forces of reaction. The only way left to save the revolution, Marx held in an article written shortly after the fall of Vienna, was "revolutionary terrorism." [39]

But when it came to practical measures, the most Marx could think of was to support the campaign of the Prussian Assembly against the payment of taxes. To this end Marx tried to rally the democratic associations in the Rhineland.[40] From the nineteenth of November the paper began printing the slogan "No More Taxes" below the masthead. But the campaign had little success and Marx soon gave it up. In a series of articles published during the following month on "The Bourgeoisie and the Counter-Revolution" Marx asserted that the two were inextricably allied and that the middle classes would inevitably support the government against the interest of the people—that is, the workers.[41] In March of 1849, on the anniversary of the revolution, the *Neue Rheinische*

[38] Marx, Engels, *Gesamtausgabe*, pt. 3, vol. 1, pp. 102, 104.

[39] *Neue Rheinische Zeitung*, Nov. 7, 1848.

[40] *Neue Rheinische Zeitung*, Nov. 15, 1848. Marx did not even go so far as his fellow democrats of the *Neue Kölnische Zeitung*, who advocated (Nov. 15, 1848) a general strike against all "traitors to the people."

[41] *Neue Rheinische Zeitung*, Dec. 10, 1848, and the issues following.

Zeitung saw no cause for rejoicing but suggested that, whereas the people of Berlin had taken "*Jesus, meine Zuversicht*" as the hymn of the revolution, they might in 1849 sing instead "*Wrangel, meine Zuversicht!*" Though a year had passed since the revolution, Marx doubted that his newspaper would last till it too was a year old.[42] In April 1849 the paper began printing its survey of political events in Berlin, of the government and the monarchy, under the simple if despairing title "*Klatsch*"!

In the spring of 1849 Marx also admitted that the paper had perhaps concentrated too much on political issues and ignored the economic side. He set out to remedy this fault and to provide an explanation of the "economic relations which form the basis of the present class struggle and national struggles" and of the "subjugation of the working class which February and March [of 1848] had brought about." There followed the celebrated essay on "Wage-Labor and Capital" which sketched the ideas which Marx was later to develop in his *Critique of Political Economy* and in *Capital*.[43] Though these articles marked a change in the subject matter which normally appeared in the paper, and though they are justly celebrated in the history of Marxist thought, they scarcely provided an answer to the objections of the workers who felt the *Neue Rheinische Zeitung* to be written at a level far above their comprehension and to ignore the actual efforts of the workers to snatch some improvement in their conditions from the political developments of the revolution.

❋

Marx had, however, with the defeat of the democrats, begun to take a greater interest in the activities of the

[42] *Neue Rheinische Zeitung*, Mar. 18, 1849.
[43] *Neue Rheinische Zeitung*, Apr. 5-8, 11, 1849.

workers' association in Cologne, though initially at least this interest was aimed at supporting the democratic movement. The Cologne Workers' Union had been in fairly close alliance with the democratic group ever since the arrest of Gottschalk and Anneke in July.[44] After the riots in Cologne at the end of September and the declaration of a state of siege, the Workers' Union was forced to reorganize itself. Marx himself was asked to be president and accepted the offer, declaring that he had no intention of changing the orientation of the club. His first act as president, however, was to call upon the group to send a representative to the Democratic Congress about to convene in Berlin.[45] The first newspaper of the Workers' Union had been suspended during the state of siege and banned in a press trial on October 22; a new one was announced on the twenty-sixth, to be called *Freiheit, Brüderlichkeit, Arbeit* (Freedom, Brotherhood, Labor). The paper followed the same lines as the old one had done since the arrest of Gottschalk, dealing more in general comment on political matters than in discussion of the workers' demands and interests.[46]

Marx and the *Neue Rheinische Zeitung* did not escape the legal persecution to which most of the democrats were subject during the autumn and winter of 1848-1849. Marx, together with others of the staff of the paper, was arraigned on December 20, 1848, on the charge of slandering various government officials, and, when this charge failed, he was prosecuted on February 8, 1849, for incitement to rebellion during the antitax campaign.

[44] *Der Wächter am Rhein*, Oct. 8, 1848.

[45] *Neue Kölnische Zeitung*, Oct. 18, 1848; Stein, *Der Kölner Arbeiterverein*, pp. 77-78.

[46] Fritz Brügel, "Zur Geschichte des Kölner Arbeitervereins," *Die Gesellschaft, Internationale Revue für Sozialismus und Politik*, vol. 1 (1930), pp. 112-116; Stein, *Der Kölner Arbeiterverein*, p. 80.

Marx's defense was a piece of pure sophistry; he claimed that his actions were entirely legal, since they were in support of an act by the same legislative body, the Prussian Assembly, which had passed the laws under which he was being tried. Or, alternatively, if his campaign had been illegal, then so was the trial conducted under these laws. The case was dismissed for lack of evidence.[47]

Also under trial in Cologne was the former leader of the Workers' Union, Andreas Gottschalk, who had been in prison since July of 1848. Gottschalk too was acquitted, though his defense was a somewhat more impassioned affair. He appeared together with Friedrich Anneke and Christian Joseph Esser, both former members of the committee of the Workers' Union, on the charge of seeking to change the state by force through the Union and its newspaper, which, it was held, exhibited "tendencies working for communism and the overthrow of the existing order." In his speech in defense of his actions, Gottschalk claimed that even if the purpose of his writings had been as indicated, they should be allowed under the right of free speech. The whole trial he condemned as a "spectacle of medieval barbarism."[48] Gottschalk and his colleagues were acquitted. The Workers' Union attempted to hold a torchlight procession to celebrate their release but the police banned such demonstrations.[49]

*

Upon his release from prison, and in spite of the attempted procession, Gottschalk found that the Work-

[47] *Neue Rheinische Zeitung,* Feb. 25, 27, 1849.

[48] The indictment was printed in the *Neue Rheinische Zeitung,* Dec. 22, 23, 1848; see also Andreas Gottschalk, *Meine Rede vor dem Geschworenengericht zu Köln am 23. 12. 1848,* Bonn, 1849.

[49] *Neue Kölnische Zeitung,* Dec. 27, 1848.

ers' Union was largely in the control of the Marxists and was no longer interested in his advice or leadership.[50] He therefore began arrangements for a new paper for the Cologne workers which would present his point of view and attack the alliance with the democrats. The paper, *Freiheit, Arbeit* (Freedom, Labor), appeared from January 14, 1849, and was edited by W. Prinz; a red flag was printed on the top of the masthead. Gottschalk tried to get it adopted as the official paper of the Workers' Union, in place of *Freiheit, Brüderlichkeit, Arbeit,* but failed.[51] He then went into exile from Cologne, staying first with his invalid sister near Bonn and then in Brussels. He continued to contribute to the paper, however, and was probably responsible for the vitriolic attack on Marx and his position which appeared late in February. The article took the form of an open letter, "To Herr Karl Marx, editor of the *Neue Rheinische Zeitung*": [52]

> We . . . are no prophets. We do not know what will become of our revolution. For us there are, apart from the possibility presented by you as necessary, the rule of the bourgeoisie, still other possibilities, for example, a new revolution, a permanent revolution. . . . For us, the party of the revolutionary proletariat who know no middle ground, there is no fear—least of all of a throwback into medieval barbarism.
>
> For you such fear exists. Naturally. You have never been serious about the emancipation of the repressed. The misery of the worker, the hunger of the poor has for you only a scientific, a doctrinaire interest. You are elevated above such miseries. Like a learned Sun-god you merely shine down upon the parties. You are not

[50] Stein, *Der Kölner Arbeiterverein,* p. 89.
[51] *Freiheit, Arbeit,* Jan. 21, 1849.
[52] *Freiheit, Arbeit,* Feb. 25, 1849.

touched by that which moves the hearts of human beings. You do not believe in the cause which you claim to represent. Yes, in spite of the fact that you prune the German revolution every day according to a pattern of completed events, in spite of your "Communist Credo," you do not believe in the revolt of the working people, whose rising flood begins already to prepare the destruction of capital, you do not believe in the permanence of the revolution, you do not even believe in the capacity for revolution.

It seems perhaps a strange attack on the founder of modern communism and the prophet of the proletarian revolution, and it was no doubt prompted largely by personal bitterness; Gottschalk was sharply criticized by some members of the Cologne Workers' Union for his assault on Marx and accused of seeking his own ends.[53] Yet Gottschalk's was perhaps the natural reaction of one who had sought from the early days of the revolution to gain some benefit for the working class and was faced with Marx's policy of seeking alliance with the left-wing democrats and ignoring the efforts and organizations of the working class.

Marx himself seemed in the spring of 1849 to doubt that his policy had been the wisest one or at least to decide that alterations must be made. He attended two "democratic banquets" in Mülheim am Rhein and in Cologne toward the end of February to celebrate the anniversary of the French revolution of the preceding year; there were songs by a workers' chorus, cheers for the "universal democratic-social republic" and innumerable toasts, several offered by Marx himself.[54] But Marx's heart no longer seemed in it.

[53] Letter from two members of the Workers' Union, "in the name of many comrades," *Neue Rheinische Zeitung*, Apr. 22, 1849.
[54] *Neue Rheinische Zeitung*, Feb. 18, 28, 1849.

At the end of February the Workers' Union in Cologne, under Marx's leadership, was reorganized; the group took as its purpose "the education of our members in political, social and scientific subjects." There was no mention, however, of political activity or of such practical measures as cooperative production or the establishment of various sorts of savings funds; nor was membership in the *Verbrüderung*, which promoted such activities elsewhere in Germany, mentioned. The club was subdivided into nine filial clubs in the hope that, when one of them was suppressed, the others might still continue.[55] In April Marx, together with Karl Schapper, Friedrich Anneke, Hermann Becker and Wilhelm Wolff, announced his decision to resign from the Rhineland district committee of the democratic clubs in order to seek "a closer connection with the workers' associations." The current democratic organization, Marx claimed, contained "too many heterogeneous elements."[56] There was danger, it was argued, of the Cologne democratic club "drowning in the general waters of democracy, which today has taken over the position of the old 'liberalism.'"[57]

There was also a movement in the spring of 1849 to reconstitute the old Communist League which Marx had dissolved in the previous year. Joseph Moll, who had opposed Marx's decision in 1848, set up a new central authority for the League in London and proceeded to Germany in search of members. In Cologne he was joined by Karl Schapper, Peter Rösler, Peter Nothjung and others, but Marx, together with Engels and Wolff, held aloof, still arguing that the revolution had removed the need for a secret, subversive organization such as the

[55] *Verbrüderung,* Mar. 6, 1849.
[56] *Neue Rheinische Zeitung,* Apr. 15, 1849.
[57] *Neue Kölnische Zeitung,* Apr. 15, 1849.

League.[58] Instead Marx carried out his new, rather belated program of seeking closer ties with the workers' organizations. He announced the establishment of a new workers' association for the Prussian Rhineland and Westphalia on April 26, 1849; he even hoped that this new group could be joined with Born's *Verbrüderung* and called for the election of delegates to the workers' congress to be held in Leipzig in June under the auspices of the *Verbrüderung*.[59] Before this plan could be carried out, however, the second revolution had begun.

Marx's eleventh hour realization of the futility of the democratic cause and his new-sought alliance with the workers' movement had one further result in Cologne. "A large number" of members of the Workers' Union announced their resignation and wrote to their old leader, Gottschalk, asking him to return to the city and take command of a new association. The recent separation of the democratic club and the Workers' Union, formerly presented as a necessary union, was, they claimed, "the best testimony to the fact that the previous leaders of the Workers' Union [that is, Marx and his colleagues] did not themselves know what they wanted and do not know what they want." [60] It was evident to the workers in Cologne that Marx's policy of alliance with the democrats had been bound to fail and that their interests lay in their own organizations and the possibility of self-help. And even Marx turned in the end to the *Verbrüderung*.

[58] See the testimony of Rösler in Mänchen-Helfen, Nikolajewsky, *Karl und Jenny Marx,* esp. pp. 151-153.
[59] *Neue Kölnische Zeitung,* Apr. 26, 1849.
[60] *Freiheit, Arbeit,* May 6, 1849.

CHAPTER 11

THE GROWTH OF ORGANIZATION

THE *Verbrüderung* issued on September 18, 1848, in Leipzig a "Circular Letter from the Central Committee of German Workers to All Workers and Workers' Unions of Germany." [1] The letter was signed by Franz Schwenniger, Georg Kick and Stephan Born, who called for the unity and organization of the working class. The revolutions of February and March, it held, had shown the power of the working class and revealed its new position in society; the Berlin Congress sought to utilize this power, recognizing that there was no longer an opposition between masters and journeymen, a false distinction preserved by the medieval guilds. For the Berlin Congress and the *Verbrüderung* there was only the modern social opposition between capitalists and workers. Therefore, the Central Committee concluded,

> *We workers must help ourselves;* that is the principle from which the Berlin Congress started. It formed its decisions on the basis of the necessity of self-help . . . Germany's workers must strive to form a moral power in the state, to become a strong body which defies every storm and presses ever forward. . . . Workers of Germany, we call upon you once more: unite, then you will be strong and need fear no obstacle! You can vanquish all, but only through united strength.

This letter marked the opening of the campaign of the *Verbrüderung* to recruit all workers into a national

[1] The letter was published in the committee's newspaper, *Die Verbrüderung*, Oct. 3, 1848; it also appeared in the *Berliner Zeitungs Halle*, Oct. 14, 1848.

organization, a campaign which was waged with considerable vigor during the autumn and winter of 1848-1849 and indeed continued beyond the defeat of the spring uprisings of 1849.

❋

The central offices of the *Verbrüderung* were located in Leipzig and were to serve as the nucleus of a whole series of regional and local branches which would reach into all parts of the German Federation and embrace the workers of all trades. The choice of Leipzig as the center for the new organization deserves some comment. The decision to move to Leipzig was reached at the Berlin Congress in August and early September. No mention of the reasons for this decision appeared either in the proceedings of the congress or in any of the subsequent histories of the workers' movement. In part the decision may have been prompted by caution. Considerations of the danger of increased police activity and of the possibility of the banning of all working-class associations in Berlin must not have seemed remote in the mounting tension of the autumn of 1848. Saxony on the other hand was one of the quieter and, superficially at least, more contented areas in the German Federation.[2]

But the decision also marked in a sense a retreat from the revolution and from revolutionary aims. Berlin was in many ways the emotional as well as the actual center of the revolution in Germany. There the barricades had been erected in March of 1848, and though Frankfurt may have been regarded as the focus of the national movement during the early months of the summer, when the Assembly was beginning its work, the prestige of Frankfurt as a revolutionary center dwindled rapidly

[2] *Verbrüderung*, Nov. 17, 1848.

after the eighteenth of September.[3] The move to Leipzig by Born and his followers was thus a move away from the center of the revolution. It may also have been regarded as a gesture in the direction of proving that the *Verbrüderung* was not simply an organization of Prussian workers but was truly an all-German body.

Finally it must be noted that the move was away from one of the most industrialized cities in Germany, a city where there were a number of factories and where factory workers played a large and recognizable role in the working-class movement, to a town in which the influence of the guilds was still largely unshaken. The Kingdom of Saxony had preserved the legal rights and position of the guilds as strongly as any of the German states. The workers of Leipzig were not noticeably opposed to guild organization; indeed the journeymen printers had refused to take part in the August strikes organized by the national printers' union: this had been a severe blow to the movement, since Leipzig was a center of the printing trade. On the other hand, the town did have an independent radical tradition, and it was perhaps this which prompted the Berlin Congress to choose it as the headquarters for the *Verbrüderung*.

❊

From October 3, 1848, the Central Committee brought out a newspaper for the organization, entitled *Die Verbrüderung*, and subtitled "Correspondence Sheet for all German Workers." The paper was published initially by the firm of Brockhaus in Leipzig; later, from January 2, 1849, it was printed on the presses owned by the Leipzig Workers' Union. It appeared twice a week with sub-

[3] The democrats certainly regarded Berlin and not Frankfurt as the center of the revolution. "Berlin . . . is the German Paris," wrote one radical paper, *Die Reform*. Quoted by Ernst Bammel, *Frankfurt und Berlin in der deutschen Revolution*, Bonn, 1949, p. 20; cf. Arnold Ruge's letter to his wife, Sept. 22, 1848, quoted in Lüders, *Die demokratische Bewegung*, p. 35.

scriptions, including postage, fixed at 14 neugroschen per quarter. The columns of the *Verbrüderung* were devoted exclusively to the affairs and interests of the workers; much of the writing was done by Born, as in the case of his earlier newspaper, *Das Volk,* but this time there was a greater number of articles by others; both his colleagues on the Central Committee and even foreign supporters of the workers' movement such as Louis Blanc and Proudhon contributed leading articles.

The newspaper took little notice, however, of foreign affairs and events. It expressed distrust of Russia, the mainstay, so the workers believed, of reaction, but never went so far as to advocate war against Russia as a means of saving the revolution, a policy adopted by Marx and the *Neue Rheinische Zeitung.*[4] There was a general hostility to foreigners, foreign produce and foreign competition, and more than a hint of anti-Semitism.[5] Even such attention as was paid to their socialist colleagues abroad was half-hearted. News of a "Socialist Confederation" to be formed in Paris to unite all schools of socialism was noted, but little interest was shown.[6] The articles by foreign socialists were accompanied by a note disclaiming adherence to their views. The editors smugly regarded the *Verbrüderung* as embodying everything of value in Blanc's article on "The Right to Work."[7] In connection with an essay by Proudhon they pointed with pride to the absence of intellectual leadership in the German workers' movement:

We German workers can congratulate ourselves that we have put no prophets, no famous writers at the head of our enterprises. . . . If you look for their "inventor," you will not discover their names; the

[4] *Verbrüderung,* Apr. 27, 1849.
[5] See the article on "Modernes Judenthum," *Verbrüderung,* Dec. 19, 1848.
[6] *Verbrüderung,* Dec. 1, 1848.
[7] *Verbrüderung,* Oct. 17, 1848.

associations have sprung up freely from a living and self-sacrificing people, everything has been done by our workers themselves.[8]

What the *Verbrüderung* did do was to report in full the growth of workers' organizations in Germany, publishing letters from the various local clubs and presenting reports of the series of regional congresses which were held during the winter of 1848-1849 in an effort to draw new members and new areas into the movement. It also published articles analyzing the condition of the workers in various industries and sections of the German economy.[9] And its columns were filled out with aphorisms, epigrams and weak puns which, it was thought, would appeal to the workers.[10]

✿

The editors of the *Verbrüderung* also attempted to expound at length in its columns the position of their

[8] *Verbrüderung*, Apr. 20, 1849. The attack on writers and "prophets" in the labor movement may have been a reference to Marx, though there is no indication that this is the case.

[9] See, for example, the discussion by Schwenniger of the plight of the wool weavers in the *Erzgebirge, Verbrüderung,* Jan. 30, Feb. 9, 1849.

[10] A typical story then current was of the worker who, when asked if he drank coffee, replied, "Nein, ich trinke lieber Tee (Liberté)!" There were such *Lesefrüchte* as: "The surfeited stomach of a king and the empty stomach of a peasant are dangerous things." The *Verbrüderung* published on Mar. 9, 1849, "The Ten Commandments of the Workers," which in a rough way sum up the demands of the workers' movement in 1848-1849: "1. Thou shalt work. 2. Thou shalt tolerate no slackers. 3. Thou shalt undertake no slave labor. 4. Thou shalt demand a just wage for thy work. 5. Thou shalt suffer no hunger. 6. Thou shalt not wear tattered clothing. 7. Thou shalt enjoy thy life. 8. Thou shalt live in honor. 9. Thou shalt shut thy ears to priests. 10. Thou shalt love thy neighbor as thyself." All of these commandments, the article noted, were broken by the workers not of their own will but by the force of the new conditions of work. The editors of the *Verbrüderung* thought well enough of this list of commandments to have it printed and sold as a special pamphlet.

organization and the role which they felt the workers must play in the revolution and in the changing economy of Germany. Most notable in this respect was a series of seven articles written by Born and published between October 3 and December 12, 1848. The articles were well thought out, planned as a unit and prepared in advance of publication. Born later regarded the series as propaganda and stated that "the style was not characterized by cool measuredness and quiet." [11] But the general tenor of the articles was one of moderation; the author searched for a middle way between the more extravagant theories of the socialists and democrats and the complete acceptance of the status quo; above all, the author sought to persuade the workers that through organization and self-help they could gain immediate and practical improvements. Born admitted that the problems of the workers could not be separated from the solution of political questions; he acknowledged that the workers' interests were "closely and firmly tied" to the democrats.[12] Class opposition was at the root of the "social question," but Born distinguished the situation in Germany sharply from that in England and France. For Born the key fact was that in Germany there existed between the class of capitalists and workers a large middle class of master artisans and small farmers who should be brought into alliance with the workers.

Such an alliance, Born argued, could be forged in the associations which were to be organized by the *Verbrüderung*, even if this meant the temporary exclusion of the poorest and least skilled workers. "Mankind obtains freedom only layer by layer, class by class," Born

[11] Born, *Erinnerungen*, p. 181.
[12] *Verbrüderung*, Oct. 16, 1848. After the failure of the Democratic Congress, Born was disillusioned even with the democrats and urged the workers to arm themselves in preparation for independent action. *Verbrüderung*, Nov. 24, 1848.

maintained. The *Verbrüderung* was to be open to all workers, but would aim more particularly at the upper level of workers, the skilled handicraftsmen who were capable of organization and self-help. Associations thus formed could improve the position of the workers through a variety of means: cooperative production, mutual aid funds, wage negotiations. They could seek government support for the right to work. They could prevent solutions to the problem of "overpopulation" which treated the lower classes as superfluous and the bourgeoisie as the most necessary element in society.[13]

Though Born and the *Verbrüderung* were interested primarily in the skilled handicraft workers, they were by no means supporters of the old guild system which had fostered this class nor were they opposed to all forms of modern industry and mechanized production as were some of the more ardent supporters of the guilds. Born published a second series of articles on the various schemes for regulating industry, condemning the supporters of the guilds in strong terms: [14]

> Whoever wants the guild system also wants absolutism; whoever wants the sole power in his trade is a despot. He places his personal interests above the general; he wants monopoly, the selfish exploitation of a business, and all his fellow citizens exist for him only in that they help increase his own riches. The guild system is a relic of the medieval caste-state.

The role once played by the guilds was to be taken over by the new associations, which would look after the workers' interests.

✳

The main interest of the *Verbrüderung* was thus in the spread of an alliance of workers' associations throughout

[13] *Verbrüderung,* Nov. 12, Dec. 12, 1848.
[14] *Verbrüderung,* Feb. 16, 1849.

Germany; most of the space in its newspaper was devoted to this end and to this end were bent most of the efforts of its Central Committee and particularly the leading figure on that committee, Stephan Born. During the autumn and winter of 1848-1849 the reports of the formation of local associations and the allegiance of both the newly formed groups and the older workers' unions to the *Verbrüderung* came into the offices of the Central Committee in Leipzig. The first issue of the *Verbrüderung* newspaper contained notices of branch clubs in Berlin and Leipzig only, but there were soon reports from organizations elsewhere as well. The different skilled trades were all represented in these associations, though factory workers and unskilled labor were rarely mentioned.[15] Some groups remained matter-of-fact in their aims, corresponding with the central body strictly on questions of organization and the immediate economic interests of their members; others spoke in more high-flown language of the role of the workers in history and the opportunities of the new era. "This is not just an ordinary new period in history," wrote the rather overly enthusiastic Workers' Education Union in Munich; "no, a new world-age is on the march!" [16]

The Central Committee made every effort to proselytize for the new organization. Kick appears to have stayed in Leipzig to manage affairs there, but both Born and Schwenniger went on a number of trips during the winter of 1848-1849, seeking to persuade the workers that organization on a national level was the best way of improving conditions of work and gaining power for the workers. Between them they visited Dresden, Altenburg, Magdeburg, Halle, Nuremberg, Heidelberg, Mainz, Co-

[15] The Industrial Union of the Wupperthal, located at Bielefeld, wrote that a special effort would have to be made to attract factory workers in order to organize them to bargain against the unfair competition of capital. *Verbrüderung,* Jan. 26, 1849.

[16] *Verbrüderung,* Nov. 7, 1848.

logne and Essen during the early months of the *Verbrüderung.*[17] Sometimes they were joined by other leading members of the *Verbrüderung* on these expeditions; Bisky from the Berlin Regional Committee went to Magdeburg, for example, to help with the campaign there.[18]

Some of these trips were in connection with regional congresses which were organized by the *Verbrüderung* in order to further the growth of organization. The first of these congresses was held in Leipzig on December 27-28, 1848. The congress was attended by nineteen representatives from the workers' associations in the Kingdom of Saxony, the Saxon duchies and the Prussian province of Saxony, together with six delegates from the Commission for the Discussion of Industrial and Labor Conditions in Dresden and the three members of the Central Committee of the *Verbrüderung.* Since delegates were elected at a ratio of one for every two hundred members of the local associations, the congress represented approximately 3,800 workers in the various parts of Saxony.[19]

The debates of the Saxon congress opened on a political note. The congress voted petitions to the Saxon Diet, protesting the exclusion of workers from the franchise, and to the Frankfurt Assembly, expressing the disappointment of the workers with the results thus far achieved by the revolution. But the address to the National Assembly went on to extol the workers' associations as the one way of achieving "material freedom" and fulfilling the promise of the revolution.

[17] *Verbrüderung,* Mar. 16, 1849; Born, *Erinnerungen,* pp. 190-191; Adler, *Geschichte der Arbeiterbewegung,* p. 179; Quarck, *Erste deutsche Arbeiterbewegung,* p. 232.
[18] *Verbrüderung,* Oct. 17, 1848.
[19] *Verbrüderung,* Dec. 8, 29, 1848, Jan. 2, 5, 1849; Quarck, *Erste deutsche Arbeiterbewegung,* pp. 219-224.

However diverse the methods may be which you will seize upon for the better existence of the working class—we await them with an anxious heart—the undersigned permit themselves to recommend one method to the Exalted Assembly and to plead for its adoption most urgently, that is, the association of workers. Just as the association of capitalists has produced great discoveries, the mines and factories which separate our time in essence from the past, so now the associations of workers will give a new, powerful form to economic activity; they will, as part of the historical development of mankind, bring more and more men into the circle of the independent and free, assuring more and more men a human existence.[20]

The final clause of this address to the National Assembly caused considerable debate, occupying most of the first session. For the address concluded by calling on the Assembly and the local legislative bodies of the various states to grant monetary support to the workers' associations in order to further their activities. The state was to be the ally of the workers in their effort to improve their condition.

The remaining sessions of the Saxon Congress were devoted, however, to a discussion of what the workers could do for themselves through their associations. The disillusionment expressed in the petitions was based on the fact that the workers saw less and less to be achieved through purely political activity. Government support for the associations would be welcome, but most of the delegates, as the debates revealed, regarded it as unlikely. Instead they explored the possibilities of the workers' associations with emphasis on the educational activities of the groups, libraries and lectures and the like, and on the plans for association workshops and

[20] *Verbrüderung*, Dec. 29, 1848.

retail outlets. The local branches of the *Verbrüderung* were to set up funds which could be used in case of illness and unemployment as well as for the support of the widows and children of deceased members. The funds were also to serve as the capital with which to establish workshops for the production and distribution by the association of various types of goods. The exact nature of these workshops was to depend on local needs and trades, but the establishment of these funds and workshops was to become one of the major activities of the *Verbrüderung* in the course of 1849.

A second congress was held by the *Verbrüderung* at the end of January in Heidelberg, a congress which drew delegates from several states in southwest Germany and marked an important step toward the organization's aim of including the workers from all parts of Germany. The Heidelberg Congress also marked a victory for the opponents of the guild system, for its main result was to incorporate the journeymen's organization set up at Frankfurt into the *Verbrüderung;* it thus marked a complete break with the guilds. The Heidelberg Congress was, finally, the scene of a debate between the leaders of these two branches of the workers' movement, Karl Georg Winkelblech and Stephan Born, who summed up between them many of the conflicts which prevailed within the workers' movement. The congress attracted a good deal of national attention and was reported more widely than were any of the other meetings of the *Verbrüderung.*

The *Neue Rheinische Zeitung* saw the debate at the Heidelberg Congress in terms of "the opposition between the lower middle classes or counterrevolutionary group and the revolutionary position of the workers." [21] And Born followed this line in his memoirs in condemning

[21] *Neue Rheinische Zeitung,* Feb. 4, 1849.

Winkelblech's position as reactionary, romantic and medieval.[22] On the other hand, later supporters of Winkelblech have praised his system of federated guilds and accused Born of trying to fit the German workers' movement into a Marxist pattern.[23]

Yet the contrast between Born and Winkelblech should not be overemphasized, for to do so is to exaggerate the clarity with which class distinctions prevailed among the German workers and artisans in the mid-nineteenth century. Both Born and Winkelblech were in fact the leaders of a movement which was largely based on the artisans; both were opposed to the extreme claims of the master craftsmen, supporting against them the journeymen and assistants. According to one contemporary account, the majority of the delegates to the congress, including the supporters of both the Frankfurt and the Leipzig committees, the adherents of both the Journeymen's Congress and the *Verbrüderung*, were equally reactionary, desiring to "return to outdated restrictions and other small or petty preventative measures."[24] Some of these supporters were willing to class themselves as "workers" and others were more interested in preserving their existence as artisans through the guild system. Yet both groups were much the same in composition and both faced the same problem, the decline of the handicraft trades.

Born's Marxism was so modified by his experiences in 1848 that it can scarcely be described as such, while Winkelblech was by no means seeking to restore intact the powers of the guilds and the guild masters. Winkelblech did emphasize the role of guilds more than did Born, who hoped that his more adaptable "associations" would perform many of the same functions as had the

[22] Born, *Erinnerungen*, pp. 191-193.
[23] Biermann, *Winkelblech*, vol. 2, pp. 284-286.
[24] *Neue Kölnische Zeitung*, Feb. 4, 1849.

guilds and permit at the same time a gradual adjustment to the new methods of production. It is in this relatively small area that the difference between the two men lay.

The Heidelberg Congress was less concerned with these ideological issues than it was with the actual mechanisms of organization. Its chief result was the amalgamation of the two groups which had been set up at the Berlin and Frankfurt congresses in August and September, each of them claiming to represent all workers in Germany. From the Heidelberg Congress, rather than the rival congresses of the summer, may be dated the first all-German workers' association.

The congress met in Heidelberg on January 28-29, 1849. The delegates came from the workers' associations in Baden, Württemberg, Rheinhesse and the Bavarian Palatinate in addition to Kick and Born for the Leipzig Central Committee and Winkelblech for the journeymen's committee in Frankfurt. There were also a number of guests who came as observers, including the philosopher Ludwig Feuerbach, the radical editors of the *Neue Deutsche Zeitung*, Otto Lüning and Joseph Weydemeyer, and three members of the National Assembly, Martini, Kapp and the democrat Julius Fröbel. Fröbel was elected as an impartial chairman of the proceedings.[25]

The first day of the congress was devoted entirely to the debate between Winkelblech and Born. The official report of this congress did indeed describe the debate as a "struggle between principles," but the principles which were held to be involved were those of Winkelblech's rather specialized "federal system" and "the free

[25] It is interesting to note that Fröbel did not bother to mention the Heidelberg Congress in his autobiography, *Ein Lebenslauf, Aufzeichnungen, Erinnerungen und Bekenntnisse*, 2 vols., Stuttgart, 1890-1891. His indifference is symbolic of the attitude of most of the 1848 democrats to the workers' movement.

associations of workers." Moreover Winkelblech himself admitted in the course of the debate "the usefulness and significance of the workers' associations and their workshops"; his own proposals he regarded as "merely a later task for the society of the future." When Winkelblech spoke disparagingly of communism, it was not one of the workers' delegates but the observer Otto Lüning who protested against his "false and petty" presentation.[26] The issue was thus not as clear cut as some have made out; the journeymen of Frankfurt and the Central Committee in Leipzig acknowledged their common aims and interests. Winkelblech resigned from the congress after the first day and left the workers' movement, but his absence made little difference.[27]

The decisions of the Heidelberg Congress were regarded above all as a step in the direction of unity for the workers' movement rather than a victory of any specific theory or approach. The Central Committee presented the decisions of the congress with the proud declaration that, "No matter how torn apart Germany may still be, its workers are united in pursuit of their common goal, of social and political freedom." [28] The chief results of the congress were matters of organization. The Leipzig and Frankfurt committees were united; one member of the Frankfurt group was to take up residence in Leipzig in order to work with the Central Committee; the others were to stay in Frankfurt to form the regional committee for southwest Germany. The *Verbrüderung* was accepted as an organ for the workers' movement for all Germany. The decisions of the Berlin Congress of the previous summer were to be used as the basis for

[26] *Verbrüderung*, Feb. 2, 1849.
[27] Biermann, *Winkelblech*, vol. 2, pp. 305-307; after the Heidelberg Congress, Winkelblech devoted himself to writing on economic problems. He made no reference to his defeated efforts.
[28] *Verbrüderung*, Feb. 9, 1849. Cf. also Balser, *Sozial-Demokratie*, pp. 59-62.

the formation of local and regional associations. In the meantime the two united committees were to constitute an "All-German Workers' League" under the Leipzig committee. Preparations were to be made for a nation-wide congress which would draw up the statutes for this new, amalgamated organization as well as a "social creed" for all German workers. This congress would be the first general workers' congress to include representatives from all parts of Germany; the congress would thus be in fact what several of the congresses of the preceding summer had claimed to be.

Four other regional congresses of the *Verbrüderung* were held during the late winter and early spring of 1849 before the arrangements for the general assembly of the workers' associations could be completed. Born presided over a congress held in Hamburg on February 10-14, 1849, and attended by thirty-two representatives of workers' associations in fifteen towns in the various states of north Germany, while Schwenniger was chairman of a similar congress held in Altenburg February 11-12 for thirteen representatives from eight towns in the Thuringian states. On March 4, 1849, a congress of representatives of eleven towns in Württemberg was held in Göppingen, and on April 3-4, seventeen delegates from forty towns in Bavaria met in Nuremberg under the chairmanship of Born to discuss the affairs of the *Verbrüderung*. In general the discussion at these congresses confined itself to the immediate schemes for self-help, education, cooperative production and the like. The Thuringian delegates also voted that the small states they represented should be united with Saxony, a step toward unification which few of the middle or upper classes of Germany would have been willing to take.[29]

[29] *Verbrüderung*, Jan. 19, 30, Feb. 20, 23, Mar. 13, 20, Apr. 6, 1849; Adler, *Geschichte der Arbeiterbewegung*, pp. 182-184; Meusch, *Die Handwerkerbewegung*, p. 62; Biermann, *Winkel-blech*, vol. 2, pp. 304-305.

One weakness in the whole movement came into the open at the Hamburg Congress and an effort was made to remedy it in the course of the spring of 1849. Delegates from the workers and peasants on the estates of Damelock and Petersdorf in Holstein raised the problem of how to help the country workers, a problem which occupied the congress for two sessions. It was decided that the principle of organization should be applied to agricultural workers as well and that the Central Committee should give special consideration to their problems.[30]

The question of workers outside the city was thus raised rather late in the revolutionary period, but it is interesting that it was considered at all. The revolutionaries of 1848 have often been charged with ignoring completely the interests of the countryside; the revolutions, it is claimed, were purely the product of the city.[31] And though this is to a large extent true, there was in the course of the revolutions of 1848 in Germany a good deal of agrarian unrest. Moreover the line between urban workers and agricultural ones was often not easy to draw; industry was not always located in the larger towns, and workers often moved from agricultural work to one or the other of the handtrades with comparative freedom, a state of affairs which the guild masters in the cities, as revealed in the petitions to the Frankfurt Assembly, deplored.

The *Verbrüderung* was at first almost entirely the product of urban organization, but the issue raised at the Hamburg Congress was one which considerably concerned the working-class leaders. A series of articles had

[30] *Verbrüderung,* Feb. 23, 1849.

[31] The charge was perhaps first made by Bakunin in his critique of the German revolutions in his "Confessions," *Beichte,* p. 60. It has been echoed by a number of subsequent historians; see, for example, A. J. P. Taylor, "1848: Opening of an Era," *From Napoleon to Stalin, Comments on European History,* London, 1950, p. 49.

already begun to appear at the end of January in the organization newspaper on the "Rural Proletariat," analyzing and attempting to reconcile the interests of the urban and country workers.[32] The *Verbrüderung* hoped to include agricultural workers as well within its ranks and began to pay more attention to their needs.[33] The attempt, however, proved to be too little and too late.

*

There is no accurate information about the number of members in the *Verbrüderung*, either at any one time during the course of its existence or, far less, over the whole two years of its history.[34] Contemporary figures vary widely, from as few as 12,000 to as many as 800,000; the former figure probably underestimates the extent of the movement, though the latter may well be the attempt of a police spy to prove the necessity of his profession. A figure of 18,000 has been offered as a reasonable estimate.[35] Up to the end of April 1849 mem-

[32] *Verbrüderung*, Jan. 26, 1849. The articles were written by Kick.

[33] See, for example, the article on the demands of the workers and peasants in the Mecklenburgs and Silesia, *Verbrüderung*, Apr. 10, 1849.

[34] The Central Committee tried to collect information from all local branches during the spring of 1849; the survey would have included information about local economic conditions as well as membership in the *Verbrüderung*, but renewed revolution interrupted the work before even one reply had been received. *Verbrüderung*, Apr. 14, May 18, 1849. The lack of accurate statistical information has perhaps led some writers to underrate the role of the *Verbrüderung:* cf. Hamerow, *Restoration, Revolution, Reaction*, p. 140.

[35] The estimate is by Balser, *Sozial-Demokratie*, pp. 72-74, which provides the best discussion of the problem; it is based on the 15,404 workers "represented" at the Leipzig Congress of February 1850, together with the estimated membership of the Cigar Workers' Association which then joined the *Verbrüderung*. Cf. Bernstein, *Geschichte der Berliner Arbeiterbewegung*, vol. 1, p. 84; Stadelmann, *Soziale und politische Geschichte*, p. 209 n. 187. The figure of 800,000 is cited by Obermann, *Zur Geschichte des*

ber associations of the *Verbrüderung* were mentioned in some eighty-seven different towns. Many of these towns had several branch associations, all of which belonged to the *Verbrüderung*; there were seven branch clubs in Berlin, for example, including the old Artisans' Union and a number of specific trade groups. The associations were to be found in all parts of the German Federation except the Austro-Hungarian monarchy; the organization was *klein-deutsch* in fact if not in theory. Many of the clubs had one or two hundred members and several had many more. The workers' associations in Halberstadt claimed over one thousand members and that in Munich was supposed to have two thousand.[36] Whatever the exact size of the organization, it seems clear that the *Verbrüderung* had gained widespread support by the spring of 1849.

The associations which joined the *Verbrüderung* were largely devoted to programs of working-class self-help. They were similar to the features of working-class life in England represented by Lovett's Workingmen's Education Association, the Friendly Societies and the early cooperative groups. Above all the associations sought to educate the working man, providing him with a chance to read and discuss subjects of interest to the development of the working class. A typical group, the Workers' Education Union in Regensburg and Stadtamhof, held weekly meetings and discussions, ran an association library where the members could read the latest newspapers and pamphlets, encouraged correspondence with

Bundes der Kommunisten, p. 81, from a report to the Prussian Ministry of the Interior; it is at least evidence for what a harassed and frightened government might have been willing to believe.

[36] *Verbrüderung*, Nov. 14, 1848; Meyer, *1848*, p. 11. There were over 5,000 members in 24 workers' clubs in Bavaria in May 1849, though it is not clear that all of these clubs belonged to the *Verbrüderung*; at least 16 of them did. Koeppen, *Die Anfänge der Arbeiter- und Gesellenbewegung*, pp. 102-103.

workers' groups elsewhere and organized frequent lectures. The Workers' Union in Schwerin provided instruction in writing, drawing, world history, geography and physics in addition to having a branch devoted to singing. The weekly program of the Brunswick Artisans' Union ran as follows: Monday evening, writing or singing; Tuesday, arithmetic; Wednesday, spelling; Thursday, political discussion; Friday, lecture or recital; Saturday, singing; Sunday, drawing.[37]

The associations also tried to improve the material position of the members. All of them had their "assistance funds" (*Unterstützungskassen*) to be devoted to various purposes, the care of the sick and the unemployed, the payment of a small amount toward workers' funerals, the support of traveling journeymen during their *Wanderjahre*. In April 1849 the Berlin Regional Committee formed a central Health Care Union for all Berlin, the *Gesundheitspflegeverein*, which united the sickness funds of eight different trade organizations in that city.[38] But most of the smaller workers' associations had some sort of fund for the support of the needy as well. In addition some of them established general savings funds which the provident worker could use to store away a small amount of money. These funds were one of the more important aspects of the workers' associations which grew up in 1848; they continued in existence and continued to attract the support of the workers long after the defeat of the revolution.

A second major type of activity aimed at helping the workers was started by the more advanced of the associations during the autumn of 1848 and gained considerable ground; this was the cooperative production and cooperative consumption of a number of essential

[37] *Verbrüderung*, June 30, Oct. 30, 1849; *Concordia*, Apr. 28, 1849.
[38] *Verbrüderung*, Aug. 7, 1849.

goods. Cooperative production was first attempted in Berlin in October of 1848, when the regional committee set up the Berlin Workers' Society for the Common Manufacture of Shirts. Members of the *Verbrüderung* were to be allowed to subscribe for two shirts per year at the rate of 1 thaler to 1 thaler, 5 silbergroschen per shirt to be paid in weekly installments of 5 silbergroschen. The cloth was to be purchased from poor weavers in Silesia through the weavers' associations in Breslau and Reichenbach; the shirts were to be made in Berlin by local seamstresses who would be hired by a special women's committee. The scheme was slow in starting, since there was some trouble in obtaining the material and the Berlin group turned first to the production of stockings. By 1849, however, the Berlin committee was producing a variety of clothes, had started the cooperative production of cigars and decided, in January of 1849, to produce bread as well. In February the Berlin committee was employing an average of nine workers full time on clothes alone. The production figures of the cooperative enterprises in Berlin for that month were 22 coats, 7 waistcoats, 42 pairs of trousers, 10,299 cigars and 15.75 cwt. of bread, which had just been added to the list of products. The figures for March 1849 were 44 coats, 66 pairs of trousers, 8 waistcoats, 8 pairs of gaiters (sic), 8,800 cigars, and 136 cwt. of bread; they remained at roughly this level in April and May.[39]

Similar efforts at cooperative production were made elsewhere by other branches of the *Verbrüderung* in the spring of 1849. In addition there were plans for cooperative retail outlets for special trades. The tailors and shoemakers in Leipzig opened stores, as did the carpenters of Altenburg and the weavers in Ulm. In

[39] *Verbrüderung*, Oct. 17, 20, 27, 1848, Feb. 13, July 27, 31, Aug. 3, 7, 1849.

Krimmitsschau it was hoped to open a cooperative res‧ taurant under the auspices of the *Verbrüderung*. The iron workers in Ober-Meissen arranged for the cooperative purchasing of bread. In Silesia there were a number of cooperative associations among the handloom weavers. All of these groups were small; almost none of them lasted beyond the reaction of 1850. Yet they marked an important beginning, the seed of the German cooperative movement which later developed under Schulze-Delitzsch.[40]

✻

By the spring of 1849 the *Verbrüderung* had become the only outlet for workers who sought some means of organization and some form of united activity. Many of the more prosperous masters no doubt held aloof from this organization, but they made no attempt to provide an alternative group or to compete for the allegiance of the journeymen and workers. They relied almost solely on the guild system. Occasionally the masters tried to interfere with the formation of a local branch of the *Verbrüderung,* but such activity was not frequent.[41] Some groups tried quite specifically to dissociate themselves from the working classes. The machine builders in the railway workshops in Dortmund formed an association and went on strike, but they insisted that they be called "artisans" and not just workers, and they refused to allow politics to be discussed in their club.[42] Similarly, the porters at the Berlin railway stations applied for permission to join the Honored Union of German Rail-

[40] Schulze-Delitzsch himself was active in the branch of the *Verbrüderung* in Eilenburg in 1848. *Verbrüderung,* Mar. 9, 27, Apr. 17, 20, Nov. 17, 1849; Adler, *Geschichte der Arbeiterbewegung,* p. 186; Quarck, *Erste deutsche Arbeiterbewegung,* pp. 206-207; Balser, *Sozial-Demokratie,* pp. 616ff.

[41] *Verbrüderung,* Nov. 7, 1848.

[42] *Neue Rheinische Zeitung,* Oct. 13, Nov. 8, 1848.

way Officials, claiming that they were not mere workers and should be classed as officials.[43]

A few further meetings of the master artisans did take place in the early part of 1849 in order to arouse support for the proposals of the Frankfurt Artisans' Congress. There was a congress for the masters of the Rhenish Palatinate and Hesse held at Neustadt an der Hardt on the fourteenth of January and a similar meeting at Halle for the province of Saxony on the eleventh of March; another was called for the Rhineland at Trier for the end of April. But no further action resulted from these meetings. The masters counseled peaceful behavior and the support of law and order; they gave their allegiance to the governments of the German states and whatever plans for economic legislation these governments might bring forward. The masters offered little opposition to the *Verbrüderung*.[44]

❊

The *Verbrüderung* also tried to make good its claim to represent all the workers of Germany by persuading the various trade groups to join. This campaign took place mainly on a local level; the shoemakers' association in one city and the spinners' in another would be persuaded to cast their lot with the regional committee and the national organizations. But two groups, the printers and the cigar makers, had already established national organizations of their own during the summer of 1848 and the *Verbrüderung* sought the allegiance of both.

---

[43] *Petition der Gepäckträger deutscher Eisenbahnen an den Verehrlichen Verein der deutschen Eisenbahn-Beamten, Berlin, den 12. Sept. 1848*, Berlin, 1848. The demand was symptomatic of the workers' concern with status.

[44] *Verbrüderung*, Mar. 16, 1849; *Kölnische Zeitung*, Apr. 20, 1849; Meusch, *Die Handwerkerbewegung*, p. 61; Biermann, *Winkelblech*, vol. 2, pp. 158-159; Goldschmidt, *Die deutsche Handwerkerbewegung*, p. 49; Adolf Schmiedecke, *Die Revolution 1848-1849 in Halle*, Halle, 1932, p. 135.

311

The printers' union, the Gutenberg League, founded at the Printers' Congress in Mainz in June, declined following the failure of the August strikes. Evicted from Frankfurt after the September riots, the committee of the organization moved to Berlin, hoping to publish there the printers' paper, *Der Gutenberg*. However, the non-Prussian members of the committee were expelled almost immediately upon their arrival and the whole committee was pronounced illegal by the Brandenburg Ministry in November. The newspaper offices were moved once again, to Neumarkt in Silesia, but the leaders of the organization quarreled and the paper soon ceased to appear.[45] A number of local leaders were persecuted as well. The leaders of the August strike in Berlin were put on trial in January of 1849 and condemned to fourteen days in prison under a law of 1845; the decree of April 6, 1848, granting freedom of association was held to be invalid.[46] Born, in the meantime, urged the printers to join the *Verbrüderung*, but the journeymen in that trade refused to make common cause with the other workers, arguing that their interests were best preserved through independent action.[47] The printers thus represent one of the few trades in Germany which refused to join with the other workers' groups, and this in spite of the fact that they had set an example to others in the early days of the revolution.

The cigar workers remained similarly separate from the *Verbrüderung* during the period before the outbreak of the second group of revolutions in the spring of 1849, though they were considerably more friendly. They had established a national association of their own in September 1848 and proceeded to spread their organization

[45] *Beschlüsse der ersten National-Buchdruckerversammlung*, p. 2.
[46] *Verbrüderung*, Feb. 9, 1849. The case was appealed, but the appeal failed. *Verbrüderung*, Apr. 13, 1849.
[47] *Verbrüderung*, Oct. 17, 1848.

through many of the larger cities, particularly those in northern Germany. The leader of the cigar makers, Kohlweck, working from a base in Berlin, was almost as active as Born and Schwenniger in traveling and organizing local branches of his group. The cigar workers' newspaper contained a number of reports of successful negotiations and peaceful relations with the employers in their trade.[48]

The group was at first reluctant to attempt any activity beyond the immediate concerns of the cigar industry. A congress in Berlin in February of 1849 reported great strides in the organization of the industry;[49] at the same time the cigar workers' newspaper began to appear. It was at first very much a trade affair, listing import prices and tobacco sales, giving news of the opening of factories and the availability of jobs in different parts of Germany.[50] Like the *Verbrüderung*, the cigar makers' association was interested solely in self-help and rejected proposed appeals to the government.[51]

The cigar workers were, however, less narrow in their viewpoint than the printers' union. The Hamburg branch, for example, called on all German cigar workers to refuse offers of jobs in England as strike breakers against the London workers.[52] A number of local branches also supported a move to join the *Verbrüderung*. Four local branches, led by the Hamburg group, urged the Central Committee in March 1849 to seek an alliance with the *Verbrüderung*.[53] The proposal was not immediately successful, and the Hamburg branch somewhat angrily

[48] *Concordia*, Mar. 17, 24, Apr. 14, May 5, 1849.
[49] *Concordia*, Feb. 15, 1849.
[50] A number of employers, it was reported, found the paper useful enough to subscribe to it themselves. *Concordia*, Apr. 14, 1849.
[51] *Concordia*, Mar. 24, 1849.
[52] *Verbrüderung*, Mar. 9, 1849; *Concordia*, Mar. 10, 1849.
[53] *Concordia*, Mar. 24, 1849.

urged all workers "to forget all egotistic, self-seeking purposes and intentions and to join hands unanimously in the great work of the *Verbrüderung*."[54] The Central Committee of the cigar makers had not, however, refused the proposal outright, but had asked merely for more time in which to allow the local branches to consider. They issued a call on May 1, 1849, for a second general assembly of the cigar workers of Germany to meet in Berlin on the tenth of June; the issue of allegiance to the *Verbrüderung* would be discussed.[55]

❖

At the same time the *Verbrüderung* itself had announced a nationwide assembly of representatives of the local and regional branches which had been set up since the founding of the organization at the Berlin Congress in August and September of 1848. This congress, which had been planned since the amalgamation of the Leipzig and Frankfurt committees at Heidelberg in January, was to be the first all-German workers' congress which could justly claim that title. It was to meet in Leipzig in June.

Before either the cigar makers' or the general congress could meet, however, events in the political sphere forced a postponement. The revolutionary governments and the Frankfurt Assembly failed to achieve their aims; they failed also to appease the workers or to grant their demands. A second revolution broke out and went down to defeat.

[54] *Verbrüderung,* Apr. 13, 1849.
[55] *Verbrüderung,* Apr. 20, 1849; *Concordia,* May 5, 1849.

CHAPTER 12

THE FAILURE OF THE

GOVERNMENTS

WHEN THE German workers joined in the riots and fighting of the March Days of 1848, they had hoped that the revolution would produce governments for the various German states and for Germany itself sympathetic to the workers' cause and the activities of the workers' organizations. It was in this hope that they had acquiesced in the limited franchise rights which had been granted for the elections of the spring of 1848; it was in this hope that they had held their congresses during the summer of 1848 and had drawn up petitions to the National Assembly in Frankfurt. By the spring of 1849 the hopes of the workers for support and aid from the government had been destroyed.

During the autumn and winter of 1848-1849 the Frankfurt Assembly continued its discussions of the new constitution for Germany; in the course of these discussions the problem of the workers was raised several times. Some concessions were made to the workers' demands. In particular, the Assembly granted the right of universal manhood suffrage, partly on the advice of the Economic Committee; the workers were to have the vote though they had been excluded from the elections to the Assembly which gave it to them. But, apart from this concession and the rather less momentous decision to ban lotteries and gambling in Germany, the advice of the Economic Committee was ignored by the Assembly; the proposals for an industrial ordinance to regulate the affairs of the workers were quietly shelved. The Economic Committee's recommendations on this subject gave little enough to the workers; the Assembly as a whole refused to go even as far as the Committee. The same indifference was found in the governments of the separate states; both Prussia and Saxony held conferences during the early part of 1849 on the subject of the position of the artisans but neither made any real progress toward fulfilling the demands of the mass of the workers.

The work of the Frankfurt Assembly was stopped and its whole purpose challenged by Frederick William's refusal to accept the imperial crown of the new German state. A second German revolution broke out in May 1849 in response to the call of the Assembly to defend its work. In this revolution, as in the March Days, the workers and artisans played an important part, providing the corps of the troops of the revolution. Many had been driven by the failure of the governments, the failure of the first revolutions, to accept the need of the second. But many more, indeed a majority of the workers, had passed beyond even revolution, had turned inward, hoping through the remaining organizations of the working class to salvage what they could from the events of 1848-1849 and despairing of any form of political action.

*

The first signs of the failure of the governments were the severe limitations on public works projects which came in the autumn of 1848.

The uneasiness of the Prussian government about this form of aid to the unemployed and impoverished workers had been evident from the late spring. But, with the autumn, the government used the excuse of the approach of bad weather and its effect on outdoor projects to call a halt to the whole scheme. On the fourth of November the Minister of Finance in the Pfuel

316

government, von Bonin, who was also serving tempo-
rarily as Minister for Trade, Industry and Public Works,
announced a major reduction of the public works projects, advising all workers employed on these projects
to seek private employment. Public workers were reduced not only in Berlin but in other cities as well, and
lower wages were paid to those who remained on the
job.[1]

The real weakness of the policy of the individual
German states, even the most advanced of them, was
revealed in the conferences which were organized by
the Prussian and Saxon governments to consider the
problems of the workers. Representatives of various
working-class groups were summoned to these conferences, but the method of selection was limited and even
those representatives who did come were not listened to
seriously.

The Prussian conference was summoned for January
17, 1849, by the new Minister of Trade, August von der
Heydt, the fourth to hold that office. Heydt, who had
been appointed when the "decreed" constitution was
promulgated by Frederick William at the beginning of
December, was the head of a banking house in Elberfeld
and an adherent of liberal economic theories; he had
little sympathy with the workers, least of all with the
artisans of the old guilds. In any case Heydt was ill
during much of the latter part of January and appeared
at only the last session of the conference on the thirtieth
of the month.[2]

The conference was attended by twenty-four artisans
elected by the artisans' associations of Prussia with three
delegates, two masters and one journeyman, for each

---

[1] *Plakate,* Ratsbibliothek, Berlin, portfolios 8 and 9; *Neue Rheinische Zeitung,* Oct. 17, 1848, Jan. 5, Feb. 4, 1849; *Neue Kölnische
Zeitung,* Oct. 18, 1848; *Verbrüderung,* Oct. 20, 1848.

[2] Tilmann, *Einfluss des Revolutionsjahres,* p. 24.

province.[3] These met with twenty merchants and factory owners to discuss the amendments which were submitted by the minister to the Prussian Industrial Ordinance of 1845. A number of workers' associations refused to participate in the scheme; the journeymen's committee in Breslau announced that the only salvation for the workers lay in free association and rejection of cooperation with the master artisans.[4]

The conference was widely believed to be a mere "election maneuver" in the campaign for the legislature which was to be elected in February 1849 under the decreed constitution of December. Heydt is reported to have remarked to one of the delegates from Westphalia when he finally met with the conference on the thirtieth of January: "Now you can see how compliant we are; be grateful and don't send us too many democrats." [5] The delegates were also flattered by an interview with the king, who complimented several of them on the peaceable behavior of the workers in their districts but instructed the delegate from Hirschberg to inform his fellow workers that he would never visit their town again as a punishment for the unrest in the district.

The conference was known as the "artisans' parliament"; it seemed to many to fulfill the demands of the workers for a branch of the legislature which was composed of and considered the artisans. It was in fact narrow and reactionary in its decisions. The delegates represented the more conservative groups among the

[3] Veit's report, *Akten des volkswirtschaftlichen Ausschusses,* vol. 2.

[4] The protest of the Breslau journeymen was printed in the *Neue Rheinische Zeitung,* Jan. 16, 1849; cf. the similarly unfavorable reaction of the Cologne journeymen, *Neue Kölnische Zeitung,* Jan. 10, 1849.

[5] *Neue Rheinische Zeitung,* Feb. 3, 4, 1849; *Neue Kölnische Zeitung,* Feb. 7, 1849.

artisans, and the program which the conference adopted aimed at a defense of the rights of the guilds and the masters without any provision for the new trends in industry, for the rights of the journeymen or for the self-help activities of the new organizations. The masters called on the Prussian government to maintain and extend compulsory guild membership and to protect native industry through tariffs. Aid was to be given to the handicraft industries through loans, free industrial schools and favorable taxes as well as through such negative measures as the abolition of production in prisons and military establishments, the prohibition of peddling and the removal of the unemployed through financed colonization. There were to be no more public works. Finally the masters called for an "industrial chamber" elected by the artisans to pass further legislation.[6]

The Prussian government promised to fulfill as many of these demands as possible; in fact the Industrial Ordinance which was decreed by the government on the ninth of February ignored the more extreme of the suggested measures, hoping to satisfy the more conservative master artisans through support of the guilds. There was no mention in the ordinance of the ninth of February of an "industrial chamber" or of direct aid to the workers, but the guild system was preserved and made legally binding in seventy different trades; there were provisions for the formation of new guilds and for the administration of the guild examinations. The number of assistants under any one master was limited. The ordinance marked a sharp break with the policy of the Industrial Ordinance of 1845 which had aimed at opening as many trades as possible to free competition; as

[6] *Kölnische Zeitung*, Feb. 3, 1849; *Neue Rheinische Zeitung*, Feb. 3, 1849.

such it represented a major success for the guild movement of 1848-1849.[7]

The ordinance of February 9, 1849, was, however, a narrow document; it appealed only to the established artisans. Many of the masters were satisfied by it and henceforth lost all interest in the revolution. But the poorer masters, the journeymen and the unskilled workers were united in opposition. They regarded it as the "decreed industrial law," the parallel of the "decreed constitution" of December 1848.[8] The mass of workers resented both the narrow basis of the conference which the government had consulted and the limited nature of the resulting law. When one of the delegates tried to explain the provisions of the proposed law to a meeting of workers in Cologne, he was shouted down with cries of, "Down with the guild masters! Down with the traitors! Down with the turncoats!"[9] The *Verbrüderung* held meetings of protest throughout Prussia and organized petitions against the compulsory guild membership.[10]

The Saxon government had also called for a commission on workers' affairs as early as the spring of 1848. This workers' commission had been duly formed, had evolved a questionnaire and had arranged for the election of local subcommittees during the summer of 1848. The commission and its subcommittees met from August 12, 1848, till April 17, 1849.[11]

[7] Schmoller, *Geschichte des deutschen Kleingewerbe,* pp. 85-87; Goldschmidt, *Die deutsche Handwerkerbewegung,* p. 52; Biermann, *Winkelblech,* vol. 2, pp. 182-186; Wendel, *Evolution of Industrial Freedom,* pp. 82-84.

[8] The *Neue Rheinische Zeitung,* Mar. 29, 1849, reported the protest of the guilds of Elbing against the "*oktroyierte Gewerbegesetz.*"

[9] *Neue Kölnische Zeitung,* Feb. 6, 1849.

[10] *Verbrüderung,* Mar. 6, 1849.

[11] Lipinski, *Arbeiterbewegung in Leipzig,* vol. 1, pp. 174-176.

Yet nothing was accomplished and considerable bitterness was aroused by the worker delegates to this commission, who, it was held, were merely parasites on the government.[12] The commission made a number of recommendations, supporting the demand for a ministry of labor and for arbitration courts, calling for state wage regulations and reform of the guild system. But both the commission and the government delayed and, in spite of protests from a number of the Saxon workers' associations, failed to decide on any legislation. Finally, in April of 1849, the Saxon government abandoned the commission entirely and called for the election of a further set of delegates from industrial and artisan circles to meet in Dresden at the end of the month to draw up an industrial ordinance. Stephan Born, among others, was elected as the delegate for the Leipzig Workers' Association. The new conference had only held one session when the second revolution broke out in Dresden.[13]

The policy of both Prussia and Saxony and many of the other German states as well was characterized by a mixture of procrastination and protection. Many did nothing, many hinted at concessions. But the actual laws which were passed supported the guilds without satisfying the majority of workers. In addition to the Prussian ordinance, laws favorable to the guilds were passed in Bavaria, the Thuringian states, Hanover, Württemberg,

[12] A cartoon, published in the *Deutsche Reich-Bremse* in Leipzig in 1849 (no other date given), showed a candidate for the commission in the summer of 1848, poorly dressed and avowing his loyalty to the workers, and the same man in the winter of 1849, now a delegate to the commission, richly dressed and declaring, "The wretches don't know what they want. I am a worker too, but I am completely content with existing conditions." The *Verbrüderung* published critical accounts of the proceedings of the commission. Nov. 24, Dec. 1, 1848.

[13] Born, *Erinnerungen*, p. 201; Lipinski, *Arbeiterbewegung in Leipzig*, vol. 1, pp. 176-179.

Baden and even liberal Nassau.[14] The governments thus managed to retain the loyalty of many of the guild members; some of the working-class discontent which lay behind the March Days was assuaged. From the point of view of the master artisans at least, the revolutions of 1848, regarded by historians as failures, were in fact a success; they gained the legal protection they desired—but from the established states, not from Frankfurt. At the same time the unsatisfied journeymen and the poorer workers came to despair of getting anything from the government or of profiting from the revolution.

*

Developments in the National Assembly in Frankfurt increased the despair of the mass of the workers and accelerated the process of their loss of faith. The long-awaited work of the Economic Committee was completed; the proposals of the Frankfurt Assembly for the economic conditions of the new Germany were brought out in public. No one group achieved its goals, neither the guild members who hoped for the maintenance of their position nor the mass of workers who hoped for an improvement in their lot. The Economic Committee, true to the background of most of its members, ultimately decided for a middle-class policy, a policy favorable to the industrialists and merchants who dominated the group and were the most outspoken members of the Assembly on economic issues. Yet in the proposed economic regulations the remnants of the guild system remained as well. No one was satisfied. The economic ordinance which the committee presented was submitted to the National Assembly in the middle of the crucial debate on the franchise law; it was not discussed either at that time or later in the general assembly of the

[14] Goldschmidt, *Die deutsche Handwerkerbewegung,* p. 67; Biermann, *Winkelblech,* vol. 2, pp. 186-188.

Parliament. Nor did the work of the Economic Committee arouse sufficient enthusiasm in any group in the country to unite support for the Assembly on economic grounds during the May risings.

The doubts of the workers about the extent to which they could hope for relief from the Frankfurt Assembly grew during the autumn of 1848. Apart from its proposals for the trade and customs unity of Germany, which were finally passed on the eighteenth of December, the Economic Committee did little and the affairs of the workers were not raised in the National Assembly. The "right of association," the right to organize, was included in the Basic Rights (paragraph 30), but not for the sake of the workers. Rather it was considered to be merely part of the liberal middle-class demands with which the National Assembly was concerned. The Economic Committee was, in the meanwhile, occupied with preparing reports on such issues as the limitation of the use of the railways for freight in order to protect shipping interests and the proposals for a national authority for doctors and physicians.[15] The only positive measure which they considered was the abolition of gambling houses and lotteries. The committee adopted this proposal on September 29; it did not come before the Assembly till January 9, 1849, when it was accepted.[16]

In the face of this delay the workers naturally became discouraged; petitions continued to be sent to the Assembly, but at a slower rate than during the summer. Many of those the Assembly did receive during this period expressed the impatience and disillusion of the workers. One petition from the Ruhr read: [17]

[15] *Akten des volkswirtschaftlichen Ausschusses,* vol. 2, reports of Oct. 13, 29, 1848.
[16] *Akten des volkswirtschaftlichen Ausschusses,* vol. 3; *Stenographischer Bericht,* vol. 6, pp. 4492-4493.
[17] *Akten des volkswirtschaftlichen Ausschusses,* vol. 17.

The undersigned printers and pattern makers in Elberfeld and Barmen, and with them all related business colleagues in Germany, greeted with joyous hopes in the March Days the political awakening of our German Fatherland. The moment appeared to have arrived when a hearing would at last be given to our just wishes and complaints.

Exalted Assembly! Trusting in this, we have sent petitions and commissions, sacrificing money so that our family lived in want, yet up till now we have seen no materially favorable result from this.

The sentiment of this group was typical of that of many workers; the paper of the *Verbrüderung* refrained from covering the activities of the National Assembly or criticizing its work in detail, "since it has destroyed itself." [18]

❖

The National Assembly did in fact consider some of the more extreme demands of the workers in a debate on the eighth and ninth of February, which discussed and rejected the call for the "protection of work" or the "guarantee of work" as presented in a number of workers' petitions.

The Economic Committee had been instructed to prepare a report on these various demands for government protection, and the subject was discussed in a meeting of the committee on the third of February. The committee was sympathetic to the workers' cause but felt that there was little it could do. One member, Professor Hildebrand, pointed out the distinction between guaranteeing work and protecting it, and took the position that the most that could be done was to guarantee the "right" to work through the prohibition of mo-

[18] *Verbrüderung*, Dec. 29, 1848.

nopoly; more than this—a guarantee of actual jobs or of a certain wage or the protection of all work through tariffs was, he argued, beyond the duty of the government.[19] The Economic Committee voted to reject the amendments which would place the guarantee or protection of work in the Basic Rights, but referred these demands to the Ministry of Trade of the German government. Carl Degenkolb was selected to draw up the committee's report to the National Assembly, stating their reasons for this position.

Degenkolb's report was presented on the eighth of February.[20] Degenkolb claimed that the evidence pointed to an improvement in the workers' conditions over the past few years, that the government should not in any case interfere with the course of economic events. To attempt to protect labor would prove to be an intolerable burden for the state, the dangers of which could be seen from the example of recent events in France. It would also put the government in the position of being a competitor in the economic market, and this, Degenkolb noted, citing the conclusions of the Frankfurt Artisans' Congress, was "not only not desired by those in industry but would be rejected as appears from a number of protests." Moreover, for the state to guarantee wages would lead to dire results for the whole nation: "the power of the nation would relax, the spur to beneficial action, competition, would fall away and spiritual attrition would necessarily follow physical laziness." In other words, Degenkolb and the Economic Committee took the liberal stand of laissez-faire. "Need creates work. . . . The free interaction of work and monetary capital, however, creates need."

[19] *Akten des volkswirtschaftlichen Ausschusses,* vol. 10, minutes for the session of Feb. 3, 1849. The committee devoted two and a half hours only to its discussion of this issue.
[20] *Stenographischer Bericht,* vol. 7, pp. 5100-5103.

The report of the Economic Committee was not accepted by the National Assembly without debate; discussion of the problem of a guarantee of work continued throughout the eighth of February and occupied most of the session of the ninth as well, though a number of members paid little heed to the debates.[21] Twelve speakers discussed the subject, five of them in favor of a guarantee and seven of them opposed, often in spite of their expressed sympathy with the workers' cause.

Even the most ardent supporters of the "protection of labor" were somewhat apologetic about their position. Karl Nauwerck of Berlin, who proposed in an amendment that the "right of subsistence" be included among the Basic Rights and that the state provide work and support to all "involuntarily" unemployed, went on to explain that this measure would serve as a means of preserving order. The right of subsistence was, he maintained, "the right not to starve" and "the last freedom, the freedom of existence." It was to be viewed not as a socialist measure but as the very opposite: "if socialism and communism have up till now formed a picture of horror, then it is beyond doubt that a principle which assures everyone subsistence is indispensable for revealing the true nature of this picture." Nauwerck denied that he was a communist and allowed that he was "socialist only in so far as it was acknowledged that society cannot be a collection of lions." [22] Another supporter of the measure, Dekan Schütz from Mainz, called for a guarantee of "the holy right to work" as a means of relieving the "frightul sickness" from which many

[21] *Stenographischer Bericht,* vol. 7, pp. 5100-5120, 5127-5146. One member complained of the monotony of the debates at this time, "the greatest and most perfect test of patience one could look for," and took the occasion of the debate on the ninth to go for a walk. Friedrich von Raumer, *Briefe aus Frankfurt und Paris, 1848-1849,* Leipzig, 1849, vol. 2, p. 229.

[22] *Stenographischer Bericht,* vol. 7, pp. 5105-5107.

were suffering, the sickness of poverty and starvation; yet he also spoke of the dangers of bloodshed and the mistakes of France.[23]

Only a few speakers were openly hostile to the workers; Moritz Mohl from Stuttgart drew a distinction between those willing and those unwilling to work and painted in vivid colors the picture of France in the June Days, when those who refused work "raised the red flag and wanted to murder those people who work"—a remark which was greeted with loud applause from the right and center.[24]

Other speakers opposed the motion in spite of their sympathy with the workers' cause. Eisenstuck from Chemnitz, also a member of the Economic Committee, regarded many of the workers' demands as just but argued that the sole solution lay in granting workers political rights. Wedekind from Bruckhausen declared himself in favor of social reform "in order to evade the progress to social revolution." [25] Beseler from Griefswald pointed to the growth of working-class organizations and maintained that the solution to social problems lay in "the German spirit of association" rather than through government action.[26]

But in spite of the considerable amount of sympathy shown, or at least expressed, for the workers, the Frankfurt Assembly had no intention of including the "right to work," a guarantee of work or protection to labor, among the rights of the citizens of the new Germany. The various amendments such as Nauwerck's which would have modified the negative report of the Economic Committee were swept aside in a single vote with a majority of 317 to 114; the committee's report was

23 *Stenographischer Bericht,* vol. 7, pp. 5127-5130.
24 *Stenographischer Bericht,* vol. 7, p. 5109.
25 *Stenographischer Bericht,* vol. 7, p. 5119.
26 *Stenographischer Bericht,* vol. 7, pp. 5141-5142.

accepted without further vote and the most the assembly would do was to assent to a measure whereby the various petitions on the subject would be turned over to the *Reichsministerium* with instructions to that ineffectual body to consider "means to develop the national power of labor as much as possible." [27]

✱

The debate on the "guarantee of work," though discouraging to workers observing the proceedings of the National Assembly, was not the crucial test of the policy of the Assembly; few had really hoped for such a measure and many of the masters and guildsmen had openly opposed it. Far more important was the issue of the industrial ordinance (*Gewerbeordnung*) which the Economic Committee had been instructed to draw up. It was in an attempt to influence the drafting of the industrial laws of the new Germany that the workers and artisans had held their congresses and drafted their petitions in the summer of 1848. On this issue the workers' support for the National Assembly might be won or lost.

The length of time which it took the Economic Committee to prepare its draft of the industrial ordinance was in itself discouraging. The task had been commissioned by the National Assembly on July 21, 1848. The committee and its subdivisions spent considerable effort in considering various specific points and recommendations, and Moritz Veit prepared a summary of the contents of the petitions submitted on the subject; but the full committee did not begin discussing the industrial ordinance till the eighth of December.[28] Even then disagreement was found to be so great on many issues that

[27] *Stenographischer Bericht,* vol. 7, pp. 5143-5146.
[28] *Akten des volkswirtschaftlichen Ausschusses,* vol. 10.

discussions continued well into 1849.[29] There were questions in the National Assembly on the eighteenth and the thirtieth of December, asking for the cause of the delay and urging all possible speed in drafting the proposed law, since it was needed for the completion of the work on the Basic Rights.[30] The attempt by one member of the committee, Philip Schwarzenberg from Kassel to force the issue by calling for a discussion of the proposals of the Journeymen's Congress and the minority report of the Artisans' Congress on the floor of the *Paulskirche* in late January was forestalled; the petitions of the two congresses were never discussed.[31] The report of the committee, including both Veit's summary of the workers' demands and the proposals for the new law together with a number of minority amendments, was not presented to the National Assembly till February 26, 1849.

The fact was that the Economic Committee found itself sharply divided on a number of crucial issues involved in the industrial ordinance. Some complained that most of the proposals would "set us back five hundred years, . . . would lead us into a medieval condition." [32] Others argued that the proposals were "a denial of the principles for which the National Assembly had declared itself with an overwhelming majority, . . . that it would introduce a new class with great privileges." [33] Still others, Carl Degenkolb and Adolph Lette among them, supported the rights of the guilds and argued

[29] The delay was increased by the fact that the Economic Committee recessed for Christmas from the eighteenth of December till the tenth of January.

[30] *Stenographischer Bericht,* vol. 6, pp. 4224, 4408.

[31] *Stenographischer Bericht,* vol. 7, p. 4922.

[32] Speech by Moritz Mohl from Stuttgart at the meeting of the Economic Committee on Dec. 8, 1848, *Akten des volkswirtschaftlichen Ausschusses,* vol. 10.

[33] Speech of Heinrich Schirmeister from Insterburg, *Akten des volkswirtschaftlichen Ausschusses,* vol. 10.

that trade freedom would be disastrous in some areas, leading to overcrowding in single industries. Lette defended the principles of guild regulation, embodied in a subcommittee report, as being in accordance with the freedom for which the revolution had been fought: [34]

The proposals proceed from the standpoint of industrial freedom; they only seek regulation of business in the interest of the public and of the tradesmen themselves, in the sense, however, not of bureaucracy but of self-government. The subcommittee does not want French institutions which only protect big business against the nakedness of the small artisan, and the committee believes therefore that its suggestions rest on a truly democratic basis, so much the more so since they create in the place of state officials independent industrial organs.

But these arguments were not accepted by the majority of the committee. In particular the defense that the proposed guild regulations were meant to apply only to artisans, since the petitions came only from them, was rejected; it was impossible to distinguish in the current state of German economic development between artisans on the one hand and factory workers and other types of industry on the other. The proposed regulations would inevitably cut across these groups.

After three debates on the proposals for an industrial ordinance, the Economic Committee appointed on December 11, 1848, a new subcommittee to draft a compromise law. The subcommittee included Veit, Hildebrandt, Stahl, Osterrath and Hollandt. It was this subcommittee's proposals that were submitted to the National Assembly on February 26, 1849. But even with considerable efforts at compromise the draft law failed

[34] *Akten des volkswirtschaftlichen Ausschusses,* vol. 10, minutes for the meeting of Dec. 8, 1848.

to achieve the support of a majority of the Economic Committee, and several minority reports were submitted at the same time.

It should be noted that the Economic Committee paid scant attention to the more extreme of the workers' congresses. In particular the suggestion of a social parliament or industrial chamber to work along with the Economic Committee received but brief and unfavorable attention in the debate in the Economic Committee on the seventeenth of January.[35] It was admitted that "anarchy" had been "easily caused by the unruly summoning of the congresses"; but the proposal was emphatically rejected. It would allow industrial or trade interests to "express too strong and therefore too harmful an influence on political choices"; the summoning of such a workers' parliament would merely serve to increase the number and confusion of opinions offered on economic issues. Finally the example of recent events in France was once more held up to point the danger of paying too great attention to working-class demands.

If the compromise which the Economic Committee decided upon failed to unite the members of the Economic Committee itself, it was also repugnant to most of the workers and artisans; by attempting to satisfy all demands the committee gained for the National Assembly the support of no single group among the working classes.

The compromise proposals were defended by August Hollandt in an introduction to the report of the Economic Committee.[36] Hollandt quite specifically defended the action of the committee in ignoring the advice and wishes of many of the workers. "If a remedy for sick conditions is to be sought, then the sufferer must be

[35] *Akten des volkswirtschaftlichen Ausschusses,* vol. 10.
[36] *Akten des volkswirtschaftlichen Ausschusses,* vol. 2.

listened to; he must explain the symptoms of the sickness and his view of the cause of the same. But the sick person is not called upon to prescribe the remedy." Hollandt, in behalf of the Economic Committee, rejected a return to the old guild system. "The salvation of social life in our time cannot lie in the introduction of greater or newer regulations. The reason for suffering lies deeper: our time has become a completely different one." The use of steam and machines, the rise of the factory system and the growth of communications, these, Hollandt argued, were transforming Germany. "When work is replaced by machines and reduced by capital, when whole branches of earning a living cease to exist, then the transformation to another type of industry must not be rendered difficult but made more easy."

The purpose of the compromise proposals of the Economic Committee was to speed this transformation and not to protect the workers.[37] The first section of the proposed industrial ordinance was headed "the abolition of industrial limitations": all privileges, concessions and monopolies were to cease. The second section was the key to the whole ordinance, for it dealt with the conduct of industry and the practising of the various trades. The right to conduct any trade was to be open to German citizens without restrictions, provided they had reached the age of twenty-five and were able to pass examinations set by an independent industrial council; any means of learning a trade was legitimate and the advance from apprentice to journeyman to independent craftsman was to be determined solely by examination. The guilds were

[37] The compromise proposals were submitted to the Economic Committee on Feb. 10, 1849, and a copy is contained in the minutes for that day, *Akten des volkswirtschaftlichen Ausschusses*, vol. 10. A further copy, with a few alterations, may be found in the report of the Economic Committee to the National Assembly, *Akten des volkswirtschaftlichen Ausschusses*, vol. 2. The proposals are reproduced in Biermann, *Winkelblech*, vol. 2, pp. 166-170.

to be allowed to continue in existence, but the section which was devoted to them provided that "no guild may assume exclusive rights in a trade, and membership in a guild may not be made binding on a tradesman." The guilds were to have no official part in the selection of the industrial councils which tested the ability of applicants in the various trades; instead the councils were to be chosen by all those practising a trade in a given area, including journeymen and assistants. In other words, the privileged position of the guilds and the master artisans was to be destroyed at one blow.

The Economic Committee thus proclaimed itself, and the National Assembly, the enemy of the artisans of the guilds. The master craftsmen could never accept the proposals of the committee, while the increased rights which were conceded to the journeymen in fact did little to protect or improve their position. And nothing was done for the unskilled worker outside the guild system.

The fact that a number of the members of the committee itself chose to submit minority reports did little to mitigate the negative effect of the Economic Committee's report. One group, to be sure, including Carl Degenkolb, Moritz Veit, Rudolf Lette and Friedrich Becker, called for a restoration of the powers of the guilds as a block against the open competition and individualism of modern times; but they found no support among their fellow committee members. On the other hand, Moritz Mohl, Heinrich Schirmeister and Ernst Merk called in a second minority report for even greater freedom of trade; they would have removed even the requirement that tradesmen be tested by an industrial council.

The proposed industrial ordinance attracted little attention when it was presented by Hollandt to the

National Assembly on February 26, 1849.[38] The Assembly voted to have the proposals of the Economic Committee and the minority reports printed; further discussions were to take place once the members of the Assembly had had time to study the various positions. Nothing more was heard of the industrial ordinance during the remaining debates of the Frankfurt Parliament.

❋

The proposals of the Economic Committee were presented in the midst of the debate on the franchise law of the new German constitution. The Constitutional Committee of the Assembly had proposed a law which would have excluded from the vote all those who were not "independent and blameless" (*selbständig und unbescholten*). The voteless classes under this law were to include the majority of the workers; servants, artisans' assistants, factory employees and daily wage earners were all considered to be dependent, if blameless.

The debate on the electoral law lasted twelve sessions, from February 15 to March 2, 1849. The left wing of the Assembly, led by Heinrich Simon from Breslau, argued for a modification of the law; in return for the promise of the left to support the principle of the hereditary emperor and the election of Frederick William IV of Prussia, the Assembly agreed to universal manhood suffrage as the basis for elections in the new Germany.[39] The left found an unexpected ally in the

[38] Von Raumer again complained of the tedium of the proceedings on Feb. 26; he wrote in a letter on Feb. 27, 1849, of the previous day, that "the weather [was] abominable and the course of the debates and decisions equally melancholy and depressing." *Briefe aus Frankfurt und Paris,* vol. 2, p. 280.

[39] Erich Brandenburg, *Die deutsche Revolution, 1848,* Leipzig, 1912, pp. 113, 115; Valentin, *Geschichte der deutschen Revolution,* vol. 2, pp. 336ff.; Mommsen, *Grösse und Versagen,* pp. 99, 151; Hamerow, *Restoration, Revolution, Reaction,* p. 131.

Economic Committee, which joined in the protest against the exclusion of the workers from the vote.[40] The proposed qualification of "independence" was rejected by a vote of 422 to 21, but the final election law, which gave the vote to "every blameless German who has reached the age of twenty-five," was accepted by only a narrow margin. The vote was 232 to 224.[41]

Nonetheless the working classes were further alienated by the suggestion that they might be excluded from the vote. The proposals of the Constitutional Committee were attacked with considerable violence as a betrayal of the workers "to whom the revolution owes its existence." A mass campaign of petitions and protests was organized against the proposed law.[42]

With the passing of the electoral law and the compromise of the issue of hereditary emperor, the work of the Frankfurt Assembly was almost complete. The election of Frederick William IV to the imperial throne on March 28, 1849, caused great rejoicing among the delegates to the Assembly. Yet increasingly the Assembly was operating in a vacuum, thinking that they could decide by narrow votes, with majorities of but ten or twenty delegates, questions which were of the greatest importance to Germany.[43] They were soon disillusioned. Frederick William, after some hesitation and several reversals of opinion, yielded to the pressure of his court and threats from Austria and refused the offered crown, declaring, in a phrase that must have seemed galling to

[40] Speech of Professor Hildebrand, *Stenographischer Bericht,* vol. 7, p. 5285.

[41] *Stenographischer Bericht,* vol. 7, pp. 5339, 5342.

[42] *Concordia,* Mar. 10, 1849; *Verbrüderung,* Feb. 19, 1849; Quarck, *Erste deutsche Arbeiterbewegung,* pp. 254-257.

[43] Von Raumer pointed out the false atmosphere and the blind faith involved in the decisions of the Frankfurt Assembly as early as Jan. 27, 1849. *Briefe aus Frankfurt und Paris,* vol. 2, pp. 190-191.

a legislative body which in fact contained so few workers or artisans, that he would not accept a throne "from Master Butcher and Baker." [44]

The Frankfurt Assembly continued its work. Some twenty-eight states accepted the new constitution, and von Gagern hoped to persuade Frederick William to reconsider. The Economic Committee too continued to meet, considering in its last sessions a scheme for internal colonization, using urban unemployed on the farms and discussing a petition from a group of actors for the improvement of working conditions in the theaters! [45] But the Economic Committee had in fact nothing to offer the workers and the Assembly had no means of imposing its will on the German states.

＊

The workers' faith in the Frankfurt Assembly and the governments of the separate states had long been destroyed. The decline in government aid, the failure of the artisans' commissions summoned by Prussia and Saxony, the narrowly liberal legislation proposed by the Economic Committee of the Frankfurt Assembly, in spite of the social concern of some of its members, had convinced almost all groups among the workers that there was no hope for action either from the conservatives or from the middle-class liberals in Frankfurt. The election of the German emperor was not greeted by the workers' *Verbrüderung* with the same joy that prevailed in Frankfurt; its paper commented on learning the news that "through the breast of the men of the people twitched a passionate pain for the betrayed and lacerated Fatherland, for raped and prostituted freedom." [46]

[44] Valentin, *Geschichte der deutschen Revolution,* vol. 2, p. 360.
[45] *Akten des volkswirtschaftlichen Ausschusses,* vol. 10, minutes for the meetings of Apr. 27, 28, 1849.
[46] *Verbrüderung,* Apr. 3, 1849.

The workers paid little attention to the last efforts to save the work of the Frankfurt Assembly.[47]

> So long as it is only a question of the imperial constitution, we can expect no revolt of the German people, for there is nothing more contrary to sense than to wish to make a revolution for the hereditary emperor, to wish to force a king to accept a crown.

Yet in spite of their disillusionment, or perhaps because of it, many of the workers came out again in support of revolution, joining in the May uprisings of 1849.

[47] *Verbrüderung,* May 4, 1849.

SECTION V
DEFEAT AND DISSOLUTION
1849 AND AFTER

CHAPTER 13

THE MAY UPRISINGS AND THE
WORKERS' ASSOCIATIONS

REVOLUTION BROKE out again in Germany in May of 1849. Once again there were barricades in the streets of the quiet "residence cities" of the German states and armed bands in the countryside; once more the call went out to the workers and peasants, to "the people," to rise and defend their liberties.

Yet the May uprisings were far different from the March Days.

In the first place, the governments and the forces of conservatism were ready for them. There was no question of the surprise and hesitation which prevailed in 1848, no question of bowing before the "inevitability" of revolution. Indeed some conservatives welcomed the new risings as a chance to make short work of their enemies; von Gerlach wrote on May 2, 1849: "So it has come at last to war against the *Paulskirche*, that is, against the revolution—that we could not have hoped for a year ago." [1] Moreover, the risings appeared as unconnected and unrelated events and not as part of a vast upheaval which was sweeping across all of Europe. There was no "revolutionary fever" in 1849; that had raged the year before and had subsided. The revolutions of 1849 could be treated as the isolated events they were and dealt with locally. The "year of revolutions" had passed.

Second, the participation of the workers in this second revolution was far less extensive and far less spontaneous. Carl Schurz, who fought in Baden and the Palatinate,

[1] Gerlach, *Denkwürdigkeiten*, vol. 1, p. 317.

noted that the workers were in general in favor of the revolution, but this was only in a passive way.[2] In southwest Germany the response to the call for troops was very slow; in spite of the adherence of the Baden army and the acquisition of a number of volunteers, the size of the troops which were opposed to the Prussian army was totally inadequate.[3] And the revolution lasted longer there than anywhere else in Germany.

In the Rhineland and the Ruhr the nucleus of the revolt was formed by the civil guard, from which the workers had been excluded throughout 1848. Moreover, the Security Commission in Elberfeld, the center of the Ruhr uprising, expelled such socialists as Gottschalk and Anneke from the city and refused to have any contact with social or economic demands which might have appealed to the workers.[4] In Dresden the workers came to the barricades but their support was inadequate in the face of the royal troops, reinforced by part of the Prussian army. The leaders of the revolt in Dresden included the head of the *Verbrüderung*, Stephan Born, who happened to be there at the time for the Saxon

[2] *The Reminiscences of Carl Schurz*, London, 1909, vol. 1, p. 223. Schurz also felt that the mass of troops were in a holiday mood and failed to take the revolution seriously. "There was a kind of general Sunday afternoon atmosphere, a real picnic humor," he wrote, "very cheerful, but not at all corresponding with the conception which I had formed of the seriousness of the situation" (p. 179).

[3] Hamerow, *Restoration, Revolution, Reaction,* p. 195. Other sources noted that there was at least a special corps of worker-volunteers who served as tailors, smiths, saddlemakers and the like to the revolutionary army, and it has been claimed that the real problem was not the lack of volunteers but the lack of weapons with which to arm them. Bamberger, *Erlebnisse,* p. 62; Schurz, *Reminiscences,* vol. 1, p. 186. The inclusion of Klaus Schreiner's *Die badischpfälzische Revolutionsarmee 1849,* Berlin, 1956, in the series *Gewehre in Arbeiterhand* is perhaps overstating the case.

[4] *Kölnische Zeitung,* May 16, 1849.

conference on workers' conditions. But also prominent in the uprising were figures as alien to the German working class as Richard Wagner and the Russian, Michael Bakunin.[5] In a list of those who were wanted by the police for their part in the Dresden affair after its failure, only 24 workers are included out of a total of 119.[6]

Elsewhere the workers did little. The Leipzig Workers' Club demanded that the city council distribute arms as soon as the revolution had started in Dresden, but, apart from the erection of a few barricades in Leipzig on the night of May 7-8, nothing was done.[7] The barricades in Breslau, once thought to be a center of radical working-class activity, lasted only a day. The central committee of the workers' associations in Württemberg issued a declaration of support for the National Assembly on the thirteenth of June and announced that "the hour of decision comes ever closer, when it will be decided whether the German people is capable of winning its freedom or whether it should live in eternal servitude." [8] But nothing was done beyond this declaration. There was widespread fear of working-class revolt, but the fears were often unrealized; in Bamberg in Bavaria, for example, the troops were called out and a number of the wealthier families left town because of possible "attacks

[5] Bakunin's role in the Dresden rising has often been discussed, possibly because this was one of the few revolutions in which this professional revolutionary actually took part. In fact he did little even in Dresden. Wagner commented that he merely "walked about smoking his cigar and making fun of the naïveté of the Dresden revolution" (*My Life,* London, 1911, vol. 1, p. 478), and Born spoke of him with a mixture of bitterness and amusement as "ein hundert Kilo schweres, naives Kind, ein *enfant terrible,* wenn man will, immerhin ein *enfant.*" (*Erinnerungen,* p. 172.)

[6] *Verbrüderung,* June 12, 19, 1849.

[7] *Verbrüderung,* May 4, 1849; *Neue Rheinische Zeitung,* May 11, 1849.

[8] *Verbrüderung,* June 26, 1849.

by the proletariat"—but the attacks never took place.[9] Many of the workers' groups behaved as circumspectly as possible in an effort to avoid repression by the government and to preserve what gains they had made.[10]

Also it was unclear just what the purpose of the various risings was. The revolt in Dresden broke out on the third of May when the king of Saxony, contrary to his promise, yielded to Prussian pressure and denounced the new national constitution; on the following day the republic was proclaimed in Saxony. In the southwest radicals at first talked of the revolution as the result of the betrayal of the people by the Frankfurt Assembly.[11] Later the National Assembly tried to enlist the support of the rebellion in Baden and the Palatinate in its own aid; the left of the Assembly issued a call to arms in its defense in mid-May, and in early June the remaining delegates, meeting as a "Rump Parliament" in Stuttgart, established a provisional government and called upon all to support the constitution.[12] But the revolutionaries in Baden set up their own provisional government and did nothing to save the work of the *Paulskirche*. The civil guard which led the revolution in Elberfeld did, on the other hand, announce its loyalty to the National Assembly.[13]

But the workers themselves had very little interest in the form of government and none whatsoever in protecting the work of the National Assembly which had done so little for them. "The proletariat," said the *Verbrü-*

[9] Koeppen, *Die Anfänge der Arbeiter- und Gesellenbewegung,* p. 73.

[10] See the report of the Workers' Union in Freiburg in Baden, which carefully remained aloof from the revolution. *Verbrüderung,* Nov. 13, 1849. In spite of this many members stayed away from the association's meetings.

[11] Valentin, *Frankfurt am Main,* p. 419.

[12] *Neue Kölnische Zeitung,* May 13, 1849; Valentin, *Geschichte der deutschen Revolution,* vol. 2, p. 503.

[13] *Neue Kölnische Zeitung,* May 2, 1849.

derung, in explaining the indifference of the workers to the defeat of the May uprisings, "is tired of fighting for the tyranny of the money bags against the tyranny of the bayonets and of securing with its blood power for the bourgeoisie." [14]

Without the support of the workers and with the Prussian government determined to defeat the revolution, the uprisings were soon defeated. Born and his colleagues were forced to flee from Dresden on the ninth of May; the risings in Elberfeld, Solingen, Düsseldorf and other towns in the Ruhr and Rhineland were put down by the middle of May. The revolt in Baden lasted longer; a number of battles were fought in June and one town, Rastatt, held out against the Prussian troops till July 23, 1849. Defeat seemed as endemic in Europe in the summer of 1849 as revolution had appeared to be in the spring of the previous year. The Roman Republic had already surrendered on the first of July; the Hungarian army under Görgey capitulated to the Russians at Világos on the thirteenth of August. The revolutions were over.

✿

There were a number of casualties to the reaction in Germany. The Frankfurt Assembly, or what remained of it at the Rump Parliament in Stuttgart, was dismissed by the troops of the king of Württemberg. There was no struggle, the soldiers merely used the flat of their swords against a procession of the remaining delegates and they dispersed. The only wounds were those of the delegates who fell in the confusion beneath the hooves of the Württemberg cavalry, and even they probably suffered more from the dirt and loss of dignity.[15] But the passing

[14] *Verbrüderung,* July 27, 1849.
[15] Valentin, *Geschichte der deutschen Revolution,* vol. 2, p. 507.

of the Frankfurt Assembly made little difference to the workers' movement.

There were also several leaders or would-be leaders of the working class who were forced by the events of May 1849 to leave Germany or to retire. Chief among these was Stephan Born, the driving force behind the *Verbrüderung*. Having taken part in the uprising in Dresden, he could no longer remain safely on German soil. He fled first to Bohemia, but soon returned to Germany on a forged passport, traveled across Saxony and Bavaria and eventually reached Switzerland.[16] He went into journalism and printing but turned ultimately to teaching; by the end of his life, in 1898, he had risen to the rank of professor of German literature in Basel. He had no further direct influence on the *Verbrüderung* or on subsequent German workers' movements.[17] A second member of the Central Committee, Georg Kick, was also forced to flee in May, so that only Franz Schwenniger remained to operate the newspaper of the *Verbrüderung*.

The *Neue Rheinische Zeitung*, which had claimed to speak for the workers, also fell victim to the reaction. The paper was banned and Marx was ordered into exile on the sixteenth of May. One last issue appeared on the nineteenth, printed in red and declaring that the editors' "last word everywhere and always will be: *Emancipation of the working class!*" The editors also advised the workers of Cologne not to join in a further revolution or attempted *putsch*, which they felt—rightly—would be bound to fail.[18] With this last gratuitous piece of advice to the workers, the *Neue Rheinische Zeitung* disap-

[16] Born, *Erinnerungen*, pp. 219ff., gives a somewhat sensational account of his escape.

[17] For a sketch of Born's career after 1849, see Quarck, *Erste deutsche Arbeiterbewegung*, pp. 131-132.

[18] *Neue Rheinische Zeitung*, May 19, 1849.

peared from the scene. The last copy soon sold out and secondhand ones were being retailed in Berlin at a rate of 1 thaler.[19] The radical *Neue Kölnische Zeitung* appeared in a black-bordered edition, lamenting the end of Marx's paper and promising to fill the gap which it left.[20] But the end of the paper, in spite of its bold "last word," probably made little difference to the workers. Marx himself left for Paris and then London, where he was joined by Engels, and the two of them endeavored to reconstitute the Communist League.

Marx's rival for the leadership of the Cologne workers, Gottschalk, also left the workers' associations and returned to his medical practice; he devoted much of his time, however, to free care of workers stricken with cholera. He contracted the disease himself and died on September 8, 1849.[21] Born's chief rival in the organization of the workers throughout Germany, Karl Georg Winkelblech, had already been in retirement since his defeat by Born at the Heidelberg Congress in January. He was elected to the Diet of Electoral Hesse in June, but refused to serve, having been convinced by the revolutions of the hopelessness of social reform. Instead he attempted to embody his ideas of guild socialism in a three volume study which appeared in the 1850s.[22]

Yet in spite of the defeat of the revolution, and in spite of the loss of a number of the protagonists of the workers' movement, the associations which had been

[19] *Westdeutsche Zeitung,* May 26, 1849.

[20] *Neue Kölnische Zeitung,* May 20, 1849. Marx turned over all articles and dispatches of the *Neue Rheinische Zeitung* to the *Neue Kölnische Zeitung* before he left and gave its editors the right to publish any more which might arrive.

[21] Stein, *Der Kölner Arbeiterverein,* pp. 104-105.

[22] Biermann, *Winkelblech,* vol. 2, pp. 357ff. Winkelblech's masterwork, *Untersuchungen über die Organisation der Arbeit-oder System der Weltökonomie,* was published in Kassel, 1850-1859, under the pseudonym of Karl Marlo.

formed in the course of 1848-1849 continued in existence for some time.

Indeed the May uprisings appear on the surface to have made little difference to the workers' associations. The newspaper of the *Verbrüderung,* for example, missed three issues at the beginning of May, but continued from the eleventh of May as before. The reports of the "progress of organization" still filled the paper's columns; attempts were made to attract the cigar makers and others into the organization, to found new branches and to widen the range of the association's activities. In particular, the period following the May uprisings saw the development of funds to support traveling journeymen, and a great deal of the space in the newspaper was taken up with this scheme. Finally, the *Verbrüderung* prepared to hold a congress in Leipzig, the congress which had been expected since the Heidelberg meeting, scheduled for June of 1849 but put off on account of the risings.[23]

Rather than succumbing immediately with the defeat of the revolution, the *Verbrüderung* and its related associations gradually drifted into oblivion; the workers' movement of 1848 ended not with a bang but a whimper. The debates and issues which filled the columns of the workers' newspapers became increasingly petty and parochial. The leaders of the movements which had grown up in the course of the revolution dissipated their energies in vain attempts at organization throughout the remaining months of 1849.

✻

The *Verbrüderung* and its local branches did experience some difficulties as a result of the defeat of the

[23] The only detailed discussion of the last years of the *Verbrüderung* is to be found in Balser, *Sozial-Demokratie, passim.*

revolution. Though the clubs were not yet closed, the members of them were constantly subject to arrest. Seven officers of the Nuremberg workers' association were imprisoned at the end of June; several members of the Leipzig workers' group were arrested in August; the head of the Hanover workers' union was exiled in September, and the chairman of the workers' association in Schwerin went to prison in October. Worst of all, the last remaining member of the Central Committee, Franz Schwenniger, was arrested on the twelfth of June and not released until the second of November. Even then he was not allowed to remain in Leipzig or to continue to edit the *Verbrüderung*. Attempts by the workers to demand concessions were of course repressed with considerably greater severity than they had been during the period of the revolutions. Ninety-two tailors' apprentices were expelled from Gera, for example, for merely petitioning for the right of workers to quit with two weeks' notice.[24]

Yet these difficulties did not stop the *Verbrüderung*. The newspaper was taken over by Carl Gangloff, a Leipzig compositor who had been active in the local association and had already been working for the paper under Stephan Born. The paper started collecting a defense fund for Schwenniger, and though the total collected was small (only 21 thaler, 13 neugroschen had been received by the beginning of July), it was nonetheless significant that a large number of workers did send in their few groschen. The *Verbrüderung* also sponsored a more general Committee for the Aid of German Refugees which advertised in its columns for the support of the workers. In an effort to attract more customers, the paper published articles of wider interest, discussing, for example, the various cures for cholera, and

[24] *Verbrüderung*, June 19, July 20, Aug. 14, Sept. 21, Oct. 5, 30, Nov. 9, 1849.

lowered its price from 15 to 9 neugroschen per quarter.[25]

The real difficulty for the *Verbrüderung* in the period of reaction lay in persuading the workers to take an interest in the activities of so dangerous sounding an organization. Many members seemed afraid to attend meetings and stayed away on account of the reports of police action in various cities. Others were merely unconcerned by the issues which had aroused them a year or so before. During the summer of 1849 the branch in Bremen complained of the "laziness" of the workers in the face of the reaction, the branch in Kiel reported slow progress on account of internal dissension and the Leipzig branch noted with regret the "indifference" of most of the trades in the area to organization. Some local associations even complained that their colleagues in other associations refused to answer letters of inquiry.[26]

Yet these difficulties too were overcome. Many clubs reported a reduction in their membership for the two months or so following the May revolts. But after the end of this period, after it seemed that the reaction had done its worst and that the workers' clubs would be allowed to remain in existence, the membership began to increase gradually.[27] New clubs were founded and new branches of older groups appeared.[28] Moreover the clubs managed to stay in existence by altering their approach or at least by emphasizing the more peaceable side of it. All question of political agitation disappeared from the programs of the associations attached to the *Verbrüderung*. Rather the clubs concentrated entirely on workers' education and self-help. The annual report

[25] *Verbrüderung*, July 3, Aug. 14, Sept. 18, 21, 1849.
[26] *Verbrüderung*, July 24, Aug. 10, Dec. 11, 1849.
[27] *Verbrüderung*, Oct. 12, Nov. 13, 1849.
[28] The Berlin branch of the *Verbrüderung* reported for the third quarter of 1849 that it had 28 affiliated branches, most of these being the clubs of the various trades in Berlin. *Verbrüderung*, Dec. 25, 1849.

from the workers' club in Halle in the autumn of 1849 mentioned only two achievements, the acquisition of twenty-five books and the purchase of a blackboard for lectures.[29] A number of associations went so far as to change their names, both to convince the authorities that they really were harmless and to persuade their fellow workers to join. The workers' union in Cologne became in July the Reading Union for Workers and in October the Educational Union.[30] Similarly the workers' society in Nuremberg which had been dissolved after the arrest of its leaders in June was reconstituted in October of 1849 as the Workers' Union for Education and Support. Other groups seemed to devolve into purely social clubs. The former workers' association in Schwerin became the Workers' Singing Union, and admission was granted only after a candidate had passed an "examination" set by the club's singing teacher, a curious echo of guild procedure.[31]

The various cooperative schemes for production and self-help continued and indeed were given a higher priority after the defeat of the revolution. The Berlin regional committee continued to be the leader in this sort of activity. Its cooperative production of clothing continued during the summer of 1849, though perhaps at a somewhat slower rate than before, but the production by the Berlin cooperatives of bread remained about the same and the production of cigars increased, reaching a peak of 15,000 cigars in September 1849, the last month for which statistics were printed. The Berlin committee also inaugurated on May 1, 1849, a health

[29] *Verbrüderung*, Nov. 20, 1849.
[30] Stein, *Der Kölner Arbeiterverein*, p. 104.
[31] *Verbrüderung*, Oct. 5, Nov. 6, 1849. The editors of the paper felt compelled to censor the "foundation festivities" of one of the workers' associations, which, they argued, had little in fact to celebrate in the way of achievement. (Oct. 23, 1849.)

insurance scheme which was the first of its sort in Germany. The Health Care Union offered to provide the services of a doctor, medicines, splints, spectacles, baths and "all other necessities" to its members, who contributed 2.5 silbergroschen per month with a special rate of 1.5 silbergroschen per head to the sickness funds of the various member associations of the *Verbrüderung*. There were only 327 members when the scheme started; by the end of September 1849 there were 5,110 members and the Union had treated 1,070 cases.[32]

Another form of self-help organized by the *Verbrüderung* rose to considerable prominence during the latter part of 1849. The various branches had talked considerably during the period of the revolution of the possibility of establishing funds to contribute to the maintenance of the traveling artisan, but it was only after the defeat of the revolutions that this scheme was taken up on any widespread basis. By the end of 1849 the leaders of the *Verbrüderung* boasted that the establishment of the support funds for travelers was the one great achievement of the organization during a period when "the political sky became ever more overcast, the air ever more sultry and oppressive."[33] The funds were, of course, aimed primarily at the journeyman on his *Wanderjahre;* in the emphasis on them, the *Verbrüderung* revealed once again how closely it was tied to the guild system and how much it depended on the lower ranks of the guilds for its support.

In the course of 1849 and 1850 over sixty local associations informed the *Verbrüderung* that they had established support funds for traveling workers. Any member of a local branch of the organization could, upon presenting his membership card, receive a small sum of

[32] *Verbrüderung*, Dec. 25, 1849, Feb. 26, Mar. 1, 5, 8, 1850.
[33] *Verbrüderung*, Dec. 28, 1849.

money to help him while passing through. The contributions were indeed small, never more than a few kreutzer or groschen, but they were probably welcome assistance to the penniless journeyman in search of employment. Occasionally one of the local groups would complain that there were not enough others participating in the scheme and would confine its contributions to the journeymen of those associations which they were sure would help their own.[34] But these complaints were heard mainly during the early months of the program and by the end of 1849 the scheme seemed to be operating smoothly throughout most of Germany.

The *Verbrüderung* also continued the series of regional congresses in the period following the defeat of the revolution in an effort to increase the size of the organization. Little was in fact achieved at these congresses, which mainly served to reveal the growing weakness of the organization. But the fact that they were held at all is indicative of the resilience of the workers' movement in the face of reaction. The regional congresses were also designed to prepare the way for a national congress of the associations belonging to the *Verbrüderung*.

The first of these congresses was held at Reutlingen on September 23, 1849, for the representatives of the workers' associations of Württemberg. The delegates reported that the movement had "come to something of a standstill," and though they assumed that this was for the present only, they had very little to suggest in the way of remedies for the situation beyond a motion which called on the Central Committee to pay for the postage of all correspondence with the local clubs. In addition it was agreed to unite with various gymnastic societies (*Turnvereine*) in Württemberg and a motion was passed

[34] See the complaint of the Hanover Workers' Union in the *Verbrüderung*, Aug. 24, 1849. Balser, *Sozial-Demokratie*, pp. 624ff., gives a list of these funds.

"to avoid politics, since individual members or clubs are not permitted to join political organizations." [35] Efforts at education and self-help remained the only activities left to the local associations in Württemberg.

A second congress, held at Hanover on October 29, 1849, attracted delegates representing 1,500 members of the *Verbrüderung* in northern Germany and came to similar conclusions. The debates at Hanover dealt mainly with the establishment of support for traveling journeymen and with the regional committee which was to supervise the funds and prevent fraud. The associations represented at Hanover also passed a motion in favor of uniting with the workers' gymnastic societies in the area.[36]

A final regional congress was held at Augsburg on November 13-14, 1849. The main purpose of the congress, according to the Bavarian regional committee in Munich which made the arrangements, was to further the formation of traveling funds in Bavaria. The congress ran into opposition, however, from some of the local clubs. In particular the Workers' Education Union in Regensburg refused to send delegates and wrote to the *Verbrüderung,* complaining about the holding of unnecessary congresses and pointing out that the money might much better be spent on the traveling funds themselves. They also protested against the fact that the congress had been called for a Tuesday and not a Sunday and would thus waste working time.[37]

In spite of these protests the congress was held, though with relatively few delegates; only thirteen members of the *Verbrüderung* were present, representing the workers in eight different towns in Bavaria. Again the representatives of the local branches lamented the lack of

[35] *Verbrüderung,* Oct. 9, 1849.
[36] *Verbrüderung,* Nov. 20, 1849.
[37] *Verbrüderung,* Oct. 26, Nov. 16, 1849.

interest. It was hoped that such schemes as unification with the gymnastic societies and the extensive adoption of funds for travelers and for the old and sick would gain greater support for the *Verbrüderung*. The delegates also passed a resolution in favor of greater centralization, giving more power to the central and regional committees. Finally, the congress, like its predecessors in the autumn of 1849, disclaimed any political intent; it adopted a resolution declaring that "the purpose of the workers' associations is to strive for the moral and spiritual education of its workers as well as to counteract the condition of material need among the workers." [38] No mention was made of government action.

There was a sequel to the congress, for the quarrel between the regional committee in Munich and the Regensburg branch about the necessity of the congress was carried on for over a month in the columns of the *Verbrüderung*. The issue was in fact a minor one, and the two sides soon lapsed into a vitriolic debate about which of them had the true interests of the workers and working-class unity at heart, a debate unbacked by any substantial arguments on either side. The editors of the paper had finally to terminate the correspondence, commenting that the whole affair was merely a misunderstanding which "brothers" should overlook.[39] The episode was, however, symptomatic of the decline of the workers' associations.

❋

The various trade groups founded during 1848 continued in existence for a period at least following the May uprisings, and the *Verbrüderung* continued to report their activities in the hopes of attracting them into the more general organization. The printers, for example,

---

[38] *Verbrüderung*, Nov. 30, 1849.
[39] *Verbrüderung*, Dec. 4, 18, 1849, Jan. 4, 1850.

made one final effort to achieve an organization which would include both the journeymen printers and the masters or employers. A congress was held in Berlin from September 30 to October 2, 1849, and attended by thirty-six journeymen and fourteen employers coming from all parts of Germany; the delegates debated statutes for the proposed organization and discussed such measures as sickness and savings funds. The congress was dispersed after its third session, however, by the Berlin police, who took the names of all present and ordered "foreigners" into exile from Prussia.[40] The Printers' League was soon banned in a number of states—Bavaria, Saxony and Prussia—but remnants of the organization remained as late as 1852, when the last branches were finally dissolved. In spite of the lack of success of the organization, however, the journeymen printers still refused to join the *Verbrüderung*.[41]

Negotiations to amalgamate the cigar workers' association with the *Verbrüderung*, though perhaps unnecessarily tortuous, were ultimately successful. The cigar makers had originally planned to discuss the question of joining the *Verbrüderung* at their congress in June of 1849. But because of the spring uprisings the congress had to be postponed, first from the beginning of June till the end of the month, and then from the end of June till some indefinite date later in the summer.[42] The issue of amalgamation with the *Verbrüderung* continued to be discussed in the columns of the cigar makers' newspaper, *Concordia*. The chairman of the Central Committee of the cigar makers, Kohlweck, argued in favor of the amalgamation, though less from practical reasons

[40] *Verbrüderung*, Aug. 31, Oct. 5, 1849.
[41] Krahl, *Verband der deutschen Buchdrucker*, suppl. to vol. 1, p. 3; Adler, *Geschichte der Arbeiterbewegung*, p. 194; Quarck, *Erste deutsche Arbeiterbewegung*, p. 213.
[42] *Concordia*, May 22, June 30, 1849.

than in support of the ideal of working-class unity. An article by the chairman of the Berlin regional committee of the *Verbrüderung*, Bisky, explained that his group sought united action by the working classes and avoided the disadvantages of "single circles of association, of corporations, of guilds." Moreover, it was pointed out that the current willingness of the employers of the cigar workers to negotiate would not necessarily last and that the help of other workers' groups might prove useful in the event of a strike.[43]

But the union was opposed by others who felt that the sole concern of the cigar workers should be the interests of their own trade and the immediate improvement of their own conditions. "The union with the workers' *Verbrüderung*," it was argued, "can, in respect to the improvement of our business, do us no earthly good." The union would be either vague and general or else one-sided and restrictive; but, in any case, it was held that it would be without practical advantage.[44] In the meantime the association was occupied with more pressing issues such as negotiations with the Berlin employers and an attempt to persuade all workers to stay away from a firm in Leipzig which had dismissed sixteen members of the local cigar workers' union.[45]

The cigar workers' congress finally met in Leipzig on September 3, 1849. The debate over the union with the *Verbrüderung* continued among the twenty-one delegates who came as representatives of the cigar workers in seventy-seven cities, but no final result was reached. It was decided to publish the cigar workers' paper as a supplement to the paper of the *Verbrüderung*, but the actual union of the two groups was to await discussion

[43] *Concordia*, June 30, July 14, 28, 1849.
[44] Letter from M. A. Arronge from Duisberg, *Concordia*, June 30, 1849.
[45] *Concordia*, May 22, July 28, 1849.

in the local associations and the election of delegates to the next general congress of the *Verbrüderung*. The congress also discussed various concerns of the trade, the problem of negotiating with employers, the proper length of time for apprenticeships as cigar workers and similar issues. Kohlweck was reelected to the office of president, but an opponent of the *Verbrüderung*, Arronge from Duisberg, was elected as vice-president. The central offices of the association were moved from Berlin to Bremen, where the local branch of the cigar workers was larger than any of the others.[46]

The amalgamation of the two newspapers, the *Verbrüderung* and *Concordia*, did take place, though not until December rather than in October as planned. Indeed once the amalgamation had taken place the cigar workers' section occasionally failed to appear altogether owing to lack of manuscripts. The cigar workers also went ahead with their plans to elect delegates to the general assembly of the *Verbrüderung;* letters were sent to the various local branches explaining the purposes of the congress and pointing out that the proposed union would not limit the activities or restrict the independence of the cigar workers' groups in any way.[47]

*

In the meantime the *Verbrüderung* as a whole had been preparing for its general congress, the first since it had been founded in Berlin in September 1848. The general congress had originally been called for June 1849 but had been repeatedly delayed, partly because of the arrests of the local leaders of some of the associations as well as the remaining member of the Central Committee,

[46] *Concordia,* Oct. 26, Nov. 1, 9, Dec. 7, 1849; Frisch, *Organisationsbestrebungen in der Tabakindustrie,* p. 12; Adler, *Geschichte der Arbeiterbewegung,* p. 195.

[47] *Verbrüderung,* Oct. 5, Dec. 11, 1849, Jan. 22, 25, 29, 1850.

Schwenniger. By the end of 1849 the congress was scheduled for either late January or the early part of February 1850. Finally, on the eighth of January, instructions went out to the local associations to elect delegates for a general congress which was to meet on the twentieth of February.[48]

The congress marked what was in a sense the first all-German workers' congress, the first to be held since the journeymen of southwest Germany had joined the *Verbrüderung* at Heidelberg in January 1849. At any rate, its claim to the title was as good as, if not better than, those of any of the other congresses of workers and artisans which had met in Germany during the course of 1848 and 1849. Schwenniger, who had been released from prison in November, urged his fellow workers to have a due regard for the significance of the event.[49]

> The first general assembly of German workers is then one of the most important moments in the history of the workers' movement since the year 1848; on it depends whether the worker can be recognized as a class or whether he will live eternally as a slave who curses his chains but never has the courage to break them.

Thus the final achievement of the workers' movement of 1848, and its final test, came long after the defeat of the revolutionary movement.

[48] *Verbrüderung*, Sept. 7, Dec. 28, 1849; Jan. 22, 1850.
[49] *Verbrüderung*, Feb. 8, 1850.

CHAPTER 14

THE FINAL CONGRESS AND THE
END OF THE ASSOCIATION

THE FIRST, and last, general congress of the *Verbrüderung* met in Leipzig from the twentieth to the twenty-sixth of February, 1850. The congress was attended by twenty-five delegates, representing two hundred and fifty workers' associations in Germany, together with six delegates from the cigar workers' organization.[1] The delegates took as their object the reorganization of the *Verbrüderung* in the face of the losses it had suffered from the reaction. Yet the atmosphere was not one of despair but of hope; the delegates assumed that it would be possible to go on enlarging their associations. One speaker at the congress described the period since the March Days as consisting of "three epochs: revolution, reaction and restoration." The worst, it was believed, had passed; the wave of arrests and suppressions which had followed the defeat of the May uprisings had subsided. The workers would maintain their loyalty to the revolution; they were after all "children of the revolution." But their chief task lay in the promotion of their organization.[2]

The reports of the delegates on the progress of their local organizations occupied the major part of the first two days of the Leipzig Congress and confirmed the belief that the epoch of reaction had passed and the restoration begun. Almost every delegate acknowledged that his club had suffered a severe decline at the time of

[1] The congress was reported in the *Verbrüderung*, May 18–June 29, 1850; cf. Adler, *Geschichte der Arbeiterbewegung*, pp. 201-204; Balser, *Sozial-Demokratie*, pp. 86-122.
[2] *Verbrüderung*, June 15, 1850.

the May uprisings; but all reported that the number of members had once again begun to rise, though totals were still far below what they had been in the early part of 1849. The delegate from Glauchau reported that his association, which had numbered one thousand before May 1849, was now down to one hundred members, though this figure marked a considerable "recovery." Similar reports came from such places as Freiburg, Schwerin, Königsberg, Hamburg and Bremen. The delegate from Frankfurt am Main reported that his club had been completely abolished for a time but was now back to forty members.

The remainder of the congress was devoted to a discussion of the ways in which the local associations could increase their membership and expand their activities. Under the president of the congress, Bisky from Berlin, and the secretary, Gangloff from Leipzig, the delegates listened to reports on the various sorts of relief funds which could be set up, on the means of financing lectures and libraries, on the progress of the producers' and consumers' cooperatives. All these projects were urged upon the local clubs. The congress also called for the expansion of the system of funds to support traveling journeymen, for the erection of guest houses for these journeymen and for the establishment of local bureaus, run by the associations, which could provide information on employment. Also among the items on the agenda of the congress were a discussion of the expansion of the workers' singing groups and the consideration of the introduction of a *Verbrüderung* song book. It was to such measures of "self-help" that the revolutionary workers' associations of the March Days had been reduced by the time of their first general congress.

The congress also dealt with a number of plans for expanding the scope of the *Verbrüderung*. Some delegates hoped that the workers' organization could join with the German gymnastic societies which were planning to hold a congress of their own at Eisenach. Others wanted to incorporate a women's branch into the society.[3] Finally, the congress discussed the question of the admission of the cigar workers to the *Verbrüderung*. The six delegates from the cigar workers' association had at last agreed to the proposed amalgamation, and after some negotiation the two groups were united at Leipzig. The cigar workers were persuaded to alter their regulations in conformity with the *Verbrüderung's* principle of equality of opportunity; they were to admit women to their trade and to remove the restrictions on the number of apprentices.

Beyond this the delegates to the Leipzig congress saw little that they could do to further the cause of working-class organization. A new Central Committee was elected, consisting of Schwenniger, Gangloff and Reuss of Würzburg. The newspaper of the *Verbrüderung* was to continue to be published, but was to appear only once a week. With this, the Leipzig Congress was over.

❋

The Leipzig Congress represents the last effort of the *Verbrüderung* to accommodate itself to the changed conditions which followed the defeat of the revolution. All attempts by the workers to keep clear of political issues and to concentrate on the simple organization of their class for purposes of self-help were in vain. The governments of a number of the German states turned to the problem of the workers' associations in the spring of 1850, ruled that they were inherently political and

[3] Luise Otto-Peters had founded a weekly woman's newspaper, *Die Frauenzeitung,* and had applied for the admission of a women's branch of the *Verbrüderung* nearly a year before. *Verbrüderung,* May 4, 1849.

ordered them banned. The first of the governments to promulgate a law against the workers' associations was Bavaria; on February 26, 1850, the very day the Leipzig Congress closed, the Bavarian law "on associations and assemblies" required all organizations to hand over copies of their statutes and lists of their members to the authorities. On the twenty-seventh of March the Bavarian government ruled that all workers' associations were political and were therefore outlawed.[4] Similar laws were enacted in Prussia on the eleventh of March and in Saxony on the third of June.[5] The columns of the *Verbrüderung* were filled with accounts of searches through the papers of the various local branches, of forced resignations, of the arrest of a number of the leaders and of the dissolution of many of the associations. Schwenniger and Reuss were both exiled from Saxony, leaving Gangloff once again to carry on the paper by himself.[6]

In spite of repression, the organization hoped to continue. Members were urged to go on reading the paper at the weekly meetings of the local associations and to reject offers of employers and others who would lead the workers out of their own organizations with promises of cooperation and financial aid.[7] The Saxon law which forbade political clubs forced the *Verbrüderung* to take some action. The last issue of the newspaper on June 29, 1850, announced the dissolution of the central and regional committees of the organization; it was hoped that at least some of the local groups might survive as non-political societies. More than this, the editors of the

---

[4] Koeppen, *Die Anfänge der Arbeiter- und Gesellenbewegung,* p. 82.

[5] *Verbrüderung,* June 29, 1850; Adler, *Geschichte der Arbeiterbewegung,* p. 207.

[6] *Verbrüderung,* Apr. 30, 1850.

[7] *Verbrüderung,* Mar. 29, Apr. 20, 1850.

Verbrüderung announced that they had applied to the Saxon authorities and hoped soon to convince them that their organization was not in fact involved in politics. They still hoped to continue the paper; the final issue contained an advertisement for further subscriptions.

Yet on the whole they were aware of the failure of the *Verbrüderung* and the workers' movement of 1848. Shortly before the Saxon government banned the organization, the editor of the paper, Gangloff, tried to analyze the causes for this failure. Curiously enough, he did not take the easy way out and blame either the middle-class liberals or the conservative governments of Germany; the failure of the workers' associations was not merely a by-product of the failure of the revolution as a whole. The causes of the failure of the associations lay, rather, in the workers themselves, though the immediate cause of their dissolution was the action of the governments.

But beyond this lay the disunity of the German working class. The Frankfurt congresses of the master artisans and the journeymen had done much to distract from the unified organization which Born and his colleagues had tried to form in Berlin. More importantly, Gangloff argued that the workers and artisans had never realized the true nature of the principles of the *Verbrüderung;* these were summed up in "the proud sentence: *We are workers and will help ourselves.*" The form of the principles was adopted by many of the associations, but "never the essence, never the thought expressed in them of growing humanity." This, for Gangloff, was the reason for the failure of the associations.[8] And the same thought was echoed in a poem which was published in the last issue of the *Verbrüderung* and began, "My child, you have long been out of your mother's cradle, now help yourself." [9]

[8] *Verbrüderung,* June 15, 1850.
[9] *Verbrüderung,* June 29, 1850.

The *Verbrüderung* was banned in Saxony at the beginning of July as a league of political unions. Gangloff tried with Schwenniger's aid to bring out another newspaper, *Prometheus,* but the paper closed within the month for lack of funds. Both editors were arrested; after six months Schwenniger was sent once again into exile while Gangloff was condemned at the end of a year's investigation to six months in prison.[10]

The banning of the Central Committee of the *Verbrüderung* did not mean the immediate end of the workers' associations. Although a large number of the local branches were dissolved in the spring and summer of 1850, others lasted for several months and in some cases years.[11] A number of the cooperative shops continued, but these were taken over by private owners. The Health Care Union in Berlin was in existence till April of 1853 when it was dissolved by the police for "criminal tendencies." In 1854 the Diet of the German Federation passed a law, proposed by Bismarck for Prussia and von Prokesch-Osten for Austria, banning all clubs or associations considered to have political, socialist or communist purposes. The remaining branches of the *Verbrüderung* came under this law, though the last three associations, in Saxe-Weimar, Schwarzburg-Rudolstadt and Luxemburg, were not closed until 1856.[12]

❋

The dissolution of the *Verbrüderung* left the workers in what appeared to be the same position as they had held in the pre-March period. Their only outlets were secret societies such as Marx's Communist League or

[10] Adler, *Geschichte der Arbeiterbewegung,* pp. 207-208.
[11] The associations in Württemberg were particularly active; see Balser, *Sozial-Demokratie,* ch. 5, pp. 337ff.
[12] Adler, *Geschichte der Arbeiterbewegung,* pp. 209-210; Bernstein, *Schneiderbewegung,* p. 85; Valentin, *Frankfurt am Main,* p. 511.

the traditional workers' organizations, the guilds. Both of these were inadequate to meet the needs of the workers, yet both underwent a revival of sorts during the early part of the 1850s. The more radical of the workers joined the Communist League as long as it was in existence, though the police kept fairly close track of it and membership was unsafe. A much larger group joined in the revived guilds, sponsored in many states by the conservative governments. The workers' movement of 1848 ended where it began.

Marx and Engels arrived in London in the autumn of 1849 and immediately began to make arrangements for the revival of the Communist League. Such a revival had already been attempted the previous spring by Joseph Moll, but Marx and Engels had held back from Moll's efforts, Moll himself had been killed in the fighting in Baden and the Palatinate and the incipient revival had been stopped. Marx and his colleagues, however, were more careful in preparing their ground; the winter of 1849-1850 was spent in London in a series of consultations on the new League, and the first address of the reconstituted central authority was not issued until March of 1850. The address published then took as the slogan of the new League the phrase "the revolution in permanence," a phrase which had been urged upon Marx in the course of 1848-1849 by Gottschalk and others in Cologne and since then by some of the followers of Blanqui in Paris. The central authority called on the workers of Europe to prepare for the proletarian revolution, cooperating with the petty bourgeois parties where possible but holding themselves in readiness for the final struggle.[13] Yet even in the period of reaction and even in London, Marx's consistency in advocating revolu-

[13] Marx, Engels, *Selected Works*, vol. 1, pp. 98-108; Gustav Mayer, *Friedrich Engels, A Biography*, London, 1936, p. 118. For Marx's changing attitude to revolution, see Lichtheim, *Marxism*, pp. 122ff.

tion seemed to waver. By the autumn of 1850 Marx and his followers broke with the revolutionary Willich-Schapper group in the League, because, he held, the increasing prosperity of Germany had removed all chance of revolution. Marx transferred the seat of the central authority of the League to Cologne in order to avoid further controversy.[14]

In Germany the League had made considerable headway. By June of 1850 the London committee had received reports which indicated that many of the more militant workers had joined; the League claimed to have made converts in all of the remaining workers' associations and to have attracted the support of the more influential members or ex-members of the *Verbrüderung*.[15]

Yet the League lasted only a short time. One of its officers, Peter Nothjung, a tailor from Cologne, was arrested at the railway station in Leipzig on May 10, 1851, while trying to buy a ticket for Berlin; on Nothjung were found copies of many of the more important documents of the League, including the addresses of most of its leaders in Germany. The arrest of Nothjung led to the apprehension of a number of the other members, some of whom made further confessions, so that within a few months the League had ceased to exist in Germany. Several of the leaders were put on trial in Cologne in October and November 1852. Although the government had forged much of its evidence against them in a vain effort to prove a connection between the German group and a similar conspiracy in Paris, and the forgery had to be admitted, the leaders were convicted, receiving prison sentences ranging from three to six years. The

[14] Marx, Engels, *Selected Works*, vol. 2, pp. 320-321; for a defense of Marx's action, see Obermann, *Zur Geschichte des Bundes der Kommunisten*, pp. 36ff.; also Marx, *Enthüllungen*, pp. 94ff.

[15] Marx, *Enthüllungen*, p. 141.

League in London dissolved at the same time and the dissident group under Willich and Schapper also disappeared. Marx was never again to advocate a revolutionary conspiracy. The history of the Communist League in Germany had come to an end.

It is doubtful, however, whether the League had ever had a great influence over the mass of German workers and the sort of associations which had been founded in 1848 and had joined the *Verbrüderung*. The Prussian police, in an effort to convict as many as possible at one time, attempted to show a direct connection between the League and the workers' *Verbrüderung;* but even using the most tenuous of arguments and indulging in the reasoning of guilt by association, they had only been able to show "communist" connections for eleven of the twenty-five delegates to the last congress of the *Verbrüderung* in Leipzig.[16] Also many of the local branches of the League in Germany probably had little interest in the theoretical debates in which Marx engaged in London; they were rather the vague sort of discussion groups which had existed secretly before 1848 and had come into the open in the workingmen's educational unions and reading clubs of 1848-1849. "The communist tendencies of the artisans" were, in the eyes of one observer in the period following the defeat of the May uprisings, nothing new; they merely afforded further evidence for the fact that "since olden times the ineradicable penchant for religious and political enthusiasms has been peculiar to our artisans." [17]

❖

The same observer cited the old guild system, "with its peculiar enthusiasms and poetry," as another example of this phenomenon. Indeed the spread of communism

[16] Wermuth, Stieber, *Die Communisten-Verschwörungen,* vol. 1, pp. 306-312.
[17] *Die Geissel, Tageblatt aller Tagblätter,* July 31, 1849.

was partly seen as a result of the decline of the guilds. The basic problem of the artisans was a question of "the honor of their class," which was "no longer respected from outside." The restoration of the guilds was all that was needed to regain the loyalty of the mass of artisans.

A revival of the guilds, if not a restoration, did take place in the years following the defeat of the revolution. Indeed this revival was one of the chief results of the artisans' movement of 1848-1849. The Prussian industrial ordinance of February 9, 1849, had set the pace for a number of the states of Germany which continued the regulations for compulsory guild membership and even restored these regulations to a number of trades which had been open to free competition. In Prussia alone the new industrial ordinance led to the foundation or re-constitution of 4,600 craft corporations. The proportion of artisans to total population increased in the period of the revolution and the years immediately following, reaching a peak between 1849 and 1852, after which it began to decline. In general, the years immediately following the revolutions brought a brief respite to the artisans between the severe depression of the 1840s and the period of rapid expansion of industrial capitalism which began in the 1850s. Wages rose in 1850 and the problem of unemployment was eased by the large amount of emigration which took place in the years following the revolution as well as by a decreased rate of population growth.[18]

[18] Schmoller, *Geschichte der deutschen Kleingewerbe*, pp. 70-71. Tilmann, *Einfluss des Revolutionsjahres*, p. 50; Hamerow, *Restoration, Revolution, Reaction*, pp. 208, 210, 229. Emigration from Germany had slackened considerably during the years of the revolution but rose again sharply from 1851 on, reaching a figure of 251,931 in 1854. See Viebahn, *Statistik*, vol. 2, pp. 241, 247. For an extremely interesting and intelligent discussion of the complex relation between the revolution and emigration, see Mack Walker, *Germany and the Emigration, 1816-1885*, Cambridge, Mass., 1964, especially chapters 4, 5 and 6.

The guilds continued to offer to the artisans the one form of organization which they were allowed. Indeed long after the end of the requirement of guild membership and the establishment of trade freedom, the guilds provided an outlet for the workers' drive to organization and remained of considerable importance, while trade unions, even when legal, were slow to make progress among the more skilled of German workers.[19] Trade freedom did not destroy the artisans, contrary to their own predictions. In many areas they still outnumbered the factory workers as late as the 1860s. In Prussia in 1863 there were over a million artisans and only 770,000 factory workers; in the Grand Duchy of Hesse the proportion was three to one.[20]

But the skilled handicraft trades upon which the guilds were based were doomed, not to extinction but to a gradual decline in importance. The 1850s marked the first great period of speculation, the *Gründerzeit*, during which Germany definitely passed into the stage of modern industrial capitalism. Production in a number of significant fields increased rapidly in the course of the decade after the revolutions. The value of the produce of all the mines in the countries of the Zollverein rose from 15 million thaler in 1848 to 46 million thaler in 1857; the numbers of workers employed in the mines increased in the same period from 88,000 to 169,000. In the same years the iron and steel produced in the Zollverein rose from 21 million thaler to 57 million thaler,

[19] Clapham, *Economic Development of France and Germany*, pp. 288, 329, 333-334.

[20] Ernst Schraepler, "Linksliberalismus und Arbeiterschaft in der preussischen Konfliktszeit," *Forschungen zur Staat und Verfassungen, Festgabe für Fritz Hartung,* ed. Richard Dietrich and Gerhard Oestreich, Berlin, 1958, p. 388; Wilhelm Ullmann, *Die hessische Gewerbepolitik von der Zeit des Rheinbundes bis zur Einführung der Gewerbefreiheit im Jahre 1866 insbesondere das Handwerk und das Hausiergewerbe,* Darmstadt, 1903, p. 62.

and the number of workers employed in the iron industry increased from 28,000 to 46,000. The amount of coal mined annually in the Zollverein in this period increased from 148,000 cwt. to 355,000 cwt. The amount of railway track in Germany rose from 5,822 km. in 1850 to 11,026 km. in 1860. At the same time, or at least after about 1852, a large number of the handicraft trades began to show declining numbers of masters and journeymen.[21]

Following the depression of 1857, pressure to open all trades to free entry increased sharply. Paradoxically perhaps, Austria was the first of the German states to introduce *Gewerbefreiheit*: a law of December 20, 1859, opened all trades to free entry as of May 1, 1860. Nassau followed in 1860, Prussia in 1861, Württemberg, Baden, Saxony and the Thuringian duchies in 1862-1863, when Bavaria also passed a law which would lead ultimately to the right of free entry into all trades in 1868. In 1866 there were only eleven states in the Zollverein that had retained the guild system intact, and these were all among the smaller members. There were another four states which were in a transition between the guild system and complete freedom of trade, but the other seventeen members had all granted this freedom. Following the formation of the North German Confederation, the right of free entry was proclaimed among all its member states. A law of July 8, 1868, established trade freedom and ended the exclusive rights of the guilds throughout the Confederation; the same law was extended to the new German Empire from January 1,

[21] For a list of these trades, see Schmoller, *Geschichte der deutschen Kleingewerbe*, p. 93; also Werner Sombart, *Die deutsche Volkswirtschaft im neunzehnten Jahrhundert und im Anfang des 20. Jahrhunderts, Eine Einführung in die Nationalökonomie*, Berlin, 1927, pp. 84, 493; Viebahn, *Statistik*, vol. 2, pp. 407, 487.

1872.[22] The guild movement of 1848 appeared also to have suffered a complete defeat.

✷

Yet though the guilds had lost their privileged position, though the Communist League had been exposed and its leaders imprisoned or driven into exile, though the workers' associations established in the course of the revolutions had been dissolved, the workers' movement of 1848-1849 influenced to a large extent the form which the German workers' movement would take once it began to revive. The issues which the workers debated in 1848 and 1849 were the same ones which were discussed again in the 1860s. Indeed the opposition between reform and revolution which was at the core of the debates of 1848 produced as well what has been called the "great schism" in the twentieth century German socialist-labor movement.[23]

By 1860 a number of the forms of self-help which had been inaugurated under Born and the *Verbrüderung* had been revived.[24] The liberal Hermann Schulze-Delitzsch

[22] Schmoller, *Geschichte der deutschen Kleingewerbe,* pp. 1, 107, 109, 151; Schmoller held that the new law would make little difference to the handtrades, which would remain or continue to decline according to such factors as competition and the development of industrial techniques, irrespective of their legal status. Cf. also Viebahn, *Statistik,* vol. 3, p. 556; Josef Kaizl, *Der Kampf um Gewerbereform und Gewerbefreiheit in Bayern von 1799-1868,* Leipzig, 1879, p. 24; Paul Möslein, *Die Gewerbegesetzgebung der Thüringer Herzogtümer im 19. Jahrhundert bis zur Einführung der Gewerbefreiheit,* Weimar, 1909, pp. 69ff.; H. A. Mascher, *Das deutsche Gewerbewesen von der frühesten Zeit bis auf die Gegenwart,* Potsdam, 1866, pp. 709ff.

[23] The phrase is Carl Schorske's; see *German Social Democracy, 1905-1917, The Development of the Great Schism,* Cambridge, Mass., 1955.

[24] Balser also emphasizes a continuity of personnel between the *Verbrüderung* and the workers' movement of the 1860s. *Sozial-Demokratie,* pp. 18, 21, 479-496.

became the advocate of cooperative production and gained considerable success in this field, hoping thus to wean the artisans from the workers and win them for the liberal cause in the constitutional struggle.[25]

The artisans in fact remained leaders of the German labor movement. Working-class parties gained their first success in the areas of handicraft production and not in the large industrial cities; socialist and union leaders with "proletarian" origins were more often former journeymen than former factory workers. The concern of the guildsmen for education and working-class culture was an abiding interest of the German labor movement.[26] Guild attitudes influenced socialist organizations as well; the guild acceptance of a hierarchical society may account for the ease with which the sociologist Robert Michels was able to derive his "iron law of oligarchy" from the example of the German Social Democratic Party of the early twentieth century.

The line between "guild" and "labor union" was often hard to draw; some workers' organizations changed from one label to another with surprising and confusing frequency.[27] The guilds themselves even regained some of

[25] That Schulze-Delitzsch aimed primarily at the artisans and not the workers in general is made clear in Krieger, *German Idea of Freedom,* p. 395; yet he made the same mistake as the liberals of 1848, attacking the guild system. Cf. his pamphlet, "Die arbeitenden Klassen und das Assoziationswesen in Deutschland," Hermann Schulze-Delitzsch, *Schriften und Reden,* Berlin, 1909, vol. 1, pp. 202ff.; cf. vol. 2, pp. 394ff.

[26] See Gerhard A. Ritter, *Die Arbeiterbewegung im Wilhelminischen Reich,* Berlin-Dahlem, 1959, p. 9, and the chapter on "Die Arbeiterbewegung als Emanzipations- und Kulturbewegung," pp. 218ff.

[27] See P. G. J. Pulzer, *The Rise of Political Anti-Semitism in Germany and Austria,* New York, 1964, p. 25. Pulzer also notes (p. 24) that the continued existence of large "pre-capitalist" groups such as the artisans provided fruitful soil for the growth of anti-Semitism; all of the anti-Semitic political parties appealed for artisan support.

their legal position. A series of laws passed after 1878 and Bismarck's break with the liberals encouraged master craftsmen to join the guilds, and a law of 1897 allowed local authorities to make guild membership once again compulsory. By 1904, the last prewar year for which statistics are available, there was a total of half a million craftsmen to be found in some six thousand different guild organizations, in half of which membership was compulsory. The guilds remained important; guild membership probably equaled and may have exceeded trade union membership as late as the 1890s, and only after the turn of the century did the trade unionists greatly outnumber the members of the craft guilds.[28]

Yet a changed political orientation was already discernible in the 1860s, a split, as it has been called, between bourgeois and proletarian democracy.[29] The Leipzig workers' educational association, the heir of the *Verbrüderung*, set itself up as the Central Committee for the Convocation of a German Workers' Congress and met on May 23, 1863, to form the General German Workers' Union, the parent organization of what was to become the Social Democratic Party. The issues of self-help or state aid, economic or political action, cooperation or hostility toward the middle classes—all of these

[28] In 1895 the trade unions claimed only 269,000 members out of a total industrial working force of 8 million; membership in trade unions rose to 1 million in 1902, 2 million in 1906 and 3 million in 1909. Clapham, *Economic Development of France and Germany,* pp. 329, 334-335.

[29] Gustav Mayer, "Die Trennung der proletarischen von der bürgerlichen Demokratie in Deutschland (1863-1870)," *Archiv für die Geschichte des Sozialismus und der Arbeiterbewegung,* vol. 2, 1911-1912, pp. 1-67; also by the same author, "Die Lösung der deutschen Frage im Jahre 1866 und die Arbeiterbewegung," *Festgabe für Wilhelm Lexis,* Jena, 1907, pp. 221-268; and the more recent study by Ernst Schraepler, "Linksliberalismus." Even here, one should note, the split was as much between the different groups of artisans as it was between the artisans and the industrial workers.

once more came under discussion. Lassalle, in his *Offenes Antwort-Schreiben*, which he wrote at the request of the Leipzig committee, opposed the doctrine of self-help and immediate economic action which Born had advocated in 1848; he called for universal suffrage and the control of the state by a working-class political party. He rejected the liberal alliance and even made overtures privately to Bismarck. Lassalle's position, though attacked by many, notably by Wilhelm Liebknecht and August Bebel (another artisan) and the party which they set up at the Eisenach Congress in 1869, as well as by Marx, was to form the basic creed of the German workers' movement in the second half of the nineteenth century. It was accepted in substance if not in form when the working-class parties united behind the Gotha program of 1875. It was in many ways the opposite of the program which Born and his colleagues had followed in the course of the German revolutions.

Speculations, fascinating though fruitless, have often been made about what would have been the fate of Germany if the revolutions of 1848 and 1849 had succeeded, if the architect of German political unity had been Heinrich von Gagern and not Otto von Bismarck. Equally fascinating would be the history of the German workers' movement if it had been instigated by Stephan Born and not by Ferdinand Lassalle. But the speculation must ignore the fact that the workers' movement of 1848 was a failure; it is equally fruitless.

CONCLUSION

THE WORKERS' movement of 1848, like the revolutions themselves, was a failure. Indeed the two failures are directly connected. The workers' movement was both a cause and a result of the revolutions. The barricades were erected and the March governments were set up because the artisans and laborers of Germany were willing to join in the revolution. But the revolution in turn gave rise to a series of strikes and the demand for organization among the workers. In fact the workers' movement seems to have followed one stage behind the revolution throughout 1848 and 1849. The workers' congresses met only after the summoning of the Frankfurt Assembly; the workers turned to self-help and cooperative enterprises only after September of 1848 when the National Assembly had rejected the popular movement. The final congress of the workers' movement, the first to include all groups within the movement, was held only after the defeat of the May uprisings of 1849 and the triumph of reaction. The workers' associations disappeared in a flurry of minor, self-centered debates at a gesture from the forces of the government.

But the workers' movement failed from internal problems as much as from the defeat of the revolution, as Gangloff pointed out in one of the final issues of the *Verbrüderung*, and this failure removed the force which lay behind the revolution.

There was no unified, class-conscious workers' movement in 1848. The beginnings of class consciousness were there, and Born, Winkelblech and others strove to produce some sort of unity, but without success. The various groups within the workers' movement, the master craftsmen, the poor journeymen, the factory workers and the

376

unskilled day laborers, all had different interests and different goals. Neither the romantic glorification of the medieval guilds and the dignity of the artisans, as expounded by Winkelblech and others at the two Frankfurt congresses, nor the hesitant use of socialist vocabulary and the elements of Marxist thought, as employed by Born and his colleagues at the Berlin Congress, could disguise the real rifts within the working classes.

The chief of these rifts, the one most fatal to the working-class associations, lay within the guild movement, the conflict between journeymen and masters; the clash between their interests was in fact more dangerous—because it was less obvious—than that between artisans and industrial workers. As Born put it, "there were two age levels, not two classes." The journeymen split from the masters at Frankfurt and formed the core of the workers who were organized by Born in the *Verbrüderung.* Even so the line between the two groups should not be drawn too sharply; many of the poorer masters felt themselves slipping into the ranks of the proletariat and made common cause with the journeymen.

Where factories did exist and the workers were employed in industrial organizations, the response was even less adequate and less unified than among the artisans. The machine builders in Berlin flirted with revolution in the early months of 1848, but they were careful to maintain their position and prestige; in the autumn they attempted to intervene between the rioting workers and the middle classes, only to be attacked by both sides. At the end of 1848 the machine builders dissolved their own associations long before the more militant groups among the artisans were willing to give up the struggle.

Nor was pure Marxism, as expounded in the columns

of the *Neue Rheinische Zeitung*, the answer to the disunity of the working classes. Marx was ignored by the workers of Cologne and bitterly attacked by their leader, Gottschalk.

The disunity of the workers played into the hands of the conservatives and the governments of the German states. During the early months of the revolutions, the governments were able to buy off the poorest and most desperate of the workers, the unemployed and starving, with a measure of direct aid, a number of public works projects and promises of further help. Later, when conditions were improved and order had been restored, the promises were broken and the projects stopped. But by this time the governments could enlist the aid of the middle classes; even the civil guard, the great defender of the revolution, turned on the workers in Berlin on October 16, 1848. Finally, the governments sought the allegiance of the more prosperous master artisans. Both Prussia and Saxony held artisans' conferences to discuss the restoration of the guilds and the Prussian law of February 9, 1849, set the pattern of an attempted legal revival of the guilds.

The Frankfurt Assembly, on the other hand, failed to fulfill the hopes of the workers which it had aroused. The flood of petitions to the Assembly and its Economic Committee indicated the desperation of the workers; self-centered, often naïve and convinced that the revolution had achieved everything, the petitioners demanded that the National Assembly prohibit freedom of trade, protecting the interests and preserving the status of the artisans. The Economic Committee could not, however, satisfy all the demands of the workers; these were too diverse and conflicting. In fact the committee in its proposed industrial law satisfied none. Free entry into all trades was to be established and nothing was done for the poorer journeymen. Moreover, economic considerations were ignored by the mass of middle-class delegates to the Assembly; the industrial ordinance, submitted on February 26, 1849, was never debated, and the Assembly concentrated on the political constitution of the new Germany. When the constitution was complete, when Frederick William IV of Prussia had been elected to the office of hereditary emperor and had rejected it, the workers showed little enthusiasm for defending the work of the *Paulskirche*. Many fought in the May uprisings of 1849, but not out of loyalty to the Frankfurt Assembly, and the revolution went down to defeat.

Yet in spite of their disunity the working classes of 1848 presented an overpowering threat in the minds of many liberals. The strikes, the congresses and associations, the clothing of traditional demands for defense of the guilds in the modern vocabulary of revolutionary socialism, all these factors contributed to middle-class fear of the "proletarian revolution" and the "red republic" which was to follow. Though the June Days in Paris had little effect on the German workers, apart from underlining the need for organization and self-help, they alarmed many of the middle classes. Speaker after speaker in the debates in the Frankfurt Assembly on the "right to work" cited the French example as proof of the danger of making too many concessions to the working classes. The fact that most of the artisans and workers saw their demands as a means of preventing the rise of the proletariat and the worst excesses of socialism and communism made little difference.

As predicted, 1848 was a revolution with social aims as well as political ones. It was different from the assumed pattern of the revolutions of the past; it was not a direct imitation of 1789. But if the events of 1848-1849 did not follow the pattern many middle-class liberals expected of them, the pattern of the revolution-that-had-been, neither did they follow the prescribed course of the revolution-that-was-to-be, the proletarian revolution of Marx's *Manifesto*. The demands of the artisans and laborers led to the outbreak of the revolution; the disunity and conflicts in these demands assured its failure.

THE FOLLOWING list is designed to indicate the range of sources on which this book has been based. It does not make claim to be a complete bibliography of the revolutions of 1848-1849 or of the mid-nineteenth century German workers' movement. In particular, secondary works are included only for purposes of reference when they are cited more than once in the notes.

For a more complete list the reader should consult Dahlmann-Waitz, *Quellenkunde der deutschen Geschichte*, Leipzig, 1931-1932, 2 vols. There is a useful bibliographical essay in Valentin, *Geschichte der deutschen Revolution*, vol. 2, pp. 595-613; Jacques Droz, *Les révolutions allemandes*, pp. 11-22, Theodore S. Hamerow, *Restoration, Revolution, Reaction*, pp. 265-287, and Frolinde Balser, *Sozial-Demokratie*, pp. 22-40, also provide critical bibliographies which survey works published more recently than Valentin's history.

SOURCES

1. Collections of Manuscripts and Documents

Akten der Nationalversammlung, Volkswirtschaftlicher Ausschuss, 55 vols., Bundesarchiv, Frankfurt am Main. The collection contains the minutes of the meetings of the Economic Committee of the Frankfurt Assembly together with the reports and amendments drawn up by the committee and its subdivisions in addition to the petitions which were submitted to the Frankfurt Assembly on economic issues.

Akten des Handwerker-Kongresses zu Frankfurt am Main, 3 vols., Stadtarchiv, Frankfurt am Main. The collection contains the minutes of the Artisans' Congress, the mandates of the various delegates to the congress and the petitions which were submitted by various groups of artisans throughout Germany.

Plakate und Flugschriften zur Revolution 1848/49, 11 portfolios, Ratsbibliothek, Berlin (East).

2. Records of the Workers' Associations

Beschlüsse der ersten National-Buchdrucker-Versammlung zu Mainz am 11., 12., 13. und 14. Juni 1848, Flensburg, 1898.

Beschlüsse des Arbeiter-Kongresses zu Berlin, vom 23, August bis 3. September 1848, Berlin, 1848.

Entwurf einer allgemeinen Handwerker- und Gewerbe-Ordnung, Beraten und beschlossen von dem deutschen Handwerker- und Gewerbe-Congress zu Frankfurt am Main vom 15. Juli bis 15. August 1848, Augsburg, 1848.

Entwurf zu den Vorlagen für den volkswirtschaftlichen Ausschuss bearbeitet von den Mitgliedern des hiesigen Gesellen-Congresses, Frankfurt am Main, 1848.

Ordnung des Bildungsvereins für Arbeiter in Hamburg, Hamburg, 1847.

Petition der Gepäckträger deutscher Eisenbahnen an den Verehrlichen Verein der deutschen Eisenbahn-Beamten, Berlin, den 12. September 1848, Berlin, 1848.

Programm und Statuten des Arbeiter-Vereins zu Nürnberg, Nürnberg, 1849.

Satzungen des allgemeinen Arbeiter-Vereins in Cassel, Kassel, 1848.

Satzungen des Arbeiter-Lese-Vereins in Frankfurt am Main, Frankfurt am Main, 1850.

Satzungen des demokratischen-socialen Vereins zu Kassel, Kassel, 1848.

Sechster Jahresbericht des Hülfs-Verein oder der Gesellschaft zur gewerblichen und moralischen Unterstüt-

zung nothleidender Handwerksmeister an Löbliche Bürger- und Einwohnerschaft, Frankfurt am Main, 1851.

Statuten des Arbeiter-Vereins in Esslingen, Esslingen, 1848.

Statuten des Bildungs- und Unterstützungsvereins für Arbeiter in Nürnberg, Nürnberg, 1850.

Statuten des Bildungs-Vereins für Arbeiter in Stuttgart, Stuttgart, 1848.

Statuten des Demokratischen Vereins in Mainz, Mainz, 1848.

Statuten des Gewerbe-Vereins in St. Pauli. Gestiftet am 25. September 1848, St. Pauli, 1848.

Statuten des Vereins der Maschinenbauarbeiter zu Berlin, Berlin, 1848.

Verhandlungen der ersten Abgeordneten-Versammlung des norddeutschen Handwerker- und Gewerbestandes zu Hamburg, den 2.-6. Juni 1848, Hamburg, 1848.

Verhandlungen des ersten deutschen Handwerker- und Gewerbekongresses, gehalten zu Frankfurt am Main, vom 14. Juli bis 18. August, 1848, ed. by G. Schirges, Darmstadt, 1848.

3. Newspapers and Periodicals of the Workers' Associations

Concordia, Organ der Assoziation der Cigarrenarbeiter Deutschlands, Berlin and Bremen, February 1849–February 1850.

Deutsche Arbeiter-Zeitung, Organ für Arbeiter und Arbeitgeber, ed. by F. Behrend and Schmidt for the *Handwerkerverein,* Berlin, April–June 1848.

Freiheit, Arbeit, Cologne, January–June 1849.

Mittheilungen des Centralvereins für das Wohl der arbeitenden Klassen, Berlin, 1849-1851.

Die Verbrüderung, Correspondenzblatt aller deutschen Arbeiter, Leipzig, October 1848–June 1850.

Das Volk, Organ des Central-Komites für Arbeiter, Eine sozial-politische Zeitschrift, Berlin, June–August 1848.

Zeitung des Arbeiter-Vereins zu Köln, Cologne, April–October 1848.

4. Other Newspapers and Periodicals

Aufwärts, Ein Volksblatt für Glauben, Freiheit und Gesittung, Vienna, July–October 1848.

Die Barrikaden: Unterhaltungsblätter der Gegenwart, Berlin, July–December 1848.

Berliner Grossmaul, Berlin.

Berliner Zeitungs Halle, Berlin.

Die Constitution, Tagblatt für constitutionelles Volksleben und Belehrung, Vienna, March–May 1848.

Der Demokrat, Vienna, July–October 1848.

Deutsche Arbeiter-Zeitung, ed. by Lubarsch and Bittkow, Berlin, April 1848.

Deutsche Reichs-Bremse, Leipzig, 1849.

Deutsche Reichs-Zeitung, Brunswick, July–August, 1848.

Deutsche Zeitung, Heidelberg, Frankfurt, April–December 1848.

Die Ewige Lampe, Ein Oppositionsblatt, Berlin, Leipzig, June–December 1848.

Die Geissel, Tageblatt aller Tageblätter, Vienna, July 1848–August 1849.

General-Anzeiger für Deutschland, Volkszeitung, Leipzig.

Grossherzoglich Badisches Regierungs-Blatt, Karlsruhe.

Illustrierte Zeitung, Leipzig.

Kölnische Zeitung, Cologne.

Locomotive, Monatschrift für den deutschen Michel, Halle, July–October 1843.

Locomotive, Zeitung für politische Bildung des Volkes, Berlin, April–December 1848.

Neue Kölnische Zeitung für Bürger, Bauern und Soldaten, Cologne, September 1848–July 1849.

Neue Rheinische Zeitung, Organ der Demokratie, Cologne, June 1848–May 1849.

Der Urwähler, Berlin, October–November 1848.

Der Volksfreund, Berlin, April–May 1848.

Wanderer, Vienna.

Die Westdeutsche Zeitung, Cologne, May–June 1849.

Zeitung für das deutsche Volk, Brunswick, March–June 1848.

5. Pamphlets, Memoirs, Government Publications and Other Contemporary Sources

Bakunin, Michael, *Michael Bakunins Berichte aus der Peter-Pauls-Festung an Zar Nikolaus I,* ed. by Kurt Kersten, Berlin, 1926.

Bamberger, Ludwig, *Erinnerungen von Ludwig Bamberger,* ed. by Paul Nathan, Berlin, 1899.

Bamberger, Ludwig, *Erlebnisse aus der pfälzischen Erhebung im Mai und Juni 1849,* Frankfurt am Main, 1849.

Bamberger, Ludwig, *Politische Schriften von 1848 bis 1868,* Berlin, 1895.

Banfield, Thomas C., *Industry of the Rhine,* 2 vols., London, 1846-1848.

Bauer, Bruno, *Die bürgerliche Revolution in Deutschland seit dem Anfang der deutsch-katholischen Bewegung bis zur Gegenwart,* Berlin, 1849.

Betrachtungen eines deutschen Proletariers, Munich, 1848.

Bismarck, Otto von, *Gedanken und Erinnerungen,* Munich, 1952.

Boerner, Paul, *Erinnerungen eines Revolutionäres: Skizzen aus dem Jahre 1848*, 2 vols., Leipzig, 1920.

Born, Stephan, *Erinnerungen eines Achtundvierziger*, Leipzig, 1898.

Born, Stephan, *Der Verein zur Hebung der arbeitenden Klassen und die Volksstimme über ihn*, Leipzig, 1845.

Contre-Revolution in Berlin oder Bürger und Arbeiter, Berlin, 1848.

Dieterici, F. W. C., ed., *Mittheilungen des statistischen Bureaus in Berlin*, Berlin, 1849.

Douai, *Das Recht und der Schutz der Arbeit*, Altenburg, 1848.

Douai, *Volkskatechismus der Altenburger Republikaner*, Altenburg, 1848.

Dronke, Ernst, *Berlin*, Berlin, 1953 (originally published, 1846).

Friedrich Wilhelm IV, *Briefwechsel mit L. Camphausen*, ed. by Erich Brandenburg, Berlin, 1906.

Fröbel, Julius, *Ein Lebenslauf, Aufzeichnungen, Erinnerungen und Bekenntnisse*, 2 vols., Stuttgart, 1890-1891.

Gerlach, Leopold von, *Denkwürdigkeiten aus dem Leben Leopold von Gerlachs, Generals der Infantrie und General-Adjutanten König Friedrich Wilhelms IV.*, 2 vols., Berlin, 1891.

Gneist, Rudolf, *Berliner Zustände: Politischen Skizzen aus der Zeit vom 18. März 1848 bis 18. März 1849*, Berlin, 1849.

Gottschalk, Andreas, *Meine Rede vor dem Geschworenengericht zu Köln am 23. 12. 1848*, Bonn, 1849.

Harro-Harring, *Historisches Fragment über die Entstehung der Arbeiter-Vereine und ihren Verfall in communistische Speculationen*, London, 1852.

Hochwirtiges der Gegenwart in Sieben Bildern, betr. die gegenwärtigen gedrückten Verhältnisse des Mittel-

standes, nämlich: der Handwerker u. Arbeiter sowie des Handels u. aller Gewerbe in Deutschland und wie diesem wichtigen Stand des dt. Volkes geholfen werden kann, Vom einem Mitgl. d. Gewerbevereins zu Dresden, Dresden, 1848.

Kinkel, Gottfried, *Handwerk, errette Dich! oder Was soll der deutsche Handwerker fordern und tun, um seinen Stand zu bessern?,* Bonn, 1848.

Koch, Louis, *Berliner Witzhagel gefallen in der Barrikadennacht vom 18. und 19. März und Später,* Berlin, 1848.

Marx, Karl, *Enthüllungen über den Kommunistenprozess zu Köln,* Berlin, 1952.

Marx, Karl, and Engels, Friedrich, *Historisch-Kritische Gesamtausgabe, Werke/Schriften/Briefe,* ed. by D. Rjazanov, Frankfurt am Main, Berlin, Moscow, 1927-1935.

Marx, Karl, and Engels, Friedrich, *Revolution and Counter-Revolution or Germany in 1848,* ed. by Eleanor Marx Aveling, London, 1896.

Marx, Karl, and Engels, Friedrich, *Selected Works,* 2 vols., Moscow, 1951.

Müller, E. H., and Schneider, C. F., *Jahresbericht des statistischen Amtes im k. Polizei-Präsidio zu Berlin für das Jahr 1852,* Leipzig, 1853.

Nees von Esenbeck, C. G., *Das Leben der Ehe in der vernünftigen Menschenheit und ihr Verhältniss zum Staat und zur Kirche,* Breslau, 1845.

Raumer, Friedrich von, *Briefe aus Frankfurt und Paris, 1848-1849,* 2 vols., Leipzig, 1849.

Schäffle, "Vorschläge zu einer gemeinsamen Ordnung der Gewerbebefugnisse und Heimathrechtsverhältnisse in Deutschland nach den Grundsätzen der Gewerbefreiheit und der Freizügigkeit," *Deutsche Vierteljahr-Schrift,* vol. 22 (1859), pp. 218-298.

Scheidtmann, Gustav, *Der Communismus und das Proletariat*, Leipzig, 1848.

Schirges, Georg, *Der Berliner Volks-Aufstand*, Hamburg, 1848.

Schlöffel, Gustav, *Schöffels des jüngeren Pressprocess verhandelt vor dem Kammergericht in Berlin*, Berlin, 1848.

Schulze-Delitzsch, Hermann, *Schriften und Reden*, 2 vols., Berlin, 1909.

Schurz, Carl, *The Reminiscences of Carl Schurz*, 2 vols., London, 1909.

Stenographischer Bericht über die Verhandlungen der deutschen constituirenden Nationalversammlung zu Frankfurt am Main, ed. by Franz Wigard, 9 vols., Frankfurt am Main, 1848-1849.

Temme, J. D. H., *Erinnerungen*, ed. by Stephan Born, Leipzig, 1883.

Tocqueville, Alexis de, *The Recollections of Alexis de Tocqueville*, trans. by Alexander Teixera de Mattos, ed. by J. P. Mayer, New York, 1959.

Verbesserungs-Anträge des Ausschusses für Volkswirtschaft zu dem Entwurfe des Verfassungs-Ausschusses über die Befugnisse der Reichsgewalt, Frankfurt am Main, 1848.

Verbesserungs-Anträge des Ausschusses für Volkswirtschaft zu den Grundrechten des deutschen Volkes auf den Grund seines Berichts vom 20. Juni, 1848, Frankfurt am Main, 1848.

Verhandlungen der Versammlung zur Vereinbarung der Preussischen Staats-Verfassung, 3 vols., Berlin, 1848-1849.

Verwaltungs-Bericht des Ministers für Handel, Gewerbe und öffentliche Arbeiten für die Jahre 1849, 1850, 1851, 1852, 1853, 1854, 2 vols., Berlin, 1855.

Verzeichnisse der Abgeordneten der Frankfurter National Versammlung, Frankfurt am Main, 1848-1849.

Viehbahn, Georg von, ed., *Statistik des zollvereinten und nördlichen Deutschlands,* 3 vols., Berlin, 1862-1868.

Wagner, Richard, *My Life,* 2 vols., London, 1911.

Weitling, Wilhelm, *Garantieen der Harmonie und Freiheit,* Berlin, 1908.

Wermuth and Stieber, *Die Communisten-Verschwörungen des neunzehnten Jahrhunderts,* 2 vols., Berlin, 1853-1854.

Wesenfeld, C. F., *Beschränkte oder unbeschränkte Gewerbefreiheit, Eine Zeitfrage, Allen Gewerksgenossen gewidmet,* Berlin, 1848.

Wirth, Max, *Geschichte der Handelskrisen,* Frankfurt am Main, 1858.

Winkelblech, Karl Georg (Karl Marlo), *Untersuchungen über die Organisation der Arbeit oder System der Weltökonomie,* 3 vols., Kassel, 1850-1859.

Wohnungsliste der Mitglieder der constituirenden Nationalversammlung, Frankfurt am Main, 1848.

Wolff, Adolff, *Berliner Revolutionschronik,* 3 vols., Berlin, 1849-1854.

SECONDARY WORKS

1. Books

Adler, Georg, *Die Geschichte der ersten sozialpolitischen Arbeiterbewegung in Deutschland,* Breslau, 1885.

Balser, Frolinde, *Sozial-Demokratie 1848/49-1863. Die erste deutsche Arbeiterorganisation "Allgemeine deutsche Arbeiterverbrüderung" nach der Revolution,* Stuttgart, 1962.

Benaerts, Pierre, *Les origines de la grande industrie allemande,* Paris, 1933.

Bernstein, A., *Revolutions- und Reaktionsgeschichte*

Preussens und Deutschlands von den Märztagen bis zur neuesten Zeit, 3 vols., Berlin, 1882.

Bernstein, Eduard, *Die Geschichte der Berliner Arbeiterbewegung*, 3 vols., Berlin, 1907-1910.

Bernstein, Eduard, *Die Schneiderbewegung in Deutschland, Ihre Organisation und Kämpfe*, vol. 1, Berlin, 1913.

Biermann, Wilhelm Eduard, *Karl Georg Winkelblech (Karl Marlo), Sein Leben und sein Werk*, 2 vols., Leipzig, 1909.

Blum, Hans, *Die deutsche Revolution 1848-1849, Ein Jubiläumsgabe für das deutsche Volk*, Leipzig, 1898.

Brandenburg, Erich, *Die deutsche Revolution, 1848*, Leipzig, 1912.

Brunner, Ludwig, *Politische Bewegungen in Nürnberg im Jahre 1848 bis zu den Herbstereignisse*, Heidelberg, 1907.

Clapham, J. H., *The Economic Development of France and Germany, 1815-1914*, Cambridge, 1936.

Cornu, August, *Karl Marx et la révolution de 1848*, Paris, 1948.

Droz, Jacques, *Les révolutions allemandes de 1848*, Paris, 1957.

Freyer, G. A. U., *Das Vorparlament zu Frankfurt am Main im Jahre 1848*, Greifswald, 1913.

Friedensburg, Wilhelm, *Stephan Born und die Organisationsbestrebungen der Berliner Arbeiterschaft bis zum Berliner Arbeiterkongress (1840–Sept. 1848)*, Leipzig, 1923.

Frisch, Walther, *Die Organisationsbestrebung der Arbeiter in der deutschen Tabakindustrie*, Leipzig, 1905.

Goldschmidt, E. F., *Die deutsche Handwerkerbewegung bis zum Siege der Gewerbefreiheit*, Munich, 1916.

Hamerow, Theodore S., *Restoration, Revolution, Reac-*

tion, *Economics and Politics in Germany, 1815-1871*, Princeton, New Jersey, 1958.

Hook, Sidney, *From Hegel to Marx, Studies in the Intellectual Development of Karl Marx*, New York, 1946.

Kaeber, Ernst, *Berlin, 1848*, Berlin, 1948.

Klein, Tim, ed., *Der Vorkampf deutscher Einheit und Freiheit, Erinnerungen, Urkunden, Berichte, Briefe*, Eberhausen bei München, 1914.

Koeppen, Werner, *Die Anfänge der Arbeiter- und Gesellenbewegung in Franken (1830-1852), Eine Studie zur Geschichte des politischen Sozialismus*, Erlangen, 1935.

Krahl, Willi, *Der Verband der deutschen Buchdrucker, Fünfzig Jahre deutscher gewerkschaftlicher Arbeit mit einer Vorgeschichte*, 2 vols., Berlin, 1916.

Krieger, Leonard, *The German Idea of Freedom, History of a Political Tradition*, Boston, 1957.

Laufenberg, Heinrich, *Geschichte der Arbeiterbewegung in Hamburg, Altona und Umgegend*, vol. 1, Hamburg, 1911.

Lenz, Max, *Geschichte der Königlichen Friedrich-Wilhelms-Universität zu Berlin*, 3 vols., Halle, 1910-1918.

Lichtheim, George, *Marxism, An Historical and Critical Study*, London, 1961.

Lipinski, Richard, *Die Geschichte der sozialistischen Arbeiterbewegung in Leipzig*, vol. 1, *Bis 1857*, Leipzig, 1931.

Lüders, Gustav, *Die demokratische Bewegung in Berlin im Oktober 1848*, Berlin, 1909.

Lütge, Friedrich, *Deutsche Sozial- und Wirtschaftsgeschichte, Ein Ueberblick*, Berlin, 1952.

Mänchen-Helfen, Otto, and Nikolajewsky, Boris, *Karl und Jenny Marx: Ein Lebensweg*, Berlin, 1933.

Maurice, C. Edmund, *The Revolutionary Movement of 1848-9 in Italy, Austria-Hungary and Germany*, London, 1887.

Mehring, Franz, *Geschichte der deutschen Sozialdemokratie*, 4 vols., Stuttgart, 1922.

Meusch, Hans, *Die Handwerkerbewegung von 1848/49, Vorgeschichte, Verlauf, Inhalt, Ergebnisse*, Eschwege, 1949.

Meyer, Hermann, *1848, Studien zur Geschichte der deutschen Revolution*, Darmstadt, 1949.

Mommsen, Wilhelm, *Grösse und Versagen des deutschen Bürgertums, Ein Beitrag zur Geschichte der Jahre 1848-49*, Stuttgart, 1949.

Müller, Hermann, *Die Organisationen der Lithographen, Steindrucker und verwandten Berufe*, Berlin, 1917.

Namier, L. B., *1848: The Revolution of the Intellectuals*, London, 1946.

Obermann, Karl, *Die deutschen Arbeiter in der ersten bürgerlichen Revolution*, Berlin, 1950.

Obermann, Karl, *Die deutschen Arbeiter in der Revolution von 1848*, Berlin, 1953.

Obermann, Karl, *Zur Geschichte des Bundes der Kommunisten 1849 bis 1852*, Berlin, 1955.

Pinson, Koppel S., *Modern Germany: Its History and Civilization*, New York, 1954.

Potjomkin, F. W., and Molok, A. I., eds., *Die Revolution in Deutschland 1848/49*, trans. by Werner Meyer, vol. 1, Berlin, 1956.

Quarck, Max, *Die erste deutsche Arbeiterbewegung, Geschichte der Arbeiterverbrüderung 1848/49*, Leipzig, 1924.

Rath, R. John, *The Viennese Revolution of 1848*, Austin, Texas, 1957.

Roehl, Hugo, *Beiträge zur Preussischen Handwerkerpolitik vom Allgemeinen Landrecht zur Allgemeinen Gewerbeordnung von 1845*, Leipzig, 1900.

Rohr, Donald G., *The Origins of Social Liberalism in Germany*, Chicago, 1963.

Schilfert, Gerhard, *Sieg und Niederlage des demokratischen Wahlrechts in der deutschen Revolution 1848/49*, Berlin, 1952.

Schmoller, Gustav, *Zur Geschichte der deutschen Kleingewerbe im 19. Jahrhundert, Statistische und nationalökonomische Untersuchungen*, Halle, 1870.

Schnabel, Franz, *Deutsche Geschichte im Neunzehnten Jahrhundert*, 4 vols., Freiburg, 1947-1951.

Stadelmann, Rudolf, and Fischer, Wolfram, *Die Bildungswelt des deutschen Handwerkers um 1800, Studien zur Soziologie des Kleinbürgers im Zeitalter Goethes*, Berlin, 1955.

Stadelmann, Rudolf, *Soziale und politische Geschichte der Revolution von 1848*, Munich, 1948.

Stein, Hans, *Der Kölner Arbeiterverein (1848-49), Ein Beitrag zur Frühgeschichte des rheinischen Sozialismus*, Cologne, 1921.

Stern, Leo, ed., *Archivalische Forschungen zur Geschichte der deutschen Arbeiterbewegung*, Berlin, 1954.

Tilmann, Margret, *Der Einfluss des Revolutionsjahres 1848 auf die preussische Gewerbe- und Sozialgesetzgebung (Die Notverordnung vom 9. Februar 1849)*, Berlin, 1935.

Todt, Elisabeth, and Radandt, Hans, *Zur Frühgeschichte der deutschen Gewerkschafts-Bewegung 1800-1849*, Berlin, 1950.

Valentin, Veit, *Die erste deutsche Nationalversammlung, Eine geschichtliche Studie über die Frankfurter Paulskirche*, Munich, 1919.

Valentin, Veit, *Frankfurt am Main und die Revolution von 1848-49*, Berlin, 1908.

Valentin, Veit, *Geschichte der deutschen Revolution von 1848/49*, 2 vols., Berlin, 1930-1931.

Wendel, Hugo C. M., *The Evolution of Industrial Freedom in Prussia, 1845-1849*, Allentown, Pa., 1918.

Wittke, Carl, *The Utopian Communist, A Biography of Wilhelm Weitling, Nineteenth-Century Reformer*, Baton Rouge, Louisiana, 1950.

2. Articles

Conze, Werner, "Staat und Gesellschaft in der frührevolutionären Epoche Deutschlands," *Historische Zeitschrift*, vol. 186 (1958), pp. 1-34.

Conze, Werner, "Vom 'Pöbel' zum 'Proletariat,' Sozialgeschichtliche Voraussetzungen für den Sozialismus in Deutschland," *Vierteljahrschrift für Sozial- und Wirtschaftsgeschichte*, vol. 41 (1954), pp. 333-364.

Czobel, Ernst, "Zur Geschichte des Kommunistenbundes, Die Kölner Bundesgemeinde vor der Revolution," *Archiv für die Geschichte des Sozialismus und der Arbeiterbewegung*, vol. 11 (1923/25), pp. 299-335.

Hamerow, Theodore S., "The Elections to the Frankfurt Parliament," *Journal of Modern History*, vol. 33 (1961), pp. 15-32.

Hamerow, Theodore S., "The German Artisan Movement, 1848-49," *The Journal of Central European Affairs*, vol. 21 (1961), pp. 135-152.

Hammen, Oscar J., "Economic and Social Factors in the Prussian Rhineland in 1848," *The American Historical Review*, vol. 54 (1949), pp. 825-840.

Nicolaevsky, B., "Towards a History of 'the Communist League' 1847-1852," *International Review of Social History*, vol. 1 (1956), pp. 234-252.

Schraepler, Ernst, "Linksliberalismus und Arbeiterschaft in der preussischen Konfliktszeit," *Forschungen zur Staat und Verfassungen, Festgabe für Fritz Hartung*, ed. by Richard Dietrich and Gerhard Oestreich, Berlin, 1958, pp. 385-401.

INDEX

"Address to German Handicraft Workers," 49
ADFV (*Allgemeine deutsche Föderalisten-Verein*), 212
Agricultural workers
demands of, 184
growth of, 18
industrial use of, 184
pre-March, 18-19
unemployment among, 19
Verbrüderung and, 305-6
Agriculture
bad harvests in, 32
improvements in, 18
Albrecht, "Prophet," 45
Allgemeine deutsch Föderalisten-Verein (ADFV), 212
All-German Association for the Protection of National Work, 236
All-German Workers' Congress in Berlin, *see* Berlin Congress of German Workers
"All-German Workers' League," plans for, 304
Altenburg, 297
cooperatives in, 309
Verbrüderung congress in, 304
Altona, 174
workers' organizations in, 48-49
Ami du Peuple (Marat's newspaper), 109
Amnesty of March, 43
Anarchy, fears of, 243
See also Communism; Socialism
Anneke, Friedrich, 63, 64n, 283
arrest of, 258, 284
expelled from Elberfeld, 342
trial of, 285
wife of, 268n
Anti-Semitism, 51, 157
March Days and, 61-62

Anti-Semitism (cont.)
in workers' organizations, 293
strike movement, 129
Antitax campaign
failure of, 266
Marx's, 266-67, 282
of Prussian Assembly, 279, 282
Apprentices
Berlin Workers' Congress on, 220
Journeymen's Congress on, 208
in manufacturing industries, 20
in printing trades, 197
as proportion of handicraft workers, 24
in Prussia, 21
training of, 246
fixed periods, 29
Architects, status of, 29
Army
public hostility toward, 67, 75
See also Civil guard
Arnold (workers' leader), 211
Artisans
aims of, 222
early drive for organization of, 4
fears of proletarianization, 242-43
guilds supported by, *see* Guilds, workers' support for
in May uprising, 316
organizations, *see names of specific organizations*
poverty of, 183
predominance in working class of, 11, 164
in 1848, 3
in pre-March period, 21-23
after Revolution, 370, 373-74

Artisans (cont.)
  reaction and, 281
  revolutionary activities of, 164
  underestimated by Marxists, 9
  Verbrüderung and, 296-98, 310-11
  See also Apprentices; Journeymen; Master artisans
Artisans' Union, 51, 143, 168, 174
  Berlin
    appeal for congress, 165
    pre-March activities, 48
  Brunswick, 308
Assembly of Delegates of the North German Handicraft and Industrial Class, *see* Hamburg Pre-Congress of Artisans
Association, right of
  in Basic Rights, 323
  Prussian decree on, 124
Atheism, fears of, 243
Auerswald, Rudolf von, 257, 261
Augsburg Congress, 354-55
Austria
  concessions to workers in, 254
  Economic Committee delegates from, 229
  free trade in, 371
  petitions from, 237
  population growth in, 18
  Prussia threatened by, 335
  Verbrüderung in, 217
  workers' organizations dissolved in, 365
    pre-March suppression, 49
  See also Vienna; *specific cities*

Baden
  anti-Semitism in, 61
  free trade in, 371
  guilds in, 322
  May uprising in, 341, 344

Baden (cont.)
  sabotage in, 256
  Verbrüderung in, 302
Bakunin, Michael
  on March Days, 57
  in May uprising, 343
Bally (Economic Committee delegate), 232
Bamberg, in May uprising, 343
Barbers, 127
Barmen, 115, 324
Barricades
  in March Days, 57
  workers' belief in, 98
  See also March Days; May uprisings; September uprising
Basic Rights, 252
  right of association in, 323
Bauer, Bruno, 47, 51
  analysis of Revolution by, 59
Bauer, Heinrich, 112, 115
Bavaria, 354
  Economic Committee delegates from, 229
  franchise law condemned in, 219
  free trade in, 371
  guilds in, 30, 321
  May uprising in, 343
  workers' organizations in, 182, 307*n*
    dissolution, 363
    petitions to Frankfurt Assembly, 237
  See also specific cities
Bavarian Industrial Club, 182
Bavarian Palatinate, *Verbrüderung* in, 302
Bebel, August, 375
Becker, Friedrich, 333
Becker, Hermann, 118, 288
  arrest of, 268
Belgium, exile groups in, 41, 45, 52-53
Berends, Julius, 48, 51

Berlin, 174, 213-14
civil guard in
  collaboration with workers, 256-57
  disbanded, 279
cooperative organizations in, 309
Democratic Congress in, *see* Democratic Congress
early workers' movements in, 47-48
explosiveness of, 291
growth of, 19
health care groups in, 308, 352, 365
industry near, 15
liberal organizations in, 124
machine builders in, *see* Machine builders
March Days in, *see* March Days, in Berlin
merchant petitions from, 239-40, 243
October riots in, 270-73, 277-78
"potato revolution" in, 35-36
pre-March riots in, 34
printers' strike in, 199-201
public works projects in, 270-73
reaction in, 279-81
  behavior of workers, 281
  democrats defeated, 280
  early growth of, 90
  public meetings prohibited, 258
  Wrangel's occupation, 279
riots in, 256-57
  October, 270-73, 277-78
strikes in, 34, 128-33
Verbrüderung in, 307
wages in, 31
workers' organizations in, *see* *specific workers' organizations*
See also Prussia

Berlin Artisans' Union
  appeal for congress by, 165
  pre-March activities of, 48
Berlin Central Committee of Workers, 128
  affiliation to *Verbrüderung* by, 217
  appeal for congress by, 168
  Born's function in, 142
  duties of, 142
  formation of, 136-45
  officers of, 142
  organ of, 143-49
  regular meetings of, 143
Berlin Central Workers Club, organization of, 76
Berlin Congress of German Workers (master artisans), 164, 167
  class consciousness of, 174
  future plans of, 175
  importance of, 173
  program of, 174-75
  representation at, 174
Berlin Constitutional Club, 124
Berlin Deputation for the Abolition of Need, 138-40
  assembly called by, 73
  demands of, 74-75
  ineffectiveness of, 140
  report on employment in public works projects, 77
Berlin Deputation for the Consideration of the Well-Being of the Working Classes, 72
Berlin Health Care Union, 308, 352
  dissolution of, 365
Berlin Journeymen's Union, 48
Berlin Ladies' Union for the Abolition of Need Among Small Manufacturers, 87
Berlin Political Club, 124, 140
Berlin Society for Publicly Useful Constructions, 72

Berlin Union of Machine Builders, 154-55
Berlin Workers' Congress (journeymen), 212-20, 290,
303
address of, 215, 243
Born's activities in, 214-15
Chartist movement compared
with, 213
Frankfurt Assembly and, 217-
19, 243
Frankfurt Journeymen's Congress compared with,
216, 220
handicraft character of, 220
initiators of, 212
program of, 215-20
apprentices, 220
guilds, 216, 219
masters' examinations, 219
political demands, 218-19
self-help measures, 218
regional character of, 214
representation at, 213-15
"social question" in, 212
suffrage laws condemned by,
219
summoning of, 212
uniqueness of, 216
Berlin Workers' Society for the
Common Manufacture
of Shirts, 309
Berlin Workers' Union, 136-37
Berliner Zeitungs Halle, 132,
143, 201
Bernstein, Eduard, Born praised
by, 152n
Beseler, Georg, 327
Bielefeld, 214
workers' organizations in, 181
Bisky, L., 74, 87, 140, 175, 298,
356, 361
in Berlin Workers' Congress,
215
in Central Committee of
Workers, 142

Bisky, L. (cont.)
in Hamburg Pre-Congress of
Artisans, 168, 170, 174n
Bismarck, Otto von, 12, 82, 223,
365, 375
unification policy of, 6
Blacksmiths, need for, 26
Blanc, Louis, 144, 293
influence of, 76
Blanqui, Auguste, 366
Blanquists, conspiracies of, 44
Blum, Robert, 52, 92
on Committee of Fifty, 95
death of, 278
memorial meetings, 279
workers' support for, 79
Boerner, Paul, 74n
Bohemia, *Verbrüderung* in, 217
See also specific cities
Bonin, Eduard von, 271, 317
Bookprinters, *see* Printers
Born, David, 87
Born, Stephan, 24n, 71, 96, 100,
115, 175, 202, 212, 214,
279, 290, 302, 313, 321,
372, 375
in Berlin Workers' Congress,
214-15
Bernstein's praise for, 152n
in Central Committee of
Workers, 142
in Central Workers' Club, 76
Communist League and, 118-
19
early association, 78
membership, 53
rejection of, 149-52
Engels' relations with, 52-53,
148
exile of, 346
flight from Dresden, 345
in Hamburg Pre-Congress of
Artisans, 168
Lette's debate with, 139-40
life of, 51-54
later years, 346
in May uprising, 342

Born, Stephan (cont.)
  Marx's relations with, 123,
    131
    differences in views, 148-
      52, 301-2
  policies of, 145-52
    Democratic Congress, 276-
      77
    Frankfurt Assembly, 96-97
    insights, 151-52, 376-77
    moderateness of views,
      137-40
    on printers, 198n, 200-1
    Verbrüderung, 220, 297-98,
      300-4
    writings, 52, 145-52
  printers and, 198n, 200-1
    strike leadership, 131-33
  Schlöffel's relations with, 109-
    10
  in Verbrüderung
    functions, 297-98, 304
    influence, 220
    moderate views, 300-3
  Winkelblech's debate with,
    300
  writings of, 52, 145-52
Borsig works, 64-65, 72, 87
  labor force of, 20
Bourgeoisie, see Manufacturers;
    Middle class
"Bourgeoisie and the Counter-
    Revolution, The"
    (Marx), 282
Brandenburg, 174
  Prussian Assembly removed
    to, 279
Brandenburg, Count von, min-
    istry of, 279
Breisgau, anti-Semitism in, 61
Bremen, 159, 168
  May uprising in, 350
  Verbrüderung's decline in,
    361
Breslau, 174, 214
  growth of, 19
  liberal organizations in, 154

Breslau (cont.)
  merchant petitions from, 239-
    40
  printers' strike in, 134, 201
  workers' organization in, 152
  pre-March, 48
  regional congresses, 172-73
  riots, 256
  strikes, 34
Breslau Democratic Club, 154
Breslau Singing Union, 48
Brill (workers' leader), 175
Britain, see England
Brno, Verbrüderung in, 217
Brotherhood, see: Verbrüderung
Bruck, Karl von, 231
Brunswick, 168
  workers' organizations in, 308
Brussels, exile groups in, 41, 45,
    52-53
Bühring, C., 212
Bürgers, Heinrich, 120, 268
  Neue Rheinische Zeitung and,
    121
Buttermilch, Meyer, 51

Cabinet makers, strikes of, 130
Café d'Artistes, 51, 75-77
Cahiers des doléances, 11-12
Calico workers
  in Silesian revolt, 34
  strikes of, 129
Camphausen, Ludolf, 63, 70,
    117, 157
  fall of, 88
  Schlöffel's attack on, 110
Capital (Marx), 283
Carpenters
  cooperatives of, 309
  guild membership of, 29
  March Days casualties of, 68
  need for, 26
  in Silesian revolt, 34
  strikes of, 130
  trade groups of, 80
"Casino" faction, 229n
Casualties in March Days, 68

Cavaignac, Gen. Louis Eugène, 269
Censorship
opposition to, 63
relaxation of, 36
in Silesian revolt, 34n
Central Committee
Democratic, 269
of Journeymen's Congress, 211
of Verbrüderung, 218, 303
of Workers, see Berlin Central Committee of Workers
Central Union for the Well-Being of the Working Classes, 36-87
aims of, 47
official support for, 47
Central Workers Club of Berlin, organization of, 76
Chartist movement, 144
Berlin Workers' Congress compared with, 213
weavers in, 3
Chemnitz, workers' organizations in, 156
Cholera epidemic, 255
Christian communist theories, 40
Christian reform movements, 45
Cigar makers
amalgamation with Verbrüderung, 356-58, 362
congresses of, 27, 193, 203-4, 257-58, 312-14, 356-58, 362
demands of, 204
economic problems of, 27
independence of, 312-14
Leipzig Congress of, 257-58
union of, 203-4
Cities, growth of, 19
See also specific cities
Citizens' Association of Lallenberg, petition by, 240-41

Civil guard
demand for, 63
disbanding of, 279
establishment of, 63
in May uprisings, 63, 342, 344
in October riots, 271-72, 278
workers and, 70
collaboration in Berlin, 256-57
exclusion of workers, 69
October riots, 278
suspicion between, 70
Civil servants
in Economic Committee, 228
in Frankfurt Assembly, 224
Classes
conflict of, 272-73
Born's views on, 149
Schlöffel's views on, 108
estates compared with, 16-17
See also Middle class; Peasants; Workers
Clothing workers, cooperatives of, 309-10
See also Tailors; Textile workers
Clouth (publisher), labor policy of, 123
Club for Employers and Employees of Cologne, 118
Code Napoléon, 115n
Cologne, 297-98
Communist trial in, 367-68
growth of, 19
liberal organizations in, 120
Democratic Congress, 268
suppression of, 268-69
March Days in, 62-64
civil guard established, 63
demands of people, 63
socialist leadership, 64
pre-March radical press in, 37
public works projects in, 117
reaction in, 258
workers' organizations in, 115-23, 152, 351

Cologne, workers' organizations in (cont.)
  conflict with Marx, 116, 286-87, 289
  demands, 117-18
  Gottschalk's leadership, 116-17, 122-23
  riots, 284
  success, 118
Cologne Club for Employers and Employees, 118
Cologne Democratic Union, 120
Cologne Educational Union, 351
Cologne Reading Union for Workers, 351
Cologne Workers' Union
  Marx and, 115-23, 258
    alienation of workers, 116, 286-87, 289
    conflict with Gottschalk, 116, 286-87
    control of union, 284-89
  reorganization of, 284, 288
  structure of, 288
Commerce, see Economy; Free trade; Industrial Revolution; Industrialization
Commission for the Discussion of Industrial and Labor Conditions in Dresden, 298
Committee for the Aid of German Refugees, 349
Committee for the Planning of the Constitution (Frankfurt Assembly), 226
Committee of the Berlin Bookprinters, 200
Committee of Fifty, 94
  membership of, 95
Committee for Priority Questions (Frankfurt Assembly), 226
Committee for the Relations of Workers, Industry and Trade, see Economic Committee

Committee of Seven, 92
Communism
  Born's rejection of, 149-52
  Christian, 40
  fears of, 243
  workers' rejection of, 79
Communist League, 151
  Born and, 118-119
    early association, 78
    membership, 53
    rejection of, 149-52
  Cologne trial of, 367-68
  crushing of, 367-68
  Engels in, 41
  final dissolution of, 367-68
  formation of, 41, 45
  League of the Just and, 41
  in March Days, 64, 100
  Marx and
    dissolution of League, 118-19, 123
    domination of League, 41, 114
    Marx's aloofness, 288
    outbreak of Revolution, 114-15
  May uprising and, 347
  Moll and
    protests dissolution, 119
    revives League, 120, 288
  post-revolutionary revival of, 365-67
  splits in, 367
  statutes of, 45
  workers' leaders and, 78
Communist Manifesto (Marx and Engels), 380
  aims of, 113
  1848 statement compared with, 112
  predictions of, 1
  writing of, 41
Communist Party of Germany, statement on 1848 revolution of, 111-12
  adoption by Democratic Congress, 276

Communist Party of Germany (cont.)
  Communist Manifesto compared with, 112
  obscurity of, 115*n*
Communists, 128
  activities of, 43-44
    study groups, 44
  workers' organizations and, 46
  formation of cells, 49
Competition, growth of, 27
Compositors, *see* Printers
Concordia, 356
  Die Verbrüderung amalgamated with, 358
  establishment of, 203
Condition of the Working Class in England in 1844, The (Engels), 37
Conferences of workers' organizations
  journeymen, 156-57
  master artisans, 157
Congresses of workers' organizations, 331, 376
  divisiveness of, 165
  earliest summons for, 159-60
  Frankfurt Assembly and, 12, 174, 189-91, 193, 195-97, 217-19, 243, 298-99
    Economic Committee, 233-34
  guilds and, 170-71, 176, 178-80, 183-89, 216, 219
  journeymen
    Berlin Workers' Congress, 212-20, 243, 303
    cigar makers, 27, 193, 203-4, 257-58, 312-14, 356-58, 362
    Frankfurt, *see* Journeymen's Congress in Frankfurt
    printers, 26-27, 80, 131-35, 158-59, 193-202, 312, 356, 382

Congresses of workers' organizations, journeymen (cont.)
  regional, 298-304, 353-55
  master artisans, 163-220
    Frankfurt, *see* Frankfurt Artisans' Congress
    Hamburg, *see* Hamburg Pre-Congress
    regional, 311
  regional, 171-74, 311
    Augsburg Congress, 354-55
    Hanover Congress, 354
    Reutlingen Congress, 353-54
    Verbrüderung, 298-304, 353-55
Conspiracies, importance of, 4
Constitutional Club of Berlin, 124
Constitutional Committee of Frankfurt Assembly, 226
  franchise law proposed by, 334-35
Constitutions
  decreed, 317
  demands for, 59
    March Days, 63
    Pre-Parliament and, 94
  in Prussia, 317
  of workers' organizations, 153, 195, 198, 217
Construction workers, status of, 29
Consumer cooperatives, 310
"Contribution to the Theory and Practice of Marxism, A" (Quarck), 10
Cooperatives, 309-10
  consumer, 310
  producer, 309-10
  revival of, 372-73
  in *Verbrüderung*, 308-10, 351-53
  workers' demand for, 218
Counter-Parliament, 274
  convocation of, 269, 273

Counterrevolution, *see* Reaction
Credit banks, workers' demands for, 172, 218
Crefeld, 214
  artisan petition from, 221-22
  riots in, 256
Critique of Political Economy (Marx), 283
Crüger, Friedrich, 212
  in Berlin Workers' Congress, 214
Cutlery industry in Solingen, 20

Damelock, agricultural workers in, 305
Day workers, 19
  in Prussia, 21
Defense funds in May uprisings, 349
Degenkolb, Carl, 329, 333
  report of, 325-28
Democratic Central Committee, convocation of, 269
Democratic Club of Breslau, 154
Democratic Congress, 225n, 278, 284
  Born's criticism of, 276-77
  convocation of, 273
  demands of, 266
  failure of, 275
  program of, 276
  representation in, 274
  "social question" in, 275-77
  Viennese revolutionaries supported by, 273, 275, 277-78
  workers and, 275-77
Democratic movement
  defeat of, 279-80
  Frankfurt Assembly and, 267-68
  isolation of, 268
  Marx and
    break with democrats, 267, 283, 288

Democratic movement, Marx and (cont.)
  Cologne Democratic Union, 120
  support for democrats, 112-13, 120-23
  middle class and, 267
  suppression of, 258, 268-69, 280
  See also Liberalism; Liberals; Middle class
Democratic-Social Union of Kassel, 154
Denmark, war with, 259
Deputation for the Abolition of Need, *see* Berlin Deputation for the Abolition of Need
Deputation for the Consideration of the Well-Being of the Working Classes, formation of, 72
Deutsche Arbeiter Zeitung, 126, 143
Deutsche-Brusseler Zeitung, 53
Deutschen Arbeiter in der ersten burgerlichen Revolution, Die (Obermann), 10
Dieterici, Friedrich, 21
Dresden, 297, 321
  growth of, 19
  May uprising in, 342-45
  workers' organizations in, 91, 156
  printers' strike, 134
Dresden Commission for the Discussion of Industrial and Labor Conditions, 298
Dronke, Ernst, on *Neue Rheinische Zeitung*, 121
Duckwitz, Arnold, 249
Duncker (police director), 87
Düsseldorf
  May uprising in, 345
  public works projects in, 87

Economic Committee, 189, 267, 322-36
artisans opposed by, 333
Austrian delegates in, 229
Bavarian delegates in, 229
class composition of, 228
criticisms of, 230
failure of, 378
guilds opposed by, 333
importance of, 167
middle class policy of, 322-24
electoral law, 335
guild issue, 333
industrial ordinance, 328-34
laissez faire approach, 330-34
workers' congresses, 233-34
work-guarantee issue, 324-28
officers of, 230-31
powers of, 232
public meetings rejected by, 232
representation in
geographical, 229
officers, 230-31
professional, 228
subcommittees of, 231
Economic crises of 1840's, 32
Economy
financial panic in, 60
growth of, 18
guilds and, *see* Guilds
improvements in, 255
industrialization of, 15, 18, 370
effect on workers, 20-21, 23, 151-52
human cost, 151-52
major areas, 15
workers' fears, *see* Machinery
in March Days, 60, 70
public works projects, 84-86
unemployment, 64-65, 70

Economy (cont.)
poverty and, 4, 31-33, 244
free trade, 244
in Prussia, 21
See also Economic Committee; Unemployment; Free trade
Education, workers' demands for, 213, 219
congresses and, 174, 209
in March Days, 63, 75
See also specific educational groups
Educational activities of *Verbrüderung*, 307-8
Educational Club for Masters, 159
Educational Society for the Improvement of the Working Class, 48
Educational Union
Cologne, 351
Stuttgart, 153
Eichel (workers' leader), 212
Eisenach Congress, 375
Eisenstuck, Bernhard, 93, 231, 249, 327
Elberfeld, 324
May uprising in, 342, 344-45
Elberfeld Security Commission, anti-worker policies of, 342
Electoral Hesse
electoral law in, 96
French reforms in, 30
workers' militancy in, 256
Electoral law, 334-35
Economic Committee and, 335
indirect features of, 96
Pre-Parliament and, 93
qualifications in, 96
Schlöffel's demonstration on, 110
See also Franchise
Emigration, post-revolutionary, 369n

Emigration rights and Frankfurt Assembly, 251
Employment bureaus
pre-March, 47
workers' demand for, 218
Engelhardt (workers' leader), 137
Engels, Friedrich, 64, 112, 115, 122, 151
aloofness toward Communist League, 288
attitude toward workers, 121
Born's relations with, 52-53, 148
in Communist League, 41
Communist Manifesto by, see: *Communist Manifesto*
Condition of the Working Class in England in 1844, The, 37
exile of, 347
flight from Cologne, 269, 282
on Frankfurt Assembly, 225n
fund-raising activities of, 120-21
London exile of, 366
on *Neue Rheinische Zeitung*, 121
writings on Revolution, 7-8
England
Chartist movement in, 5, 144, 213
exile groups in, 40-41, 45, 365-67
factory system in, 244
Industrial Revolution in, 244
population growth in, 17
Equality, Born's rejection of, 150
Esselen, Christian, 154
Essen, 297
Esser, Christian Joseph, trial of, 285
Estate, class compared with, 16-17

Estate owners in Economic Committee, 228
See also Agriculture
Estates General in French Revolution, 12
Exile groups
in Brussels, 41, 45, 52-53
in London, 45, 365-67
conflicts, 40-41
in Paris, 115, 365-67
post-revolutionary, 365-67
in pre-March period, 50
workers' organizations and, 50

Factories
apprentices in, 20
in England, 244
in France, 244
in Germany
number, 20-21
Prussia, 20
See also Industrial Revolution; Industrialization; Machinery
Factory workers
attitudes of, 16
class consciousness, 127
conservativism, 377
casualties in March Days, 68
concessions to, 71
increase in, 370-71
in Prussia, 21
reaction and, 281
in Silesian reovlt, 34
strikes of, 130
in *Verbrüderung*, 297
Famines, 32
Farmers
in Economic Committee, 228
in Frankfurt Assembly, 224
See also Agricultural workers; Peasants
February revolution in France, 53
impact on Germany, 57, 71

Federated guilds, 210
  Winkelblech's concept of, 300-2
Feierabend Verein of Altona, 48-49
Fellner (workers' leader), 215
Feuerbach, Ludwig, 302
"Few Words about the Union of Workers and Employers, A" (Stegen), 192
Financial panic in March Days, 60
First German Handworker and Industrial Congress, *see* Frankfurt Artisans' Congress
Fischhof, Dr. Abraham, 90
Flocon, Ferdinand, 114
Food prices, 32
Fourier, Charles, influence of, 76
France
  1848 revolution in
    February uprising, 53, 57, 71
    June Days, *see* June Days in Paris
  exile groups in, 115, 365-67
  factory system in, 244
  fear of, 327
  guild reforms in, 30
  Industrial Revolution in, 244
  Napoleonic reforms in Germany, 30
  National Workshops in, 78, 85, 244
  1789 revolution in, 4, 13-14, 34-35
  workers' attitudes towards, 244
  See also Paris
Franchise, 219
  Bavarian condemnation of, 219
  for Frankfurt Assembly, 95-96, 223, 267

Franchise, for Frankfurt Assembly (cont.)
    workers, 252
  Pre-Parliament and, 93
  workers' demands for, 63
    exclusion, 219
    Frankfurt Assembly, 252
    Journeymen's Congress, 209
    March Days, 75
  See also Electoral law
Frankfurt, 214
  decline as revolutionary center, 291-92
  Democratic Congress in, *see* Democratic Congress
  public works projects in, 87
  September uprising in, 260-61, 265, 268-69
  workers' organizations in, 152
    artisans' congress, *see* Frankfurt Artisans' Congress
    masons, 135
    Journeymen's Congress, *see* Journeymen's Congress in Frankfurt
    pre-March activities, 48
    printers congress, 202
    Verbrüderung, 302-3
Frankfurt Artisans' Congress, 164, 167, 205-6, 311
  Committee on the Affairs of the Journeymen in, 180
  Economic Committee and, 234
  Frankfurt Assembly and, 12, 189-91, 193
  guild system supported by, 183-89
  left wing of, 186-87
  master–journeymen split at, 176, 178-80
  plan for, 169
  program of, 181-89
  protests against, 180-81
  representation at, 177-79

Frankfurt Assembly (National Assembly), 5, 159-60, 163-64
charges against, 230
class composition of, 223-25, 228
collapse of, 316
defeat by reaction, 345-46
committees of, 226
Constitutional Committee of, 226, 334-35
declining importance of, 253
democrats and, 267-68
difficulties of participating in, 96
economic attitudes of, 227-28, 349-50
  free trade issue, 237, 239-41, 248-49, 330-34
  industrial ordinance issue, 252, 328-34
  work-guarantee issue, 324-28
Economic Committee of, *see* Economic Committee
electoral law of, *see* Electoral law
emigration rights and, 251
Engels on, 225n
failure of, 314, 378
  mistakes, 225, 230
  timidity, 260-61, 379
franchise for, 95-96, 223, 252, 267
Frederick William IV elected as hereditary emperor by, 334-35
  crown refused, 267, 316, 335-36
free trade and, 237, 239-41 248-49, 330-34
left-wing of, 260, 273
  electoral-law issue, 334-35
legalistic attitude of, 225
Marx on, 225n
masses feared by, 260-61
May uprisings and, 344

Frankfurt Assembly (cont.)
nicknamed "parliament of professors," 96
September uprising and, 261
Truce of Malmoe and, 223, 259, 269
unreality to people of, 252
Verbrüderung's address to, 298-99
workers and
  congresses, 14, 174, 189-91, 193, 195-97, 217-19, 243, 298-99
  demands, 77, 238-48, 250
  disillusionment, 232, 260-61, 266, 322-24, 336-37
  early attitudes, 97, 221-23
  emigration rights, 251
  franchise, 252
  industrial ordinance, 252, 328-34
  laissez-faire approach, 330-34
  petitions, *see* Petitions of workers
  slovenly treatment of demands, 250
  work-guarantee issue, 324-28
Frankfurt Gymnastic Union, 48
Frankfurt Journeymen's Congress, 219
  Berlin Workers' Congress compared with, 216, 220
Frankfurt Printers' Congress, 202
Frankfurt Workers' Union, 260-61
Franz (printer), 211
Frauen Zeitung, 268n
Frederick the Great (King of Prussia), 32
Frederick William IV (King of Prussia), 16, 75, 379
  decreed constitution of, 317
  early liberal policies of, 36

Frederick William IV (cont.)
  elected as hereditary emperor,
    334-35
  crown refused, 267, 316,
    335-36
  in March Days, 58
    concessions to workers,
      82-86
    duplicity, 82n
    Radowitz's program, 82-83
  workers and
    concessions, 82-86
    petitions, 35
    workers' organizations sup-
      ported, 47
Free association, Prussian decree on, 124
Free trade
  extension of, 28-29, 371
  Frankfurt Assembly and, 237,
    239-41, 248-49, 330-34
  guild opposition to, 157
  Hamburg Pre-Congress and,
    169-70
  journeymen and, 170-71, 208
  petitions on, 237, 239-41
  poverty of workers and, 244
  workers' attitudes toward, 27-
    28, 157, 166n, 176, 193,
    224, 237, 239-41, 248
    Hamburg Pre-Congress,
      169-70
    journeymen, 170-71, 208
Freiburg
  printers' strike in, 201
  Verbrüderung's decline in,
    361
Frei handel, see Free trade
Freiheit, Arbeit, 286
Freiheit, Brüderlichkeit, Arbeit,
  284, 286
Freiligrath, Ferdinand, 121
Friendly Societies in England,
  307
Fröbel, Julius, 302
Fröhlich, Karl, 202
Fromm (workers' leader), 137

Gagern, Heinrich von, 92, 190,
  226, 233, 336, 375
  September uprising con-
    demned by, 260-61
Gangloff, Carl, 349, 361, 362-
  63
  arrest of, 365
General German Workers' Con-
  gress, see Journeymen's
  Congress in Frankfurt
General German Workers' Un-
  ion, formation of, 374
Gerlach, Leopold von, 83, 97,
  127
  on reaction, 341
German National Bookprinters'
  Union, statutes of, 195,
  198
General amnesty of March,
  1848, 43
German Handworker and In-
  dustrial Congress, see
  Frankfurt Artisans' Con-
  gress
German-French Yearbooks, 45
German legion, 114
German states, see specific states
German Workers' Union (Lon-
  don exile group), 40
  See also Workers' Union
Geschichte der deutschen Rev-
  olution von 1848/49
  (Valentin), 8
Gesellschaftsspiegel, social ori-
  entation of, 37
Gewerbefreiheit, see Free trade
Glachau, Verbrüderung's de-
  cline in, 361
Gneist, Rudolf, 57-58
Goldschmidt (workers' leader),
  140
Goldschmidt factory, 129
Goldsmiths, strikes of, 130
Göppingen Congress of Ver-
  brüderung, 304
Görgey, Gen. Arthur von, 345

Gospel of the Poor Sinner, The
  (Weitling), 40
Gotha, 158
  guilds in, 158
  workers, organizations in, 152
    regional congress, 171
Gotha program (Social Demo-
    crats), 375
Gotha Zeitung, 158
Gottschalk, Andreas, 63, 77,
    366, 378
  arrest of, 258, 284
  Cologne workers led by, 116-
    17, 122-23
  class-consciousness of, 116
  Communist League and, 64
  early association, 78
  death of, 347
  expelled from Elberfeld, 342
  Marx's conflict with, 116,
    286-87
  new union of, 289
  policies of, 116, 286-87
  release from prison, 285
  socialist views of, 116
  theory of permanent revo-
    lution of, 286-87
  trial of, 285
Government aid
  Struve's program on, 92
  workers' demands for, 77, 209
  See also Public works' pro-
    jects
Great Britain, *see* England
Gross, Dr. (administrator of
    workers' bank), 89
Grün, Karl, 38
  journalistic activities of, 37
Grüneberg, public works' pro-
    jects in, 87
*Guarantees of Harmony and
    Freedom, The* (Weit-
    ling), 40
Guilds
  absolutism and, 238-39
  in Baden, 322

Guilds (cont.)
  as bar to self-improvement,
    32
  in Bavaria, 30, 321
  conditions of workers and,
    23-31
  congresses on, 170-71, 176,
    178-80, 183-89, 216, 219
  decline of, 15, 372
    concern over, 30-31
  Economic Committee and,
    333
  extension of, 319-22
  federated, 210
    Winkelblech's concept,
    300-2
  in France, 30
  free trade opposed by, 157
  in Gotha, 158
  in Hanover, 90, 321
  in Hesse, 157-58
  importance of, 11
  influence of, 155-57
  in Leipzig, 155-57
  March Days and, 62
  master-journeymen splits
    over, 24-25, 156, 192-
    94, 247-48, 377
    congresses, 170-71, 176,
    178-80
    Verbrüderung, 310-11
  in Nassau, 322
  in Offenbach am Main, 157-
    58
  petitions of, 185
  post-revolutionary revival of,
    369-75
  pre-March, 23-31
  in Prussia, 24
    extension, 319-20
    limitations, 29
    regulation, 29
    revival, 369
  reforms of, 28, 30
    French, 30
  restoration of, 90
  in Saxony, 30

Guilds (cont.)
structure of, 32
tests of, 188
in Thuringia, 321
trades in, 29
traditions of, 4
training programs of, 246
Verbrüderung and, 296, 310-11
workers' opposition to, 192-94
workers' support for, 155-58, 222
  congresses, 171, 183-89, 216, 219
  journeymen, 25, 192-94, 196, 208-11
  March Days, 62
  master artisans, 3, 165-67, 246
  petitions, 185
in Württemberg, 301, 321
Guild socialism, 347
Guizot ministry, fall of, 53
Gutenberg, Der, 202, 312
establishment of, 198
national influence of, 11*n*
Gutenberg League, 312
Gymnastic societies, 48
early importance of, 4
workers' organizations from, 154, 355, 362
Gymnastic Union in Frankfurt, 48

Halberstadt, *Verbrüderung* membership in, 307
Halle, 174, 297, 311
workers' organizations in, 351
Hamburg, 168, 174, 213-14
artisan congress in, *see* Hamburg Pre-Congress of Artisans
growth of, 19
merchant petitions from, 243
printers' demands in, 134
strike movement, 201

Hamburg (cont.)
Verbrüderung's decline in, 361
workers' organizations in, 152
pre-March activities, 48
Hamburg Congress of *Verbrüderung,* 304-5
Hamburg Educational Club for Masters, 159
Hamburg Educational Society for the Improvement of the Working Class, 48
Hamburg Pre-Congress of Artisans
appeal for, 159-60, 164
delegates to, 165
free-trade issue in, 169-70
journeymen and, 170-71
Hamm, workers' petitions from, 245
Handicrafts, *see* Apprentices; Artisans; Journeymen; Workers; *specific crafts*
Handloom weavers, *see* Weavers
Hanover, 168
electoral law in, 96
guilds in, 321
restoration, 90
petitions from, 237
Hanover Congress, 354
Hardenberg, Prince Karl von, reforms of, 28
Hätzel, August, 44, 76, 78
Hatzfeld, Countess Sophie von, 259*n*
Health Care Union, 308, 352
dissolution of, 365
Hecker, Friedrich, 60, 62, 92, 94, 110
Hegelian philosophy, influences on socialist theories of, 36, 38
Heidelberg, 158, 204, 297
anti-Semitism in, 61
workers' organizations in, 180, 300-3

Heidelberg Congress of *Ver-
brüderung,* 300-3
    as all-German workers' asso-
    ciation, 302
    organizational achievements
    of, 303
Heidelberg Worker's Club, 180
Heine, Heinrich, on Weitling,
40
Held, Friedrich Wilhelm Alex-
ander, 92, 102
    decline of reputation, 107-8
    life of, 103-4
    machine builders and, 103-4,
    107
    popularity of, 100
    printers' strike condemned
    by, 132
    views of, 104-7
Hempel, Friedrich, 156
Henry LXXII (prince of Reuss-
Lobenstein-Ebersdorf),
59*n*
Herwegh, Georg, 114
Hess, Moses, 38, 115-16
    journalistic activities of, 37
Hesse, Electoral
    electoral law in, 96
    French reforms in, 30
    workers' militancy in, 256
Hesse, Grand Duchy of
    artisans in, 311, 370
    concessions in, 90
    guilds in, 157-58
    merchant petitions from, 247-
    48
Heydt, August von der, 317-18
Hildebrand, Bruno, 231, 324
Hlubek, Franz Xaver von, 229
Hoffmann von Fallersleben, 51
Hollandt, August, 330-34
Holstein, 168
    rural workers in, 305
Home work, 20
Honored Union of German Rail-
way Officials, 310-11

Hours, working
    length of, 31
    workers' demands on, 172,
    213
    Journeymen's Congress,
    209
    printers, 197
    strikes, 128-31
*Humanity as It Is and Ought
To Be* (Weitling), 40
Hungarian revolutionaries, de-
feat of, 345
Hunger marches, 35

Imperial Diet of 1731 (Prus-
sia), 28
Income taxes and Pre-Parlia-
ment, 94
Industrial Club (Bavaria), 182
Industrial councils, workers'
    demands for, 244
Industrial freedom, *see* Free
    trade
Industrial ordinance
    of Frankfurt Assembly, 252
        Economic Committee, 328-
        34
    in Prussia, 29, 319-20
Industrial Revolution
    in England, 244
    in France, 244
    in Germany, *see* Industriali-
    zation
Industrial Union of the Wup-
perthal, 297*n*
Industrialization
    centers of, 15, 18, 20, 370
    human cost of, 151-52
    pre-March, 20-21, 23
    working class and
        effects, 20-21, 23, 151-52
        fear of industrialization,
        see Machinery
Insurance programs, *see* Social
    insurance programs
Intellectuals and socialist theo-
ries, 36

Iron workers
  guild membership of, 29
  strikes of, 130

Jacoby, Johann, 95
Jellačić, Baron Joseph, 278
Jena, 182
Jews, see Anti-Semitism
Joseph II (Emperor of Austria), 32
Journeymen, 318
  casualties in March Days, 68
  class consciousness of, 127
  conferences of, 156-57
  congresses of
    Berlin Workers' Congress, 212-20, 243, 303
    cigar makers, 27, 193, 203-4, 257-58, 312-14, 356-58, 362
    Frankfurt, see Journeymen's Congress in Frankfurt
    printers, 26-27, 80, 131-35, 158-59, 193-202, 312, 356, 382
    regional, 298-304, 353-55
  foreign influences on, 50
  free trade and, 170-71, 208
  frustrations of, 15-16
  guilds and, 25
    influence of guilds, 156-57
    opposition to guilds, 192-94
    support for, 25, 192-94, 196, 208-11
  increase in, 24
  in manufacturing, 20
  masters' conflict with, 24-25, 156, 192-94, 377
    congresses, 170-71, 176, 178-80
    guild system, 247-48
    Verbrüderung, 310-11
  pre-March riots of, 34
  proportion of handicraft workers, 24

Journeymen (cont.)
  in Prussia, 21
  self-help activities of, 352-53
  social origins of, 16
  strike movement of, 129-35
  Wanderjahre of, see: Wanderjahre
Journeymen's Congress in Frankfurt, 167, 204-12, 329
  appeal for delegates, 206-7
  decisions of, 207-11
    apprentices, 208
    education, 209
    free trade, 208
    government aid, 209
    guilds, 208-11
    hours, 208-9
    scope, 210
    universal suffrage, 209
    wages, 209
  flag adopted by, 211
  organization of, 211
  representation in, 204-5
Journeymen's Union, 44
  Berlin, 48
  Leipzig, 156
Judges in Frankfurt Assembly, 224
June Days in Paris, 144, 379
  defeat of proletariat in, 2
  effect on German workers, 163
  September uprising compared with, 261
  social revolutionary importance of, 3

Kapp, Friedrich, 302
Karlsruhe, merchant petitions from, 240
Kassel, 168
  liberal organizations in, 154
  workers' organizations in, 153
Kick, Georg, 290, 302
  exile of, 346
  in Verbrüderung, 218, 297

Kiel, 174
  May uprising in, 350
Kleinbürgertum, *see* Middle
    class; Petty bourgeoisie
Koblenz, 178
  public works' projects in, 87
Koch (workers' leader), 212,
    214, 216
Kohlweck, Franz Wenzel, 204,
    313, 356, 358
Kölnische Zeitung, 269
Königsberg
  growth of, 19
  Verbrüderung's decline in,
    361
Köpenick, guild petitions from,
    185
Krause, Ernst, 175, 212
Kriege, Hermann, 275
Krupp factory, 20
Kuhlmann, George, 45

Labor dues, abolition of, 18
Labor force, size of, 17-18, 20
  See also Unemployment;
    Workers
Labor ministry, *see* Ministry of
    labor
Ladies' Union for the Abolition
    of Need among the Small
    Manufacturers (Berlin),
    87
Lallenberg, merchant petitions
    from, 240-41
Land owners in Economic Com-
    mittee, 228
  See also Agriculture
Langenbielau, weavers' revolt
    in, 34
Lasalle, Ferdinand, 259*n*
  policy of, 375
Lauenburg, 159
Lawyers
  in Frankfurt Assembly, 224
    Economic Committee, 228
  in Prussian Assembly, 254

League of Cigar Workers, or-
    ganization of, 203-4
League of the Just, 39, 44
  Communist League and, 41
  factions in, 44-45
  London remnant of, 40
  in Switzerland, 44
  Weitling's influence in, 44
Leipzig, 201, 213, 278
  cooperatives in, 309
  guilds in, 155-57
  May uprising in, 343, 350
  workers' organizations in, 80,
    91
    conference of journeymen,
      156-57
    guild influence, 155-56
    May uprising, 343, 350
    pre-March demonstrations,
      35
    printers' movement, 134,
      199, 201, 357-58
    regional workers' con-
      gresses, 171-72, 298-99
    Verbrüderung, 291-92,
      298, 303, 362-65
Leipzig Congress of Cigar Mak-
    ers, 357-48
Leipzig Congress of *Verbrüder-
    ung*, 360-62
Leipzig Journeymen's Union,
    156
Lenin, Vladimir Ilyich, 122
Lette, Adolph, 329-30, 333
  Born's debate with, 139-40
  in Economic Committee, 233
Lewissohn, Louis, 101
Liberalism, 2
  of Frederick William IV, 36
  Pre-Parliament and, 94
  republicanism, 92
  See also Democratic move-
    ment; Middle class
Liberals
  March Days and, 58-59
    demands, 63
    fear of workers, 71-72

Liberals (cont.)
  organizations of
    Berlin, 124
    Breslau, 154
    Cologne, 120, 268-69
    Kassel, 154
    See also Democratic movement; Middle class
Lichnowsky, Prince Felix, death of, 261
Liebknecht, Wilhelm, 375
Linke (workers' leader), 211
Linz, *Verbrüderung* in, 217
List, Friedrich, popularity of, 27
Locksmiths, strikes of, 130
Locomotive, Die, 103-4, 107
London
  exile groups in, 45, 365-67
    conflicts, 40-41
  Marx's exile, 366-67
Lovett (Chartist leader), 213
  Workingmen's Educational Association of, 307
Lübeck, merchant petitions from, 243
Lucht, A., 212
Lüchow, J. C., 75-76, 137
  in Central Committee of Workers, 142
Lumpenproletariat, formation of, 15-16
Lüning, Otto, 38, 302-3
  journalistic activities of, 37

Machine builders
  casualties in March Days, 68
  Held's leadership of, 103-4, 107
  in October riots, 278
  reaction and, 281
  social attitudes of, 16
    artisan outlook, 310
    conservatism, 377
  status of, 29
  strikes of, 130

Machine-building factories in Prussia, 20
Machine Workers Union, 154-55, 273
Machinery, workers' hostility toward, 127, 197-98
  March days, 57, 74
  petitions, 239-41
  Rhineland, 35
  Silesia, 57
Magdeburg, 297-98
Mainz, 158, 297
  anti-Semitism in, 61
  workers' congresses in, 165
    printers, 133, 158, 194-99, 202, 312
  workers' organizations in, 152
Malmoe, truce of
  Frankfurt Assembly and, 223, 259, 269
  workers' reactions to, 253
Mannheim, 204
  merchant petitions from, 247
Mäntel, Christian, 43-44
  influence of, 50
Manufacturers
  in Frankfurt Assembly, 224
    Economic Committee, 227
  small scale of, 20
  social origins of, 16
Manufacturing industry, craft workers in, 20
  See also Factories; Factory workers
Marat, Jean Paul, Schlöffel's emulation of, 109
March amnesty, 43
March Days, 57-80, 237, 315
  anti-Semitism and, 61-62
  Bakunin on, 57
  barricades in, 57
  in Berlin, 64-80
    armed clashes, 67
    barricades, 57
    burial procession, 69
    casualties, 68

March Days, in Berlin (cont.)
concessions of government, 68-69, 71-72
financial panic, 60
organization of workers, 70, 72-77
public works, 72
reaction of middle classes, 71-72
unemployment issue, 64-65
workers' demands, 70-71, 73-80
Zelten meetings, 65
casualties in, 68
causes of, 376
in Cologne, 62-64
civil guard established, 63
demands of people, 63
socialist leadership, 64
Communist League in, 64, 100
economic problems and, 60, 70
unemployment, 64-65, 70
public works' projects, 84-86
enthusiasm during, 57-58
financial panic in, 60
government policies and, 81-97
concessions, 58-59, 71-72, 82-91
early indecision, 81-82
Frederick William IV, 58, 82-86
Hanover, 90
Hesse-Darmstadt, 90
Nassau, 90-91
Pre-Parliament, 91-97
Prussia, see Prussia, March Days in
Saxony, 91
Vienna, 90
guilds and, 62
liberals and, 58-59
demands, 63
fear of workers, 71-72

March Days (cont.)
machine breaking in, 57, 74
Marx's views on, 100, 111
middle class and, 58-59
demands, 63
fear of workers, 71-72
in Munich, 80
peasant uprisings and, 59-61
Prussia, see Prussia, March Days in
short-lived unity of, 99
in Silesia, 57
"social question" in, 59n
socialists in, 64, 100, 111
students in, 68
unemployment and, 64-65
in Vienna, 57
workers in
casualties in fighting, 68
concessions to workers, 71-72, 82-86
demands, 63, 70-71, 73-80
initiative, 59-60
liberals' fear of, 71-72
organizational activities, 70, 72-77, 124-28
Marriage, workers' attitudes towards, 46n
Martini (Frankfurt Assembly delegate), 302
Marx, Karl, 1, 15, 64, 143, 151, 223, 375
antitax campaign of, 266-67 282
artisans underestimated by, 9
attitude toward March Days, 100, 111
surprised by events, 113-14
Born and, 123, 131
differences in views, 148-52, 301-2
in Brussels, 52-53
Communist League and
dissolution of League, 118-19, 123

Marx, Karl, Communist League and (cont.)
  domination of League, 41, 114
  Marx's aloofness, 288
  outbreak of Revolution, 114-15
  Communist Manifesto of, 1, 41
  democratic movement and
    break with democrats, 267, 283, 288
    Cologne Democratic Union, 120
    support for, 112-13, 120-23
  failure of, 377-78
  final exile of, 366-67
  on Frankfurt Assembly, 225*n*
  Gottschalk's conflict with, 116, 286-87
  influence of
    League for the Just, 45
    theoretical, 38-39
  in London, 346-47
  writings of
    economic, 283
    on 1848, 9-10, 100, 260
    journalistic activities, 37, 120-23
  Neue Rheinische Zeitung and, 120-23
    editorial board, 120-21
    financial support, 120-21
    hostility of workers' organizations, 122-23
    labor policy of publishers, 123
    views of newspaper, 121-23
  post-revolutionary policies of, 366-68
  prosecution of, 284-85
  Russian policy of, 293
  on September uprising, 260
  Weitling's conflict with, 40-41
  workers' movement and, 100-1, 111, 122-23

Marx, Karl, workers' movement and (cont.)
  alienation of workers, 116, 286-87, 289
  aloofness, 8-9
  Cologne Workers' Union, *see* Cologne Workers' Union, Marx and
  conflict with Gottschalk, 116, 286-87
  relations with Born, 123, 131, 148-52
  shift toward workers, 283
  Verbrüderung, 289
Märzschwarmerei, *see* March Days
Masons
  guild membership of, 29
  need for, 26
  in Silesian revolt, 34
  strikes of, 130
Master artisans, 317
  class consciousness of, 127
  conferences of, 157
  congresses of, 163-220
    Frankfurt, *see* Frankfurt Artisans' Congress
    Hamburg, *see* Hamburg Pre-Congress
    regional, 311
  divisions among, 25-26
  fears of proletarianization by, 25-26
  frustrations of, 15-16
  gains of, 322
  guilds supported by, 3, 165-67, 246
  journeymen conflicts with, 24-25, 156, 192-94, 377
    congresses, 170-71, 176, 178-80
  guild system, 247-48
  Verbrüderung, 310-11
  in manufacturing, 20
  proportion of handicraft workers, 24
  in Prussia, 21, 370
  regional congresses of, 311

Master artisans (cont.)
  in Rhenish Palatinate, 311
  Verbrüderung and, 296-97,
    310-11
  See also Artisans
Masters' examinations, Berlin
    Workers' Congress on,
    219
May, Johannes Martin, 177,
    181*n*, 186*n*, 187, 233-34
May uprisings, 337, 341-59
  in Baden, 341, 344
  in Bamberg, 343
  in Bavaria, 343
  Born in, 342
  in Bremen, 350
  cause of, 316
  civil guard in, 63, 342, 344
  Communist League and, 347
  defense funds in, 349
  in Dresden, 342-45
  in Düsseldorf, 345
  in Elberfeld, 342, 344-45
  Frankfurt Assembly and, 344
  in Kiel, 350
  in Leipzig, 343, 350
  middle-class character of, 342
  newspapers banned in, 346-
    47
  in Prussia, 345
  radical leaders and, 346-47
  in Rastatt, 345
  in Rhineland, 342
  in Ruhr, 342, 345
  in Solingen, 345
  in Stuttgart, 344
  workers' organizations and
    artisans, 316
    lack of workers' support,
      341-45, 350
    repressions, 348-49
    *Verbrüderung, see: Ver-
      brüderung,* in May up-
      risings
Mazzini, Giuseppe, 44
Mechanization, *see* Industriali-
    zation; Machinery

Mecklenburg, 168
  franchise laws condemned in,
    219
Mecklenburg-Schwerin
  marauding workers in, 256
  petitions from, 237
  See also specific cities
Medical care of workers, 308,
    352, 365
Medieval ideal of hierarchy, 16
Meisterrecht, 220
Mendelsohn, Joseph, 87
Mentel, Christian, 43-44
  influence of, 50
Merchants, 318
  petitions of, 239-41, 243-44,
    247-48
  See also Middle class
Merk, Ernst, 249, 333
Metal workers, trade groups of,
    80
  See also specific metal crafts
Michaelis (workers' leader), 87,
    137, 140
  in Central Committee of
    Workers, 142
  political approach of, 138
Michels, Robert, 373
Middle class
  democrats and, 267
  Economic Committee and,
    322-24
    electoral law, 335
    guild issue, 333
    industrial ordinance, 328-
      34
    laissez faire approach, 330-
      34
    workers' congresses, 233-
      34
    work-guarantee issue, 324-
      28
  in Frankfurt Assembly, 223-
    25, 228, 322-24
  March Days and, 58-59
    demands, 63
    fear of workers, 71-72

Middle class (cont.)
  Marx's views on, 113
  organizations of
    Berlin, 124
    Breslau, 154
    Cologne, 120, 268-69
    Kassel, 154
  peasants and, 60
  socialism feared by, 243, 379
  weakness of, 16
  working class and, 5
    fear of working class, 71-72, 379
    lower middle class and, 16
Miners, 370
Mining, peasants in, 20
Ministry of labor, 72, 87-88
  Struve's program on, 92
  workers' demand for, 65-66, 74, 77, 172, 213
Ministry for Trade, Industry and Public Works (Prussia), 72
  establishment of, 87
  failure of, 88
Minkus (Frankfurt Assembly delegate), 223
Mohl, Moritz, 228, 327, 333
Moll, Joseph, 40, 112
  Communist League and protests dissolution, 119
    revives League, 120, 288
  death of, 366
  influence of, 45
Monecke, Eduard, 109
Morality, workers' attitudes toward, 46n
Moravia, Verbrüderung in, 217
Mühlheim, anti-Semitism in, 61
Müller (workers' leader), 137, 211
Munich, 214
  growth of, 19
  March Days in, 80
  printers' strike in, 201
  riots in, 256

Munich (cont.)
  shoemakers' strike in, 135
  Verbrüderung membership in, 307

Napoleonic Code, 115n
Nassau, Duchy of
  concessions in, 90-91
  free trade in, 371
  guilds in, 322
  peasant uprisings in, 61
National Assembly, see Frankfurt Assembly
National Assembly of Book Printers, 133, 194-99, 202, 312
  apprentices and, 197
  documents issued by, 195-99
  Frankfurt Assembly and, 195-97
  guild system criticized by, 196
  hour demands of, 197
  machinery and, 197-98
  newspaper of, see: Gutenberg, Der
  organizational regulations of, 198
  representation at, 194
  strike threat of, 197
  wage demands of, 197
National Guard in Vienna, 90
National Workshops in France
  mistakes of, 244
  public works projects compared with, 78, 85
Nationalism, importance of, 2
Nauwerck, Karl, 326
Nazis, on Weitling, 39n
Neckarbischofsheim, anti-Semitism in, 61
Nees von Esenbeck, Christian, 154, 175, 214
  life of, 215n
Neue Deutsche Zeitung, 302
Neue Kölnische Zeitung, 347
Neue Preussische Zeitung, 201

Neue Rheinische Zeitung, 148, 300
  Bürgers in, 121
  level of, 283
  Marx and, 120-23
  policies of
    antitax campaign, 266
    Democratic Congress, 275
    June Days, 163
    middle class, 281
    Russia, 293
    "social question," 11
    workers' movement, 11, 281-82
  prosecution of, 284-85
  suspension of, 269, 346
Neuss, riots in, 256
Neustadt an der Hardt, congress in, 311
Newspapers
  pre-March radical, 37
  "social question" and, 11
  workers' associations ignored by, 11
  See also specific newspapers
Nothjung, Peter
  arrest of, 367
  in Communist League, 288
Nuremburg, 297
  congress of *Verbrüderung* in, 304

Oberländer (Saxon minister), 91, 254
Obermann, Karl, *Die deutschen Arbeiter in der ersten bürgerlichen Revolution*, 8
Ober-Meissen, cooperatives in, 310
O'Connor, Feargus Edward, 213
October riots
  in Berlin, 270-73, 277-78
  civil guard in, 271-72, 278
  class war in, 272-73
  issue in, 270-73
  outbreak of, 271-72

October riots (cont.)
  Prussian Assembly and, 277-78
  reactions to, 272-73
  workers in, 272-73
Odenwald, peasant uprisings in, 60
Offenbach am Main, guilds in, 157-58
Offenes Antwort-Schreiben (Lassalle), 375
Officially sanctioned workers' organizations, 47-49
Oldenburg, 168
"On the Relation between Politics and the Social Question" (Born), 277
Organization as end in itself, 4
  See also Liberals, organizations of
Organization of Work and Its Practicability, The (Lüchow), 75-76
Osterrath (Frankfurt Assembly delegate), 250, 330
Otto-Peters, Luise, 362*n*

Palatinate
  May uprising in, 341
  workers' petitions from, 249
Paris
  exile groups in, 115, 365-67
  February revolution in, 53, 57
    enthusiasm, 71
  German workers in, 115, 365-67
    socialist influences, 50
  June Days in, *see* June Days in Paris
  See also France
Patow, Erasmus von, 132
  policies of, 88-90
Pawnbrokers, attacks on, 72
Peasants
  bought off by Hapsburg Monarchy, 2
  conservatism of, 144

Peasants (cont.)
  demands of, 60-61
  emigrate to towns, 19
  in Frankfurt Assembly, 224
  in March Days, 59-61
  middle class and, 60
  in mining, 20
Pelz, Eduard, 154
People's Club of the Zelten
  aims of, 102
  formation of, 101
  leaders of, 102-11
  limitations of, 103
  moderate views of, 126
Permanent revolution, Gotts-
    chalk's theory of, 286-87
Persecution of workers' organi-
    zations, *see* Reaction
Petersdorf, rural workers in, 305
Peterswaldau, weavers' revolt
    in, 34
Petitions of merchants, 239-41,
    243-44, 247-48
Petitions of workers, 315
  to Frankfurt Assembly, 13-14,
    97, 193, 221-23
    congresses, 234
    consideration of, 226
    decline in number, 323-24
    demands, 238-48
    Economic Committee, 234
    form and character, 236-38
    free trade, 237, 239-41
    by localities, 236-37
    number, 235, 323
  guild, 185
  to Frederick William IV, 35
  pre-March, 35
  to Prussian Assembly, 254
Petty bourgeoisie and working
    class, 16
  See also Middle class
Pfuel (Prussian minister), 316-
    17
Piece rates, hostility of workers
    toward, 130

Pieper (*Handelsmeister* of
    printers), 132
Pinson, Koppel, 8n
Political Club of Berlin, 124,
    140
Pomerania
  merchant petitions from, 244
  workers' petitions from, 246
Population growth and condi-
    tion of workers, 17-18
Porters, middle-class outlook of,
    310
Potato famine of 1845, 32
"Potato revolution," 35-36
Potschapel, workers' organiza-
    tions in, 156
Potters, strikes of, 130
Poverty of workers, 4
  free trade and, 244
  horror stories of, 31n
  in pre-March period, 31-33
Prague, *Verbrüderung* in, 217
Prater, battle of, 259
Pre-Congress, *see* Hamburg
    Pre-Congress of Artisans
Pre-Parliament, 91-97, 164
  adjournment of, 94
  Committee of Fifty elected
    by, 94
  constitutional policy of, 94
  electoral law and, 93
  function of, 92
  liberal policies of, 94
    republicanism, 92
  Struve's program for, 92
  tax policy of, 94
  unrepresentative nature of, 93
Prices
  demand for fixing of, 204
  food, 32
  riots over, 256
Printers
  apprentice, 197
  Born and, 131-33, 198n,
    200-1
  congresses of
    Berlin, 356

Printers, congresses of (cont.)
  Frankfurt, 202
  Mainz, 133, 158, 194-99,
    202, 312
  demands of, 131-32, 197-98
  decline of, 356
  economic problems of, 26-27
  independence of, 312
  strikes of, 131-35, 199-202
    effectiveness of strike, 132-
      33
    failure, 200-2
  trade groups, 80
  See also: Gutenberg, Der
Printers' League, banning of,
  356
Prinz, W., 286
Producer cooperatives, 309-10
Professors in Frankfurt Assem-
  bly, 224
  Economic Committee, 228
Prokesch-Osten, von (Austrian
  minister), 365
Proletarianization, artisans'
  fears of, 242-43
Proletariat
  definitions of, 22
  as scare word, 242
    attitude of workers, 74
  See also Factory workers;
    Master craftsman; Jour-
    neymen; Workers
Protective tariffs
  Committee of Fifty on, 95
  Frankfurt Assembly and, 249-
    50
  workers' demand for, 222
Proudhon, Pierre Joseph, 143,
  293
Provisional Central Committee
  for the Employment of
  the Workers, 254
Prussia
  artisans in, 21, 370
  Austrian threats to, 335
  conference on workers' prob-
    lems, 316

Prussia, conference on workers'
    problems (cont.)
  demands, 319
  opposition to, 318, 320
  representation, 317-19
  results, 319-20
  constitution decreed in, 317
  day workers in, 21
  delegates in Economic
    Committee, 229
  factory workers in, 21
  free association decreed in,
    124
  free trade in, 371
  guilds in, 24
    extension, 319-20
    limitations, 29
    regulation, 29
    revival, 369
  industrial ordinances in, 29,
    319-20
  journeymen in, 21
  machine-building factories in,
    20
  March Days in
    Berlin, see March Days in
      Berlin
    concessions to workers, 71-
      72, 82-86
    government policies, 58-59,
      68-69, 82-90
    Ministry for Trade, Indus-
      try and Public Works,
      87-88
    public works projects, 84-
      86
  May uprising in, 345
  parliamentary bodies in,
      see Prussian Assembly;
      United Diet for Prussia
  petitions from, 236
  pre-March workers' actions
    in, 34-35
  reaction in, 34-35, 279-81
    behavior of workers, 281
    democrats defeated, 280
    early growth of, 90

Prussia, reaction in (cont.)
    public meetings prohibited, 258
    Wrangel's occupation of Berlin, 279
  servants in, 21
  steam engines in, 20
  strikes in, 34-35, 124-33
  Wanderjahre regulated in, 29
  workers' organizations dissolved in, 363, 365
  See also Berlin; *specific cities*
Prussian Assembly
  antitax campaign of, 279, 282
  class composition of, 254
  dissolution of, 266
  October riots and, 277-78
  petitions to, 254
  removed to Brandenburg, 279
  workers' relationships to, 254-55
Prussian National Assembly, *see* Prussian Assembly
Prussian Statistical Bureau, 21
Public education, 213, 219
  congresses and, 174, 209
  in March Days, 63, 75
Public works projects
  in Berlin, 270-73
  in Cologne, 117
  curtailment of, 270
    October riots, 270-73
  in Düsseldorf, 87
  failure of, 85-86, 90
  in Frankfurt, 87
  in Grüneberg, 87
  in Koblenz, 87
  March Days and, 84-86
  National Workshops compared with, 78, 85
  proposals for, 65
  in Prussia
    March Days, 84-86
    restrictions, 316-17
  riots over, 86
  strikes on, 130

Public works projects (cont.)
  in Vienna, 90, 259
Puttkamer, Robert von, 89

Quarck, Max, "A Contribution to the Theory and Practice of Marxism," 8

Radowitz, Joseph Maria von, 3
  social policies of, 82-83
Railway workers
  artisan outlook of, 310-11
  in Silesian revolt, 34
  strikes of, 35
Railways
  growth of, 27
  sabotage of, 256
Rastatt, May uprising in, 345
Reaction
  artisans and, 281
  beginnings of, 253, 258-61
    arrests of workers' leaders, 257-58
    June Days compared with, 253
    restrictions on civil rights, 258-59
  in Cologne, 258
  democratic movement and, 268-69
  dissolution of workers' organizations by, 258-61, 362-65
  factory workers and, 281
  Frankfurt Assembly defeated by, 345-46
  May uprisings and, 341
  mechanism for, 255
  in Prussia, 34-35, 279-81
    behavior of workers, 281
    democrats defeated, 280
    early growth of, 90
    public meetings prohibited, 258
    Wrangel's occupation of Berlin, 279

Reaction (cont.)
  strength of, 345
Reading groups, Communist, 44, 351
Reading Union for Workers of Cologne, 351
Red flag, 271, 280, 286
Reflections of a German Proletarian (anonymous), 21-22
Regensburg, workers' educational societies in, 307
Reichensperger, Peter, 23
Reichenbach, workers' petitions from, 249
Reis, Dr. (workers' leader), in Central Committee of Workers, 142
Religion, socialist critique of, 40
Republic
  Pre-Parliament and, 92
  Struve's proclamation of, 268
Reuss (workers' leader), 362
  exile of, 363
Reuss-Lobenstein-Ebersdorf, 59n
Reutlingen Congress, 353-54
Revolution and Counter-Revolution in Germany in 1848 (Marx and Engels), 7-8
Rheinhesse
  anti-Semitism in, 61
  Verbrüderung in, 302
Rheinische Zeitung, social orientation of, 37
  See also: *Neue Rheinische Zeitung*
Rhenish Palatinate
  anti-Semitism in, 61
  free trade demands of, 239
  master artisans in, 311
Rhineland, 214, 260-61
  democratic movement in, 268
  food prices in, 32
  free trade in, 28
  industry in, 15
  machine breaking in, 35

Rhineland (cont.)
  May uprising in, 342
  riots in, 256, 284
  See also specific cities
Riesenstein, 158
Riots, 284
  increase in, 256-57
  October, *see* October riots
  pre-March, 34-36
  price, 256
  over public works projects, 86
Roman Republic, defeat of, 345
Rönne, Friedrich von, 227-28, 230, 233, 249
Rösler, Peter, 288
Ruge, Arnold, 277
Ruhr, May uprising in, 342, 345
Rump Parliament, 344
  defeat of, 345
Rural workers, *see* Agricultural workers; Peasants
Russia
  counterrevolutionary role of, 345
  Marx's policy toward, 293

Sabotage, 256
Sachsenhausen, riots in, 256
Salis (student), 109
Saxon Diet, 91
Saxons! What is Necessary and What is Blum Doing? (Semmig), 79
Saxony
  conference on workers' problems in, 316, 320
    recommendations, 321
  franchise laws in, 219
  free trade in, 371
  guilds in, 30
  industry in, 15
    textile, 20
  petitions from, 236
    merchants, 240-41
  political freedom in, 291-92
  workers' commission for, 91

Saxony (cont.)
  workers' organizations in
    concessions to, 91
    demands, 79
    dissolution, 363-65
    regional congresses, 171-72, 298-99
    Verbrüderung congress, 298-99
    See also Dresden; *specific cities*
Schapper, Karl, 40, 115, 288, 367-68
  arrest of, 268
  in Communist League, 288
  dissolution protested, 119
  influence of, 45
Schassler, Max, 101
Schirges, Georg, 187
Schirmeister, Heinrich, 333
Schleswig-Holstein, 259
  petitions from, 237
Schlöffel, Gustav Adolf, 102, 108
  anti-capitalist speech of, 138-39
  arrest of, 110
  Born's relations with, 109-10
  Camphausen attacked by, 110
  death of, 111
  life of, 108-11
  Marat emulated by, 109
  policy on electoral law, 97
    franchise demonstration, 110
  popularity of, 100
Schmoller, Gustav, 222, 372*n*
Schnapper, Karl, 112
Schulze-Delitzsch, Hermann, 310, 372-73
Schurz, Carl, 341-42
Schütz, Dekan, 326
Schwarzenberg, Philip, 234, 329
Schwarzer (Austrian minister), 254
Schwarzwald, peasant uprisings in, 60

Schwenniger, Franz, 290, 304, 313, 346
  arrest of, 349
  in Berlin Workers' Congress, 215
  exile of, 363, 365
  release from prison, 359
  in *Verbrüderung*, 218
Schwerin, 349
  workers' organizations in, 308, 351
    Verbrüderung's decline, 361
Schwerin Workers' Singing Union, 308, 351
Security Commission of Elberfeld, antiworker policies of, 342
Security Committee of Vienna, 90
Selencka (Pre-Congress delegate), 169
Self help by workers
  Berlin Workers' Congress program for, 218
  growing orientation toward, 46-50, 261, 265-66
  journeymen and, 352-53
  revival of, 372
  Verbrüderung's proposals for, 218, 351-53
  See also Cooperatives; Social insurance programs
Semmig, Hermann, 38, 79
September crisis, 265-67
  effect on workers' organizations of, 266
  results of, 266-67
September uprising in Frankfurt, 265, 269
  democrats blamed for, 268
  Frankfurt Assembly and, 261
  June Days compared with, 261
  Marx on, 260
  workers in, 260

Serfs, freeing of, 15, 18
  See also Agricultural workers;
    Peasants
Serge makers, strikes of, 130
Servants in Prussia, 21
Shipbuilders, status of, 29
Shoemakers
  cooperatives of, 309
  economic problems of, 26-27
  strikes of, 135
  trade groups of, 80
Sick aid, 308, 352, 365
Silesia
  censorship in, 34*n*
  cooperatives in, 310
  industry in, 15
    textile, 20
  machine breaking in, 57
  March Days in, 57
  regional workers' congress in,
    172-73
  strikes in, 34, 129
  weavers' revolt in, 34
  See also specific cities
Silk makers, strikes of, 130
Simon, Heinrich, 334
Singing clubs, 4
  in Breslau, 48
Sittenfeld (employer), 133
Skrobek (workers' leader), 79,
    91
Social Democratic Party, origins
    of, 374
Social insurance programs
  Radowitz's, 82-83
  workers' demands for, 79,
    172, 213, 218
  See also Self help by workers
"Social question"
  in Berlin Workers' Congress,
    212
  in Democratic Congress, 275-
    77
  early controversies over, 37
  in March Days, 59*n*
  nature of, 2
  newspapers interested in, 11

Socialism, 38-43
  conflicting definitions of, 42-
    43
  Die Verbrüderung and, 293-
    94
  guild, 347
  intellectuals and, 36
  Marxian, *see* Marx, Karl
  middle class fear of, 243, 379
  "true," 38-39, 78
  utopian, 45, 78
  workers' organizations and,
    34-54
    antisocialist sentiments, 79,
      243-44
    discussions of socialism,
      35-38
    early unrest and, 34-35
    influence of utopians, 78
    leaders, 50-54
    revolutionary groups, 43-
      46
    self-help groups, 46-50
  *See also specific socialist
    theoreticians*
*Socialism and Communism in
    Contemporary France*
    (von Stein), 37
Socialists, 128
  artisans underestimated by, 9
  in March Days, 64, 100, 111
  Marx's influence on, 38-39
  utopian, 45, 78
  See also Communist League;
    Communist Party of
    Germany; Marx, Karl;
    Social Democratic Party;
    Weitling, Wilhelm; *spe-
    cific socialist theoret-
    icians*
Society for Publicly Useful Con-
    structions of Berlin, 72
Solingen
  cutlery industry in, 20
  May uprising in, 345
Spiegel (workers' leader), 202

427

Stadtamhof, workers' educational societies in, 307
Stahl, Wilhelm, 228, 330
State, society compared with, 17
State governments, *see specific German states*
Status, class compared with, 16-17
Steam engines in *Zollverein*, 20
Stegen (workers' leader), 192, 258
Stein, Lorenz von, 37
Stein, Baron Heinrich vom, reforms of, 28
Steinhauer, F. E., 212
Stettin, 174
  population increase in, 19n
  workers' organizations in, 47
Stock exchange, decline in March Days of, 60
Stolp, workers' petitions from, 246
Stralsund, merchant petitions from, 244
Strikes
  anti-Semitism and, 129
  in Berlin, 34, 128-33
  in Breslau, 34, 134, 201
  of cabinetmakers, 130
  of calico workers, 129
  of carpenters, 130
  in Dresden, 134
  of factory workers, 130
  in Freiburg, 361
  of goldsmiths, 130
  in Hamburg, 201
  of journeymen, 129-35
  of locksmiths, 130
  of machine builders, 130
  of masons, 130
  in Munich, 135, 201
  of potters, 130
  of printers, 131-35, 199-202
    demands, 131-32
    effectiveness, 132-33
    failure, 200-2
  in Prussia, 34-35, 124-33

Strikes (cont.)
  on public works projects, 130
  of railway workers, 35
  of serge makers, 130
  of shoemakers, 135
  significance of, 2, 192-93
  in Silesia, 34
  of silk makers, 130
  of tailors, 129
  of textile workers, 129-30
  of weavers, 130
Struve, Gustav von, 60, 62, 94, 110, 113
  German republic proclaimed by, 268
  policies of, 92
Students, 108
  in March Days, 68
  workers' organizations and, 178
Study groups, Communist, 44
Stuttgart
  May uprising in, 344
  Rump Parliament in, 344
  workers' organizations in, 153
Stuttgart Educational Union, 153
Suffrage, *see* Electoral law; Franchise
Suppression of Revolution, *see* Reaction
Switzerland
  German workers in
    League of the Just, 44
    socialist influences, 50
  Young Germany group in, 44, 50

Tailors
  congresses of, 193, 203
  cooperatives of, 309
  demands of, 203
  economic problems of, 26-27
  pre-March riots of, 34
  strikes of, 129
  trade groups of, 80

Tariffs, protective
  Committee of Fifty on, 95
  Frankfurt Assembly and, 249-
    50
  workers' demand for, 222
Taxes
  nonpayment campaign on
    failure, 266
    Marx's, 266-67, 282
    Prussian Assembly, 279,
      282
  Pre-Parliament policy on, 94
  Struve's program on, 92
  workers' demands on, 213
Temme, Jodocus, 274n
Temperance societies, early im-
    portance of, 4
"Ten Commandments of the
    Workers, The," 294n
Tests, guild, 188
Textile industry, craft character
    of, 20
  See also Textile workers;
    Weavers
Textile workers
  in Silesian revolt, 34
  strikes of, 129-30
  See also Weavers
Thuringia
  free trade in, 371
  guilds in, 321
  See also specific cities
"To the German Workers"
    (address of Berlin
    Workers' Congress), 215
"To the Workers' and Journey-
    men's Associations of
    Germany" (Workers'
    Association of Frank-
    furt), 207
Tocqueville, Alexis de, 1
Towns, growth of, 19
  See also specific towns and
    cities
Trade protection, merchant de-
    mands for, 240-41
  See also Free trade

Trade unions
  importance of, 4
  membership of, 374n
  See also: Verbrüderung;
    specific workers' organi-
    zations and unions
Tradesmen, see Merchants;
    Middle class
Trier, 311
Trotsky, Leon, insights of, 3n
"True socialism"
  appeal of, 38
  influence on workers' leaders
    of, 78
  theoretical principles of, 39

Ulm, cooperatives in, 309
Unemployment
  agrarian, 19
  growth of, 18-19
  March Days and, 64-65, 70
  post-revolutionary decline in,
    369
  programs against, 84-86
    private, 86-87
    public, see Public works
      projects
  workers' demands on, 78
Unification of Germany, Bis-
    marck's policies on, 6
Union of Handicraft Masters of
    Bielefeld, 181
Union for the Improvement of
    the Working Classes and
    the Opinion of the
    People, The (Born), 52
Union of Machine Builders in
    Berlin, 154-55
United Diet of Prussia, 89
  demands for, 63
  summoning of, 70
Urban (veterinary), 73
Utopian socialism, 45
  influence on workers of, 78

Valentin, Viet, 83n
  on Economic Committee, 230

Valentin, Viet (cont.)
  limitations of, 6
Veit, Moritz, 235, 237, 252, 328,
  330, 333
Venedy, Jacob, 95, 261
Verbrüderung, 283, 290-314
  address to Frankfurt Assem-
    bly by, 298-99
  artisans and, 296-97, 310-11
  Born and
    functions, 297-98
    moderate views, 300-3
    writings, 293
  branches of, 217, 291-92,
    302-3, 307-10, 362-65
  Central Committee of, 218,
    303
  central offices of, 291-92
  cigar workers' amalgamation
    with, 356-58, 362
  class consciousness of, 290
  congresses of, 353-55
    Altenburg Congress, 304-5
    Augsburg Congress, 354-55
    Goppingen Congress, 304
    Hamburg Congress, 304-5
    Hanover Congress, 354-55
    Heidelberg Congress, 300-3
    Leipzig Congress, 360-62
    Nuremburg Congress, 304
    Reutlingen Congress, 353-
      54
    Saxon Congress, 298-99
  cooperative activities of, 308-
    10, 351-53
  decline of, 361
  Democratic Congress and,
    275
  dissolution of, 362-65
  educational functions of, 307-
    8
  establishment of, 217
  factory workers in, 297
  final congress of, 360-62
  growth of, 297
  guild system and, 296, 310-11

Verbrüderung (cont.)
  handicraft workers and, 296-
    97, 310-11
  Marx and, 289
  master artisans and, 296-97,
    310-11
  in May uprisings, 342, 348-59
    change in aims, 350-52
    fate of leaders, 346-47, 350
    reductions in membership,
      350
    regional congresses, 353-55
    repressions, 348-49
    self-help activities, 251-53
  membership of, 306-7
  motto of, 379
  newspaper of, *see*: *Verbrü-
    derung, Die*
  organizational structure of,
    218, 291-92, 303
    statutes, 217
  Prussian industrial ordinance
    denounced by, 320
  recruitment campaign of, 290-
    91, 297
  rural workers and, 305-6
  scope of, 220
  self-help measures of, 218,
    351-53
  trades represented in, 311-14
  Winkelblech's policies in,
    300-3
Verbrüderung, Die (newspa-
    per), 149, 276, 346, 362
  accepted as all-German
    workers' organ, 303
  Born's contributions to, 293
  credo of, 294*n*
  Concordia amalgamated with,
    358
  establishment of, 218
  on Frederick William's elec-
    tion, 336
  May uprisings and, 348-50
  moderate views of, 294-96
  socialism and, 293-94

Verbrüderung, Die (cont.)
  topics reported in, 293-94, 306
Vereinblatt der Maschinenbauer zu Berlin, 155
Vienna
  August uprising in, 261
    battle of Prater, 259
  growth of, 19
  March Days in, 57
  National Guard in, 90
  October uprising in
    democratic support for, 266, 270, 273, 275, 277-78
    failure, 278
  printers' demands in, 134-35
  public works projects in, 90, 259
  Verbrüderung in, 217
Villages, excess labor in, 18-19
  See also Peasants
Virchow, Robert, 71
Volk, Das, 200
  character of, 143-45
  Born's policy in, 145-52
Volksfreund, Der, 109-10
Volksverein unter den Zelten, *see* People's Club of the Zelten
Vossische Zeitung, 65, 201

Wage demands
  of cigar makers, 204
  of printers, 197
  of Journeymen's Congress, 209
  minimum, 172, 174
"Wage-Labor and Capital" (Marx), 283
Wages, 71
  in Berlin, 31
  food prices and, 32
  postrevolutionary increase in, 369
Wagner, Richard, 343

Waldeck, Dr. (workers' leader), 175, 277
  in Central Committee of Workers, 142
Wanderjahre
  effects on journeymen of, 251
  funds for, 352
  Prussian regulations on, 29
  workers' defense of, 183, 246
Warmbrunn, communist "conspiracy" in, 43
Weavers
  in Chartist movement, 3
  cooperatives of, 309
  economic problems of, 27
  Silesian revolt of, 34
  strikes of, 130
  See also Textile workers
Wedekind (Frankfurt Assembly delegate), 327
Weerth, Georg, 121
Weights and measures, reforms in, 249
Weimar, printers' strike in, 201
Weimar Republic, 8, 188n
Weitling, Wilhelm, 152n
  influence of, 44, 50
  life of, 39
  Marx's conflict with, 40-41
  Nazis on, 39n
  theories of, 40
    proposal for equal pay, 275
  writings of, 40
Weserdampfboot, 37
Westfälische Dampfboot, 37
Weydemeyer, Joseph, 302
Wheat, price increases in, 32
Wiesbaden
  peasant uprisings in, 61
  workers' congress in, 49
Wig makers, 27n
Willich, August von, 63, 64n, 367-68
Wigend (publisher), 52
Windischgrätz, Prince Alfred von, 278

Winkelblech, Karl Georg, 154, 170, 173, 210, 220, 303, 376-77
  background of, 154n
  Born's debate with, 300
  guild concepts of, 300-2
  later life of, 347
  radicalism of, 186
  in *Verbrüderung*, 300-3
Wischmann (Pre-Congress president), 169
Wolff, Ferdinand, 121
Wolff, Julius, 258
Wolff, Wilhelm, 112, 115, 288
  on *Neue Rheinische Zeitung*, 121
Women's branch of *Verbrüderung*, 362
Women's rights, workers' attitudes toward, 46n
Women's societies, 6, 87
Woniger, Dr. (workers' leader), in Central Committee of Workers, 142
Work guarantees and Economic Committee, 324-28
  See also Public works' projects
Workers, 2, 275
  agricultural
    demands, 184
    growth, 18
    impoverishment, 18-19
    industrial use of, 184
    pre-March, 18-19
    unemployment, 12
    Verbrüderung, 305-6
  antisocialist sentiments of, 243-44
  artisans preponderant in, 9, 164
    in 1848, 5
    in pre-March period, 21-23
    after Revolution, 370, 373-74
  belief in barricades by, 98
  civil guard and

Workers, civil guard and (cont.)
  collaboration in Berlin, 256-57
  exclusion of workers, 69
  October riots, 278
  suspicion between, 70
  communism rejected by, 79
  definition of, 22
  democratic attitudes of, 127
  Democratic Congress and, 275-77
  disenfranchisement of, *see* Electoral law; Franchise
  economic demands of
    credit banks, 172, 218
    employment bureaus, 218
    free trade, *see* Free trade, workers' attitudes toward
    government aid, 77, 209
    guilds, *see* Guilds
    hours, *see* Hours, working
    industrial councils, 244
    machinery, *see* Machinery
    March Days, 70-71, 73-80
    moderateness, 126, 153-55
    public works, *see* Public works' projects
    wages, *see* Wage demands
  Engels' attitude toward, 121
  factory, *see* Factory workers
  Frankfurt Assembly and, *see* Frankfurt Assembly, workers and
  Frederick William IV and
    concessions, 82-86
    petitions, 35
    workers' organizations supported, 47
  guilds and, *see* Guilds
  handicraft, *see* Apprentices; Artisans; Journeymen; Master artisans
  in March Days
    casualties in fighting, 68
    concessions to workers, 71-72

Workers, in March Days (cont.)
demands, 63, 70-71, 73-80
initiative, 59-60
liberals' fear of, 71-72
organizational activities, 70, 72-77, 124-28
Marx's attitude toward, see Marx, Karl, workers' movement and
in May uprisings, see May uprisings, workers' organizations and
middle class and, 5
fear of working class, 71-72, 379
lower middle class and, 16
moral attitudes of, 46n
naïveness of, 125
in October riots, 272-73
organizational failure of, 264
dissolution of organizations, 49, 362-65
weakness, 376-77
political influence of, 2
demands, 75
weakness, 16
pre-March conditions of, 15-33
agrarian workers, 18-19
disunity, 15-17
guild system, 23-31
industrialization, 20-21, 23
population growth, 17-18
poverty, 31-33
predominance of artisans, 21-23
revolutionary influences, 34-35
riots, 34-36
Silesian revolt, 34
Pre-Parliament and, 91-97
radical leaders and, 99-123
reaction and, see Reaction
revolutionary role of, 2
in September crisis, 266
in September uprising, 260

Workers (cont.)
socialism and, see Socialism, workers' organizations and
spontaneity of, 59-60, 127, 260-61
strikes of, see Strikes
self help by, see Self help by workers
See also specific workers' organizations; German cities and states
Workers' Association
in Breslau, 256
in Cologne, 258
in Frankfurt, 207
Workers' bank, 88-89
Workers' Club of Heidelberg, 180
Workers' commission of Committee of Fifty, 95
Workers' Education Union, 297, 307, 354
Workers' Singing Union in Schwerin, 351
Workers' Union
in Berlin, 136-37
in Cologne
demands, 117-18
formation, 116
Marx and, 115-23, 258, 284-89
in Frankfurt, 260-61
in Kassel, 153
in London, 40
in Schwerin, 308
Working hours, see Hours, working
Wrangel, Count Friedrich von
Berlin occupied by, 279
machine builders and, 281
Wupperthal Industrial Union, 297n
Wurm (communist), 43
Würtemberg
electoral law in, 96

Würtemberg (cont.)
  free trade in, 371
  guilds in, 321
    regulations, 30
  peasant uprisings in, 60
  petitions from, 236
  Verbürderung in, 302, 304
  See also Stuttgart; *specific*
    cities

Young Europe movement, 45
Young Germany group, 44
  ideological influence of, 50

Young Hegelians, 36, 38, 51

Zacharias (journalist), 74
Zelten district in Berlin
  as agitational center, 101
  public meetings in, 65
  See also People's Club of the
    Zelten
Zollverein, 30, 184
  defects of, 249
  economic foundations of, 15
    handicrafts, 27
    steam engines, 20